A Burton Railwayman

David Fleming

Copyright David Fleming 2005

Published by David Fleming ISBN 0 9550847 0 9

Printed by Tresises, Stanley Street, Burton upon Trent DE14 1DY.

CONTENTS

Chapter 1

In the Beginning

It was a dull rainy August Monday morning in 1936 when I first announced my arrival into the world in response to the midwife's smack on my derriere. Not the last time upon which it was to receive such treatment by any means but certainly the only occasion with such good intention.

In no time at all I was being introduced to the world of railways for, living in Burton-on-Trent, it was not possible to travel far in the town without passing over a level crossing, of which there were no less than thirty three within the Borough boundary.

From our home in Shobnall Street, a perambulation into town involved crossing over the railway bridge by the station upon which were situated the booking hall and canopy covering the forecourt, followed by the level crossing of Ind Coope & Allsopp, whose bright green engines made many journeys across each day. Next came the Station Street crossing of Bass & Co, where road traffic was frequently held up for some considerable time while a shiny red engine performed a series of shunting movements, to and fro, much to the consternation of the waiting multitudes. My mother assured me that even at the tender age of six months or so, I used to get quite excited at the sight, sound and smell of all this activity.

As our family had no railway connections at all, my father working on the Post Office and my various uncles being joiners, turners and brewery workers or engineers, my early interest was all the more surprising. One of my Grandfathers had earned his living on rails, being a tram driver, throughout the entire life of their operation in Burton from 1903 to 1923, having moved to Burton from Dudley on their introduction, to train new drivers and then serving as stated for the entire duration of their service, until their demise. Interestingly, a colleague of his Mr Felthouse, who also I understand came with my Grandfather at the inception, drove the first and last tram in the town on public service, these being the corporation trams of course, not the Burton and Ashby light Railway trams of the Midland Railway which also operated over the corporation system. The short section of tramline where it made a right angle crossing with the railway lines on the brewery level crossing remained in-situ long after the trams finished, the longest lasting piece sharing the Bass & Co crossing previously mentioned in Station Street, which lasted until the railway lines were replaced in the 1950's.

Prior to the Second World War and indeed for some years afterwards, it was the popular and necessary thing to rent and cultivate an allotment and my father was no exception. Some of my earliest memories are of accompanying my parents to this plot of ground. It was situated alongside the Trent and Mersey Canal on the very edge of the town. Indeed one of the cast iron boundary posts was sited on the canal towpath just the other side of the hedge from the plot. When the war began it was covered with an earthenware pipe filled with concrete on the assumption that an invading force would not know where they were if they could not read it. However let it be said that we children knew where there were two more which never received the treatment, probably because the authorities did not know they were there being hidden in one case in a hedge and the other in a thicket where blackberries flourished, both I might add away from any form of public highway or right of way and there may have been others in other parts of the town.

No. 22822 The Engine which started the authors interest in railways at the tender age of three years old. Photo: Authors Collection.

But I digress. Reaching the allotment, other than down the canal towpath, was by way of Bass Maltings. This involved crossing the Shobnall Crossing over which shunting operations connected with the said Maltings, the Bass Cooperage and Bottling Stores and also Marston's Brewery were taking place constantly through-out the day. It was these shunting movements, which fascinated me so much. I can see even now in my mind's eye an immaculate old Midland Double Frame 0-6-0 No.22822 with the legend L.M.S in red edged, straw coloured numbers and letters, pristine against a new matt black background, its outside cranks whirring round as it ran up and down, propelling the wagons too and fro. At the end of each shunt, her driver was clearly visible in the cab as he heaved at the reversing lever to set back and start another run. My father, in his dear ignorance, thought that the reversing lever was the hand brake and pointed it out to me as such. As it did indeed resemble the motor vehicle hand brakes of the time, albeit considerably larger, he is to be forgiven for such an obvious mistake. It does how-ever remain an abiding memory for me, that he would spare ten minutes or so of his time for me to watch this scene of activity when he would have much rather have been hoeing up his potatoes or weeding his onion patch or whatever. Little did I think then that 13 or 14 years later I myself would be shunting at that very spot, albeit not, sadly, with 22822 but, even so, with ex Midland veteran class 1F 0-6-0 Tank of the1870's vintage.

Burton Station forecourt circa 1950's now demolished. Photo: Photo: Authors Collection.

Came the war and my father was conscripted into the RAF and in consequence the allotment was given up after a valiant attempt by my mother to keep it on single-handed.

But, as with all things, time marched on and my younger comrades and I grew older and our sphere of activity became larger. As I lay in bed at night the sound of trains lulled me to sleep and I soon realised that the noise was not coming from Shobnall Sidings but further afield - the main line no less - and the sound was of trains pulling out of the station to climb over Moor Street Bridge. Moor Street Bridge and its trains were visible from the top of our street, just about half a mile away.

Shobnall sidings, Bass signalbox and Banner signal on left and BR (ex midlands) box an the right. Photo: Authors Collection.

3

In no time at all, our intrepid band ventured that way and what a world opened out for me. Whereas my comrades had just a passing interest in all this railway activity laid out before them, I was totally captivated and wished to be in no other place.

On arriving home that night I couldn't wait to tell my mother of all the wondrous things I had seen but she, being worried as to my whereabouts all day, greeted my enthusiasm with another chastisement on my nether regions. No midwives smack this, but a full-blown attack! Still, bless her heart, she had no husband to help her bring me up, thanks to Mr Hitler. She did however come to realise that railways and I were inseparable and came to accept it.

Burton Station (South) signalbox and level crossing. Circa 1968 level crossing now disused and most crossing boards removed. Photo: Authors Collection.

All my holidays and Saturdays were being spent at "Steamer Gates," as the Moor Street Bridge location was known. It should be explained that the bridge has a headroom clearance of only nine feet to road traffic. To the one side, the railway had seen fit to install a set of level crossing gates for road traffic too high to pass underneath. This saw occasional use but drivers of such vehicles invariably faced long waits, while a clear path over all four running lines could be arranged. Such was the intensity of traffic at this time that drivers with local knowledge avoided this route altogether and crossed over the main line by means of the Station Bridge previously mentioned.

At the signalbox (Burton Station South) end of the gates, was located the fuel bunker for the box. As we got older (following the example of the older boys) we, in our turn would sit on the side of this bunker with our feet resting on the gates. As boys are notorious for not sitting still, the gates tended to move backwards and forwards against the locking stop, which in turn made the lever in the box kick slightly and the winding wheel also rock to and fro. This of course annoyed the signalman who periodically came out of his box to move us off. Being the Forties and not the Nineties, however, we complied with his commands without argument, creeping back twenty minutes or so later to start the whole round again. After all it was far better to view the proceedings from over the gates than through them.

And what a view! All four lines were busy with a constant procession of trains. Ex-Midland 2F, 3F and 4F 0-6-0's; 1P 2-4-0's; 2P, 3P and 4P Compound 4-4-0's; LMS 4F Class "5"'s (Blackies); Garratts; Jubilees and 8F's. Even the 7F 0-8-0. Ex LNW Super "D's"' put in an occasional appearance also, and an LNW 2F 0-6-0 was not unknown. Patriots were rare and Scots never appeared. Both the Fowler and Stanier versions of the 3P 2-6-2 and 4P 2-6-4 tanks were seen. During 1942 and 1943 there were three Southern Railway Class F1 4-4-0's allocated. Although meant for local passenger work, I only recall once seeing one thus used, on I think the Leicester working, their more usual duty being on local transfer freights. We rarely saw the "Tutbury Jinny" engines - Ex Midland Class 1P 0-4-4 tanks, unless one was used on a trip working, as they operated the push and pull service to Tutbury out of the north end bay of the station, starting their day before we arrived at the gates and finishing long after we had gone home.

United States Transportation Corps. 2-8-0 No. 2088. Photo: P. Groom.

1943 brought new surprises in the shape of Riddle's War Department 2-8-0's and US Army Transportation Corp's S160 2-8-0's. Whilst the American engines were only around for about twelve months, the "Austerities" as they became known never totally went away again.

As winter came on year by year, we occasionally spent a penny of our all too sparse pocket money to buy a platform ticket and do our spotting from the station itself. Here we discovered other delights to amuse us between trains. A machine on the platform allowed you to stamp out 25 or 26 letters and numbers on to a metal strip for the princely sum of one penny. A favourite subject would be the number and name of a Jubilee, which had just run in on a train for Bristol or Bradford. 5612 JAMAICA for instance followed by 5590 TRAVANCORE. An argument would arise as to the spellings of the names. Was the 'I' before or after the 'C' in Jamaica? Was it 'TRAVAN' or 'TRAVEN'-core? After all we were only eight or nine years old at the time. Whilst we were discussing these important issues (arguing would better describe it) someone would sneak away and punch a Z or a Q or something in to spoil it. After all it wasn't his penny in the machine. This invariably caused a fight between the offender and the offended and the inevitable end resulted in all and sundry, whether involved or not, being escorted off the station and onto the street. Another feature of the station platform on the Derby side was a drinking fountain, which bore the legend MR 1883. A plunger was pressed and the water was ejected out of a nozzle into a cast iron basin, whence it drained away rather like a sink. A cast iron drinking vessel, rather like a cup without a handle, was hung on a chain, the purpose of this saliva edged receptacle being to catch the water and drink from it in a more civilised manner. This contrivance generated much sport, with water from the nozzle being redirected in directions for which it wasn't meant to go, by grubby fingers judiciously placed over it. Alternatively, one of our gang, feeling thirsty, would be genuinely partaking of a drink from the cup when another of his "friends" would hit the bottom of it with the inevitable results. Again a fight and a premature return to the street being the outcome.

LNER Class K2 2-6-0 crosses over the LMS mainline at Wetmore. Bound for Burton (LNER) yard. Photo: Authors Collection.

1943/44 brought the United States into the war and we always hoped that an American Troop train would stop in the station when we were on the platform. The soldiers always seemed to have plenty of sweets and chocolates, (candies they called them) which they threw out to us. We would scramble about the platform for them, much to their delight and our profit. Who cared what they called them, so long as they threw them.

"Got any gum, chum?" we would shout, and out of the window came the goodies.

The war in Europe ended in 1945 and in the East in 1946. My father returned home and very soon obtained bicycles for us all so we could get out into the country for picnics. To me however, it meant a quicker journey to Moor Street Bridge. We heard tell of another engine shed at Horninglow and decided to venture forth into the town to try and find it. Perhaps we would have better luck getting round it as most of our attempts to bunk the Midland shed ended in disaster.

Another factor, which made me wary, was the unfortunate fact that one of the railway policemen lived only three doors away from us, so that - giving a false name and address if caught was not a good idea on my part. In any case, driver Charlie Wallace also lived only six doors away and could be persuaded to take me with him occasionally when he went to collect his wages. So off we went to discover the delights of Horninglow Ex LNW Shed, only to find that it contained just two engines, both belonging to Burton 17B and frequently seen at Steamer Gates.

Further exploration of the area, with a little guidance from the local kids, did however reveal the existence, hereto unknown, of the LNER in the town. At Wetmore Bridge no less, I recall, after having been there only ten minutes or so, a B17- "Doncaster Rovers," hove into view, tender first. Imagine our delight. Needless to say we found ourselves at this "new" location quite often in the future, as most of the traffic that crossed over Moor Street passed under the footbridge or Road Bridge, there. Ian Allan's "ABC of LNER Locomotives" was therefore added to our libraries along with the LMS issue which most of us already had.

September 1947 saw our graduation to the senior school and also the parting of the ways of our little gang, as we were divided up between three different schools depending on our academic ability. I found myself alone at my new school but soon made friends who had similar interests. Attending my new school meant a cycle ride under Moor Street Bridge every day and this, at least in the mornings, revealed activities I had until then been unaware of, previously being rarely there much before 10 am. It was on one of these school journeys that I first saw Ex Caledonian "Pug" No. 56020, looking superb in its fresh coat of black gloss, with the number on the cab side and the legend "BRITISH RAILWAYS," in off white, along the sides of the saddle tanks. No one would believe me when I arrived at school and related what I had seen on the bridge shunting wagons into Ind Coope's, Mosley Street premises. Two of my mates met me there the next day only to find the usual Deeley Tank on this duty. Months were to pass by before one of them entered the shed successfully and saw her there for himself.

Ex Caledonian RLY No. 16020 (BR 56020). Photo: Authors Collection.

It was about then that we heard about the West Coast Main Line, which until then I hadn't realised, was as close as Lichfield. That weekend we resolved to go and oiled our bikes accordingly. With a saddlebag full of egg sandwiches and a bottle of water for what, at least my parents thought, was a day at Wetmore, we set out for Lichfield Trent Valley, twelve miles away along one of the busiest trunk roads in the county. Most lorries then only travelled at 30 miles per hour and it wasn't long before we abandoned pedalling and commenced tailgating. If only one's parents knew what we really did, bless them!

Within minutes of our arrival it was like Wetmore all over again, only better as our first "Duchess" came roaring through. Hillary and Tensing, when they reached the summit of Everest, couldn't have been more excited than we were that day. We had just arrived at Lichfield to find our very first express headed by a "Duchess." Its name and number have now been forgotten but sufficient to say that over the next 2½ years I saw them all, plus the Princess Royals and the "Scots" as well. This one - 46103 "Royal Scots Fusilier," I was destined to be pulled by, from Leeds to Glasgow "St Enoch" some eight years later whilst in the army doing my National Service.

When, many trips later, mother found out we were cycling along that "dangerous road" as she put it (if only she knew how dangerously we were doing it!) she put a block on it, or rather got my father to. He, being ever resourceful, suggested that I went by train; about one shilling 'return' a child's fare was then; however I had to earn it of course. "You get nothing for now't in this world my lad" he quoted.

Thus - I am up and out of the house on a Saturday morning by twenty to six. I push one of our neighbour's (an old gentleman by the name of Mr Ward) wheelbarrows to Sharps and Knights wood-yard, about half a mile away, and join the stampede when the gates open at six, into the yard. Here I load up this huge, and believe me it was huge, contrivance with firewood, for which I pay sixpence, race back home, unload, race back to the yard, fill up again, paying another sixpence and race back to Mr Ward's house with his load, unloading that as well. Then I would get my bag with the usual egg sandwiches, bottle of water, pencil and ABC's therein and, with the fare in my hand, run to the station to catch the 8.18 train for Walsall out of the South bay, alighting naturally at Lichfield T.V. How I never nodded off to sleep, to waken in some carriage sidings in the West Midlands, I'll never know. But the first 'Semi' of the day soon wakes me up and I am all-alert again.

Ex LMS 'Jubilee" Class 4-6-0 runs into Lichfield (Trent Valley) low level with a southbound working. Photo: L. Cairns.

The only Pacific to be still streamlined was 46243 "City of Lancaster" at the time allocated to Camden shed (1B) who only cleaned the number on the cab side. Underneath the grime she was painted all over black, a legacy from the war and it wasn't long before her turn to enter Crewe works came, from which she emerged in de-streamlined form. The only one clue to her previous streamlined state being the sloping front of the smoke box like the rest of her unfrocked sisters, and thus referred to in train spotting circles as "Semis." The never stream-lined engines of the class were referred to as "Duchesses," whilst the Princess Royal Class were known as ""Prinnies." Leastwise they were at Lichfield T.V.

Some other engines which could be observed at Lichfield during these early BR days, even if not so prestigiously as "City of Lancaster," were nevertheless of great interest to me. I saw, for instance, my first Ivatt Class 4, 2-6-0, "flying pig" there, No. M3002, on a tripper from Nuneaton. I recall how she blew a double smoke ring from her chimney as the driver reversed his gear. What a smart, modern looking, engine I thought, which was probably at complete odds with what her crew were thinking, particularly the fireman, as they were not famed for being good steamers in their original double chimney form.

The last three surviving Ex LNW "Prince of Wales" Class 4-6-0's used to turn up on local workings from Stafford. "Queen of the Belgians," "Lusitania" and an unnamed member, No. 25752. Although these three engines were all allocated BR numbers in the 58xxx series, they never carried them and went to the scrap yard still carrying their LMS ones.

Claughton number 6004 was the last survivor of her class also and went to an early grave once in the service of BR. The only time I saw her she was going very well with a Crewe-bound fitted freight.

An enterprising chap started visiting the train spotting fraternity about this time at both Lichfield T.V and, I am told, Tamworth as well. He was selling quite reasonable photographs of LMS BR (M) engines for sixpence a time. So, how did I earn another sixpence? Not by fetching another barrow of wood for anyone that's for sure!

Ex LMS compound No. 41095 leaves Burton station on a local working for Birmingham. Note the pathway on the left from Moor Street to the Midland Loco sheds. Photo: P. Webb.

Now! My father used to have a bottle of beer now and again, from the local off license, for which one penny was paid on the return of the empty bottle. This was only realising an average three pennies a week with possibly four pence on a good week. Should I encourage him to drink more? Offer to fetch it for him from the shop? Dismiss the idea! Not positive and reliable enough. Then came the brainwave! Wasn't there a bottling plant at the end of the street? Why not recycle some of them, as it were! So, with my equally hard up pal and accomplice, we proceeded to "borrow" a few bottles from the bottling stores to re-present at the many off licenses around the area. All we needed was an extra sixpence, for a photo each visit and, while we were at it, another ten pence for a bottle of Tizer. Much better than water and another bonus was that there was two pence back on a Tizer bottle, so we would only need another eight pence in future. Then my mate came up with idea number two after a few weeks. If we could find pop bottles we would make our money twice as fast and in half the time. So that became the pattern for the next few weeks but of course, the pop bottles were coming out the back of the shop and going back in the front. We were sure to be found out or caught I reasoned and in any case, I had got a paper round now and had never been so rich in all my life. So ended that little enterprise.

I suppose it was fraud really, but at twelve years old your mind doesn't work in the same way as it does when an adult, although because of my basically good upbringing, I knew it was wrong.

When I was about eighteen the proprietor of our local shop was taken ill and I took it upon myself to help out whenever I could, until he sold the shop and moved away. I wouldn't accept any payments from him as I felt I owed him something though this wasn't the declared reason for my assistance. Even so, I never told him about the pop bottles either.

Having settled into my new school routine and surroundings, I found myself taking more interest in swimming and football and less in train spotting. My interests in railways however, was still very much alive and, when eventually asked what my ambitions were with regards to employment when I left school, an apprenticeship in locomotive engineering, which basically meant that I wanted to be a loco fitter, was my choice.

This completely confounded my careers teacher who had no ideas or information about employment on the railways. In consequence he tried to sell me another career, possibly with one of the many other engineering companies in the town. However my choice was made, I wasn't going to give in without a fight and informed my father of my intentions. He in turn recruited Mr (Driver) Wallace to make some enquires and speak up on my behalf for, at the time, you had to know someone to gain employment on the railway.

Eventually an interview was obtained and down the long path from Moor Street to the Shed I trod, accompanied of course by my father.

How grand it felt to walk down that path without the need to conduct ones-self like a commando making a raid on an enemy stronghold. No dodging about and hiding for me that day. Straight down the middle with head held high.

We reported to the chief clerk who in his turn conducted us into the inner sanctum, there to be introduced to and interviewed by Mr Bertie Staines, the current shed master at the time.

After much discussion during which it transpired that there wasn't a vacancy for an apprentice at that time, a compromise was suggested. Following a number of phone calls he suggested to me that I start as a cleaner and then, in twenty months or so's time when the senior apprentice completed his training, that I be given the opportunity to take the vacancy this created.

Needless to say I was agreeing to this idea before it had barely left his lips. Whether or not the initial disappointment on hearing that there were no apprentice vacancies had shown on my face or possibly Mr Wallace had sung my praises more than a little, I do not know but the 'cleaner to apprentice' idea was a somewhat unusual an occurrence at that time.

So off to Derby for a medical which, apart from the obvious medical checks, also had quite a stringent eye sight test, with me sorting out filthy strands of wool into yellow, white, blue and so on, followed by pages of dots devised I believe by some Japanese genius, whereby a number was visible if your eye sight was correct and you were not colour-blind. I did wonder if the doctor knew what the numbers were himself or was it just a case of shout out any number with

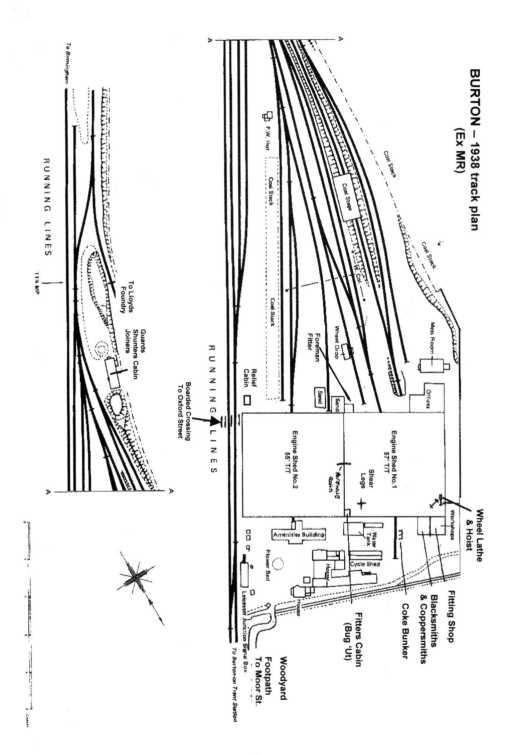

BURTON – 1938 track plan (Ex MR)

confidence, whether you could see or not. Not that I had to resort to such subterfuge, naturally. Finally you stood with the doctor at one end of a darkened room whilst different lights were switched on and off, which of course I had to identify, red, green or yellow. I called the yellow light white and after several attempts the doctor whispered to me, "Don't you think it looks yellow?" So I called yellow next time round and honour was satisfied - and to think that I nearly failed to get the job for the want of a name.

I should mention that there is a subtle difference, which came obvious when I got out on the line, between the yellow of a distant signal at caution and the back light shown by all signal lamps, at least in the semaphore days, which is white.

A letter eventually arrived confirming my fitness and advising me to commence my employment with British Railway (London Midland Region) at Burton Motive Power Depot as a locomotive cleaner on Monday, September 3rd 1951 at 7:30am.

The due day arrived and I made the first of many journeys on my trusty cycle to the sheds. On arrival I was pleased to find that one of my old school mates from junior days, Reg Finch was also starting as a cleaner at the same time. He, by reason of his name being alphabetically before mine, obtained promotion from youngest hand cleaner as soon as we walked through the door, it being my humble position during the ensuing weeks.

We were both introduced to Mr "Pom" Rose the charge-hand cleaner who lead us round to the stores where we were issued with two suits of bib and brace overalls and jackets and one of the coveted shiny topped enginemans' hats. Now we really did look the part. One of the clerks then took us into the lobby where we read out a big notice relating to discipline and conduct, signing a ledger to confirm that we had done so and understood it, to boot.

We then came back down to earth with a bump as we were presented with a wheelbarrow, shovel and brush and instructed to clean out as many of the inspection pits around the shed as we could, which didn't have an engine standing over them. Truth to say that apart from an occasional foray with a paraffin rag, cleaning cab side numbers, I never ever personally cleaned an engine at all, although some of my colleagues did, as an attempt was made to keep the "Tutbury Jinnie" engine and the 2-6-4T number 42336 (the only one allocated to Burton) clean, along with a couple of "Crabs" for the prestigious London and Bristol fitted beer trains. My artistic skills were occasionally called upon to paint the old, rusting, smoke-box and chimney black, followed by whitening the smoke-box number and 17B plate with whitewash, which called for a steady hand and delicate touch when armed only with a whitewash brush.

But most of my time seemed to be spent on the ash-pits, either emptying their contents onto the side or else from there into a wagon, a real fun job anytime, particularly if it was a windy day. Still I was reasonably happy for, wasn't I surrounded by engines and railways? and it wasn't going to be forever. Soon, I used to tell myself as yet another train steamed by, it would be my turn to be aboard the engine, with all the status that went with it.

Although I didn't realise it at the time, all the labouring duties that I performed were building up my strength and stamina for that very day when it did arrive.

After a few months of this type of work "Pom," in his wisdom or otherwise, sent me up the coal stage for a fortnight to take the place of one of the coalmen who was absent for some reason or other. This was a soul destroying task entailing the filling of tubs of coal out of wagons, then pushing them onto a tipper cradle to upend the contents onto the tender waiting below. There were three coalmen to a shift and between them they were averaging five or six wagons and occasionally more, of coal per shift, roughly sixty tons per eight hours.

Towards the end of my second muscle aching, back breaking week, George Wallace, Charlie's son and a fireman at Burton, came under the tipper with his engine for coal. On seeing me there he asked me if I was enjoying spending my bonus.

"Bonus!" I asked "What Bonus?"

"Oh, they're all on bonus up here," he answered, "After so many tons they all get it. I think they share it out between them."

"Do they" I thought, "I'm having some of that then," I told myself. So at the end of the shift I tackled the leading hand about it.

"There pulling your leg son" he replied, "Could you see the Railway doing owt as daft as that?"

Now I have always been a big lad for my age, which is probably how I got the job in the first place, plus I didn't like being messed about, particularly where money was concerned, so I pulled myself up to my full height and replied that, No, I didn't think they were pulling my leg and what's more I wanted my share now.

After further argument during which we nearly came to blows, he reluctantly handed over £2, which I accepted with great alacrity. Whether or not it should have been more I had no idea, it certainly wouldn't have been less. But I was happy to have obtained something out of him for, if it had but come to a fight, I would almost certainly have come off worse.

One of the jobs that I did enjoy was helping the steam- raiser. The first thing to be checked was the water level in the boiler. If this was showing at all in the bottom of the glass then everything was all right as when water was heated and became under pressure it had a tendency to increase in volume and therefore rise up the glass. Secondly, all control valves and in particular the regulator, were checked and closed and the engine put in middle gear. This was most important as more than one engine had been fired up with the regulator even slightly open and in gear, causing it to make steam and start off and end its journey in the turntable hole, crashing into the buffer stops or into another engine, with the resultant risk to life and limb into the bargain.

When everything was checked to satisfaction, the firebox was lined with coal and two or three firelighters lit on the shovel and placed inside the box.

Alternatively a couple of shovels full of fire from the sandhole would be added, particularly if the engine was required in a hurry. Specially adapted shovels were kept for this purpose, being firing shovel blades fitted to a shunting pole ash handle, which allowed the steam-riser to carry the shovel with its hot contents on his shoulder without burning himself. The practise of raising steam so quickly in a locomotive boiler was discouraged as undue stresses were created when the boiler and fire-box heated up too quickly and consequently, was only undertaken in very urgent circumstances.

Some depots used to use hot water for washing boilers out, the boilers then being refilled with hot water as well, with the obvious saving in time when relighting afterwards. However at Burton in common with most if not all Ex LMS depots, cold water was used for boiler washing, with the consequent penalty of a longer period of regeneration to steam.

Whatever methods were applied, the resultant fire required attention and this is what gave all us cleaners pleasure. We shovelled away with great enthusiasm, imagining who knows what while we were doing it. It may have been an old 2F or 3F in reality but in our minds eye it was a Jubilee on the "Devonian" or if our minds were really tuned in, possibly even a Duchess on the "Royal Scot." These excessive urges were all right once the fire was well burnt through, but care had to be shown in the early stages. It was possible, with over-filling, to put the fire out and one of our number actually did that very thing on a 2P one evening! Fortunately another couple of shovels full of fire courtesy of the sandhole soon put things right but, as you can imagine, living it down took quite a lot longer. Another factor to consider was that most firemen, when they came on duty, particularly if they were going to prepare and work the engine themselves, liked to find a small fire in the box so that they could make it up in their own way. I know I did when I gained a bit of experience myself. A moderate fire under the door and about 60lb-psi on the clock was the ideal to aim for. Too much fire and the engine would be blowing off all day in the shed to the annoyance of all and sundry.

So there we were then, a gang of cleaners doing just about everything but clean engines and all awaiting the day when we would meet the inspector, hopefully meeting with his approval and passing out to become Passed Cleaners and go out Firing at last.

We studied the rulebook and asked each other questions. The ones we were concerned with were those grouped under 'Protection of Trains'. These were designed to cover all foreseeable events and conditions so that everyone concerned knew immediately what action to take individually and consequently saving valuable time in both protection and warning to others.

Familiarisations of all the various controls and equipment used and the ability to operate it were also one of our concerns, along with practise firing as already mentioned when steam raising.

Finally the day came and our intrepid band were introduced to Mr Wells the firing inspector. After a brief informal chat we were taken aside individually and questioned on our knowledge of the rulebook. A visit onto the footplates of a class 3F came next, where we were asked to name the various controls and explain their function. Then a demonstration of checking the water level in the boiler followed by the operation of the injectors. On to an 8F next, where the whole procedure was repeated. A few shovels full of fuel were then fed into the firebox and we each returned to the mess room in our turn, to await the verdict.

As it transpired we were all passed as suitable and able to take our places as Passed Cleaners on the rotor. This meant, among other things, that we had to check the alteration board daily when we signed off, in case we were marked up for a duty, which required a different start time to our rostered one. We did not have long before some of our number found their names on the list, the usual turns being shed-preparing and disposal, both of which are extremely hard work.

Being the youngest hand Passed Cleaner, my name took a little longer than most to appear but as sure as eggs is eggs, there it was listed one afternoon as I checked the list, marked against R. Smith on 6am preparation. My first firing turn - three hundred and twelve to go and I am a registered fireman. A long way ahead, let's just get turn number one done first.

Arriving at the shed bright and early the next morning I introduced myself to "Dickie" Smith, who I knew of already as he was a regular shed man, being confined to shed limits after failing an eyesight test some years before. A smallish, thin built man with a very even temperament, we got on fine right from the start. He informed me that we had six engines to prepare for our day's work along with any movements which the fitting staff may require doing. So we were going to be quite busy. We already had the numbers of the first four engines to hand so we got started on the first one immediately, a Class 3F, very handily situated next to the sandhole in No.2 (New) shed. I should explain that both the two sheds and various sidings had all got names, which helped to identify the whereabouts of the individual engines. Thus the 1869-built roundhouse was known as the "Old Shed," and indicated OS alongside the engine number, the 1892-built roundhouse was always referred to as the New Shed (NS), with the siding down to the Sand-Hole being (SH) the Wheel Drop Plant road (DP) and so on.

Round to the back stores I went to obtain the engine tools and oil. These tools came in a bucket and consisted of I think four spanners, a hand brush, box of detonators, red flag, coal pick, firing shovel, two head lamps, a gauge lamp and the oil bottle and feeder. With a saturated engine, like a 3F, a bottle of saturated steam oil was also required. I was fortunate to obtain all these items and staggered back to our 3F in triumph with my equipment.

Our engine was showing a healthy 80lbs on the clock and with the boiler water out of sight in the top of the glass, I wasn't too worried about that side of things. Although I didn't know it then, this first engine was to prove to be the exception rather than the norm, but I had yet to discover this unfortunate fact for myself. I fed a few shovels in the back corners and under the door in the mistaken idea of looking professional and dropped the damper down. This brought an angry shout from "Dick" underneath, as he was standing on the open door at the time, while he oiled the crankshaft. On his not unreasonable request I opened it again. Another couple of lessons learned, one: never do anything without checking where your opposite number is first and two: that "Dickie" knew an awful lot of profanities for such a small man.

The next job was to check inside the smokebox so, armed with a $^3/_4$ x $^7/_8$ spanner, I slid round the engine, telling "Dick" at the same time where I was going.

"Just hang on and do nothing till I get there" he shouted back. "Check the sand boxes while you're waiting."

I did this and found that they all needed filling. "At least I haven't got far to carry it," I reflected "When I can find the sand buckets." These buckets resembled a large watering can with a large spout and when full must have weighed in the region of 60lbs or more. Real arm stretchers, particularly if you have far to carry them. A quick search soon revealed two rather battered specimens, which I soon had filled and was on the way back to the engine. Each of the four boxes was well down and thus required at least two buckets-full. Not easy items to find, I resolved to keep the buckets for our other five engines and hid them behind a stack of brake blocks near by.

"Right then Dave, let's have a look in the smokeboxes, slip up and put the blower on" Dick commanded. I complied with his bidding and then joined him on the front framing.

"I just thought I'd show you how to do this for the first time as there isn't much room on the front here and we don't want you falling off now do we?" Dickie said. "Now - imagine all these dogs are shut and tightened up" he continued, referring to the ring of clips which surrounded the door and when tightened up pulled the door onto its face to make it airtight.

"Undo all the dogs, leaving the one farthest from the hinge 'till' last. Then stand to one side before you knock this last one off, that way, if the door springs open, you wont get knocked off the engine and, if you're on disposing you won't get your boots full up with char either" he explained.

All good simple advice, for which I was grateful. Dickie had a look round inside and then asked me if I knew what I was looking for when I checked it myself.

"Leaking tubes, washout plugs and anything else which doesn't seem right" I answered.

He nodded in agreement and pointed out one or two more items to take particular note of, like ejector exhaust pipe gland on the side of the ring on the blast pipe cap, for instance.

On a superheated engine, which of course our 3F wasn't, he mentioned the need to notice any signs of leaks or blows from the superheater, so I wiped round the joint both on the box and the door and closed it up tightening all the clips securely.

The next job involved removing the reservoirs from the two headlamps and the gauge lamp and taking them to the front stores window. Here, on the counter, stood a tin bottle of rape oil with which to fill them. This done, I returned to the engine, replaced the reservoirs in the lamps and placed one on the front and one on the frame fitted to the side of the fireman's gauge glass.

All the fire irons were in place on the tender rack, so all that remained to do was to top up the tank with water and refuel the bunker. As I dropped out of the cab to get the turntable, I noticed that we now had 110lbs of steam showing, more than enough for the safe operations of our steed by Dick, around the yard. Dick brought her on to the turntable with gallons of water and steam spraying forth from her open cylinder drain cocks. As he came to a stop I snatched the vacuum bag off the front of the engine and, joining the tractor bag to it, shouted for Dick to "Blow up."

He pulled out the large ejector handle in the cab to comply with my call, so that I could turn the table and engine round with the vacuum motor. As he did so a gush of dirty, sooty water ejected out of the chimney and all over yours truly, much to the amusement of the early staff cleaners who had just gathered to start their duties for the day.

"It's a bit dark outside still" Dick called, trying not to laugh also, "So you'd better light the lamp Dave, better to be safe than sorry."

Handing over the controls to one of the cleaners, who was only too pleased to drive the turntable round, I fished out my lighter and applied the flame to the wicks. Having checked that the catch was securely locked on the table, I knocked the bags apart and returned the engine hose to its dummy then, walking out of the shed and seeing that he road was clear, I beckoned Dick to follow me with our 3F, to the water column.

Climbing up onto the back of the tender, I dropped the bag in the tank and called down for Dick to turn it on. These water hoses, or bags as they were called, were made of pieces of leather, riveted together with copper rivets to form a tube. When the water was turned on a fine jet of water sprayed out of one of these joints to catch me on the side of my face. In the gloom of the dawn I couldn't see where it was coming from at first and in consequence managed to direct it involuntarily down my neck as well.

"You can have a wash in the cabin" Dick called in answer to my request to turn the water off. "No need to have one up there" he grinned. "Drag them fire irons onto the back before you come down" he added "or they'll get in the way when we coal her up."

Two more lessons learned. Watch the leaks and shift the irons. There's more to preparing than you realise.

Up to the top of the yard we ran, where I dropped off to reverse the points enabling us to run down to the Old Shed doorhole. Here we reversed again to join the queue for coal under the stage. When our turn came, I go up onto the stage to help wheel the loaded tubs out over our tender.

"Spent all your money yet?" my coalman adversary of a few weeks back sneered at me.

"Yes and put it to better uses than you would" I replied, with the obvious hint that he would have had it himself if I hadn't challenged him about it at the time.

"Cheeky illegitimate child" he answered or something similar.

I decided to let it rest as I would be seeing quite a lot more of him that day with five more engines to coal, let alone what the future days and weeks would bring. After all, I had won my point and he knew it.

Dick had trimmed the coal on the tender and made sure that I knew what was required. We stabled our steed on the coal road ready for her crew to step on and away and then started the whole round all over again, this time with a 4F.

I had two more days with Dick that week on the same duty where we prepared two class 3F's two class 4F's, a "Crab" and an 8F each day.

On the second day, in addition to our preparation duties, we also pulled an Austerity off the Wheel Drop Plant with a pair of coupled wheels missing, and on the third day positioned a class 2P onto the plant to have her trailing set of driving wheels removed.

The following week saw me marked up for two disposing turns with Sid King a recently Passed Fireman. If I had thought "prepping" hard work, then disposing was to disillusion me completely.

There were two systems in operation at Burton when it came to disposing: the quota system, whereby you disposed of six engines and got away home or the other system, in which you waited to do the engines at the foreman's request but invariably found yourself on the shed for the best part of the eight hours. The only benefit being that sometimes you might not do as many engines.

As I hadn't done any disposing before Sid wisely decided on the second plan of action as he would be taking on the role of teacher, I not having a clue how to go about it.

We retired to the cabin and had a drink of tea while Sid attempted to explain roughly what went on. After about an hour the foreman's assistant, Pete Smith, came in and gave Sid our first engine. A class 3F again, what else! As we walked down the yard to her in the New Shed Ashpit, it started to rain. We had hardly reached the shelter of the cab when it really set in and literally hammered down.

"This will lay the dust" Sid remarked as he looked into the box. I snuggled up into the corner of the cab out of the rain, only to be asked by Sid to see if I could find the firebar tongs. The New Shed Ash Pits would only hold three engines and a glance out of both sides of the cab reveal no sign of them anywhere.

"You'll probably have to go over to the other pit." Sid remarked helpfully. "Mind you I should hang on a minute. We can't have you catching the flu on you first day can we!"

I waited a few minutes but the rain still came pouring down and, by the look of the sky, would continue to do so for quite some time to come so I climbed down and set across the yard to the other pit. As I got near I saw what I was looking for and, as I leant across the pile of ash alongside to reach them, a head appeared over the side of a 4F cab and informed me in no uncertain terms to forget it as he was a quota man and had first claim on them.

A searching look up and down showed what looked like the handles of a set poking up behind the ash pile about ten yards away. I dashed towards them and in my haste tripped over an old smokeplate, gashing my shin on its ragged edge. However I staggered on to my quarry and pounced upon them, only to let go even more quickly as they were very hot.

In response to my involuntary yell another face appeared over the adjacent cab side and informed me to be careful as they had just been thrown out and were red hot.

"Now he tells me," I mused. I am by now totally fed up with disposing having barked my shin, burnt my hand and got wet through into the bargain. We hadn't even put one engine away yet .Carefully holding these blasted tongs right on the end, I reared them up against the side of the cab. Sid, I saw, now had a pair of strong gloves on. He hauled the tongs aboard and inserted them into the firebox. While I had been away he had racked the fire back and exposed a section of the firebars at the front of the box. Clamping the tongs around one of these bars he coiled himself up and, with a combined leap and twist, bounced the handles of the tongs on the mouthpiece, dislodged one of the bars and lifted it out of the box. He then repeated the exercise with two more, these being relatively easy to remove, now that the first one was out.

It was then just a matter of pushing all the clinker and ash through the resultant hole, having of course opened the damper door first. I dropped down into the pit and racked all the contents out into the pit below. Then it was a case of replacing the bars, spreading the good fire back under the door and adding some fresh coal to it. I found replacing the bars a lot more difficult than removing them and that was hard enough in its self, particularly the first one. However, Sid could have all three back nearly as quickly as it takes me to write and tell you about it. I never truthfully acquired the skill and many were the bars I dropped through, into the ash-pan below. Practise makes perfect however, and I did acquire a certain expertise as time went on. I always felt that it was preferable to bailing it out through the door with the long paddle. This cumbersome piece of apparatus consisted of a shovel or paddle on the end of a ten- foot,long steel shaft with a loop on the end. When inserted into the firebox a paddle-full of fire was scooped up then the paddle withdrawn, manoeuvred out of the box and round the cab to be discharged through the doors to the ground beneath. Easy you might say, nonsense I'd say. Having been inside the firebox and over and into the fire, the steel handle, being an excellent conductor of heat, gets very hot and requires a padded cloth to hold it, to protect your hands from burning. So hot does everything become that even the cloth starts to smoke. Then, as if that isn't enough, while manipulating the paddle in the cab, the loop on the other end of the steel rod has a nasty habit of hooking itself on some projection or other in the cab or on the tender handbrake, causing it to deposit its red hot contents onto the cab floor.

Some of the newer engines were fitted with a rocking grate and hopper ash-pan. The later class 5's in the 446xxx and 447xxx series are so fitted. The remainder, and that is the majority of the class, as well as all the 8F's are not. Yet, as these engines pass through the works for overhaul, they are still not modified, but stay the same old way.

If the tank was less than half full it was the practice to top up the tender, and in the case of a tank engine, it was always filled anyway as the water capacity of even the largest tank engine was only 2,000 gallons, with most of them being considerably less.

When this was completed all that remained was to collect the tools and return them to the stores, a task usually carried out while on route to stabling the engine.

Thus was the awesome duty of engine disposal, methods varying somewhat with different engine types, but the end result being of course, the same.

Another turn that came the way of us junior Passed Cleaners, though not me personally, was that of fireman on the shed shunt engine. Although an engine was allocated to this job, it was rarely if ever used. Invariably any suitable engine in steam that was handy was pressed into service, to either place a few wagons on the Ash-Pits for loading, or possibly another six or eight loads of coal to be pushed up onto the Coal Stage, with of course the prior requirement of removing the empty ones first. This movement occurred at least once every shift. Other needs might be a van for the loading of dried sand for dispatch to an outstation like Overseal or Horninglow, or a wagon with a newly refurbished set of wheels from the works, to be shunted into the Old Shed and there positioned under the hoist for unloading.

The official engine for this duty had the honour shared between Burton's spare 0-4-0's, numbers, 51217, 51235, 56020, 41516, 41523, 41532, 41536 and 47000. As only duties for two of these four wheelers was current at the time, the first engines of this list were never or very rarely called upon to work and in consequence patiently clocked up eight miles per day between them on this duty without turning a wheel or feeling the warmth of a fire in their boilers, until they had clocked up sufficient miles to allow them to go to the works for overhaul prior to returning to their slumbers in a corner of the shed again. Alternatively some other engine in very run down conditions and overdue shopping, might find itself allocated on paper to the duty whilst hiding in another corner, awaiting the day of departure for works attention.

A trip across to Leicester Junction was also required twice a day to convey empty wagons (Ex loco coal), loads of ashes, wagons of wheelsets for works attention, sand vans and the like. On return, more loco coal would be worked in along with any other shed traffic as described. Also, wagons of scrap metal for Lloyd's foundry, situated behind the shed, was conveyed along with any rail traffic for the FNF (Fine Needles Frames) factory that had a siding off the shunting neck as well. All this traffic was handled by the shed shunt crew with their acquired engine, under the watchful eye of George Terrington, the shed shunter.

George combined these very exacting duties with that of bookies runner for the shed, a most important task and one that called for a clear head and an addiction to punctuality. Many were the 'sixpence each way' and 'shilling roll ups' or whatever, thrust into his hand each day, the selection being written on just about any type of paper imaginable, such as torn up cigarette packets, the backs of wagon labels, drivers notices and the borders of the daily papers. No official betting slips in those days as, off course, betting was illegal. Everyone always got his winnings and, if queried, it was a joy to witness George work out even the most complicated bet in his head and with a few stabs of his finger on any suitable surface, be it an engine frame, a wagon side or the mess room table, convince the poor unfortunate punter who had the temerity to a query it in the first place. It pleased me to discover, in later years, that his brother lived but a few doors away from my brother and sister in law in a tiny hamlet called Model Village, between Long Itchington and Southam in Warwickshire, over fifty miles away. Another example of that often used phrase "what a small world we live in!!

On one occasion, whilst collecting another load of scrap metal for delivery into Lloyd's Foundry, the driver noticed that one of the wagons contained a large number of spanners amongst it contents. George was informed and the wagon concerned mysteriously found itself inside the new shed instead of the foundry, to the great delight of the artisan staff, of which by then I was one myself. However the laugh was on us, for when the spanners were used, and very nice they looked too, they were all of soft metal, having not been annealed to harden and strengthen them. Hence their presence in the scrap wagon in the first place.

Whilst on the subject of shed shunting and their engines, an unusual job once came my way with one of the lesser of the 0-4-0's, 51217 to be exact. Along with one of the Passed Firemen, I forget now who, I was once again booked on control relief. On signing on again at 2pm, the foreman gave us a job right away. We were to prepare and coal, then take 51217 light engine to Tame and Rae Gas Works Birmingham. She was apparently on hire or loan whilst their own engine was being overhauled.

I had seen this delightful little bright green Peckett 0-4-0, shunting about on a couple of my trips to Birmingham. Wasn't her driver in for a shock I told myself, when he saw what we had brought him.

So we gathered up a set of tools and a bottle of oil and wandered off to find her. The cleaners had sloshed some paraffin about in a futile attempt to clean her, only succeeding in making everywhere greasy/dirty instead of just dry/dirty. All the traditionally shiny steel surfaces like hand rails, water levers, reversing lever and regulator handle were heavily rusted and covered with soot, with the brass work green with verdigris. What a mess!! Where do you start? Surprisingly a full set of short fire irons reposed on top of the tank. At least that was one blessing. One of the gauge glass protectors was also missing, but a protracted search around the shed revealed 51235, from whence I acquired the last surviving set off her! A quick run round to my locker for my gloves and I set about trying to raise some steam.

Like 41516 and their like, a firing shovel was but a hindrance on such a small engine, with its diminutive footplate and firebox. The steam raiser had filled the tank from one of the boiler-washing hydrants alongside. Noticing some broken firebrick nearby, I gathered up a shovel-full and proceeded to spread it over the bars, a handful at a time. On top of this I spread the fire with the clinker shovel and then added a few cobbles of fresh coal by hand, piece by piece. Although the blower was roaring away nicely, the clock read zero so I concluded that it, like a few more things on this engine, didn't work.

"How are you doing mate?" asked my driver.

"Ok, I think," I replied "but the gauge is bust so I don't know how much steam we've made."

"I'll see the fitter then. Anything else you've spotted that we need?"

"A smoke plate and mouthpiece shield!" I ventured.

"You'll be lucky" he grinned as he went off to find the fitters.

I dropped a few more cobbles around the box and then went to check the sand boxes. There was about half a box full in each and one of the front ones had its lid missing. Still, its contents were dry so another trip to 51235 was called for, to acquire a replacement. The steam raiser saw me and informed me that he had earlier purloined four fire bars from her for 51217 as well. "At this rate" he joked, "There'll soon only be a boiler on wheels left," and asked, if so, could he have it for a wheelbarrow!

On the way back I spotted two sand buckets and so returned, via the sand-hole, with them both full, and the purloined lid in my pocket. One bucket was sufficient to fill both sandboxes on the one side, and so triumphantly went round the engine to fill the other two, where unbelievably, the sandbox lid, ex 51235 wouldn't fit! It was too small. Yet it looked the same as the one on the other side.

As I turned towards the cab to tell my mate, the fitter was walking away.

Bang! A sound I recognised as a gauge glass breaking, reached my ears. He turned back, cursed and returned to the engine. We arrived at the cab step together.

"Don't know where you're going to find another one of those!" he snaps

"Well we ain't going without it," my mate replied. "And while you're at it, perhaps you would be so kind as to change the other one as well."

"The sandbox lid isn't big enough" I chipped in.

"Asterisks, asterisks!!" replied the fitter and stomped off. As he passed the 0-6-0 tank in front he reached across, snatched off one of its lids and threw it at me. I jumped aside as 25lbs of cast iron flew past my body, to hit the motion plate and fall in half a dozen pieces to the shed floor.

"Well done mate," my driver remarked, "He seems a bit upset about something or other doesn't he?" he added.

"What'll I do about the lid then?" I enquired.

"I might just mention it when he comes back. Lets get the glass fixed first, and for goodness sake don't mention that I broke it on purpose either." he remarked. As if in reply to my incredulous gaze he added, "This thing has stood here for months. Who knows when they were last changed. Could have gone any time."

I knew he was right in what he said and nodded in agreement.

Eventually the rotund shape of Cyril Barclay came into view with tools and new glasses and washers in his hand.

"The surly sod has sent his Mate back to do the job. He's alright. As good as they come." Said my Mate, adding mischievously, "Hope she don't tip up when he gets on."

Ex LYR 0-4-0ST No. 51217. Photo: P. Webb

I burst out laughing and we both stood aside, trying to stifle our mirth as he climbed aboard.

"That's made the springs creek" I tittered as my Mate gave my ears a playful cuff.

"You found some then Cyril" my Mate said when he had composed himself.

"Got a box full in the stores so I brought you a couple extra to take with you" Cyril puffed in reply.

The gauge was reading 70lbs psi and I was itching to add some more fuel to the flames but I would have to wait. I could hardly see the boiler beyond Cyril's bulk, let alone the fire-hole doors. Eventually both glasses were changed and he stepped down, wiping his brow with a dirty hand cloth.

As I opened my mouth to speak, my Mate put his finger to his mouth and made a "Shush" gesture. When Cyril had left us and disappeared around the turntable my Mate nipped off old 51217 and came back with the sandbox lid taken from the other side of our stable-mate and dropped it neatly over the top of ours.

The gauge was now creeping up to the 100lb mark.

"When we're on 140 we'll get the table and see if we can get rid of this thing in front, then coal up, top up the tank and get out of here. We've been messing about for long enough," my driver declared.

More cobbles are fed into the box and I watched the needle climbing round the clock. The fire was slowly building up nicely and I resolved to use the same method of firing as I had on 41516 namely a moderately thick fire. Evenly spread all over the grate. This I suggested to my Mate.

"Don't see why not," he agreed, "sounds as good as anything else. Perhaps a little bit thicker under the door and back corners. I don't know, I've never even seen it in steam before, let alone been on it."

As if to confirm our method, at that moment 51217 lifted her valves and a quick glance at the gauge saw the needle just under the 160lb mark.

A bit of fiddling about and the injectors were tested and the boiler topped up.

"Get the table, mate" is my next instruction. Having checked that no engine is about to run into the shed and onto it, I release the catch and wind it round nearly half way to line up with the "Jocko" and our valiant steed hiding behind it. Re-locking the catch, I go back to ease the hand brake on the Jocko off.

My mate eases the lever into forward gear, winds off the brake and opens the regulator. Everything disappears in a cloud of steam, but no movement occurs. Another attempt and still no movement.

"Try her in reverse," I suggest.

"Not a lot of room that way mate," my driver answers. He pulls the lever back and gives the handle a stab. Sods law immediately takes over and 51217 lurches backwards into the shed wall about six or eight feet behind before she can be reversed again, whence she dashes into contact with the Jocko and is catapulted back into the wall again for a second time as her solid wooden buffers meet up with the sprung variety as fitted to the 0-6-0. This entire happening, enshrouded in a cloud of steam, occurring in less time than it takes to tell.

"That was fun, shall we try again now that she's got the idea," my mate quips and gently eases our little bronco up to the Jocko again. I drop under the buffers and, straddling the pit, join the two engines together with the wagon coupling, which is hanging off the Jocko's draw hook. Most shunting engines return to the shed with one of these couplings hanging on the hook, as they are much lighter and easier to use by the shunter than the engine's own three-link coupling. Of course some engines are equipped with a screw coupling, which is nigh, impossible to control with a shunting pole even when stationary, let alone on the move.

Clambering out, I climb up onto the Jocko and release the brake.

"Come on then," I shout and my mate gives 51217 the works. She lurches back and forth into the buffers like a terrier on a lead but forward movement or indeed any movement of the 0-6-0 is none existent.

"Bloody silly thing," my mate curses, "Are you sure you've got that brake off?"

"Of course I have," I shout back.

All this furore attracts quite a crowd who assemble around the table-hole to watch the fun.

"Uncouple her, mate," my next order. "Get on and stop her on the handbrake. I'm going to set back and then run at her and bat her on, bloody, bloody thing!"

I do as I am requested and, setting back into the wall again, my mate literally throws 51217 at my "Jocko" only to bounce back into the wall again for the umpteenth time. They don't build walls like that today. But we are winning. I am on the move, 51217 tears into me again and the Jocko is now really moving.

Like a dog after a cat she's at my mount again and this time we are rolling on to the table with our little L&YR Pug puffing along behind. A cheer goes up and I look round to see about thirty spectators shouting and laughing. Bump, bump and my Jocko is on the table. Pause and then another bump, bump, bump and, to the accompaniment of thirty odd voices all shouting "Whoa," I wind the hand-brake on. Having come to a halt and made fast the brake, I kid myself that per-haps our spectators will wind the table round for us. As I climb down and look round the only person in sight is my mate, as I might have known.

I wind the table round a couple of roads and re-secure it so that we can shunt the Jocko off onto one of its sisters standing down the bottom of the pit. A quick check to see if anyone is working on her first, then my mate sets back with 51217 and charges into us again and away we go without any bother onto the appointed pit road. Having tied her down again I bid a fond farewell to the Jocko and rejoin my mate on the table as he winds it round to the out-going road.

"You're not going to like your fire, mate" he says, "all that excitement has really knocked it about."

I opened the doors and had a look inside. What was left of the fire had all gone to the sides of the box, leaving a hole through which the bars were visible in the middle.

Right, I though, "Drastic needs calls for drastic action."

"Wait in the door hole mate" I requested, "I shan't not be long."

With that I ran round to the sand-hole and collected a shovel full of fire from out of the furnace.

"How do you propose to get that lot into here?" asked my mate. "There's no room to turn round yourself, never mind with that great long thing."

"Pass me the firing shovel down will you?" I replied. Where upon I emptied my large pan of fire upon the shed floor then passed it up a shovel full at a time for him to deposit in the firebox.

A passing cleaner offered to return the pan to the sand-hole, so off we went to coal our little charge up. This we did by backing down to the reserve coal stack, and throwing the coal off the top into our two diminutive bunkers. When we had loaded on as much coal as we could, we topped up the tank that, incidentally only held 850 gallons. A run up to the guards relief cabin to collect our guard, followed. We required a guard, as we had to tow a brakevan with us as our wheelbase on its own was of insufficient length to operate the track circuit. As I went to inform him we were ready, I grabbed the tea can to brew up.

"Don't quite know where we are going to put it," I commented to my Mate as I got down with it.

"I'll find somewhere, don't you worry, even if I have to throw you off," he grinned.

Our guard proved to be even larger than Cyril.

"Wait till he gets on our little footplate!" I smiled to myself as I mashed the tea. "My mate will have to get off as well to make room for him." As we were going out of the cabin door, I spied a nice little guard's dustpan lying by the stove. Quick as a flash, I bob down and up again with it securely hidden beneath my overall jacket. "Could be very useful, " I reasoned. How right it proved so be.

In my absence my mate had been busy building up the fire and so with a full glass and 160lbs on the clock we were as ready to go, as we ever would be.

With all three of us somehow wedged inside the cab, we reverse down to the belling out peg. My mate shuts the regulator with the idea of free-wheeling down to it, but 51217 stops straight away without need to use the brake. So a bit more steam and we arrive at the phone.

"51217 light Engine to Leicester Junction Siding for a brake, then engine and brake Tame and Rae gas works and God bless all who sail in her," I tell the bobby.

"Wait while I get my hankie, I enjoy a good laugh" he answers, then pulls off the peg and we are away. As we pass the enginemen's relief cabin, some wag hols up a piece of string.

"You should be on the stage," our guard tells him.

"Your front wheels ain't on the rails," he shouts back. "You fat so and so!!"

"Asterisk" was the only reply from our erstwhile guard. "He wouldn't last two minutes down the Working Men's," he added turning to us.

What was he doing down the Working Mens' Club I wondered, but didn't dare say it.

After standing for about ten minutes on the end of the Shobnall branch, the dolly dropped off and we crossed over all running lines to stand on the Leicester Branch prior to getting the road into the sidings. A couple of minutes elapsed and my mate told me to go across to the phone to remind the bobby that we were there, as we wouldn't show on his circuit board.

"Come and sign the book" he said when he answered.

So I set off back across the boards to do just that. As I arrived alongside the shed, the Passenger for Leicester came out of Burton Station and up towards the junction.

"I'll just get in the box when it goes by and my mate is signalled across into the sidings," I reasoned, and so it proved to be. Still, I had come to sign the book and sign it I did. It all helps to keep the record straight.

When I got back to our little engine it was buffered up to the brake, one of the double veranda LMS 20-ton type, and our rotund guard was leaning over the front rail, awaiting me to couple up for him.

"Surely that's either your job or the shunter's while we are here?" I questioned.

"There used to be a dustpan in our relief cabin you know," he replied "been there ages it has. I wonder what happened to it?"

As I screwed the coupling up between the van and engine, I thought of one or two places to put it when I had finished with it, none of them a million miles away from where I was standing.

My mate had "knobbed" the fire up again while I had been away and it now looked like a mini volcano in there. A signal clattered over our head and a 4F came running through on 'the slow' with a load of coal.

"Reckon we'll be following him," my mate said and sure enough a soon as it was clear, the points slammed over and the dolly dropped off.

A toot on our pop whistle and over went the handle for the start of our expedition to Birmingham, for on this little thing it could hardly be called just another run.

51217 just stretched the draw hooks and then catapulted back into the van again.

"I don't believe it, he's still got his brake on, the dense 'person'," snorted my driver.

I leapt off the engine and up on to the veranda. Bursting through the door into the van I lifted the ratchet and wound the wheel off. The Ollie Hardy look-alike was setting his stall out without a care in the world.

Flopping down in his comfortable seat he moaned, "Oh dear you did give me a fright. I don't know what I thought was happening."

"Just pay attention to what's going on," I shouted over my shoulder as I left.

Leaping back onto the footplate, I shouted out, "Right away mate, you was right, he had got it on." "What a waste of space he is." I thought.

As we moved off I glanced over towards the junction box. There was both the bobby and the recorder with handkerchiefs in their hands, wiping their eyes and rocking back and forwards in mock laughter. Or perhaps it was for real!!

We trundled along, behind the brake of the 4F's train, until he stopped in a position that indicated he had another train ahead of him. After four or five minutes another freight, this time in charge of an 8F, pulled up behind our brake. Looking back, I thought I recognised the driver as my old friend Ted from Toton (see chapter six), so I dropped off to see and so it proved to be. As I went past our brake, our guard shut his door too. He probably thought that I was coming back to have another go at him.

"Like it round here do you?" I asked as I climbed aboard.

He introduced me to his mate who, coincidentally I had taken the place of that day. His face still carried the scars of the accident that had kept him off work for nearly four months. I felt a bit embarrassed in view of the reason I had met Ted in the first place and began to wish that I had not come. My mate gave a toot on the whistle and, just as I turned to go, Ted's mate noticing my feelings, shook my hand and wished me well.

When I got to Branston, the bobby put us inside and there we waited while both Ted and two more trains behind him overtook us. We filled the tank again while we waited and put in, at a guess, about 100 gallons. And we'd only gone a couple of miles as yet.

Eventually we toddled on to Barton and Walton bit by bit down the block.

When we, in out turn, arrived at the front of the queue, the bobby there had the audacity to turn us down the sand-hole sidings.

I went across to the box to see him and find out what was going on. He put me on to control who told me that we would have about an hour wait until there was a gap which would allow us to run to Wychnor at 15 miles an hour.

When I got back on to our little engine and told my mate, he seemed quite pleased.

"Money for old rope this job mate," he said, "Overtime, plenty of it, our day's half up already and we're not even a quarter of the way there yet."

Ollie Hardy called from his veranda to find out what I knew and commenced to moan again straight away. "I don't want no overtime. Working these long hours is not doing me any good."

"Carrying that barrel about in your trousers isn't doing you any good!" I mused and turned my back on him.

As the hour approached, I built up the fire with the aid of the dustpan so that, come the moment, we would be ready for our four mile, 15 mph, dash.

A compound came through going great guns with a rake of parcel vans, closely followed by a Stainer 2-6-2T with three coaches, which stopped in the platform. Away he went and then it was our turn. With one eye on the points and the other on the dolly I was able to anticipate the moment.

Slam, clang and, with a pop of the whistle, we're out and away up the main line.

Our 13" diameter cylinders are driving the 3' wheels round ever quicker as the connecting and coupling rods become a blur. I'm feeding coal in, broken up earlier with my dustpan. The injector is going on and off in short bursts and needle is very slowly falling down the clock. My mate has her pulled up two notches on the reverser. He jags the regulator over a bit more as she starts to feel the 1-in-450 pull of the grade up to Wychnor. He drops her down a notch and the noise at the chimney sound more like a 3F than what she really is. The blast is pulling the fuel straight off the pan and I'm having trouble keeping the back corners fed. Most of the fuel is ending up at the front of the box and I'm expecting a hole to appear again in the middle any minute. We are now pounding along, one notch off full gear and with the valve just open onto the main gate. Pressure, despite all my efforts, is now at 110lbs and falling. Standing up to get the small rake off the tank top in an effort to pull back some of the un-burnt fuel from under the arch, I see the junction signal for Wychnor coming into view. Both boards are at danger so we will be stopping in about a minute or so's time, however we still have to keep pounding away until we get to them, for to shut the regulator now and expect to free wheel the rest of the way just won't work with this engine as we discovered earlier.

When we did stop I first had to carry out Rule 55 again, so over to the box I went. As I was signing the book, the bobby, who I knew by sight from my tripper days, told me that I hadn't got a lamp on the front of the engine.

"We had one when we left the shed," I assured him.

"Well, you've not got one now," he answered.

On my way back I had a look and, sure enough, it had gone. 51217 had certainly done some pitching on our dash from Barton but I wouldn't have thought things had been bad enough to throw a lamp off. The other one was still on the back bracket, illegally perhaps but there was nowhere else safe to put it, so I quickly transferred it to the front middle iron. "Could have done with the wag's piece of string now to tie it on with," I thought to myself. My mate had had a go at the fire again during my absence and things were looking much rosier again, or so I thought!

A Jubilee, assisted by a 2P, came charging across the junction. I count 14 coaches in tow as they accelerate away towards Burton. The points changed, the board came off and we chugged across the junction, to reverse into Wychnor Sidings. As we came to a stop, I enquired whether or not I should make another brew.

"I'll go," my mate volunteers, "I've got to ring control. That last little sprint was a bit much for her I'm afraid. She's run three boxes hot and the fourth is a bit warmer than I like."

I got down to have a look myself. On feeling the axle end on the one nearest to me, I nearly burnt my fingers. "So that's that then, I suppose." I mused. I was getting quite attached to her in a funny kind of way. She hadn't really had a chance. Coming straight out of store like that, without having a few days running-in or pottering about the shed yard or the like. "Our guard's conspicuous by his absence as well," I thought so, creeping up the side of the brake, I peeped through the window. When my eyes became accustomed to the lower light level inside, I saw he was sound asleep, lying on one of the long lockers that stretched the full length of each side of the van, his head resting on an air pillow. Just then, my mate returned and I beckoned to him, signalling in sign language to keep quiet.

"Well, he did tell you how hard he worked and now you can see for yourself," he retorted, "Let him sleep on, his moaning gets on my nerves."

When the boxes had cooled down and, after applying all the oil both we and the Wychnor trip engine had spare, we made our leisurely way back home to Burton and on to shed.

51235 made the journey with a little more success the following week, just for the record.

The foregoing, of course, was experienced after I had been out firing for some 12 months or more.

Chapter 2

Off the Shed At Last

Having spent a few weeks sweating away, disposing and preparing engines, with various drivers and Passed Firemen, the former working out their last days and the latter just starting out on their driving careers, I felt the need to venture further afield and out onto the line, past the belling-out peg.

As with most things, patience is its own reward and there on the sheet, for the following Monday, was the legend: P/C Fleming, report Horninglow 05.00 N DIXIE.

"What's that," I asked George Swann, my Passed Fireman driver for the day. We were sat in the canteen waiting for the last two engines to put away before going home. We had already disposed of two Class 3F's and an 8F and, although my mate, as with most young drivers, had done his share, I for one was glad of the rest.

"Can't say that I've ever worked that job Dave," he replied, "But I know you're in sight of the shed most of the time. The Western Shed."that is of course. Not exactly Main Line then," I thought to myself, "But we all have to start somewhere."

N Dixie or New Dixie, as it turned out to be, was part of a complex of sidings to the east of the main line between Horninglow Bridge and Wetmore Bridge, centred on the area around Hawkins Lane where, indeed, was a public house named The Dixie. Although this had nothing to do with the railway, I found that it did figure in my driver's plans for the day.

So, on a dull, damp, Monday morning, in early October, my inner man full of egg and bacon, my mother having heroically got up and prepared about 40 minutes before, I climbed astride my trusty cycle and pedalled off, in the opposite direction to my normal journey. I was about half an hour early, as I wanted to take my time and get everything right on my first turn. On arrival at the shed, which, like most of its kind had no proper road access but involved a wander across an ill defined path, not the easiest journey on a bike, especially for the first time in the darkness. I reported to the night chargeman whose name, I think, was Nibbs.

It certainly wasn't Clarence Coles, he of the artificial leg, an ex driver who had taken on the chargeman's job following the unfortunate accident resulting in the amputation. He had a reputation for being unpredictable and bad tempered, not without reason I suppose, but I always found him quite alright myself. It was rumoured that, whenever he saw the engine that resulted in his accident, he would swear at it and hit it with his stick but I never witnessed that either. However, I grew to know that, swear – he most certainly could!

Mr Nibbs, known by all and sundry as "Nibby," was either trainer or physio' for Stapenhill Football Club, one of the top teams in the local league at the time.

"7643 is your engine, lad so you'd better get sorting her. She's outside, down the side," he informed me.

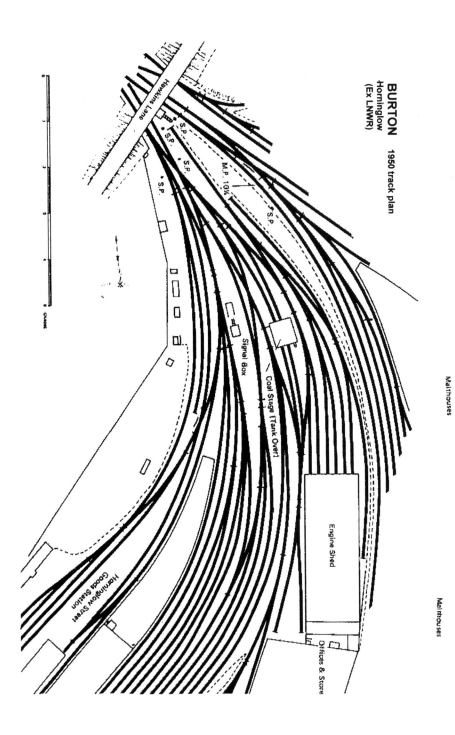

BURTON
Horninglow
(Ex LNWR)

1950 track plan

Hawkins Lane

S.P.
S.P.
S.P.
M.P. 10¾
S.P.

Signal Box

Coal Stage (Tank Over)

Engine Shed

Horninglow Street
Goods Station

Offices & Store

Malthouses

Malthouses

The Western Shed was a typical ex-LNW straight shed, originally with a north light roof but this had been replaced, in 1946, with a prefabricated concrete one as part of the post-war LMS reparation plan, being one of the first, if not the first shed to be so treated. I walked back to the shed entrance turning to walk down the outside of the wall and there she was, easy to pick out being the only one there. Whilst walking up the inside of the shed I had noticed that the smoke from the engines, which would have been lit up that morning, didn't seem to hang inside the building as it did at the Midland but carried away outside quite well.

Climbing onto 47643 and having to grope my way into the cab, which was full of smoke, I shone my bike lamp onto the gauge. She was just beginning to make steam and had about 20lb on the clock. Flames were licking around the door, which was of the ratchet type and half open. Knocking the blower on immediately pulled the flames back into the box and cleared the smoke out of the cab as well. What a mess was revealed in the beam of my lamp as I shone it round the footplate. Everything had a patina of soot and smokiness about it. "Where do I start?" I asked myself.

Sprinkling a bit of fuel on seemed a good idea, then check the sand boxes, the inside of the smokebox, making sure the door is firmly shut and air-tight, collect the tools and, most importantly, the oil for my driver. So, back round the shed wall and down to the chargehand to ask where to find them. "Come with me, lad," he said, "You've not been here before have you, so you won't know where owt is." Into the oil store, next door, where a row of buckets, complete with tools, were lined up on the floor. Alongside each was a shovel and the all important oil bottle and feeder. "The lamps should be on the engine some-where," he added, "You'll need to clean and trim them yourself."

"Is there any firebrick?" I enquired, as a bit spread onto the bars helps to prevent clinkering because the waste deposits tend to cling to the bricks rather than to the bars themselves.

The chargeman laughed, "You're not down the Midland now laddie, this is Indian Country. You'll not find luxuries like that here."

With that, I staggered off with my burden and loaded them onto our steed. I shot a round into the box and a sprinkle across the middle, being careful not to add too much coal at a time until it had really caught alight. Most of the fire was just under the door and I didn't want to spread it out too quickly and put it out. The gauge had gained another 10lbs or so in my absence and the water level, when I had cleaned the frame so that I could see it, was about half an inch up the glass. No worries there then for, when the water warms up and makes steam, it expands and consequently gives a higher reading. I tested both gauge frames and, as already described, cleaned the glasses and protectors. Putting the oil bottle on the frame plate, I took up the $^3/_4$ - $^7/_8$ spanner and went to the front of the smokebox to check inside. It all looked fine in there with no tubes leaking, washout plugs blowing or anything else. Whoever had put her away on Saturday had done a good job of cleaning out all the ash so I wiped round the joint and door ring and closed the door, tightening up all the dogs around the circumference with the spanner. Then, while I was up there, I looked in the front sand boxes, which of course, appeared to be empty. Remembering my preparing turns at the Midland, I reached in as far as I could to feel if what sand that was in there was dry or wet-through. As I found the latter was indeed the case, there didn't seem much point in adding any more. As I found the back sands to be the same, I thought I would see what the driver had to say about it when he arrived. As 7643 wasn't standing over a pit I couldn't check the ashpan properly but, as a nice red glow was beginning to appear through the damper, I assumed it must be clean. Anyway, we would have to go over a pit to oil round, I reasoned.

Burton (Horninglow) shed ex LNWR. Photo: Authors Collection.

Just as I was climbing back into the cab to check on the fire and, with a bit of luck, have enough steam to work the injector, as well to starting to clean it up, my driver climbed up the other side. A flat cap appeared, under which was a fringe of white hair and a ruddy face, followed by a portly body, which seemed to have a problem squeezing between the uprights of the cab opening. A pair of rather short legs and feet encased in boots, the shine from which would have put many a guardsman to shame, completed the picture.

"Good morning, mate," I greeted him, cheerfully, "I'm Dave Fleming from the Midland and I'm with you today. I've put the oil to warm and, when we get a bit more steam, I'll soon have this place looking nice and tidy."

He scowled back and said, "I'm the driver, not your mate. Just give me steam and we'll get on all right."

"Up yours then," I thought and climbed down again to trim the lamp.

"Where are you going now lad, watch out, I'm going onto the pit," he called, moaning, "What a bloody mess"

As we had barely 50lbs of steam by then, I thought he would have waited but, no! Next thing, he was hammering away at the handbrake with the coal pick to release it, as the steam-brake hadn't enough power behind it yet to take the weight off.

"If you'd concentrated on making this fire up instead of fiddling with the lamps and things you might have done better," he growled.

"We're going to have fun today, I don't think," I told myself, "What was he moaning about anyway. I was only just supposed to have arrived, like he had."

Eventually he wound off the brake and, throwing the engine into forward gear, he pushed open the regulator, looking over the side to perceive motion. Clouds of steam issued forth from the cylinder drain cocks and not a little from under the boiler, out of the glands but there was no progress forwards at all. To my amusement, I observed that the steam-brake was still on. 'Grumpy' snatched the regulator shut then heaved it open again with exactly the same result. Looking round, he then noticed the brake handle in the down position and with a furtive look in my direction, moved his not inconsiderable torso, to hide his hand as he gently lifted the brake handle up into the off position, whereby 7643 literally leapt forward with a great roar up the chimney and much slipping of the wheels.

"Pull that lever over would you," he said, pointing to the point lever outside, which would switch the road to let us back into the shed and over the pit. This done, he reversed down and stopped in a position suitable for oiling around underneath. I shot another charge round the firebox while he filled up his feeder. The pressure gauge was now reading 75lbs so I tested the driver's injector then, after shutting it off, put mine on. As he got off to start oiling around, I looked over the side and, seeing he was clear of the cab, started to attack the layer of soot that lay over everything. Wouldn't do to wet him, I reasoned. He was in a bad enough mood as it was. Shall I tell him about the sands now? I wondered. Why not! Get it over with, I decided.

"Just fill 'em up to the top, lad. Give 'em summat to do emptying them when they get round to puttin' 'em right. I booked 'em last week but nothin' gets done 'ere. No fitters, you see and they're not going to come up from the Midland just for that. And when they do get round to it, they'll be wet again as soon as the tank's filled." He moaned on, "Don't suppose you'd like to oil round underneath would you? I'm not as young as I was and I'm not exactly built for it now either, am I?"

I felt like saying no, after his initial attitude but just took the feeder from him and dropped down underneath. Doesn't want to get dirty, either, I mused, as I climbed up behind the middle axle and, being careful to keep my back off the firebox front, started screwing out the corks one by one and filling up the oil pots. Having completed the driving axle, I passed the feeder outside and, having checked the ashpan properly, climbed back out of the pit.

Grumpy had re-filled the feeder and, seeing the pleading look in his eyes, I took it off him again climbing up on the framing to oil the sidebars, little ends, expansion links and piston and spindle gland pots, etc. He had done the siderods, axlebox pots and brake-gear himself. As I went in search of a sand bucket or two, he climbed back into the cab to hang up his jacket and put his other traps away.

Another young fireman, who I hadn't seen before, spoke to me and said, "I see you're with that miserable old sod. Best of luck mate! I had him all last week on lates. Still, when they open, he'll be gone for an hour at least. And a bit of advice – keep out of the cabin on the Ale Dock or they'll have you."

"What do you mean?" I asked.

"Just try it if you want to find out," he rejoined, "Are you after these?" he said, indicating some buckets, "Sand's down there, through that door in the corner."

I picked up the two buckets he had indicated and strolled down to fill them up. They seemed to weigh a ton each when full and I resolved to put only one bucket full in each box. To my surprise, my driver brought the engine down the shed as far as he could towards me to save the long walk back. I emptied one bucket into the front box then endeavoured to pour the contents of the other through the keyhole at the bottom of the tank side to fill the back box. My new-found fireman friend appeared at my side at this moment with a piece of pipe, which bridged the gap between the keyhole and the sandbox lid. "Thought you might need this," he said and held it in place while I filled the box.

You've no chance of that old misery helping you," he added.

"Who would that be, then?" came my driver's voice from behind my new-found friend. We both looked around, aghast and I suddenly found myself alone with just an empty sand bucket and, of course, the driver, who had the makings of a smile on his face.

"One up to us there, kid," he said, "Just chuck a can-full in the other side and we'll fill the tank and make a start. I've filled the lubricator for you."

Filled the lubricator? I thought. What does he mean? Have I missed something? I resolved to ask him about it when I got the chance. He doesn't seem so bad after all, now he's been here a bit. I filled both sand buckets again and put the contents of one in each of the boxes on the other side, with the aid of the piece of pipe, noticeably held with much show by my driver.

General view of Horninglow yard with 35OHP diesel shunting the sidings. This was the job on which the auther had his first firing turn on Class 3F No. 47643. Photo: P.Webb.

"That'll do, kid," was his next remark, "We'll run up to the bag and top her up, then we're on our way. You'll see it sticking out of the stage wall when you get outside."

With that, I walked up the shed and outside towards the coal-stage, pulling a couple of point levers over as I went, to set the road for 7643 to follow.

When filling the tank on these shunters you had to be very careful for, if you overflowed the tank, the water ran down the sides and straight into the sand boxes. As ours was already wet I was not too bothered if this happened, although I did attempt to avoid it, just for the practice. As both tanks were connected by a balance pipe this also affected the speed with which they filled and I found that, if you shut off just as the level was coming to the top on the side you was filling from, the two tanks seemed eventually to balance out with about 50 to 100 gallons short of capacity and nicely below the top thus preventing it from slopping out when shunting back and forth. Of course, closing the lids after filling helped as well - another facet that most firemen seemed to ignore. Whilst all this was going on, I heard the driver putting a charge of coal into the box. Things are looking up, I thought.

After whistling up, the bobby in the box dropped the dolly and off the shed we went to start our day's work, initially right alongside the shed down at Horninglow Street Goods Wharf. Here we pulled the previous day's vans and wagons out of the goods shed and set them aside in a siding nearby. I fed another round of coal into the box to add to that which my driver had fed in a few minutes earlier. A glance at the clock shows that we now have 140lbs showing and with the blast of the chimney as we pull that raft out of the goods shed, the fire is really coming to life.

I slipped the injector on again and then looked out over the side to check the overflow to see that all the water is indeed going into the boiler and not wasting out of the overflow pipe below the step. A slight tap on the water handle to adjust the flow and every drop is being picked up. The tanks on 7643 hold 1200 gallons of water when full and its surprising how soon it can all be used up, so no point in wasting any.

Now we are moving onto another row of vans and these are now drawn out onto the road over the points, prior to being set back into the shed. After a bit of manoeuvring, they are set to the shunter's liking and we are hooked off to return to the original load we pulled out of the shed previously. These are then coupled back on and the shunter jumps on the step calling out, "Right away, Arnie, Take 'em round the corner."

So that's his name, Arnie is it! Arnold I suppose, I muse.

Arnie, for his part, blows a pop or two of some whistle code, whereupon the signalman, who must have been waiting for the moment, immediately pulls over the points and, as the signal drops off; one of those short arm shunting signals; he pushes open the regulator and with a little slip, 7643 gets the raft of about twenty vehicles on the move. Off we went, out past Hawkins Lane Box and under the bridge to enter the vast sidings complex on the other side.

As we rounded the curve onto the area known as New Dixie proper, we passed in front of one of Worthington's blue brewery engines waiting for the road, with

Ex LMS Class 3F No. 47643. Photo: K. Fairey

a number of open wagons loaded with beer barrels of various sizes. We reached the end of the yard, the shunter dropped off and, after pulling a few levers, I saw him calling us back.

"Right on, Arnie," I called, "Hit 'em up," and Arnie did just that, pushing the regulator well over and snatching it shut, then dropping on the brake as I shouted, "Whoa," in response to the shunter's next signal - throwing his arms up in the air. The whole raft disappeared down the sidings between two other rows of wagons with a runner keeping them company, ready to drop a couple of brakes on when he thought fit.

We then moved on to another road, collecting another raft, which we commenced to sort from road to road at the shunter's behest. This went on until about 9 o'clock, when we pulled some vans and wagons of barrels into the ale dock. As I looked out at what was going on, I noticed these big brewery labourers rolling and stacking the barrels, sorting them into groups and, after unloading one wagon, re-loading it with one of the sorted groups. As I looked closer I could see that some of these labourers were women or female at least. Their huge physique and indeed their language, did not allow the title: "ladies," to sit fairly on their shoulders.

"We'll have our snap now, kid," said Arnie. "Nip over the cabin and mash; and be quick, afore that lot have finished unloading them tubs. If they get 'old of you, you'll know about it."

I grabbed our two cans and shot off to the cabin as quick as I could. I spotted the urn bubbling away in the corner and soon had our cans full. Just as I turned to come away, I heard the door open behind me. My heart missed a beat as I looked round, to see this huge Amazon standing there.

"I hope you've not used all the water, you little 'person'," she swore, with a high melodious note, which quite belied her appearance.

"No," I stammered, "There's plenty left."

"There'd better be, you little 'person'," she repeated.

I scurried past her and out of the door like a rocket, so fast that Seb Coe would have been hard pressed to catch me, her laughter echoing in my ears. Dodging round more of her compatriots, as I dashed back to 7643, I jumped up into the cab, thinking, "Sanctuary! Sanctuary!"

Arnie sat in his corner with the suggestion of a smile on his face. "You made it then," he said. "A bit of a close call that, from what I could see," and so saying, poured himself a lid of tea and started on his breakfast. This consisted of a baked potato, which he retrieved from behind the clack box and, when cut in half, I could see was cooked to perfection. He then spread butter all over it and, along with his cheese sandwiches, ate with great relish and much smacking of his lips.

"I feel better for that, kid. Should last 'till opening time now," he remarked, butter still dripping down his chin. "Have a fry-up some mornings," he continued, "Got up a bit late this morning. Didn't have time to sort it so I just grabbed these spuds." With that, he got up and retrieved a second potato from behind the clack box on my side. "Might as well have it now. Don't know if we'll get the chance later on," he added. So saying, he went through the whole ritual again.

"What would have happened then, if I had got caught in the cabin?" I asked Arnie.

"Better you don't know, lad," he answered, spluttering baked, buttered potato down his chin. "Don't make me laugh, I'm tryin' to eat me snap."

And that was that! Who could I ask now? Who dare I ask now? Was it all a leg-pull? Some legend, passed down to alarm young fireman like myself? But, then again, I had faced the Amazon and lived to tell the tale. But, what tale?

"Better liven her up, kid," Arnie recalled me from my reverie, so I opened the damper and looked into the box. The fire had gone a bit dead so I just dropped a couple of shovels full under the door and let the ratchet top stay open, closing the bottom half. This, I felt, would better direct the secondary air over the grate when we got going. The gauge was reading about 140lbs and, with ³/₄ glass of water, I wasn't too concerned about what would happen when we started off again.

Soon we were back at it again, up and down, backwards and forwards, with wagon after wagon. Knocking them out, first down one siding then another. In between firing; and it's amazing how much steam is needed when shunting, it being all full gear work; I was trying to work out the technique that Arnie was using. When pulling a raft out, he seemed to give just a touch of steam, to gently tighten the couplings, before pushing the regulator more open to really get them going. Then, with a touch of the brake as he shut the regulator, he seemed to gather them up as the couplings slackened before making a full application, bringing the wagons under control and stopping them without any surging forward; which occurs when the wagons take over and start pushing the engine. Similarly, when propelling and making a shunt, it would initially be all-out on the regulator, followed by a slight easing, as the couplings were unhooked, before braking to a stop. This again, allowed the couplings on the wagons, still attached to the engine, to tighten and take the strain before stopping, therefore, hopefully, preventing any broken couplings. I would have loved to have a go but knew there was no chance of that happening.

All this to-ing and fro-ing with 7643 shouting loudly up her chimney, was producing quite a strong pull on the fire, which was now white hot and needing constant attention. Pressure was now holding at 160lbs and, when we stopped for a couple of minutes between shunts, the valves lifted.

"That's your back going up there, kid," Arnie chided.

"You said you wanted steam. So there you are," I shouted back.

"You'll do," he said, "Soon be having another minute, so I'd leave it if I were you."

I slipped the injector on and dropped the damper, opening the top half of the door and slacking the floor down again. Arnie's shiny boots got an accidental damping. "Now for it!" I thought. "That's bound to upset him again." But, no, he just looked down and said nothing. "Probably can't see them over his paunch," I amused myself, thinking.

"Right. Now, what's your name, I'm just off for a pint across the road. Just sit here and do nowt 'till I come back," said Arnie. "Keep your eye on things and don't move the engine, no matter what anybody says." With that he heaved his bulk through the door, climbed down the steps and trotted across the sidings quicker than I had seen him move all day.

After some 30 minutes or so, one of the shunters climbed up the steps and popped his head through the door.

"Where's Arnie then? As if I didn't know," he remarked. "Not gone walk-about again has he? You know, you'd think that pub would close if he didn't turn up every morning. He'll not be back afore 12 o'clock if I know him. No chance of you doing a quick job, I suppose?"

"You suppose right," I replied, "Much as I'd like to, of course."

"His regular Mate does, you know. In fact Alan does it all the time," he chided.

"Well he's not doing it today." Arnie's head appeared over the door on the other side. "What do you want Tom? A push up the shed?"

"Yes, when you're ready," he answered.

"Well done Arnie. Twice in one day. Are you psychic or what?" I asked.

"Twice?" puzzled Arnie. Then the penny dropped. "Oh are," he said, "Smart 'bum'. I'd forgotten about him. Eh lad, you might be right. I'll get that fireman. You see if I don't," he smiled. "Come on. Better put Tom out of his misery. He knew where I was, the old devil. He should do, he's usually with me!"

In no time at all the morning came to an end, and our relief set, both Western men who I did not know, stepped on. I was just giving the footplate floor another squirt round with the pep pipe as Arnie did his best to keep his feet out of the way. My only regret was not having the chance to clean the fire, as we had been in the middle of a shunt and had just stopped while the shunter checked his labels before knocking them out.

As we walked back to the shed, Arnie asked me how many turns I had done and I answered, truthfully, that this was my 23rd but the first time I had been off the shed.

Arnie said, "They know where to send 'em to train 'em. You're doin' alright, kid. See you again some time."

With that we signed off, Arnie booking the brakes and sands and me, more than ready for my dinner. I reflected that I never did find out about that 'lubricator' either.

The following day found me on disposing again, with Bill Clemson this time. Wednesday was a Rest Day and on the Thursday, I was put back to 12.40, working from Horninglow again. This time it was shunting at Old Wetmore with 47231, a Midland version of 47643 and beset with the same sanding faults as the standard engine. The distance to Old Wetmore from Horninglow Shed was over a mile and it had become the custom for the crew being relieved to run down, through the sidings complex to Dixie to facilitate the change over. My driver that day was Passed Fireman D. Smith, who was working his last week at Horninglow prior to transfer, to Rugby I think, for promotion to driver.

Ex MR Class 3F 0-6-0 No. 47231 which the author fired on the new Wetmore shunt. Photo: K. Fairey

47231 had been out about 8 hours when we took her over and the relief fireman said they had been so busy he hadn't had time to clean the fire. He was rather obese and I got the impression he wasn't telling the truth. She had about 120lbs on the clock, the water was out of sight in the top of the glass and the footplate looked like a farmyard.

"Nothing special about him!" I said to my new mate, who I think was called Dennis.

"No mate. He is a bit of an idle sod. He's been the same all week. He'd have to shape up a bit if he was with me regular, I can tell you," he answered.

I swept up the footboards and shovelled the rubbish into the box as we ran back through the sidings to Wetmore. When we arrived, Dennis had a look in the box and checked the condition of the fire by tilting the shovel this way and that, enabling a draught of air to be deflected over the fire-bed to see how it was. Our trip back had pulled the clock back another 10lbs so something really needed to be done before we did any real work.

"It's a bit thick under the arch and there's a fair bit of clinker in there too, mate," was his verdict.

"Right then, let's get to it," I replied and reached round the corner of the cab for the rake. I manoeuvred it into the cab and down into the box. "Do the front first," I thought and started to rake the fire back from where it was nearly solid, right under the arch. I had to be careful, as it's easy to knock a hole in the arch or even knock the lot down. After sweating away for about 10 minutes, I had near enough cleaned out the front end. Each paddle of clinker, when broken up, had to be lifted with the paddle, eased out of the box, then turned and bailed out over the side. All the irons are very hot and held, in the absence of gloves, with a couple of cloths; which are soon smoking with the heat.

"This is worse than disposing," I tell myself.

Then I fetched a couple of firebars up and pushed the lot through into the ashpan, there, to rake it into the pit.

Dennis, who had been perched up on the side of the tank out of the way, then volunteered to take over and do the back half. I was more than pleased to let him and got off the engine altogether, partly to give him room and partly to cool off.

The back end wasn't so bad and Dennis was soon spreading the good fire over the grate, adding some more fuel to help it along. All this activity had pulled the pressure down to about 80lbs. so there was only one way it could go and that was up. Although the water level was now in sight in the glass, I didn't dare put the injector on with the pressure so low. Another fireman, who I knew by sight from the Midland Shed, climbed up the steps, looking in the cab and up at the gauge.

"Blimey, mate, what's going on here?" he asked. "Have you ever been out before? If you can't make one of these steam, there's not much hope for you," all the remarks naturally, being made to me.

"Hold on there. It's not his fault," interrupted Dennis, "It's that fat idle sod (giving his name) who's to blame. Just let me have him for a couple of days. I'd soon alter his outlook on life."

"All right, calm down. I came to see if I could give you a hand," the visiting fireman retorted. "We're on the tripper and we're doing your work while you sit here.

I looked across, to see a Black 5 no less, shunting up and down. "What are you doing with that?" I asked.

"Running it in after a hot box," he answered, "My mate's not very pleased at having to wind that back and forwards I can tell you! Still, I've got enough fire in the box to last all day."

Picking up the shovel, I spread a bit more on ours, noting at the same time that the clock was reading three figures again, if only just.

"Give it another 10 minutes and we'll be ready," said Dennis.

"I'll be off then," our fireman friend said, adding, "Sorry to get you wrong, pal. See you around."

"Thanks for your help," said Dennis. "Yes, thanks," I echoed.

"I'll pop over to the cabin and tell the lads we're ready to start. Give us your can; I'll make a brew up while I'm there," said Dennis. "That should get the foreman going. Have to see if I can square the time as well. If he books it to us I'll have that bl..dy fireman or his mate."

When he got back, wreathed in smiles, I had got old 7231 nearly blowing off.

"Think I squared that one away, mate," said Dennis, "I see you've been busy too. OK, let battle commence. Get that brake off and let's get at it," and with a toot on the whistle, away down the yard we went, only to be told there was nothing to do for now as the trip engine had done it all. Told, I might add, with a hint of sarcasm.

"Drink your tea then, mate," said Dennis, "Did you say your name was Dave?"

I confirmed and so it was "Dave" for the rest of the shift.

After about a quarter of an hour, the LNER Yard shunt came round, with about 30 wagons for us to play with. Dennis told me that, until recently, an Eastern engine was used, which worked in from Slack Lane Shed at Derby on a Monday and stayed all week, being shedded overnight at the Western, but this practice had now ceased and a Midland engine was now. used. This was usually 47464 and, indeed, this was the engine in use that day. Some months later, when I was sent to relieve the ER fireman who had taken ill, 47464 was the engine again in use on that occasion.

So, we carried on until about 4.30, when the shunter joined us and we set off up the slow line under Wetmore Bridge and along to the English Grains Siding with half a dozen wagons of spent hops from Bass's Brewery. These, we shunted into the private siding and the previous day's empties drawn out, to be propelled back 'wrong line', the way we had come, back to Wetmore.

The siding at English Grains was inside a gate, which was closed and locked when not receiving or dispatching freight. Whilst this movement was going on, the normal permissive block arrangements were suspended and the shunt engine had sole occupation of that stretch of line. A similar situation also applied on the

No. 47485 shunts English Grains sidings. Photo: P. Webb

down, or south-bound goods line, when traffic was required to be delivered or collected at the Clay Mills Pumping Station, this traffic being mainly fuel for the boilers, with an occasional consignment of lime.

Our day came to an end just after 7.30, when we again trundled up through the sidings to hand over 47231; in a clean and efficient condition, with a full tank, bright clean fire and spotless footplate; to our relieving crew. Incidentally, Dennis had shown me all the vagaries of the Sight Feed Lubricator, so there was another snippet of information to add to my ever-increasing experience of a fireman's duties.

"I'll just call for a fish and chips supper on the way home," I decided. "After all that, I'm hungry and I think I've earned it!"

This was my last trip out of the shed for about a fortnight, when again I had another turn on the early New Dixie Jocko, this time with 47233. I forget who the driver was. In between time, it was back in the shed, preparing and disposing, with the odd day labouring, thrown in.

Chapter 3

On the Tripper

Having completed 29 firing turns, mostly preparing and disposing, with 4 duties off the shed, 2 being on the New Dixie shunt and one each on the Old Wetmore and Old Dixie Jocko's, it was with great pleasure that I found myself marked up for the 5.45 a.m. Horninglow Bridge Tripper, with Bob Shrive as my Mate.

This again required me to sign on about 5.00 a.m. to prepare the engine, normally an ex MR 2F 0-6-0. I resolved to arrive in plenty of time to enable me to do a good job but, in truth, I didn't make it until about ten minutes to five.

The preparing routine, being quite familiar to me by now and having been described in the previous chapter, I will not bother to detail.

As it was in the middle of the week, the engine had been in steam for a number of days and gave off a warm, comfortable ambience as soon as I stepped into the cab. Number 58221 was fitted with a Deeley cab and Belpaire boiler, the firebox of which had the usual Midland style ratchet door. The fire was reasonably made up and about 100lbs of steam was showing on the clock.

"Quite a good start," I thought as I went through the other prepping duties. Bob went round with the oilcan whilst I filled and regulated the sight feed lubricators to about three blobs per minute up the glass. This oil, of thick consistency, was known by us as saturated steam oil and was carried through to the cylinders and steam chest to lubricate their movement when the regulator was open. If the pistons and rods produced a groaning sound because they were running dry, it was a simple matter to increase the flow, thereby hopefully adding more lubrication to the affected parts. It was not unknown for a severe case to be 'cured' by pouring the oil straight down the blast pipe and into the steam chest underneath but of course, this encouraged carbonisation and was definitely not popular with the fitting department. However, 58221 was not suffering from this problem.

As time approached, we moved on to the turntable, turned to face north as the wind was blowing from that direction and moved out of the shed up to the crane to fill the tank. I managed to wet my feet and legs from the knees down, as was my way, despite all my efforts to avoid it and, suitably chastened, belled off the shed in company with a 4F that was also heading to Horninglow Bridge, setting out down the main line, through the station, to our destination.

Here we found a train already made up to Trip up to Leicester Junction and, in no time at all, we were there, ready to start our journey back. Leicester Junction is right opposite the Midland Shed, from which we had departed roughly 20 minutes before so you can see that our range of operations was not very large.

Our guard came to join us in the cab, as it's rare to have a brake van at the rear of a train when tripping within the confines of the Burton area.

"There's 43 on, equal to 50. Will you take them, Bob?" he asks.

"I usually do," he answered. "Better ask my mate, he's holding the shovel."

The guard, Fred, ignored that and me, replying, "Thought you would. I've hung the lamp on."

Even though there is no brake van at the rear of the train, a red lamp is carried on the last wagon to indicate to the signalman that the train is complete, as well as the obvious warning to following traffic.

Another train, with a 4F at its head, was standing, waiting at the peg on the slow road, for the path ahead onto the block section up to Leicester Junction so I reasoned that he would be going first and, in consequence, this would give me time to build up a decent fire enabling us to move this large load off up the line. Wrong...! Our dolly dropped off, Bob nodded towards the handbrake and heaved the reverser back ready to start. As I wound the handbrake round he gave the regulator a push and, with a wheeze, old 58221 eased backwards, yanking the load after her wagon by wagon. Quickly, I lifted the damper and, taking the shovel off the guard who was just about to push it into the tender, presumably to fire up, I spread three down each side, two across the middle, one in each back corner and another under the door, adjusting the ratchet of the top half of the door to allow an air current to pass over the fire and complete combustion. As I had already got my threequarters of a glass of water, I left the injector off for a while until the gauge looked a bit more healthy than the 125lbs it was then showing.

An ex Midland 2F, like the 3F and 4F, has a cylinder size of 18" diameter and the same 26" stroke. Only the boiler pressure is less, being 160lbs compared with 175lbs on the other two. This combines to give her a useful tractive effort of just under 20,000lbs.

58221's 4'11" coupled wheels dug into the steel rail and, with a shout up her chimney, romped away the goods line towards Burton Station North Box where, with the calling-on signal, pulled off and green flag hanging out of his box, the bobby indicated there was one more train standing ahead of us between there and the South Box.

Bob eased the regulator shut and dropped the lever down a couple of notches before pushing the handle over again. With the tremendous blast created by the exhaust, the fire was now becoming white-hot and I quickly fed another charge round the box. Bob now shut off the steam and started to gather the train together to creep down towards the bridge at the station, looking for signs of the brake van of the train in front. As he did so, 58221 blew off at the safety valves so I slipped the injector on, shut the damper and dropped the flap on the door. The brake van's red lamp showed up, just under the bridge and Bob brought us to a halt about an engine's length away.

In the bay platform opposite, 58080, another ex Midland type, this time an 0-4-4 passenger tank, was just backing on to its 2 coaches, preparatory to working the first Pull and Push service to Tutbury where it connected with trains for Crewe on the ex North Stafford line. The origins of this train dated back many years before the grouping of 1923 when North Stafford Railway enjoyed running powers into Burton and, indeed, had their own engine shed with turntable and water tower, the table lasting well into the fifties and the water tower into the eighties. These facilities were sited adjacent to the north end of the station platform, at the west side and were approached, other than by rail, from Derby Street Wharf.

"Save some of that steam, Dave," Bob shouted, "You'll need it soon, when we get away from the other end."

Ex MR Class 2F 0-6-0 No. 58186 passes Burton station on the Horninglow bridge/Leicester junction tripper. Photo: P. Webb

As the train in front moved off, we drifted down after it with just a breath of steam, once being on the move, letting the wagons push us along, only to come to a halt on the rising gradient that climbed out of the station to pass over Moor Street Bridge and the Bond End Branch. Here, the gradient stiffened to 1 in 60 for the climb and old 58221 was going to have to flex her muscles to get those 43 wagons on the move. As I have explained, I had got a good fire going as we came down. The glass now looked to be reading about ½ a glass, owing to the angle of the boiler standing on the rising gradient with the firebox end uphill. I decided to put a drop more in to be on the safe side but not too much, as she might start to prime if the boiler got too full. Once over the bridge, the gradient started to fall again very gently towards Leicester Junction so this had to be borne in mind.

Meanwhile, it was nice to watch the passengers on the platform, waiting for their train, each one standing in his or her favourite spot, awaiting the service to Birmingham and points in between, reading their morning 'papers or keeping an eye out for their yet to arrive travelling companions to join them.

In the bay at this, the south end of the station, stood an ex MR Class 2P, 4-4-0, on three coaches, forming the 7.08 service to Leicester. A Compound ran into the main platform with the Birmingham train and, minutes after it had left, the Class 2P, number 40364, followed it up the line then branching left for Leicester at the junction ahead. Hardly another minute elapsed before a Stanier 2-6-4T came rattling past with three more coaches, which it proceeded to reverse into the bay just vacated by the Leicester train, to form a working to Walsall and Wolverhampton, via Lichfield High Level.

"Keep her hot, mate," ordered Bob, "We'll be off now the Leicester's gone. Won't let that one in front, across the junction 'till she's clear."

Another few minutes passed and the signal was pulled off, then, with an all-out effort, the sands laying a trail before us, 58221 heaved her burden slowly but surely up the gradient and over the bridge, on the last leg of the short journey, the first that day, to Leicester Junction.

As we passed over Moor Street, the hooter below sounded, indicating that a vehicle approaching the bridge had broken the beam across the road and, in consequence, was too high to pass under the bridge, which had only 9' of headroom. Looking over the side from my elevated position in the cab, I saw nothing that could have caused it so presumed that it was either a vehicle on the other side of the bridge out of my sight or possibly some playful schoolboy waving his cap or bag through the beam, as I had done on occasions, only a couple of years before.

Apart from the siren going off, a flashing, illuminated sign was lit up, warning drivers to stop by displaying wording I cannot precisely recall but stating something similar to: "STOP. HEADROOM LIMITED." The beams across the road on approach to the bridge emitted from boxes at the top of posts on either side of the road and had been erected, as a safety measure because numerous vehicles in the past had struck the very low bridge when their drivers had not realised the height of their steeds would not go under. Many were the traffic hold ups caused by such incidents. One such, I recall, involved a van, which had become stuck under the bridge. The driver had tried to reverse but was unable to dislodge the van and, along with the drivers of the several vehicles held up behind, was getting more and more distressed. However, one bright spark came along and suggested he release some air out of his tyres. On doing so the van was released and driven clear, to the cheers, jeers and what-have-you, of all present, together with congratulations to the solver of the dilemma.

Having climbed over the bridge, steam was still kept on until most of the train had also passed over the summit, by which time the engine was getting quite close to the home signal gantry at the junction itself, where the necessity of keeping the train under control prior to stopping, should it be necessary, was paramount. As it happened, on this occasion we were signalled through and up the shunting neck, there to reverse into the sidings and hook off. We then ran forwards then reversed into an empty road. The Leicester Junction Jocko, another Class 2F like ourselves, then dropped our return load onto us.

In good time, we reversed our train out of the sidings and on to the Leicester line to stand at the signal and await a path back to the north end of the town. As the Leicester line climbed away from the junction at about 1 in 60, this again called for a maximum effort from our old engine. Ancient she may have been but gently treated she was not, having to work every bit as hard as she ever had. Eventually a way across the junction became available and away we went, getting a good start down the favourable gradient of the branch to pass over all the running lines and join the up - slow line going north, passing the line leading down to the left for Shobnall and the ex LNW Burton avoiding line to Stretton Junction. But, more of that anon...

Alongside the line we were now travelling on was the pathway up to the Midland Engine Shed and, as we approached the bridges over the Bond End

Branch and Moore Street again, a diversion went down the embankment to the Signal and Telegraph Department. Where these two paths separated a fog hut was situated, with a set of repeating arms for the outer home signals protecting the approach to Burton Station. A set of levers allowed the fog-man to place a detonator on either of the two running lines to create a warning to the foot-plate crews. Between the two bridges the main path sloped down to the street, with a walkway following the railway to provide pedestrian access for railwaymen going to and from the station. After crossing the second bridge, a rarely used level crossing, complete with gates, was situated, which was controlled from Burton Station South Signalbox, as more fully described in Chapter One. Immediately behind and beyond the signalbox, a line curved sharply in from Ind Coope's Bottling Stores. So sharp in fact that only 4-wheeled engines were allowed round it. The brewery kept an ex WD battery-electric loco there, to perform the rail movements within their premises and this small, green engine could sometimes be seen going about its duties. On the left of the line, as we passed through the station again, were some carriage sidings. These were used to stable excursion stock and other low-use vehicles. A clerestory-roofed dining car stood on the stop block and had done so for a number of years. During the 2nd World War an ambulance train was garaged there, I recall. A small C&W Department was also entrenched down below the bridge, at the end of these sidings.

As we passed the South Box. The bobby again had his green flag out, once more indicating we had a train standing in front of us.

"Keep you eye up for the brake van, Dave," Bob grinned, "Never mind the 'talent' on the platform."

"Typical teenager," quipped Fred, "Mind on everything but the job."

As we pulled up behind the brake van, I dropped off, nipped over to the said platform and vaulting up, took the tea can into the porter's room to mash. When I came out, Bob was moving off under the bridge behind the brake but I realised he would be stopping again at the starter opposite the platform end. The "Jinnie" had now departed from the North Bay and in its place stood sister engine 58058, with a parcels van. Two porters were unloading what appeared to be station stores.

"Pinching our hot water, I see," joked one, as I walked past. "Haven't you got enough of your own on that thing?" Whereupon his distraction caused him to drop a rather heavy looking box that the other porter was passing to him, onto his foot.

As he jumped about the platform in pain, I answered, "No need to get hopping mad about it."

A quick departure seemed prudent for, as the saying goes, if looks could kill!

Fred had seen this pantomime and, as I got back on the engine, made some remark about me not being the only one not concentrating on the job in hand.

"I'll be watching you, pal," I decided, "No one's perfect all the time."

"I've put a bit on, so you can enjoy your tea," he added, "And here's mine and Bob's cups as well."

"Cheek," I thought, as I filled their two cups and my lid.

So we sat... Nice and comfortable. The October sun had come out and warmed me from the front whilst my back was pleasantly cooking off the firebox front. With the hot tea inside me, I reflected that these trippers had a lot going for them.

A clatter of signals disturbed my reverie and, at Bob's touch, 58221 lurched into life again. We chuffed off, past Derby Street Wharf and the line into Truman's Brewery, quickly followed by a second line that branched off to the left, curving away past the ice house to cross Derby Street, Victoria Street, Dallow Lane and Victoria Crescent, to terminate at a set of buffer stops by the Trent and Mersey Canal. I was never lucky enough to work on this little branch to discover from where precisely, the traffic was generated but, by the 1950's, it was fairly light. However, it lasted until post 1968, being the last of the many Burton branch lines to close, an English Electric 350 h.p. Class 08 shunter, performing the last rites, removing remaining stock, closely followed by the demolition men.

As we stopped, yet again at Horninglow Bridge, Fred went over to the box to notify the bobby that we had some 'cripples' making up part of our load. This entailed us running up to North Stafford Junction and on to Knotty, prior to reverse them into the wagon works. There were some repaired wagons to bring back from there so these were added to the rest of our train for the return trip. Then it was back, across the road to Horninglow Bridge to start the whole round again. We did three round trips that morning, being relieved at Leicester Junction on the fourth journey. I was pleased to see that I was again marked up for the job the following day with Bob and Fred on 58221.

These two days were not my only turns on the Horninglow Tripper. It came my way a number of times over the next 12 to 15 months, usually with a 2F but, on some occasions with a Class 3F and once, which is worthy of mention, with a Class 2P, number 40436. This turn was also a popular one for initial running in of engines after attention to hot boxes.

Now, a more unsuitable engine for freight work, than a Class 2P, with its 7' driving wheels, is hard to imagine. We were on the afternoon turn and stepped on board at Leicester Junction just as Mick Brooks was finishing cleaning the fire. It was a blustery, March day with the wind blowing strong and cold from the North West. The engine was facing that way I was pleased to note.

"You'll have some fun with this, Dave," was his greeting, as I put my traps away in the tender box.

"How do you mean?" I asked, "Won't she steam?"

"Oh, she'll steam alright," he answered, "You'll find out," and with that he dropped off and followed his mate back to the shed to book off and go home.

Joe Ansacre, my driver for the day, was a quiet, unassuming type and one of the older drivers at the shed. A real gentleman.

"Everything alright your side, Dave?" he enquired.

"I reckon so," I answered.

"Only want Harold then and we're away," he commented, referring to our guard for the day.

We had my favourite threequarters of a glass of water and the gauge was just short of blowing off at 160lbs. Mick had handed her over to me in very good order with the footboards scoured white and even a nice plank of wood to substitute for the missing seat. Harold joined us and, with only six wagons forming our load, 40436 gave a bit of a slip from her 7' wheels as she reversed out of the sidings and up the branch to stand clear of the signal controlling the junction. Soon, the peg dropped and away we went, engine first, back down the slow line, through the station to arrive at Horninglow Bridge yet again.

"Nothing to it," I thought, as I sprinkled another charge around the box whilst we ran back across the road. Harold dropped off to find out about our next duty and we backed down the sidings out of the way. As I went to brew up, Harold passed me on his way back.

"There's plenty to do. 'Bout two loads I'd say. See what Joe says. Don't quite know what this engine'll do," he remarked, "Inspector reckoned they took forty-odd this morning."

"Not my worry," I thought. "I'm only the stoker. I just give them the steam and let them do what they like with it."

Having brewed up in the shunter's cabin, I returned to the engine, which had by now been moved on to its next load.

"Better get her hot, Dave," was Joe's greeting, "We've a fair few on."

"Forty-five to be exact," confirmed Harold.

"Water OK, 160lbs on the clock. I'll start on the fire when we move off," I thought. It was not considered good practice to fire whilst standing in normal circumstances.

An 8F was just starting away on the goods line with a train of bogie bolsters, loaded with steel strip and plate.

"We'll probably follow him," said Joe. "About five minutes I should think."

Throwing the dregs of my tea out over the side of the cab, I turned my baking potatoes and then, taking up the pick, set about breaking up some rather large lumps of coal that were threatening to fall and block the hole on the tender front. I had given the coal on the tender a good wetting when we filled the tank, to help lay the dust, as we were going to be running tender first again. A little trick I had learned with Bob the first time I had been on this job.

"Well, I'm ready," I told myself, "Let's get on with it."

Joe's prophecy came true as, sure enough, off came the dolly for us to follow the 8F down the goods road. I released the hand brake and Joe eased open the handle. Steam issued from the cylinder drain cocks as he slowly wound the gear back into reverse from the midgear position. 40436 gave a shudder and started to move slowly out of the siding, bringing each wagon in its turn with her, as the couplings tightened. A little bit more regulator until we were on full first valve and a little bit more on the gear until all the train was on the move. And never a slip. A superb piece of driving and a first class example of enginemanship. As those big wheels took the grip and turned round and round, the long drawn out exhausts up the chimney were almost painful to hear – as if she was telling us that this was not the sort of work for which she was intended at all. What could we do but agree with her.

I had already lifted the damper so, taking up the shovel, I shot a couple into each back corner, with three more down each side and two more under the door, each one fired over the flap. Shutting the sliding doors, I glanced up at the chimney, where it was rewarding to see the exhaust steam discoloured by the smoke from my efforts. 40436 was superheated and, having been out already for one shift, was thoroughly warmed up and producing hot, dry steam.

Now we had got them moving, Joe's next task was keeping our considerable load under control so that we could stop them when required. Harold stationed himself by the tender handbrake, ready to wind it on when the occasion demanded. This was my job really but he was an old hand and had more than likely forgotten more than I would ever know about it.

The steel train kept going, through the station and the bobby at Burton Station North had his flags out again, waving at us so, on we plodded, in its wake, with just a breath of steam on, keeping us on the move but not too much. We came to a stand as usual, by the south end of the station platform. Nothing much was happening on the station on our side, although a local service to Derby ran in behind a Class 4F on the far platform as we came to a stand. I dropped the damper and slipped the injector on.

"Mind your feet," I called and slacked the footplate down.

"A bit tidier than your regular Mate," Harold looked at Joe, "Don't think he knows what that pipe's for."

Joe, being the gentleman he was, made no comment, but what did he think? That was another matter entirely.

A whistle popped over the far side of the engine and I crossed over to Joe's side to see what was happening. A little, pale green, 4-wheel saddle tank engine came into view, with three or four wagons in tow. As it came nearer it passed a small engine shed that was situated behind the Elim Church, a corrugated iron building sited on the approach slope to the Moor Street level crossing. The engine was one of the Ind Coope & Allsop fleet and the engine shed was one of two within that company's premises, the other one being just off Horninglow Street. I am not sure which of the two constituents of the brewery erected which, prior to their amalgamation.

Our signal came off whereupon '436 and Joe faced their next challenge; that of lifting the 45 wagons out of the station and up the 1 in 60 incline to climb over the Moor Street and Bond End Branch bridges. As if on cue, it started to rain. Not the proper, wet rain but the damp, sticky, mizzling stuff. Joe tried the same method that had met with resounding success earlier. Our 2P moved off in back gear, travelling about half an engine's length and then stuck. Being on the incline, all the train was hanging on the drawhook and 40436 was attempting to move the lot and herself, all in one movement. Next thing, those big 7' driving wheels lost their grip on the rails, oiled by the rain and started slipping.

Joe slammed the regulator shut and applied the brake. Shut the tap, count to ten and have another go! Nothing but clouds of steam, slipping wheels and a volcano up the chimney. I look at the fire. What a mess in there! My nice sloping firebed is torn apart with burning coals even on top of the arch. Steam pressure is still OK though. As if to confirm this, the safety valves lift so I put on the injector to quieten her down.

A close inspection of the firebed showed a couple of holes in the middle and a heap of fire under the arch. As I reached round to lift the rake down from the tender top, Joe said, "Leave that for now. Get some ballast on the rails by the wheels. Harold's going back down to drop a couple of brakes towards the back of the train. We'll set back onto them and then have another go."

"Am I?" inquired Harold. "Yes I am," he answered himself after seeing the look on Joe's face.

So, down the side he went, towards the rear, to carry out Joe's bidding.

"Why don't we try the sands?" I asked.

"While you're down there, have a look for them and if you can find them then I'll use them," Joe replied patiently.

Down I got, to spread some ballast under the wheels, as instructed. Amazed, I observe that there is a solitary sand-pipe leading down to the rails, sited for forward running only, no provision being made for running in reverse at all. What was the designer thinking of? Didn't Mr. Johnson think his engines would ever operate a train in reverse? Obviously not, it would appear!

All this slipping and roaring by '436 had attracted the attention of the Ind Coope driver, who had brought his little engine right up to the limit of his movements, the better to watch what was going on. "Bet he's got back-sands on that," I mused.

Harold, by now nearly out of sight, was waving his arms about.

"I think Harold's ready, Joe," I shouted up into the cab.

Joe popped the whistle and, dropping '436 into fore-gear, eased her and most of the wagons back onto the braked ones. He then spun the lever back into reverse and, pushing the handle over, caused '436 to move backwards once more. I was round the opposite side by then, ballasting the rail on that side for all I was worth.

The old Class 2P kept moving on, ballast crunching beneath her wheels with small particles flying out like shrapnel, in all directions. But she had got the bit between her feet now and started forging slowly and steadily out onto the bridge, her exhaust shouting in long, measured beats loud and strong, up to the heavens. Does any other machine respond quite like a steam engine, I wonder.

Harold had lifted the wagon brakes in turn, just as the weight was about to come on, a true pro', not needing any other instruction but knowing instinctively what was required - and when. 40436 felt a slight check as the weight of the few trailing wagons, behind Harold's last braked one, were added to the load. As I was still feeding ballast under the wheels, some of the 'shrapnel' stung my hand as it continued to fly out from under those big wheels.

"So this is what 'Brookie' had meant by 'fun and games'," I reflected.

An ex LNW Super D came coughing up through the station alongside us with a coal train, overtaking us, its off-beat exhaust shouting, "I can do it, I can do it," as it passed over the top of the bank and away towards Leicester Junction.

"So can we, now," my mind shouted back, "But no thanks to Mr. Johnson. Rather – to Joe Ansacre, Harold and Yours Truly."

As we topped the gradient and started down past the bridges, I climbed back onto the footplate and sat down for a minute. Looking back over the side, the little green engine had now gone and of Harold there was no sign at all. Glancing across the cab towards Joe, we grinned at each other with a feeling of triumph at our success.

Our efforts had taken a toll of the boiler, which was down to less than a $^1/_2$ of a glass and with 120lbs on the clock I left the injector on only until I had $^1/_2$ a glass. As we were signalled through the junction and on to the shunting neck I got the rake down and started to pull some of the fire back from under the arch and over the middle of the grate. Then I spread half a dozen shovels around the box and, lifting up the flap, shut the door.

"Blimey, Joe, I wouldn't want to have to do that too often," I said.

"Don't suppose you will for an hour or so," Joe answered, "But there's still another lot down there don't forget," he qualified.

"I forgot about them," I groaned.

"You can bet they won't have," said Joe, "And got a few more to go with 'em if I know anything."

Just then, Harold arrived, very wet and equally fed up.

"You might have waited for me," he grumbled, opening the firehole door and standing before it, enjoying the heat.

I hadn't the heart to protest at his Cavalier use of my fire. Truth to say, I didn't dare say anything.

"If you can't take a joke, you shouldn't have joined," quoted Joe.

"Shall I go and make another brew?" I asked.

So off I got, once again and into the shunter's cabin to perform the honours. Where would the railway be without a lid of tea, I wondered. Walter Raleigh, or was it Drake, had a lot to be thanked for. Or was that potatoes. Potatoes!! I had forgotten about my baked potato gently cooking behind the clock box. Come on kettle! Hurry up and boil, I pleaded. Still, what difference would another couple of minutes make now I reasoned. Mr. Blooming Johnson and his sand pipes or, rather, the lack of them. All that effort for want of two penn'rth of pipe. Designers! They're all as bad as each other. What was stopping Stanier or Ivatt and Co. from having them fitted later?

The kettle's boiling now and a voice behind me enquires as to whether I'm going to mash, or what? I look round. "Sorry," I mumble. "I was miles away."

"That's all right. Don't worry. You've had all my ballast so you may as well have the water as well." He replied.

"Are you a plate-layer," I asked

"I'm the ganger," he grinned, "I don't miss a lot, lad. Now get off with you and feed Harold his tea. Tell him from me it will cost him a pint."

"It was me that put it on," I argued.

"But it was his bl..dy train," the ganger corrected.

I left before more argument. As Harold drank his tea I passed the message on.

"Ignore him," he answered, "He'll be gone home by the time we come back."

And, sure enough, he was and yes, we had to do it all again. In front of a platform full of passengers this time as well!

But that spud was done to a turn and, with a knob of butter and some shredded cheese, it went down a treat.

Of course, tripping around the town was not the only freight workings that came the way of an up and coming young firemen. Their first main line turns invariably found the anxious young passed cleaners working a tripper to either Wychnor, Overseal or – and this was most likely – to Chaddesden Sidings, Derby. I was no exception and found myself, quite unexpectedly, on the footplate of 43306, heading for Wychnor, one November, Monday afternoon.

Having worked the afternoon turn Shobnall Jocko the previous Friday with old ex MR Class 1F 0-6-0T number 41839, I had checked the work sheet to see what I was next booked out on. I noticed that my old school mate and immediate senior on the service list, Reg Finch, was booked on the late turn Wychnor trips, whilst I was just 12/0 Shed Duties.

"Probably the ashpits again," I thought and, sure enough, come Monday I was renewing my acquaintance with that very spot once more.

After about 1½ hours at this dusty, eye-stinging task, having just emptied the contents of the New Shed Pit onto the side, Freddie Kent, the list clerk, came running up, shouting and beckoning as he came.

"Do you want me?" I called back, wondering what on earth was going on that could possibly require such attention to anyone so insignificant as me.

"Get your gear and off to Branston," he puffed. "Your Mate's gone and done it for himself."

"Who?" I asked.

"Reg," he replied. "His Mate's sending him back. You want to watch him, by the way. Funny bloke is Cock," referring to driver 'Cock' Ford, "Well, get on then! He's standing waiting," he continued.

As I was rather dirty and sweaty, despite a non-too warm November afternoon, I suggested I have a wash first.

"You'll have plenty of time for that later," Fred replied. "Now, will you get a move on!"

So, after nipping over to the cabin for my traps, I set off up the yard and across the line to Branston.

Meeting Reg on the way, I asked what was to do as, up to that moment, I had thought he had met with some sort of accident but it was obvious from his appearance that this was not the case.

"I'll kill the nice gentleman." He swore. "Carrying on like that with me. 'That's your side of the engine. Stay on it', he says. So I put him right."

I knew Reg was a bit hot tempered; I suppose we all suffer from the arrogance of youth to some extent and Reg somewhat more than most. Apparently he had threatened to hit Cock with the shovel. Thus: the long walk back. This lapse of control cost him a one-week suspension with the consequent black mark on his record.

So, with some trepidation, I mounted the steps into the cab, incidentally on the right, i.e. the driver's side, to be greeted by an encouraging remark from this great bulk of a man:

"Not another b....y kid !"

Before I could say anything in reply or look at the fire, water, clock or anything else, he was whistling up for the road, which became immediately available and we were on the move.

The water, I remember, was about ½ a glass, 140lbs on the clock (a 3F was pressed to 175lbs) and there was, what seemed to me, a rather messy fire. I opened the damper and, taking up the shovel, attempted to fire a couple into each back corner, one or two down each side and a couple under the door.

"Fire her like a Jocko," I told myself.

Of the eight or ten shovels full, about five arrived where I intended, most of the rest now lying on the floor of the cab. I scooped this up and dropped it just inside the box under the door, lifted the flap and left the top ratchet half of the door on the catch. Clouds of smoke emitted from the chimney and much tut-tutt'ing from my driver (I cannot, by any stretch of imagination, call him my mate).

Ex MR Class 3F 0-6-0 No. 43342. Photo: Authors Collection.

"This guy is not another Arnie," I decided. "I can't see him mellowing as the day progresses. Stuff you then!" I thought. "Just try and do the job and keep out of his way. Let him get on with it! Going to be a long day though !"

Being somewhat ambidextrous, I never had much problem firing from either side of the cab so it was no trouble to stay on my side, as it were. I wasn't brilliant on either side in any case so there was no advantage either way.

The exhaust was crashing out of the chimney top and the whole engine was banging and knocking about. Cock hadn't pulled the lever back far out of full gear but, in my inexperience, I hadn't understood the significance of this. Was he trying to test me or was it just his temper? Both, probably, I concluded when recollecting the journey, later in the day.

The clock had now gained about 10lbs, which was not surprising, the amount of draw Cock's driving method was pulling on the fire. I put the injector on, as the water was dropping in the glass. Another round of firing, holding the back of the shovel high to keep the fuel at the back of the box, as Bob Shrive had shown me all those weeks ago. I tried to look at the firebed by holding the shovel at an angle, like George had done, but it all looked the same to me - a mess ! It was only later that I realised we had been turned out – main line, straight from the start at Branston. Quite brave of the old bobby when you think about it, with me as the fireman and an ape as the driver.

I'm firing like a demon now. The injector is on all the time and the clock is welded at about 150lbs.

"If only I could make her blow off, that would show him," I mused.

My wishes were soon to be granted for, low and behold, we had arrived at Wychnor and are backing into the sidings.

After a short consultation with the shunter, during which, to my delight, much shouting was done, particularly by Cock, as 43306 blew her head off, we knocked out the 30 or so wagons of our train and then proceeded to make up another. In due course this was collected by an ex LNWR Super D and we sorted out the train she had brought in.

"Your mate's looking a bit black. What you been doing to him?" teased the shunter to Cock who only grunted in reply.

"I had a couple of hours on the ash pit before I came out," I volunteered. "Not had time for a wash yet." I was wet through with sweat and must have looked a sight.

"We'll just knock these few off and that's it for now," the shunter added, Eric I think his name was, "Then it's packing time."

With that chore completed, we pulled down to the column to fill the tank, which entailed me climbing up to put the bag in, down again to turn the water on, then off, and back up again to lift the bag out, Cock's contribution being to lean on the reverser and stare into space.

As I climbed back into the cab, we set off up the shunting neck, which was the longest I ever came across, right up to the stop block at the far end. Considerably further than our shunting duties had required.

"Stop here until I come back," Cock uttered. The first words since his welcome remark to me when I first got on board at Branston.

I looked round in amazement.

"It speaks !" I thought. But even as I looked, his ruddy, open chest and bull like head were disappearing down the steps and away.

He followed a well-worn path, away beyond the buffers and over towards the main road.

"I know where you're off to," I thought as I spotted the roof and chimneys of the Paul Prye public house in the distance.

Filling the bucket with hot water via the pep pipe, I had a good wash, then got out my sandwiches.

"You miserable old devil," I thought. I'd not had chance to make a cup of tea. "Me who had done all the work, yet he was supping pints over there, no doubt."

"Dare I go and mash?" I wondered. It was a long way to the shunter's cabin and almost the same distance to the box at Alrewas Station, which I could see in the distance.

"Better not," I decided, "But I'll drop off and mash myself one when we get started again," I vowed.

So there I sat, on old 43306, in the dark, eating my sandwiches, feeling very thirsty and dreaming up nasty things to do to my recalcitrant driver, none of which I would dare to put into effect.

Having satisfied my hunger, I got the rake down and had a poke at the fire, pulling back the excess from under the arch. There was a lot of clinker in there and, fuelled by my angry thoughts of Cock relaxing with his pint whilst I grafted, I set about bailing out the worst of it.

As I was tidying up the footboards after my exertions, the ape-man climbed back up into the cab and grunted, "Knock off the brake."

I did his bidding and we were off back down the neck to carry on where we had left off over an hour before. I shot a charge round the box and as we came up to the cabin, without a second thought, I grabbed my tea can and dropped off to mash.

"Where you off to?" bellows Cock.

"That's only the fourth time he's spoken to me today," I reflect and, choosing to ignore him, disappear into the cabin. The urn takes about three or four minutes to boil and as I wait, I can hear our 3F banging up and down outside.

"Poor old 3306," I think, "He ain't got me to take it out of so he's taking it out of her."

Tea made, I climb back on board as he comes to a halt near the cabin. A quick look at the steam, water and fire, the latter, thanks to Cock's manifestations, now being white hot, I treat to a quick charge round then sit down and pour me out a lid of tea.

Nectar! Oh - the flavour! Oh - the thirst quenching delight!

My pet gorilla looked in and glared across the cab, his eyes shining red in the reflection from the fire.

"Just say it !" I think to myself, "And Reg won't be the only one on the carpet in the morning."

A voice floated up from along the side and Cock looked away.

"You've 12 on 5. Pull clear and I'll drop 'em on the van. Drop back, I'll hook you on and we're right away home to mother."

It was our guard. The first time I had seen him all day.

"Wonder where he hides out?" I mused.

"I bet mother won't be very pleased to see you!" I thought, of Cock.

Another round in the box, then lift the damper to wide open and the ratchet on the catch, up with the flap. "I'm ready," I told myself, "Let's get home, away from this arrogant b...."

Off we went and, after a wait at the junction for a couple of runners to pass by, both with Black 5's at their head, we were right away back to Branston. On arrival we were turned up the Birmingham Curve, where the Branston Jocko pulled off our dozen wagons and brake. Off, round the curve to the Leicester Branch, to run back down to Leicester Junction and wait for a path across the line. A few more runners cross in each direction, then we are let across to reverse into the shed, leaving 43306 on the number 2 ashpit, now full again despite my efforts earlier in the day.

As Cock gets off I assume we aren't meant to put her away, so I follow him. I suddenly feel tired and won't be sorry to climb into my bed. We walk into the lobby and Bert Sinclair, running foreman, says to my driver,

"I've marked Dave up with you for the rest of the week. Is that alright?"

The gorilla grunts something in reply and Bert says to me, "11/35 then all week lad. If you survive that you'll survive anything."

"No bother," I think to myself, "I think I've got his measure now."

With that, I climbed aboard my trusty old bike and pedalled home to bed; past the chippie - I hadn't even got the energy to call for six pennyworth.

Tuesday followed much the same pattern with 43306 as our steed.

The following day, Wednesday, with Cock having beaten 43306 into submission, we took to 43256. It soon became obvious that she was not made of the stuff of her sister and, despite Cock giving her the lash, she just didn't seem to get along as well at all. I had got plenty of steam most of the time so the boiler was OK but she didn't seem to have any pulling power.

Having arrived at Wychnor and playing with the trucks for hours on end, the time came again for my pet gorilla to go for his walk through the jungle to the Paul Prye so, up the shunting neck we went once again, me by now, fully organised with a full tea-can, sandwiches and reading materials at the ready. I decided to try a bit of footplate cooking or, to be more precise, grilling and, opening the locker door on the tender, I gave the top a wipe and covered it with a drivers notice. Upon this I opened up my cheese sandwiches, gave the shovel a good clean with the pep pipe, then held it in the firebox to heat it up. On deciding the time was right, I pulled it out and held it over the open sandwiches. In next to no time the cheese was bubbling and warming up nicely. A couple of minutes more of this treatment and my gourmet treat was ready. Delicious on a cool, November evening, washed down with a couple of lids of tea. Unfortunately it was now too dark to read my magazine so I settled down on my capacious fireman's seat, fortunately all complete, to have a snooze.

Soon. my reverie is disturbed by a voice calling from below, "Anybody there."

"Surely Cock isn't back yet," I think. "Doesn't sound like him anyway."

A uniform peak cap hoves into view up the steps. I can just make out the legend "Inspector" above the peak. The ruddy face beneath is flushed and, somewhat breathlessly utters, "What the hell are you doing right up here then?"

"Having our break," I reply.

"Where's your Mate?" the next inevitable question was asked.

"Gone for a walk," I answered. Well, it was the truth. Hope he doesn't ask "Where to?"

"Hmm. Well lad, it's like this. The Bescot Parcels will be here in a minute or two and he's got a hot box on a van at the back near the brake. He's going to run down to the junction and you're to follow him down and lift 'em off, shove the van inside and put the rest back behind him. Shouldn't take five minutes," he explained.

"Can't be done," says I.

"Why ever not?" he asks.

"'Cause my mate's not here." I said, stating the obvious.

"Well, can't you do it? Can't you drive it.. Blimey, even I could drive it." The Inspector is nearly blowing a blood vessel by now.

"Yes, I can drive but I'm not going to and neither are you," I answered, "My mate won't allow it."

"Where's he gone? Urgh, I'll be back," he promised, storming back up the siding.

A few minutes elapsed and an Austerity came clanking by with part fitted lights up. The crew looked across and both waved. I kept out of sight behind the cab sheet until they were well by. She had a good fifty-odd vans in tow and flames were coming out of one of the axleboxes, about fourth from the rear.

"He'll just fit comfortably between the junction and the points," I muse.

More minutes elapse and the whole train starts to reverse back up the line until the rear section, behind the cripple, is clear of the points. One of the shunters then nips between and uncouples, while two others throw some water over the box.

The Austerity then pulls forward again, leaving the brake and last three vans standing on the main. She then reverses the train, cripple first, into the yard, where it is uncoupled and more water is poured onto the axlebox. The Austerity again pulls forwards onto the main line, then reverses back onto and becomes re-united with the rear three and the brake van.

I could almost hear the Austerity driver swearing from my position in the cab at the top of the yard. With a derisive hoot on its whistle, the Bescot Parcels continued on its way to York. The Inspector returned, climbed up into the cab and, with a glare at me, sat down to await Cock's return.

"About another five minutes," I thought and, sure enough, to the minute, Cock returned.

"Where on earth do you imagine you've been, driver?" the Inspector raved.

"Who the hell are you?" glared Cock, "Get off my engine, now!"

"Who do you think you're talking to?" the Inspector shouted back.

"Off, before I throw you off. And I will, won't I mate?" my ape-man yelled back, turning to me.

I kept quiet. "Don't drag me into it," I thought.

The Inspector dismounted in double quick time, only to remonstrate from the safety of the floor, "What's your name, driver?"

"You know my flaming name," Cock bellowed back, "Get the brake off, mate," he said, turning to me.

"Speaking now, are we?" I think to myself as I do his bidding and wind off the handbrake.

Cock pulls the lever back and slams the regulator wide open. 43256 leaps backwards into her tender and charges off down the shunting neck to the sidings, leaving the Inspector standing, staring after us, waving his arms in the air in anger and frustration.

"And he's still got to face the long walk back as well," I think. "He'll not let this drop. You've gone too far this time, Cock my old mate. Number nine room for you," I turn away and smile. "Serve you right, you arrogant devil."

"You didn't tell him where I was, did you, kid?" Cock asked.

"I said you'd gone for a walk," I answered, "Which was true wasn't it?" then told him all that had occurred.

"Blow him. Blow 'em all," was Cock's retort, or something similar but unprintable, "Still. Thanks kid. You're not a bad lad and I've really pushed you. I know I have," he went on.

I couldn't trust myself to answer so I just gave a grin and nodded.

As we were ready to leave, the Inspector came out of his office and called up to us, "I've wrote a letter about this to you superintendent. You've not heard the last of this, driver, not by a long chalk."

"Would you like me to post it for you?" Cock shouted back and, whistling up for the road, eased our load of five and a brake down to the peg to turn us out onto the main line. This pulled off and we rattled the few hundred yards to the junction where we stopped to wait for the runners to pass again.

I went up to the box to sign the book and the bobby wanted to know all about it.

"Where was he then? Down the pub, knowing him, I bet," he stated.

"I've no idea where he went," I answered.

"Good lad. You'll do," he replied, "But you won't convince them Bescot men so easily."

The second runner was belled, so I made my way back to the engine.

"What's that clever sod got to say?" Cock asked, "I saw you talking to each other."

"Nothing particular," I answered.

"I'll bet," Cock retorted.

With that, the runner hammered by, led by the inevitable Black 5 and in no time at all we were banging and creaking along in his wake.

I had given the coal a good wetting, preparatory to our tender-first dash back to Burton but Cock seemed even more angry than usual and thrashed the poor old engine along like a mad thing. Full reverse gear and regulator nearly right across. He kept jagging the brake to hold her back. Just past Barton and Walton Station she developed a loud roar up the chimney, which was noticeable even above the cacophony that 43256 was creating in response to Cock's rough handling. I fed another round into the box, which was white hot, such was the draught being created by the exhaust.

"Leave it lad, summat's up," shouted Cock, shutting the regulator, rubbing the brake and dropping the lever into middle gear.

Everything was suddenly quiet, with only the click of the wheels on the rail joints and the rattle of the motion as we coasted long the track. Cock slowed her down some more and we came to a stand at the signals for Branston Junction. As we stopped, he went round the corner of the cab and along the framing, to peer down between the frames.

"Now what's he broke?" I wondered, "I hope they stop it out of his money."

Just then the signal came off for us to cross the junction and run up the Birmingham Curve as always. Cock climbed back into the cab.

"Can't see owt, lad. Too dark," he said, "We'll soon know anyway."

With that, he pulled her back into reverse and gently opened the regulator.

Old '3256 gave a chuff, followed by a roar and thus we moved off: chuff, roar, chuff, roar, cuff.

"Hole in the D, lad. Bet you any money," declared Cock.

"Right," I answered, not having a clue what he was talking about.

Whereupon we made our way on to the shed, to leave her standing over number 2 pit again, as always.

When I came on next day, I saw that they had marked up 43815 for Cock to wreck. Hunting out 43256, I found her with the steamchest cover off and both slide valves out. In the centre of one of the brass slide plates was a hole that you could almost put your fist through. There were no fitters around to ask about it so I resolved to mention it to Cock.

"Perhaps he would like to have a look as well," I reasoned.

But, no, he was his usual, unreasonable self. Still, I was beginning to prefer him that way. At least you knew where you were with him then. Nowhere at all!

I then realised what his problem was. I had spotted a note pinned to his card. Not surprising after yesterday's episode I reflected but I was wrong.

"Look at this, lad. Can't have my blasted holidays when I want now. Got to get a swap. What do they do in that flaming office," he grumbled.

"So, that's you upset for the day again," I despairingly mused.

We crossed over the line to step onto our engine and Bob, the driver handing over, greeted my Mate by saying, "Come on Cock, me old mate. Got another one for you to wreck. She's a good one so far so see if you can keep her that way for a change."

I glared agonisingly at him and Cock growled. Then, with a wink in my direction, Bob and his mate dropped off to leave me to the tender mercies of the ape-man for another shift.

We got through the day without any problems, Cock and the Inspector stalking each other like a pair of tomcats, keeping out of each others way. Cock still went for his pint but he was back in half an hour or so. He said nothing and I had no intention of saying anything. I had wondered why we never saw our guard and realised that he, like most, gave Cock a wide berth.

We had 43815 on Friday as well, another quiet, uneventful day, if such was possible with Cock. As we signed off that night he shouted after me,

"9.35 in the morning. Don't forget. 2 hours earlier."

For this final duty of the week we had 43306 back again, fresh from boiler washing out and repairs. We relieved Bob as usual but instead of going off to Branston, we climbed up the Leicester Line as far as Coton Park. Here we shunted a few loads of coal about, then made up a train, which we took down to Wetmore Sidings. Then it was back to the shed, where we put her away, leastways I did, Cock's contribution being to drive her into the shed and then, off the table, onto the pit after I had bailed the fire out.

So ended my first complete week on the footplate and one that I will never forget. It can only get better from here on I hoped. Cock got his letter when he signed off that Saturday evening. It was not policy to issue a reprimand before a driver started his duty, for obvious reasons of safety, etc. as any worry could be very distracting to any normal person. But then, who could describe Cock as a normal person?

Our paths crossed but once more during my firing days, this being with 42826 on the Chaddesden (Chad) Tripper and, truth to tell, on that occasion, whilst still a bit heavy handed as was clearly his style, a more pleasant turn one could not have had. He even grabbed the shovel and put a round on, with great skill, on a couple of occasions. Maybe I had passed his test of approval. I don't know. To me, at the time, it was a test of endurance.

Incidentally, Cock's real name was Harry but I never ever heard anyone either address him or speak of him by that title.

Chapter 4

Up the Branch Line to Overseal

Footplate turns were coming up thick and fast now for our little gang of passed cleaners and whenever we met each other, either collectively or singly, our individual experiences were avidly discussed. A few of our numbers had taken a turn on the Class 4F, with mixed success. With 772 of them having been built at various times, in several batches between 1911 and 1941, it was inevitable that, sooner or later, my turn would come.

Checking the sheet before signing off one Friday evening, I was pleased to see that I was marked up for two consecutive days on 89 Target, the Overseal Tripper, with Harold Slater, starting the following Monday.

Signing on at 10.15 a.m. I arrived, as usual about 30 minutes early, to prepare and then work the turn, and noted that our engine was 43286, one of Burton's allocation of ex Midland Class 3F 0-6-0's.

Having gone through the usual routine duties of preparation I swung the turntable round for Harold to ease our mount out of her bay to be turned. Lifting the vacuum pipe off its stop, I connect it to the table hose and shout to Harold, "Blow up." He pulls the large ejector handle and, with a sucking noise, the engine and table pipes unite as one. I pull the lever to release the locking catch that holds the table securely in position. Selecting the direction control, I pull the power handle to operate the vacuum motor and turn 43286 round to face south and the turntable to line up with the outgoing road. Re-engaging the locking lever, I knock the vacuum pipes apart and replace the engine pipe onto its stop.

We stop by the water crane and top up the tank then down to the bell out peg and off the shed, over to Leicester Junction Sidings, where we back onto our train. This is made up mainly of empty wagons for the pipe yards situated on the Woodville Branch, which will be dropped off at Woodville Junction plus traffic for both Bretby and Coton Park Sidings. Immediately behind the engine are five wagons of loco' coal and a van of dried loco' sand for Overseal Loco. This latter would have originated from Burton Loco, the sand having been prepared in the dryer there; a task I had helped with many times in the past.

Our guard Reg, gives us the load, almost the limit for our Class 3F, and away we go. I look back and exchange waves with Reg, give Harold the nod and get down to the task of providing steam. I felt I had the measure of these Class 3F's and old 43286 confirmed my confidence by responding to my actions very favourably.

On arrival at Bretby Junction we performed some shunting and I was reminded of an earlier occasion there with Charlie Ball on old 58236. This engine was about the most antiquated locomotive upon which I ever worked, with the possible exceptions of 41516 and 41523. She still retained her old original Kirtley boiler, fitted with a round-top firebox and Salter safety valves atop the steam dome. She was pressed to 160lbs and had 4'-11" coupled wheels, dry sands and the same Kirtley excuse for a cab that she had received when originally built in

1875. One of the jobs, I remember, called for 50 – 60 empties to be propelled up to Park Lane Colliery, which really necessitated two runs up the 1 in 50 bank to achieve. However, if this could be done in one attempt it allowed time for a pint in the White Horse pub at the top as the reward. Charlie told me to raise a full head of steam while he drew this huge load down to the stop block at the end of the sidings.

Ex MR Class 2F 0-6-0 No. 58236 tile engine this author fired on the Coton Park tripper. Photo: Authors Collection.

He then said to me, "Up on the tender back are some old brake blocks. Get them and hang them on the levers on the valves," meaning the safety valves.

This I did, not without a little alarm, whereupon 58236's 160lbs became almost 180, before the auxiliary valve on the firebox top opened with a bang. This made me jump nearly out of my skin, as I was somewhat apprehensive by this time and was looking round for somewhere safe to take cover. Let it be said that in 58236's Spartan cab such a place did not exist.

"Right, lad," says Charlie, "Now for it! Keep digging in and don't use the injector if you can help it."

Off down the sidings we thrashed, with the poor old lady working flat out to get a run round the curve and up the bank to the pit. With a nice dry rail and the sands working, we were almost guaranteed success and so it proved to be. Charlie and the shunter went for a celebratory pint, leaving me to celebrate by spending the next half hour repairing my wrecked fire – and, of course, returning the old brake blocks to the tender back. A good engineman Charlie, who knew just how far one could go to achieve a result.

Incidentally, during this, as we passed under the A444 at the top of the bank and swung away right into the colliery yard, I had noticed an overgrown and trackless cutting, climbing away to our left.

"Where did that go, Charlie?" I enquired.

"Bretby Pit, lad," he replied. "That was a real test up there. Made the old girl cough a bit, that did, I can tell you," he added.

Returning to the trip with 43286, our next port of call was Coton Park Sidings, about a mile further along the line and at the point where the

Swadlincote and Woodville Branch Loop left the main Leicester Line. All traffic to and from Cadley Hill Colliery passed through these sidings.

Then, on to Gresley, where sidings to the right of the line marked the start of the Netherseal Colliery Branch. An occupation siding on the left side, adjacent to the coal wharf, served Bonas Tape Factory and boilerhouse. At this time, 1952, Gresley Station was only just beginning to show signs of subsidence, as a result of the mining in the area but over the ensuing years it was affected to such an extent that the platform sunk to below the track level and the adjacent road bridge had to be packed and lifted by 6' or more. On this occasion we had nothing for this stop so carried on through the tunnel and up the bank to Woodville Junction. It was said that the railway owned the coal and mining rights beneath the tunnel, thereby saving it from being mined and consequential subsidence.

At the junction we dropped off our empties for the pipe yard, then continued to Moira West Junction, where we swung round to the right to enter Overseal Sidings. Here, more shunting was performed and the vanload of sand delivered to the engine shed, which was situated right alongside the sidings.

An LMS Class 4F 0-6-0 not the authors favourite engine. Photo: Authors Collection.

The fitter in charge here for many years was a chap named Saunders, I forget his Christian name. He achieved local fame by broadcasting on the BBC Radio as a contestant on Carol Lewis's Discoveries. I'm not sure, after all these years, but I think he played a trombone or something similar. Later on he left Overseal to take up a position at Market Harborough I believe.

If a temporary replacement was required for any of the six engines stabled at Overseal, usually due to them needing a boiler washout, the 89 Target engine was normally used. This day was no exception, with us bringing back a Class 2F, number 58253, which was a Derby engine, presumably on loan for a spell.

I had no trouble for steam all day with either engine and when we were relieved at Leicester Junction I was able to hand over to our relief a nice, clean, working model, a situation always to my pleasure.

The following day we were marked up to take 44436 on the job. My first turn with a 4F had come at last. 44436 was straight off boiler wash-out and repairs and consequently had been freshly fired up earlier that morning. She was just making steam and had 20lbs on the clock. The footplate was covered in the usual patina of dirt and soot and both gauge frames were smoked up. A quick nudge of the blower handle lifted the flames from around the door and back inside the box where they belonged and as the smoke in the cab followed them, things began to improve straight away.

I decided to find some broken firebrick to spread over the bars before I began to build up the fire. This can be a big help when running, as any clinker formed tends to stick to the firebrick instead of the bars and, as a result, does not impede the passage of primary air through the bars and the fire above. This achieved, I began to slowly build up the fire, as I would on a Class 3F, reasoning that the Class 4F was fitted with a superheated version of the Class 3 boiler; what was known as a Type G7 or G7S boiler, the S indicating 'Superheated.'

With the oil bottle warming up nicely on the flame plate, ready for Harold when he showed up, I then went off in search of the sand buckets. These could be anywhere around the shed as no one ever bothered to return them to the sand hole where they belonged, just dropping them where they had finished using them. This arm-stretching task completed, I turned my attention once more to the fire. There was now about 70lbs on the gauge so, checking that Harold was clear, I tried both injectors. Leaving on the right hand one (on the fireman's side) I set about cleaning up the cab and washing away the soot and grime covering everything. Soon everything was looking bright and clean with the footplate nicely scoured. It was possible to bring them up to whiteness with the high powered hot water jet from the pep pipe.

My cleaning operations had impaired the steam making efforts of 44436 and the gauge read 65lbs after my ablutions were completed so, as I was now able to devote all my attention to this task, I fed a little more coal around the box. By the time Harold had completed his inspection and oiling round, we had a healthy 150lbs showing and, with my favourite threequarters of a glass in the boiler, I felt fairly confident as we moved out of the shed to fill the tank.

"Another change-over today, Dave," Harold informed me, "3306, I think they said," he added.

"Not another 4, then," I rhetorically queried.

"No, they only have one up there (meaning Overseal) for the 'Brum' and she won't be back before we leave. Probably bring her back tomorrow," he answered. "And don't forget the letters today either. We did yesterday and old Joe (Joe Benson Sen. the running foreman) weren't very pleased."

It was the usual custom for any correspondence between Burton and Overseal Depots to be conveyed by the 89 Target in a special canvas bag provided for the purpose. I nipped back to the office for this and on return, found that Harold had filled the tank so all I had to do was climb up and haul the bag out.

Soon we were backing onto our train at Leicester Junction and 44436 rewarded my efforts on her behalf by blowing off at the valves. A glance at the clock showed her reading 170lbs, 5lbs light, so I pointed this out to Harold.

"Not very good, straight off repairs," I reflect and say so.

"If it weren't booked, the fitters wouldn't know would they? They can't tell when the engine's dead. They'd certainly have changed it if they had known. Still, Saunders can do it when we get there. We've not got time to mess about with it here," Harold decided.

Our guard arrived and gave us the load, which was similar to the previous day's, with the exception of the van of sand, being just under the limit laid down for a Class 4 engine over our route. The signal dropped and with a toot on the whistle, Harold dropped the gear down and heaved open the regulator, as I released the tender brake. Away we stormed, up the 1 in 60 of the bank to climb over the bridge across Branston Road, before levelling out to cross the viaduct over the Trent and its floodplain.

I am firing two in each back corner, three down each side, with another two under the door, as I would on a Class 3F when working hard. I check the water level as we cross the viaduct, to find it down to ½ a glass so I slip the injector on and glance at the gauge - 150lbs. Where has 20lbs gone in so short a time? I know we have been working the engine hard but then my shovel has been busy too.

Harold pulls 44436 up a bit more and settles down for the short run to Bretby Junction. I check the damper is open with the ¾" ⁷/₈" spanner wedged under the handle to keep it so. The flap is up and the fire is white hot, although the blast is nothing to shout about; not, that is, compared with a Class 3F. Pressure has lost another 5lb even though the injector is off. Taking up the shovel, I charge another round in and still the gauge goes the wrong way, 145lbs - now 140lbs. Harold shuts off, ready for Bretby Sidings, oblivious of the relief felt by his fireman.

Our sojourn here gives me a chance to examine my fire but it looks all right to me. Whilst we stand waiting for our next dash to Coton Park the boiler recovers somewhat and we set out on our second leg with a healthier 160lbs showing. I experiment with various door openings from fully closed to half open in an attempt to find the correct amount of secondary air flow to complete combustion and carry the heat produced over the arch and through the tubes. Apertures cast into the doors already cater in part for this necessity leaving the fireman to do the fine-tuning as it were. But this is all to no avail, the needle on the gauge continues on its suicide mission or should I say my suicide mission so that, by the time we complete shunting at Coton Park it is down around the 120lb mark.

"What on earth am I doing wrong?" I ask myself. Having checked everything I can think of, all I can do is watch the painfully slow climb back up the scale the needle is making again whilst we are standing. It's obvious that I'm firing incorrectly but what should I be doing that I'm not already. I could ask Harold for suggestions but that goes against my pride. What if we run straight through Woodville like we did the previous day? Would we manage to get there or would we stick in the tunnel or, more probably, on the bank the other side, short of steam. The shame of it! What if we run back through the Traps (Trap-points)?

"Shall I slip over to the box and mash?" I ask Harold.

"Yes, if you like," he replies, "Always ready for a cuppa."

So, over to the box I go with my can. As I brew up from the signalman's ever boiling kettle I casually ask him how long it will be before we are off.

"About ten minutes, straight after the passenger," he informs me.

Back on the engine I drop a couple of shovels just under the door as Harold pours the tea. The boiler has recovered once more to 160lbs I observe and the glass is full to just below the top nut.

"Not a bad drop of char this, Dave lad," Harold grins, "Just sit back and enjoy yours."

"All right for him," I think, "He's only got to drive the thing."

Soon the clang of the signal disturbs my thoughts and in no time at all one of the Leicester Black 5's come rattling by with three coaches in tow. The injustice of it all! Here we are with the old nail and about 40 wagons hanging on the hook and yet there goes the passenger with a '5' and a silly little train like that. Now, if things were the other way round I'd have no trouble at all! There's another clatter as the signal returns to danger, followed by a slam as the points go over in our favour. Off drops the dolly and I turn to wind off the hand-brake. A quick glance at the clock shows the needle to be just under our 170lbs maximum and the water level bobbing in the top nut of the glass, I having decided to abandon my favourite threequarters glass and give the engine, and consequently me, a better chance.

With a pop on the whistle, Harold yanks open the regulator and off we go, snaking out over the points onto the main line. I look back for the guard's wave but there is no sign of him although I can see that the van is coming along behind our train.

"I've not seen him, Harold," I call.

He lifts his hand in reply and calls back, "OK Dave, I've got him."

"Wish he'd make his mind up who he's waving to," I muse, "Better get on with wrestling with the fire then."

I check that the damper is still propped open, then open the doors and drop a quick round about the box, keeping the back end of my shovel up high as I do so.

"Don't put too much on," Harold interrupts, "We've got one for Bonas's today so we'll no doubt be across the road and inside again. Don't want her blowing off do we?" he continues.

"Blowing off," I remark to myself, "Some chance of that, I don't think." Then I reflect, "Perhaps there is a God after all. Didn't I hope we would have to call here today?"

Very shortly, Harold is shutting off steam again and easing the brake to gather up our train prior to stopping then reversing into Netherseal Colliery Exchange Sidings. Once inside, the points are set against us as a coal train emerges from under the A444 road bridge and comes charging past, a Coalville 4F at its head, working hard to lift its load up the gradient out of Gresley Station.

"He's going well," I think, "Must have got her measure," referring to the fireman who was hanging out of the cab and giving me a cheerful wave as they go. Just to rub salt into my wound, I think.

When he's clear we nip out with our one wagon of coal and are soon backing into Bonas's sidings, where we exchange it for its predecessor, now empty of course. We again have to wait before we can cross back to the rest of our train. The guard joins us and he helps me to finish my can of tea.

"Do guards ever mash?" I wonder, "Certainly not in my company," I reflect.

Just then another Black 5, this time on a long train of what looks like parcel vans, charges past.

"Never seen him before," remarks our guard, Reg, "I wonder if owt's up somewhere."

Hardly have the vans disappeared under the road bridge when the signals are again pulled off to herald the approach of an 8F which comes pounding past with a mixed train on Class E lights.

"Nip up to the box and see what you can find out," says Harold.

So, away I go, learning that something has happened on the Wychnor Viaducts and all southbound trains for Birmingham are being routed this way, "Over the Alps," as it is called by us local railwaymen. This diversion required traffic turning off the main Derby – Birmingham line at Leicester Junction and running up the branch as far as Moira West Junction, where the right hand fork was taken, as indeed shall we with our train – when we eventually get going. The diverted services would then continue down the joint -MR/LNW line to Nuneaton Abbey Street, bearing right at the junction to run through Stockingford and Arley Tunnel, to rejoin the main line at Coleshill. A very undulating journey with a sharp climb to Arley summit, hence its name "Over the Alps to Brum."

"We've got the Devonian coming up soon and the Newcastle to Bristol behind it, so, when I call you out, tell Harold not to hang about. Not that you'll be going up before them, mind you, but I'll try and get you back out of Bonas's and over here before then," added the bobby.

Dang, dang, go the instruments and the bobby jumps to answer. Bells ringing to his beat and needles dance across dials. Levers slam across the frame at the bobby's efficient work. A look at the box clock shows the time to be just after mid-day. I knew that the Devonian was due through Burton at 12.16 so it would be passing us any time after half past.

"Is it OK if I stop here for a bit?" I asked the bobby.

"Yes, sure you can," he replied, "Just don't get in the way."

Looking across the line I could see 44436 standing in the siding. As I watched she lifted her valves and blew off. Harold got down from his seat and dropped the damper, then opened the firehole doors and slipped the injector on.

"Don't put too much in, Harold," I said to myself. "Still, it's nice to hear those valves blow. Be a different story if we were on the move, though But, still, it's only a couple of minutes to Overseal with Woodville Junction in between and then I've made it!"

The signalbox door opened and another fireman came in, an Overseal man this time.

"What's going on, Ernie?" he asked the bobby, "Old Bill's going crackers down there. We should be in Rawden by now."

I looked round, beyond the door to see a Class 2F standing on a load of coal out of Netherseal Colliery.

"The world's gone mad today, Wal'." The bobby answered and went on to explain what was happening.

Another 8F came thundering by with a load of empty mineral wagons. Ernie leaned out of his window and waved them on with his arm. The fireman was busy shovelling away and, as the driver was on the opposite side of the cab, I wondered for whose benefit it was all for.

"We'll just get your mate back over this side now," he said to me, "Then it's the Devonian."

"Won't that '8' get in the way?" I asked.

"He hadn't better," Ernie answered, "He's supposed to be going to Coalville."

After tapping out a few more bells and receiving the replies, Ernie slammed a few levers over and pulled a few more out. Harold's whistle was heard and out of the sidings old 44436 came, with her one wagon in tow. More levers moved back and pulled over and Harold was setting back onto our train. A quick flick of his shunting pole and Reg had everything coupled up again. Ernie now had two trains waiting in the yard, the Devonian coming up the main from Burton and another coal train belled on the down.

"Gets more like Clapham Junction every day, Ern'," says Wal, "You'll need a couple of pints after this lot."

"I can handle it, don't worry yourself," Ernie replied, "Now, if you've nothing else to say, clear off and make some space for the workers."

As I made a move to follow the other fireman Ernie said, "I didn't mean you, son. Just that mouthy so-and-so. Gets right up my nose he does."

"Here she comes now, look," he observed and round the curve, into the dip opposite the box came the big, shiny, green Jubilee, "The Devonian" headboard in silvery letters standing out against the red background, catching the early afternoon sun.

"45685 Barfleur," I read on her side as she passed by. With the three-cylinder beat roaring defiance to the world, she streaked away, under the bridge and through the station, her equally smart and shiny, carmine and cream coaches following obediently in her wake.

"I'll try and get you away after the Newcastle," Ernie turned to me, "So get back and tell Harold not to hang about when I get you the road. Tell Reg to leave the lot at Woodville today. You'll not be able to mess about shunting at Overseal while this is going on. You'll probably find your changeover there anyway. It's usually on the Woodville Jocko."

Down I went to report back to Harold and Reg. Soon the unique three-cylinder beat came into earshot again and, amidst a cloud of steam hissing from piston glands and numerous other places, could just be made out a dirty Jubilee, number 45610, "Gold Coast" of Derby. A greater contrast with her sister engine, Bristol's 45685, was hard to imagine.

"Probably some of our men on the pilots," Harold remarked, "Be some money made down there today, I'll be bound. Mind you, Davey lad, the rate we're going we'll be having some ourselves."

I opened the damper and wedged the spanner under the handle again. The gauge was hovering around the 170lb mark and the fire looked good, glowing red all over. "Better leave it until we get started," I decided. With the water out of sight in the top nut and with only just a mile to go, albeit all uphill, I reasoned that we should make it alright without too much trouble.

The points clattered over and the dolly dropped off, I released the handbrake and we were on our way. Exchanging waves with the guard, I gave Harold the nod and started firing. A quick charge round the box and shut the door. 44436 had really got the bit between her teeth now and veritably hammering along. Harold wound the gear up half a turn and slammed the valve right over. We were now on full regulator and about 50% cut off.

As we crash through the station I notice the needle beginning its downward slide. Another quick round of fuel into the box and we pound into the tunnel as Harold drops the wheel into full gear. 44436 has got the lot now and is accelerating through this world of darkness. The noise of the exhaust is something to be heard. The heat is becoming unbearable as our 4F's exhaust efforts are mixed with the smoke and steam left behind by the preceding train. It's becoming hard to breathe as we burst out at the far end and into the sunshine. What a relief to breathe fresh air again. As the smoke clears out of the cab I see that the glass is down to about half and the gauge is reading 130lbs. As I watch, it visibly falls another 5lbs. I snatch up the shovel and bail another quick round in the box, leaving the injector alone for a moment or two, much as I would like to put some water back in the boiler. Harold had certainly taken it to heart when I gave him the signalman's message about not hanging about.

Another quick round in the box and, looking over the side, the home signal for Woodville Junction comes into sight. 44436 is beginning to labour now, those 40-odd wagons hanging heavily on the tender. Water is now down to a quarter of a glass and this with the firebox downhill of the gradient.

"Where would it be when we levelled out?" I wonder, "Let us just get by the peg and I'll put it on no matter what the gauge reads," I decide.

The gauge! I can't believe the gauge! 115lbs! Is that all! What on earth am I doing wrong? If this is number 4's, give me a 3F any day!

44436 gives a lurch to the right and, to my relief, we are crossing the down main to enter the sidings at Woodville Junction. I quickly flick on the injector and then fire another eight round the box. The fire is still white hot so why isn't it making steam?

We come to a standstill with just 95lbs showing on the clock. Leaving the damper open and the blower on, I knock off the injector when the glass shows half again. The foreman shunter comes up and has a word with Harold and we then push our load back into an empty road. Harold looks up and notices the gauge, which is now reading 100lbs again.

"Blimey, mate," he says, "I know I was giving her a thrashing but I didn't realise things were that bad."

"That's alright," I replied rather blousily, "You've got your job to do and I've got mine." "And," I added, "We made it. We got here." "But," I told myself, "We nearly didn't."

When the Overseal fireman, Bob Southerd, climbed into the cab, I was just scouring the boards and generally cleaning up. The gauge had recovered to about 140lbs by then so I had shut the damper and just left the blower cracked to lift the smoke.

He looked into the box and said, "What's been going on in here then?"

"It's got a bit knocked about, thrashing up from Gresley," I answered.

"Where's that then?" he asked, "Back side of Derby or somewhere?"

I decided the least said the better and forced a laugh. His sinister smile and questioning eyes said it all. He knows, I decided, that I don't know what I'm doing. And he's right. Straight round to see George tonight, if he's in, and find out what to do to make these 4's steam.

We brought 43623 back, as 43306 was stuck down at Donisthorpe or somewhere, due no doubt to the emergency workings. Our run back was quite uneventful although we passed a number of extra workings going the other way. As we parted company in the lobby when we signed off, Harold said, "No' a bad couple of days, Dave me lad but you don't like them number 4's, do you?" I just smiled and said, "Cheerio." So he did know, all the time!

This parting remark made me even more determined to lay the ghost of Mr Fowler's protégé. Being at a Midland Depot, I knew that once I found out how, I wouldn't have long to wait to put the knowledge into practice.

The cause of the diverted workings was, strangely enough, another Class 4F, which had fallen apart whilst working a train for Birmingham, over the viaduct. It took the fitters several hours to sort it out and the consequent delays and diversions took nearly all the rest of the day to recover.

I did eventually lay the ghost of the 4F's but true to say, I, in common with many other firemen and indeed drivers as well, was not happy when aboard the things, much preferring a Class 3F.

Talking about "The Branch" and the diverted Devonian, etc. travelling via Overseal and Stockinford to Birmingham, I will describe one of the eight trips that I had on this route known to the Burton men as "Over the Alps to Brum." Whereas the other seven were relatively uneventful, this one was anything but.

Signing on at the very civilised hour of 9.00 am. for Control Relief, I soon found my mate for the day, Jock Creer, holding court in the canteen. Jock, a dour Scotsman, was very much a larger than life character, whose early railway career was, to say the least, a bit of a mystery. Although a little bit intimidating for a young Passed Cleaner on his first outing, I had been out with Jock before, on the Chadd Trippers, so I knew him to be a good engineman, whose company held no fears for me.

We were soon involved in the usual game of dominoes, then, after only twenty minutes or so, Freddie Kent came in with a piece of paper detailing our task for the day. This proved to be a full load of coal for Hams Hall Power Station, which the Control, in their wisdom, had decided to route "Over the Alps" instead of the more usual route down the West of England Main Line, as described in Chapter 5. The Toton driver didn't sign for this alternative route and thus requested a conductor or relief.

Soon we noticed our train approaching slowly along the down slow from the station, with 48182, then a Toton engine but later destined for allocation to Burton, at the head. Climbing aboard, the usual pleasantries were exchanged and, for my part I was pleased to find a clean footplate, full glass of water and the gauge just short of blowing off.

"She's a good-un," was the welcoming remark from the Toton fireman, a wiry looking man in his twenties. "A bit of a rough ride but a good-un nevertheless." "Aren't they all," I answered, trying to seem more experienced than I actually was.

As the relief man got off I looked at the fire, which true to fashion was enormous, being level with the top of the flap and white-hot. No wonder he had said, "I left you a good-un," as he descended the steps. A look in the tender revealed a mixture of slate-grey lumps and some of them ovoids, which were just beginning to make their appearance on the tenders of second-rate trains.

Jock's remark on seeing the fire and the fuel was, "There'll be some clinker under that lot, laddie." He called everyone "Laddie."

We had to wait for the guard's relief, during which time 48182 opened her safety valves, despite me having dropped the damper and opening the firehole doors.

"Not much wrong in there, then," I thought. Clinker or not I wasn't going to get the irons out and have a poke around inside. A quick burst with the live steam injector soon quietened her down. I didn't dare put too much in the boiler with having a full glass already.

Our fresh, Burton guard soon arrived who, I was pleased to see, was Reg Finch, my mate's father and ex-North Stafford man, who I knew to be a good, conscientious man. He informed Jock that we were overloaded for our diversion and would we like to knock five wagons off, some 75 to 80 tons in total. The 8F's were known for their excellent brake power and this could have been the reason for Jock's decision to take them all on. I am not sure, after all these years, of the loading for an 8F over this road, if indeed I ever knew but, sufficient to say, they were not generous, indeed quite the opposite, so I knew I was going to be busy come what may. At least the Toton man had left me with a good start. He was certainly a "fill the hole and sit down for ten minutes" man, whereas I preferred to fire to the chimney and in consequence add fuel every couple of minutes or so. However, as I had inherited this furnace, I had to suffer it and look forward to a ride at least as far as Gresley before I needed to pick up the shovel.

As it was a Wednesday, the bobby held us at Leicester Junction until after the ten o'clock passenger up the branch. This was an extra working on Wednesdays and Saturdays associated with Market Days but I am not sure where, certainly not in Burton, which in those far off days implemented half day closing on Wednesdays. This working eventually came by, in charge of the inevitable Burton Class 2P, swinging across to the left, in front of us, to climb up onto the Leicester Branch proper.

I lift the damper, shut the doors and, in a moment more, the points clunk over, the peg pulls off and we are on our way. With great skill, Jock slowly eases away our 8F, gradually picking up each of our 60 or so wagons one at a time, building up a momentum to climb the 1 in 80 incline to the A38 road bridge over Branston Road and never a slip from 48182's 4'-8" wheels. Looking back from Jock's side, I exchange waves with Reg back in his van.

Thus we plodded up and over the A38, passing Birmingham Curve Junction Box on the way, to level out as we crossed over the river Trent and its floodplain, by means of Stapenhill Viaduct. Looking at the glass, the water was now just in sight below the top nut, so I left the injector off for a little while longer. A quick glance in the box revealed a white hot mass and although still of mountainous proportions, I couldn't resist sprinkling a couple or three shovels-full of ovoids onto the top of it. The gauge was rock steady on 225lbs so I sat down again to enjoy the ride. We had now passed Bretby Junction Box so, after a quick check of the level, I slipped the exhaust injector on at its pre-determined setting decided by my many predecessors, months if not years, before. Swadlincote Junction and Coton Park Sidings came and went until soon we were passing Gresley Signalbox and the Netherseal Colliery Sidings.

Jock had had our mount on full regulator climbing out of Burton but had eased her onto the first valve and a longer cut off once all the train was on the viaduct. The Toton man's remarks proved to be true as she certainly was a rough ride. However, as we passed through Gresley Station I picked up the shovel to add more fuel and Jock opened her up again onto the main valve for the climb through the tunnel and up through Woodville Junction to Moira West Junction where we would swing round to the right prior to passing Overseal Loco' Department. The sound of the exhaust was something to be heard. With four sharp, even beats shouting to the world and never a sign of a blow anywhere. There was nothing wrong with the front end. A glance at the gauge, with the needle pinned to the 225lbs red line mark, showed that there was nothing wrong with the boiler either. How different to the 4F's were these 8's, I reflected. One driver, many years later, once said to me that there was no such thing as a bad Class 5 or 8F, just that some were better than others.

Round the corner at Moira and past the shed, Jock shut off, dropped the lever to Drifting (marked with a 'D' on the reverser scale at a position about 45% cut-off) and started rubbing the brake. I looked across at him and, receiving a nod, wound the tender handbrake on then went back to my firing, putting another round on, prior to shutting the doors. I was still firing over the flap, such was the quantity of fuel in there.

As we approach Donisthorpe at the bottom of the bank, 48182 lifts her valves again as I wave to the Overseal fireman on the tripper standing in the colliery sidings there. The Measham bobby has the back-uns off as we approach his box so, as Jock opens her up again, I release the hand brake and we pass Measham Colliery Sidings on our left. Jock looks the picture of a perfect driver as he adjusts the reverser and leans back out through the open window, his cloth cap pulled down over his eyes, his pipe - one of the Sexton Blake type with the bowl on the end of a curved stem - clenched between his teeth, his right hand resting on the reversing wheel ready to dart out to shut the regulator handle, work the brake, flick the sand valve or whatever, in an instant.

Measham is on a slight embankment, the make up no doubt coming from the cutting through Donisthorpe, both being more or less the same length. As we reach the end of the embankment we pass over the Ashby Canal and proceed to follow its course for the next 13 miles on to Nuneaton. However, after only three miles or so we approach Shackerstone Junction and signalbox, where a single line comes in on the left from Coalville. The Shackerstone Bobby has his backboard on so Jock shuts off steam again and slows our train down coming to a stand in Shackerstone Station. I take the opportunity to clean up the footplate whilst we are standing, collecting up all the eggs and coal pieces that have failed to find their way into the firebox, partly due to the manic gyrations of our rough, old mount and partly through my lack of skill and experience. It's one thing to fire a locomotive when it's stationary but quite another when it's rocking and banging along like old 48182 is.

The exhaust injector has maintained the water level very nicely while we have been running and even changed over to live steam with hardly a blip when the regulator was shut. After a quick squirt round with the pep pipe I shut it off, as I don't wish to overfill the boiler while we are standing. I drop the dampers as well and open the doors to stop her blowing off.

Jock comes back from the station box after carrying out Rule 55 and tells me that we will be here for about another 15 minutes. Shackerstone Station, although complete and well maintained, had been closed to passenger traffic since the 1930's, in common with all the other stations along this stretch of line although still, at this time, open to goods traffic. Jock had taken his tea can when going to the box so we both enjoyed a lid of tea and I had a sandwich.

Almost to the minute the clattering sound of our signal being pulled off disturbs our relaxation so, with a hoot on 48182's deep throated whistle, Jock nods to the handbrake as I am winding it off and heaves the handle up to set us in motion once again. Wagon by wagon he takes up the slack as I open the dampers again, propping the $^3/_4$ x $^7/_8$ spanner under the handles to stop them shaking shut again.

A spring loaded plunger was fitted on the opposite side of the slot, through which the damper handles slide, it having to be compressed when an alteration to the setting was required, before either raising or lowering the handle the desired setting then being held in position by the plunger holding the slot in the rod in its locking place. However, in practice, due to the thumping and banging created by the rough riding of the engine, the damper operating rod would slowly shake free of its slot, eventually dropping down and closing the damper doors, hence the use of the spanner as a makeshift but effective remedy. This feature is common to most ex MR engines and is perpetuated in the Stanier designs. Mr. Hughes' Crabs however, have a screw handle with which to operate the dampers and these are no trouble at all, the damper staying in any position desired.

Looking back, I acknowledge Reg's wave from the van and turn my attentions to the boiler and fire. The water is just in sight in the top of the glass which, as we are running downhill, is to be expected, the clock is still on the red line so I just sprinkle a few more ovoids mix on the firebed over the flap then shut the doors. Jock has now got our train nicely on the move so, with just a breath of steam on to cushion the pistons, we all-but coast down to Market Bosworth.

As we run under the road bridge to enter the station the bobby has his back-uns off so Jack opens her up again for the rise to Shenton. Passing the goods yard we see the cause of our delay at Shackerstone as, standing inside, is what I believe to be a trip working from Nuneaton, with one of Mr. Ivatt's masterpieces in charge – No. 43020 – still wearing her double chimney. I blow a rude call on our whistles as we run by and her fireman acknowledges with a thumbs down wave over the cab side.

As they went through the works, all these early double chimney 'doodle-bugs' were being fitted with a single chimney and modified blastpipe following extensive trials in an attempt to improve their somewhat mediocre steaming capabilities. Indeed, 43027 ran around wearing an ugly stovepipe chimney for some considerable time during, I believe 1952, in connection with these trials. I only came in contact with them myself when on disposing duties and in consequence thought of them very favourably with their rocker grates, hopper ashpans and of course self cleaning smokeboxes. Truly a disposing fireman's dream. Otherwise, it was said that their only saving grace was their monitor type injection, which really poured the water into the boiler - on reflection, probably too quickly, considering their poor steam raising ability in their original double-chimneyed form. As more than one fireman was heard to say, "Give me a 4F any day," probably says it all.

But - back to 48182. As we get nearer to Shenton, we pass the site of a very important battle that took place in 1485. The Battle of Bosworth Field, no less. Where cattle now graze and the rural life of the community pursues its calm, serene existence, thousands of men clashed with swords, pikes, etc. and the air was rent with the sound of battle. Now, just the shout of 48182's exhaust disturbed the silence with our passing, Jock giving her more steam as the gradient increased against her, the thumping ring of her motion echoing back from the trees and hedgerows of the pastoral scene.

On the principal of 'if it works, why change it' I am still feeding this monstrous fire I have inherited and, truth to say, so far our rough old lady seems to like it. With both of our injectors working well I am confident that we shall have no problems. You see! If they fail for some reason, not a totally unknown scenario, then the fire has to be bailed out - and very quickly – to save the firebox crown. For, once it ceases to have any water above it, disaster is but moments away with the fusible plugs melting to disgorge steam at high pressure onto the fire which immediately shoots out of the firehole onto the footplate where, I am told, there is no escape from the ensuing, scalding, burning conflagration. And there was no way you would manage to bail out that mountainous fire in the time available.

As we pound down the bank towards Stoke Golding the bobby there has his distant off as well. With all the train nicely gathered up behind the tender, a slight increase in braking checks our speed, as we swing round to the right at the junction. The left hand line continues almost straight on at this point as it heads away towards Hinckley and Leicester. We flash under a bridge and there, immediately on our right, over the hedge, appears the test track of the Motor Research Institute. Cars, lorries and buses are frequently observed being put through their paces and this day was no exception with what appeared to be two Land Rovers fighting their way through some very rough and muddy terrain. Then our view is lost as we enter an ever-deepening cutting to pass under the main A5 trunk road emerging back at ground level before starting a climb onto another embankment crossing over the A444 followed by the West Coast Mainline.

The only excitement below is another 8F restarting a long train of vans with part fitted lights up. I hope she is in better nick than our steed, as they don't hang about on that line. Two quick junctions come up on our left hand side as a spur from the low level line joins us, followed immediately by a second line which has also passed over the West Coast line but avoids the station and continues on towards Hinckley and Leicester.

At this last junction the distants are firmly against us and we soon come to a stand on the loop at Nuneaton (Abbey Street). I am quickly up onto the back of the tender to add some 2,000 gallons or so to fill our tank up to capacity. This is a booked water stop for which some ten minutes or so are allowed whilst the train is examined. Jock has a walk round our engine, feeling the bearings and adding a drop of oil here and there as he does so. I spend the remaining time shovelling up all the ovoids from the footplate that have shaken out of the tender to fall all over the floor following our rattling run down from Shackerstone.

This is always a problem with a tender containing these eggs until at least half of the fuel has been used and is no doubt why the Toton fireman had got such a huge fire on. He would have started with a tender full of the things and, if the preparing man hadn't built a barrier with some large coal pieces, the ovoids would have flown onto the footplate like water as soon as the engine got on the move. Still! At least the fuel (you can't dignify it by calling it coal) comes to you and saves you having to go into the tender to fetch it out.

Having shovelled all the spillage into the firebox, I slip the injector back on to slack the footboards down. I toy with the idea of having a dig down through the great fire mass to try loosening the firebed and allow more primary air through the firebars as these dratted ovoids tend to settle into a big melted mass, unlike coal which, being harder and in consequence not so tightly packed, provides natural gaps through which the primary air flows. But, despite the doors being open and the dampers closed, 48182 lifts her valves, so I decide to leave well alone.

A Leicester to Birmingham stopper ran in alongside us, headed by a Saltley Compound, so I closed the doors and opened the dampers, ready to follow in its wake. As the Compound roared away up the unremitting climb to and through Arley Tunnel, we got the road to follow her. The gradient, though varying slightly, averages 1 in 130 for the next two miles, culminating in the dark, damp confines of the 995 yard long Arley Tunnel.

Jock set 48182 to the task of hauling our overloaded train, wagon by wagon, up the two miles or so to the summit. After exchanging waves with Reg in his van, I set to and add yet more ovoids, mixed with a sprinkling of the slate-grey stone which passed for coal, onto our fire, all delivered into our cab courtesy of the rough riding. As we are climbing with some determination and the draw bar is in tension, the violent oscillations between engine and tender reduce somewhat. I all but closed the doors and, with the needle showing 220lbs, we entered the tunnel. I had fired early to enable the smoke to disperse before we entered this Stygian hole in the ground. The fireman on the Compound before us hadn't been quite so considerate with his firing however and, as we entered, smoke was still rolling out of the tunnel mouth. With the side windows shut, I snuggled down into the corner of the cab, sitting on the floor trying to gasp some clean air.

The racket which 48182's run down motion made echoed all around and I was fascinated to see, in time with each beat of the exhaust, a constant trail of smoke and steam pour round the back edge of the cab roof and pass with a jerk back through the gap between the firedoors, all illuminated by the beam of intense light shining through that same gap in the firehole doors. With the atmosphere becoming increasingly foul, we suddenly emerged into the daylight once again.

Throwing the sliding window back, I hang over the side of the cab to draw in some very welcome lung filling gasps of air. A quick glance at the clock shows 195lbs and the glass is just showing below the top nut. As we are now pointing downhill and it is basically downhill the rest of the way to our destination, all our hard work is over, or so we think.

Jock is gathering up the wagons behind us as I wind the tender handbrake on. Down through Arley and Fillongley Station we go, with the train nicely under control. At Church End Colliery Box the bobby has his distance board on so Jock starts to gather them up even more, when suddenly, with a bang, we lurch forwards as a cloud of steam jets out from below, between the engine and tender.

I look across at Jock in alarm.

"Steam brake pipe's burst between the engine and tender," he shouts, "Get down the side and drop off," he adds. "No need for us both to get killed," he qualifies his order.

I open the side doors and climb backwards down the steps to do his bidding. By this time we are travelling at a tremendous rate, our overloaded coal train pushing away at our tender with only the handbrake and Reg in his brake van to hold them back. Prior to making the final jump I look down to see the sleeper ends going by in a blur. My courage fails me and I climb back up to take my chances with Jock on the footplate. He has by now got the whistle wide open, the handle jammed down with a piece of our slatey coal. I am at a complete loss about what to do next as I go across to Jock's side. I have the tender handbrake on as hard as it will go.

Jock takes his pipe from his mouth and says that he is going to try and 'poleaxe' her. I hadn't a clue what he meant but was soon to learn that he was going to wind the gear into reverse and, with a breath of steam on, create an hydraulic braking effect on the engine, probably doing untold damage to the motion at the same time.

By now we were flashing over Whitacre Junction. Looking across, I caught a glimpse of an express approaching along the fast line from Burton and heading, under 'clear' signals, for Water Orton Junction, to where we were also heading, some mile or so distance. As I watched, mesmerised by all the events unfolding around me, the express driver had the clear road thrown against him, in his face. He disappeared from my view behind the buildings of Hams Hall Power Station, our original destination, as we flashed across the turn-off into the sidings, to continue our headlong dash towards Water Orton.

As we shot across the junction our speed was noticeably slowing. I looked back towards the line on which the express was approaching to see a Jubilee just coming to a halt, midst clouds of steam, not 200 yards away.

We finally came to a halt in Castle Bromwich Station, where I staggered off the footplate, only to be physically sick after collapsing onto the nearest platform seat.

However, after a couple of minutes, I climbed back onto the cab and, seeing we had a full glass, shut off the exhaust injector, which amazingly had still kept going through all the gyrations, shut the dampers and opened the doors. As a finalé, 48182 lifted her valves again.

Jock, still pulling on his pipe, asked me to go to the box and request an engine to pull us off the mainline, which I did. Eventually two of the Camphill Bankers turned up, both class 3F's and, following the issuing of Wrong Line Orders, backed on to us then hauled us, train and all, into Bromford Bridge Sidings.

The quick reactions of the signalmen concerned is to be praised for, not only did they keep us going down the main line but kept us on the fast line towards Birmingham, having stopped what turned out to be a Newcastle – Bristol express which was the biggest gamble of all. Had the bobby turned us into the dead-end at Whitacre Junction, I doubt that I would have been writing this story now because of the likely resultant pile up. Similarly, had we been turned down the goods road at Water Orton onto the block, another collision would have been inevitable as trains were always stacked one behind the other there, day and night.

I reflected that the Compound ahead of us must have got a move on, as we were sniffing at his heels at Arley Station, where presumably he had stopped, not to mention Whitacre as well. Ironically, it was fortunate, if that's the right sentiment, that the brake pipe burst when it did for, if it had happened further down the bank, the outcome would have been very different.

Still! All's well that ends well and, as Jock says, "We got away with it!"

Our poor old abused and misused 8F was left at the Bromford disposal point, for the Saltley men to dispose and take care of, prior to being towed to Saltley Depot for examination and repairs, the disposal element being much to my relief as I had visions of having to chuck that huge fire out myself. This indeed, was uppermost in my mind when Jock asked me if I felt like working 48182's return-working back. Apparently, Control had asked him if we would as, after such a dramatic experience, we could have gone back home on cushions.

So we took charge of our 3F rescuer, number 43284, and ran light-engine, back to Hams Hall Power Station, where we backed onto a full load of empties for Toton Yard. Routed back over the main line via Coleshill, Tamworth and Wychnor, the only problem we had was over HasloughTroughs, where I discovered that the scoop was seized solid and in consequence we had to back our train into Wychnor Sidings to fill the tank. Relief was forthcoming at Burton, where we put the bag in again to top it up for our relief crew, a set of Toton men who told us they were hoping for a ride back on the cushions. Still, they had a nice, clean footplate to take over, a fresh, clean fire (I had chucked out the clinker at Hams Hall), a full boiler and 170lbs on the clock.

Jock made out his report and I went home to see what my mother had prepared for tea. What an exciting, not to mention, a little frightening, day I'd had. And not a minute's overtime made either!

The following day Jock and I had another run to Bromford Bridge with yet another coal train, this time with 43966, along the main line this time. When we went across the disposal point to turn, the Saltley men told us that the fitters had been over to fit a new brake pipe to 48182 and that she had been sent home, light engine, for them to worry about.

I dared to ask about the huge fire in her box and if they'd had to chuck it out.

"You must be joking," the fireman replied, "Reckon it would take her all the way home would that."

I was going to explain that it wasn't my normal way of doing things but thought better of it. He probably wouldn't have believed me anyway.

Chapter 5

Off to Brum

Signing on for 6.00 am. one Tuesday morning with a pair of grinding goggles, acquired by one of my mates from his workplace in my pocket, and anticipating yet another happy time on the ashpits, I was pleasantly surprised to hear Reg Haywood the list clerk, speak to me in, for him, quite a civilised manner, between clouds of snuff., numerous pinches of which lay comatose all down the front of his waistcoat.

"Sign on for 5.30," he said, "And go with Albert Dukes on Control Relief; he's in the canteen I shouldn't wonder." Excitement flooded over me, followed by that pit of the stomach feeling, which attacks you when facing the unknown.

I patted the goggles in my pocket. "Won't be needing you today," I thought. Off to the canteen I went, and spotting Albert sitting at a table having a shuffle of dominoes with 3 other footplate men, I bought a mug of tea from the redoubtable Mrs. Sayers, the canteen manageress, who had just opened up, and wandered over and made myself known to him.

"Can you play this game then. Art thee any good at it?" he said.

"Yes, I think so," I replied.

"Good," he said, "Because these two are off in a minute," pointing to the pair who it transpired were Toton men.

The 3rd player I knew to be an old hand Burton passed fireman who was on disposing and waiting his last engine to make up his quota of 5.

"Any on the pit?" he enquired to me by way of greeting.

"Not that I know of," I answered, wishing that I had indeed even looked to see. "I've only just come on."

"Bloody typical int it, a dead loss this 2 o'clock disposing. You hang around for hours just waiting for one more flaming engine," he grumbled.

Blimey! I thought. You've only been here 4 hours. What are you moaning about. Not that I dare say it to his face.

The Toton men got up to go and, just as I had sat down and another fireman had slipped in to the other vacant seat, in came little Ronnie Harrison, the foreman runner, to give our moaning colleague his last engine to dispose.

"42826 for you," said Ronnie, and turning to my Mate said, "Westhouses, Bromford Bridge, 8313 coming down the main in 20 minutes, just left Stenson."

Back- came the tummy chums and down went the dominoes.

"Come on mate, get your bag, we're off," said Albert, rising from his seat, "Well get him by the box and save a walk," meaning right outside the loco by Leicester Junction Signalbox. "What's your name by the way?" he asked. "I'm Albert. Have you been on an 8 before?"

A Stanier Class 8F 2-8-0. The ideal frieght engine. Photo: Authors Collection.

I had to admit that I hadn't.

"Don't worry, they're a doddle. Just do as you think and I"ll put you right if you're having trouble," he answered, though what he thought was best left to the imagination.

A plume of steam was seen in the distance as she lifted her train out of the station, over Moor Street Bridge and the Bond End Branch, then her driver shut off to approach Leicester Junction, gathering her train of coal up behind her. To my delight, as she came into view, I could see that her paintwork had still got a suggestion of a shine and her buffer beam was bright red.

"Must have known it was your first time lad, they've painted her up for you!" remarked Albert. "Not long out of shops this one. Should be a nice ride!"

The road was signalled to switch the train over on to the slow line and it became apparent even to me that there was no way it was going to stop and let us get on where we stood outside the signalbox.

"Of all the brainless idiots," or words to that effect, cursed Albert. "Now we've got to walk, half way to Branston to catch the flaming thing."

The train eventually stopped with the brake about 100 yards clear of the junction and we plodded off after it with Albert cussing and cursing as we tripped over signal wires, points rodding, rails and the like. His demeanour wasn't helped by our guard, who stepped out of their relief cabin as we passed by and strolled with us for about 20 yards before climbing up into the brake, with a parting remark, "Enjoy your walk! At least it isn't raining."

What Albert wasn't going to do to the driver when we got to the engine was nobody's business but when we did eventually climb aboard, I at least couldn't believe what I saw.

There stood two grey haired old gentlemen, one - who appeared to be the fireman - with a beard and both looking old enough to be Albert's granddad, let alone mine.

"She's a good un youth," said the one without the beard, to Albert, who himself was showing greyish white hair beneath his grease topped cap. Just as father time was about to speak to me 8313 blew off at the safety valves, effectively killing all other conversation stone dead.

Off they got and Albert checked the reverser, gave a toot on the Caledonian Hooter and, lifting the brake, gave the regulator handle a tug. 8313 started to ease the train away, one wagon at a time, whilst I had a quick check of the water in the glass and the pressure gauge, then opened the door to look at the fire. To my inexperienced eye, there looked to be enough fire in there to take us all the way to Birmingham and half way back. With opening the regulator and using some steam, the safety valves closed and, as I could now hear myself think as it were, I remembered to look back for the guard's signal to tell us that all the train was on the move. After a couple of minutes and still no sign of him, I wondered if I should mention it to Albert.

"The guard's not waved yet, Albert and we know he got on," I called to him, wondering as I did the possible folly of reminding him of the remarks recently made.

"OK mate, I've seen him," he replied. "Just wondered if you'd remember to look. Anyway if we had left him behind, we'll be stopping again in a minute. We're on the block. Leave the fire and drop the damper or we'll be waking all of Branston with that lot in there! I doubt we'll get far before 9 o'clock at any rate."

And so we stopped behind the brake of the one in front. The guard on it was very confident, as he got off and asked if he could come up and wash his hands in a bucket of hot water. He said that he didn't like eating his snap with dirty hands.

I asked him where he was from as I thought I had seen him before and he answered, "Chadd," meaning Chaddesden Sidings, Derby.

"It's always the same here on this job," he added. "Stand for ages you do. Thought I'd take my chance here, as you've no chance on the move with that mad bugger on the front."

And with that he left; and a good job too, because he had hardly got back into the van when it seemed to leap away from inertia to 15-20 miles an hour without any build up of acceleration at all.

Albert trundled 8313 down, after the brake, to stop at the signal before the box at Branston Junction. Here, a cord from the Leicester line at Birmingham Curve Junction Box curved round to Branston to form the third leg of a triangle, mainly being used by coal trains to and from the South Derbyshire and Leicestershire coalfields to Birmingham. This was the end of one permissive block section with a second commencing beyond the junction and as far as Barton under Needwood, known as Barton and Walton Station where the four-track section ended.

Another 8F from Coalville was waiting on this cord line with a load of 16T steel and ex-PO wooden wagons all loaded to the brim, like ours, with coal for Birmingham.

"Bet he goes first," says Albert and sure enough about five minutes later off came the peg and away he went, to follow our 'Chadd' guard down the slow towards Barton.

All this time a procession of passenger and fast freight trains had been overtaking us on the fast line on our right. Albert looked at his watch and said to me

"Nip up to the box and find out what's happening Dave."

So off I went to see the bobby. "Better get some coal on son, you're out after the Gloucester Passenger. That's her now," he said as the bells rang and he fiddled with the instruments then beat out a code back. As he went to pull his levers I dashed back down the steps and up onto the engine in double quick time.

"Calm down lad and take your time. We're going after the passenger, right? Thought we might. Get that damper open a couple of nicks and have a look at that fire," Albert retorted.

The fire now looked a bit dead but from past experience working block for block with the constant standing about for ages on end, I knew or hoped it would liven up once we got going. The water was showing just over threequarters of a glass so, with 220 lbs showing on the gauge, I thought, "Great," and sat down again on my seat.

Albert said nothing so what else was I supposed to do?

I looked back down the train towards Burton and spotted a plume of smoke and steam coming up rapidly towards us and, in no time at all, the Gloucester Passenger came charging by headed by a Compound with 6 coaches in tow.

"Now for it," I thought. The butterflies in my stomach took off again as, with a clunk, the points went over and clang - off came our signal, turning us out - main line - in the wake of the Compound and its 6 coach load.

Albert looked at me as I released the hand brake and said. "OK mate,"

As I nodded back he opened the steam brake, dropped the gear down and with a toot on the whistle, gave the regulator handle a gentle tug.

8313 gave a throaty chuff and settled down to the task without a slip, out over the points and on to the main line. I looked back and acknowledged the guard's wave with a toot on the horn and shouted across to Albert who nodded, stuck his head out of the cab and away we went.

From my trips to Wychnor I knew that the line climbed gently for the first 4 or 5 miles at about 1 in 250-300 so I decided - in for a penny, in for a pound - as the pressure had already dropped nearly 10 pounds and we had only gone about 3 or 4 trains length, I opened doors and taking up the shovel put one in each back corner, three down each side and one under the door. I slipped the exhaust injector on and set the feed at minimum. This did nothing for the pressure gauge, but at least it did not fall off anymore.

Albert linked her up a bit more as we passed the 'Coalville 8', our 'Chadd' guard standing on his back veranda with a sandwich in his hand. He shoved the regulator right up into the roof, took a piece of wood out of his pocket and wedged it between the quadrant and the handle. We roared through Barton and Walton Station the back-uns off and 8313 was really getting dug in. The fire was white hot now and still with threequarters of a glass in the boiler, I shot another charge around the box with 2 or 3 extra ones in the middle and an extra one under the door also. By the time I looked up we were going round the corner to the left at Wychnor Junction. Old 8313 gave a kick as she crossed over the junction, with the ex LNW line to Lichfield and Walsall/Wolverhampton curving off to the right. Cock Ford's image crossed my mind and I smiled as I remembered the incident with the hot box and the Austerity (see chapter three).

From here on, this is all new ground to me. In no time we are crossing the viaduct over the Trent and swinging to the right to cross over the A513 Alrewas to Tamworth Road then crashing through Elford Station. The platform here is very narrow and you feel that you could reach out and touch the station buildings as you run through. As we pass over the bridge I lean out of the cab window to look back down the train but, such is the dust created by our passing and from the train itself, that I cannot see the brake-van very clearly at all. We are now passing over a high embankment but I haven't got time to enjoy the scenery. I am watching the chimney and, as the smoke clears, charging another round into the box. On checking the water again, I increase the feed as the level is down to half a glass. As I stoop to feed another round into the box I spot another station out of the corner of my eye.

"Tamworth," I tell myself, as I reflect on the hours I had spent or mis-spent only a couple or three years earlier whilst train-spotting.

Are there any avid spotters here today to write down 8313's number? and boo or cheer as the case may be! or possibly ignore the high level that we are on altogether, in favour of more worthwhile engines on the Euston-Crewe line below. Probably not anyone there at all on a Tuesday morning in December!

I'm firing like a pro' now I tell myself with pressure steady at 220 lbs and the water level. These '8's are "The business," I tell myself. The tender doors are open now and I am finding a mixture of ovoids and briquettes and the further into it I get, the less coal there is amongst it.

Just then Albert shuts off, drops the gear down, gives a toot on the whistle and starts rubbing the brake.

"That'll do for now mate," he calls across. "Give that handbrake a turn or two. We'll be going round the houses in a minute from Whitacre, and we're stopping to fill the tank. We normally lift some on the troughs at Tamworth but they're out under repair at the moment."

I didn't like to admit that I didn't know there were any troughs at Tamworth or that I had not checked the gauge on the tank. either. And I thought I was doing so well.

As if he could read my mind Albert said, "You're doing all right kid. The worst is over now. I doubt we'll get a run from here into Brum."

We pulled up into the loop and I dropped the damper, shut off the injector and opened the doors, just as she lifted her valves. What a waste of steam but what a satisfying sound to a greenhorn fireman, like me. Then - over to the box to carry out Rule 55 and back up onto the tank and - in with the bag.

"OK Albert. Turn on," I shouted, over the sound of a 4F coughing and wheezing by, with a load of empties. Next moment I am yelling as a jet of icy cold water swamps my backside from a leaking hole in the bag. So - 3000 gallons in the tank and the rest where I would rather not remember.

Still, I consoled myself, as I attempted to dry out in front of the fire, it beats emptying ashpits every time.

Albert whistled up for the road, and after about ten minutes, the peg came off and we pulled out of the loop. The bobby had a red flag hanging out of the box and as we passed slowly by he held up 2 fingers. Not because he was being rude but because there were two trains standing on the block ahead of us. I opened the damper and firehole door to view the fire which looked dead again. A quick glance out of the cab ahead showed nothing in front as far as I could see but Albert still let 8313 just drift along with a breath of steam, the regulator being just off its face.

"What do you do now David?" I asked myself. "Get the dart down perhaps! But what would Albert say?"

"I'm the fireman, I told myself," so get the dart down!

Fire-irons on a Stanier tender are housed in a tunnel on the fireman's side and when you try to pull one out all the others want to come out for a look as well. So there I am trying to remember what shape the handle of the dart is and all three irons are coming out as if saying, "Choose me, choose me!!"

Albert looks across and says, "Got a bit of clinker in there mate. I'm not surprised. Reckon this old lady has come farther than Westhouses. Or else she's been turned round without anyone bothering. Leave it mate, and I'll give her a bit of stick." So saying, he indicated me to wind the tender brake on and opened her up. That soon had her hot and brought a smile to my face. We got the road through Kingsbury and ran on to Water Orton before we caught up the other two on the block. As we stopped behind the brake in front, it started to move, so we drifted down behind it to Castle Bromwich where a Saltley crew climbed aboard to take over.

The fireman, a little chap of about 20 looked in the tender, then in the box, eyed me up and down and said, "Blimey mate, you got shares in the pit or summat? Where you come from then, Scotland?" I went to reply when he added, "Never mind, kid, you'll soon get the idea."

At least, I thought to myself, the cab was clean and tidy as I had just slacked it down for the umpteenth time since leaving Branston.

We stayed on up to Bromford Bridge with this Brummie fireman giving me ear-ache all the time till we got off.

When we did Albert said, "He'll enjoy chucking that lot out. He won't have much wind left for owt then,"

In the cabin there, we had our snap and I got a bit worried as the only two engines on the pit outside were both Garratts. But I need not have worried as two sets of Toton men came in the cabin to brew up before taking them away.

I must have dropped off to sleep without realising.

Next thing, I hear Albert's voice saying, "I thought we'd have been taking that one back mate, but Saltley must have wanted her for something else. I'll give control a ring and see what's about. They'll have to be quick, our days up in 2½ hours." When he came back. off the phone he sat down and said that we had to wait while they rang us back. After about 20 minutes we hear an engine come through the sidings and stop outside the cabin.

A fireman burst through the door and said, "Who are Burton men?"

As we were the only ones in there, Albert said, "Guess!" Whereupon the fireman said, "You're to take over this old camel and take her to Burton."

This old camel proved to be a '4F', number 44272 of Gloucester and she was going LE to Derby Shops. So, gathering up our traps, off we went again.

What an old nail this thing was to. If it could knock, bounce, rattle or shake then it did. She certainly wasn't going to shops before time.

Now - I had never been happy on a number 4 and, in common with many new firemen, I had trouble making them steam. Still - having got the theory from George Wallace, following my disastrous turn on the Overseal Tripper, I saw an opportunity to put it into practice. I remembered to check the water level in the tank this time as well and as it was showing empty, I was glad I did. I had a quick look at the fire, which was right up above the flap of the door and noted that the boiler was full above the top nut in the glass. The footplate was filthy, with lumps of coal and not a few ovoid eggs, all over the floor. There was absolutely nothing to sit on across where the seat used to be.

(When ex Midland engines came out of the works after overhaul they were fitted out with nice long planked seats with a hinged door across the oil store box on the fireman's side. These were invariably, removed by some misguided person, very early on, to make, so it was rumoured, rabbit hutches and the like or more likely firewood. This situation was common throughout the system).

Even more serious, from Albert's point of view, was the lack of a drivers stand and flame guard, a piece of sleeper serving to act in its stead.

Thinking of tidying up the cab I then noted that there was no slacking pipe either with which to wash down and as I looked out after the departing fireman, I spotted it hanging over his shoulder. Of the driver there was no sign at all.

I looked across at Albert and I could see at once that he was not a happy man.

"Well you've had the cream, now you've got the scrap, kid," was his remark, or something similar.

"And the tanks empty," I replied.

"OK, we'll pull down to the column but you'll probably find that the float is broken and we have at least ½ a tank. Still we'll fill up anyway. Get the brake off, we might as well make the best of it," and with that he knocked off the catch and let her spin into full gear, yanked open the handle and off we clattered down the siding to the column.

Up onto the tender back I went and clambering over the coal round the hole, reached for the bag and fed it in. Climbing onto the pick-up dome (which covers the pipe that passes through the tank to allow it to be filled when on the move via the scoop in the troughs between the rails below), I steadied the leather water bag and called for Albert to turn it on.

"I'm not going to get another wetting this time," I told myself, only to feel the chill up my arm as yet another leak got me again. My remarks are normally represented in print as asterisks and my ardour was definitely dampened. Albert laughed and said that it was all part of the game.

As the tank was filling, another 4F came rattling in with a coal train and stopped about three roads away. An idea formed in my mind and when the tank was filled, I chucked the bag out and after looking round for the non-existent tank-lid, I climbed down and went across to this other engine.

"What yow dooin next?" I asked the fireman in a fake Brummie accent.

"Off to the shed mate, we've done," he answered.

"Then you won't mind if I nick your pep pipe will you," says I.

"Help yourself," says he, handing me the $^3/_4$" and $^7/_8$" spanner with which to remove it.

"No sooner said that done. Thanks." In my delight I answered in my normal voice.

"Doing Music Hall turns as a sideline?" the Saltley diver grinned, "You need a bit more practice yet. Be off with you or I'll foist my useless Mate on you as well!"

So I returned to poor old 4272 with my trophy in my hand, which I immediately connected up to the fitting provided.

"Bit cheeky that wasn't it mate?" chuckled Albert. "You'd not of had it if I'd been the driver."

"You get nothing without trying," I retorted and slipped on the injector so that I could damp down the footplate and lay some of the dust.

"Better knock the digger off now Dave, we don't want her priming. God knows how full up she is," reprimanded Albert.

Here I go again, I thought, solving one problem and creating another. Still of course he was right and served as yet another lesson in the art and skill of becoming a fireman.

Soon we were rattling and banging along the block to Whiteacre where we stood at the peg on the end of the platform.

"I'll just stretch my legs and go and see the bobby," Albert said as he stepped across onto the platform. "This old gel 'll be a bit rough when we really get going. See if he can find us a quiet path where we can take our time."

While he was gone I noticed the gauge was dropping back to about 150 PSI and yet the fire looked massive and I hadn't as yet touched it, apart from chucking the spillage we'd inherited off the floor onto it. What had George said to me? Keep the back corners full, just a bit down each side and plenty under the door. Keep it thin under the arch.

Right! Down with the rake and pull some back from the front if I can but be careful not to knock the arch, which looks a bit iffy to say the least. I've just got the rake down when Albert gets back on.

"What's up mate?" he asks. I point to the gauge and tell him my fears.

"Don't worry about that now lad. There's enough in there and in the boiler to take us nearly to Burton. I'd leave it if I were you. Plenty of time to mess around in there when we get to Wychnor. Just sit back and enjoy the view. We'll see how it looks when we get going in another 5 minutes or so after the Newcastle's gone through. Its on time. Then we've got 20 minutes to get clear at Wychnor."

Soon we heard the familiar 3 cylinder beat of a Jubilee working hard, coming up from behind us and although we couldn't see her, we certainly heard her and her train go roaring past on the direct line over to our left. I opened the damper a bit wider in readiness and as the peg pulled off, Albert opened the regulator and off we went in her wake. As we passed the section signal the distant pulled off beneath it.

He's not hanging about in front of us, I thought as I turned back from looking over the side of the cab to check the gauge and water. It was still out of sight above the top of the glass and the pressure had dropped 5 lbs. I'll give it another 5 minutes, I thought then attempt to do something about it.

Albert whistled up and I looked out to see another station coming up. 'Wilnecote,' it said as we passed the board. Wilnecote! just goes to show how busy I was, coming up to Brum that I never noticed it pass by.

It seemed a while before we got to Tamworth again and this time I looked out for the troughs, just as Albert whistled up to warn a gang repairing the line. A wave from the lookout and all the men standing back well clear was very reassuring.

Nothing about on the Low Level - as I could see. What must it be like to fire a Duchess I mused.

Head back in the cab again to check the gauge and water, only to see we are down to just below 130 lbs, although the water is still above the top nut. A feeling of panic hits my stomach again as I open the doors and have a look at the fire. It's white hot and there still seems to be as much of it as when we left Whiteacre.

"Put a round on," I says to myself and picking up the shovel, I shot a couple of charges into each back corner. I try for two more down each side but miss the door with the first, scattering coal all over the cab front, the largest piece bouncing back to land on Albert's right foot. He just wriggled his leg and I tried again just as we rolled through Elford Station.

44272 for some reason, gave a particularly pronounced lurch and a bounce, noticeable even with the atrocious antics which were the norm with her progress down the line, causing me to catch the side of the firehole with the blade and catapulting half the charge into the fire where I hadn't intended it to go and the other half back round my feet. The jarring pain that shot up my arm had to be experienced to be believed and in my temper I shot the shovel up the tender and learned out of the cab to cool off.

"To hell with it! And the pressure gauge! I'll sort it out at Wychnor," I told myself.

But next thing I knew we were rattling over the junction and carrying on to Barton.

What's happening now? Another quick look at the gauge. Still around 130 lbs and - low and behold, the water is appearing just in the top nut. Now, at least I know where that is, I told myself. The litter of coal on the cab floor was annoying me now, so there was nothing for it but to sweep it up and then retrieve the shovel to deposit it in the box.

On hearing me open the doors wide and appear to 'fire' the box, Albert pulled his head in and with a quick look round called out, ""Leave it mate, there's enough in there to get to Burton."

"I've no intention of putting any on, "I thought to myself, unless I really have to. My wrist hurts too much.

When we reached Barton and Walton, the Bobby still kept us main-line but, as the distant was against us and at Branston, we were again turned down the block. The Branston Junction signalman indicated four fingers meaning four in front of us and I could well believe it as we only just got inside, clear of the junction and behind the brake of the 4th train.

The bobby at Barton had taken a gamble with us as, hardly had we stopped, when another runner, this time with a 'Black 5' in charge came charging past us with its fireman over on our side wagging his finger and mouthing something as he passed that, probably it was as well we didn't hear.

As we slowly followed the procession down to the loco I put the injector on, just to top up the boiler but mainly to slack the cab down and as we were one train away from Leicester Junction I noticed that steam was down to 105 lbs so asked Albert if it would last or should I put a bit on. After all, no one wants to run on to the shed with a box full of fire if they can help it.

"Just give it a rattle round and push some of what's left under the door forward a bit, if you want to," he replied. Just then the train in front started off and we followed him down to the junction gantry.

As I'm lifting the dart into the box, two Burton men climb up into the cab, the fireman being my pal - Reg Finch of Cock Ford fame.

The driver - Charlie Smith, known as Greenlight to all though not to his face, owing to his excessively cautious attitude to everything, asks Albert, "Is everything alright? We are taking her on to Derby."

I quickly handed over the dart to Reg and, with a parting remark about what a rough old camel she was, echoing the fireman who we in our turn had relieved, dropped down onto the ballast, round the relief cabin and out of sight.

What Reg said, next time I saw him, is not for the written word and no excuses about expecting to go on to the shed would pacify him.

Albert was pretty nifty in leaving as well, I thought and as we walked back to the shed, I remarked that we would not be the most popular pair that those two would meet that day.

I only had one question left to ask Albert, one that had been on my mind all day, about the fireman who we relieved on 8313 at the start of the shift.

"Oh, you mean Gabrielle," he said. "He's a permanent fireman. He either didn't pass his driving exam or opted not to try for it."

"Is that really his name?" I asked.

Albert just smiled and said, "Who did you think it was. Father Christmas?"

We signed off at 2.15 pm and on looking at the sheet, I saw that I was marked up for 6.00 am spare again the next day. So, putting the goggles in my pocket, I collected my bike out of the rack and pedalled off home.

Will I be wearing them tomorrow on the dreaded ashpits? I wondered – or will I get lucky again?

Chapter 6

Birmingham Again

Reflecting on the way things had progressed, during what was really my first mainline job; Chadd trippers and the like apart; I was - all in all - quite pleased with myself, even though the return journey perhaps could have been performed better. Who would have thought that a light engine run could have presented me with so many little worries. Still, so long as one learns by ones faults and errors, there was nothing lost, so I told myself.

My second run to Birmingham came about quite soon afterwards and a little unexpectedly.

During the rest of the week following my triumph on 48313 I got two more footplate turns in ,both of which were preparing turns on the shed with Dickie Smith. Dick was a good man to be with and had a pleasant demeanour considering that he was permanently confined to shed duties having failed his eyesight test some years before. As he said, at least you know when your going to start and finish. Now! Preparing engines is no sinecure, as has been previously mentioned but they all count as turns towards the magic 313, after which a passed cleaner becomes registered as a permanent fireman. An unusual number 313 I always thought. Not 300 or 310 or some other nice round figure. And of course multiples of 313 governed your entire footplate career. I have often wondered how and why such a figure was arrived at. However I digress -

The following week, to my delight, on looking at the sheet for duty I found that I was 'Red Inked' for the entire five days - Monday to Friday with another Driver Smith, Fred this time, who I had known for many years as he lived in the same street as myself. Fred was another extremely nice chap, who had a bad leg, which caused him to limp and on occasions gave him quite a lot of pain and discomfort.

Our duty involved signing on at, I think, 5.10 am. to prepare and then work the Leicester Junction shunting turn, which was quite a busy operation. Throughout my entire time working at the shed, the sound of the Leicester Junction Jocko shunting up and down (all shunting turns, at least around Burton, were referred to by this Railwayman's jargon of Jocko's) had formed a background of sound to my life. Now, I was going to work the job and be instrumental in making that sound myself.

The engine normally allocated to this turn at that time was an ex MR Class 2F, though I see from my notes that the engine we had on the first morning was 3F number 43795, with 58160 from Tuesday to Thursday and 58130 on Friday.

Having prepared 43795 we belled off the shed by running up to the shed outlet signal and then advising the signalman at Leicester Junction Box, which controlled all movements on and off the shed, who you were and where you wished to go, i.e. 43795 for 6 o'clock Leicester Junction shunt.

He would then make the necessary arrangements with other boxes concerned, then pull off the signal and away you would go.

As Leicester Junction was right outside the shed and the sidings just over on the far side of the main line, most of the movements for our particular journey would be under his control, the only other box being directly involved being Leicester Junction Sidings Box. These 2 boxes incidentally, faced each other across the main running lines of the junction.

We started shunting straight away, up and down the shunting neck time after time after time. The fire was getting nice and hot and I was kept busy feeding what passed for fuel (hardly worth the name coal) into the box, dropping most of it just inside the door with a few down each side and the back corners. Trying to maintain my favourite threequarters of a glass of water was not easy when shunting backwards and forward with the water surging up and down the boiler all the time, one moment showing full to the top nut and the next minute just showing in the bottom of the glass.

Most of the traffic handled there was generated by the breweries, with some general traffic thrown in also. Amongst the trains made up were three for London, timed to leave at 4.20, 6.00 and 11.10, with two for Bristol at 1.30 and 4.20, all of these being either full or partly fitted - that is to say with a continuous vacuum brake throughout all or part of the train as with passenger coaches. These have all to be piped up by the shunters and tested by us with our engine to ensure that the system is sound and free from leaks and capable of holding 21" of vacuum, although 19" would be acceptable for a freight train. With a class 3 engine the testing was no problem as they were all fitted with vacuum brakes but sometimes when a 2F was on the job, it was one with a steam brake only. In this case one of the trip engines obliged when bringing another transfer load to be re-marshalled ready for onward dispatch to their respective destinations. As a matter of interest the engine part of both the 2F and 3F of Midland Railway design was basically the same, only the boilers being different. Indeed, with the exception of the Deeley-built Class 3's - 43775 to 43832, all the Class 3F's were class 2's re-boilered with type G7 (un-superheated) boilers pressed to 175 lbs, in place of the type G5's at 160 lb PSI originally fitted. This applied to both the 5' 3" and 4' 11" diameter wheel locos, although not many of the latter were converted.

After we had been shunting for about an hour, Fred's leg started aching so I was requested to heave the lever over each time we were required to go backwards, which naturally was very often. It wasn't long before I was doing it all, shunting and firing as well, while Fred gave advice from the fireman's seat. As I had already had a bit of practice at shunting down at Dixie and Wetmore, I was able to make a reasonable job of this, as has been described in an earlier chapter.

"Just keep your eye up for anybody as matters coming from the shed, David!" Fred kept saying about every ten minutes or so. "We don't want the sack do we?"

Then he would go on to relate a joke or two, of which he seemed to have an endless supply. After I had dealt with another raft of wagons he'd say something like

"That was a nifty" or "Pretty" or "Smart" or whatever, "Piece of shunting David," and dive his hand in his pocket to bring out a bag of sweets or caramels.

"Have a toffee?" pronounced 'Tuffy'.

Yes! A grand chap - Fred and, as I had known him for all my life, it was like being out with your Uncle or Dad. I was pleased to see him many years later after I had left the Railway to find that he had had an operation on his leg, (one of the benefits of medical advancement and technology) and was walking with no effort and more importantly still, no pain.

"Born too soon David, that's been my trouble," he joked and then added,

"But they've been grand days."

I'm sure we all agree with him there. So the pattern went on, through Tuesday and Wednesday, now with 58160, until Thursday morning. We were just making a last movement before stopping for some snap, during which time I intended to give the fire a clean, as old 58160 was jibbing a bit and the pressure dropping to about 100 lbs with the excuse for coal we were burning.

Fred remarked, "I've better stuff in my back garden than this rubbish David, and that doesn't grow spuds without a bit of manure on it."

As we ran back up the neck I saw that I was not the only one who would be fire cleaning, as the stokers at the Burton Foundry, whose Lancashire Boilers were positioned alongside the line with just a wooden fence between, were also gathering their irons together to do the same.

"Whoa up there," I heard a shout and slammed on the brake. What on earth's happened, I thought, are we off the road with the wagons or something? As we stopped in double quick time, with Fred up off his seat and winding on the handbrake, I'm across the footplate and looking over the side. We see a young cleaner - Mike Taylor, who I knew had just passed out for firing the previous week, come running up to the engine and climb on.

"Quick Dave," he said between breaths, "Crossy says (referring to Ted Cross the running foreman at the shed) you've got to go on that train there to fire it as its fireman is hurt," and pointed at an 8F which was just coming to a halt on the mainline. Sensing the urgency I gathered up my bag and jacket and, as Fred drove back down towards the junction, I shouted

"Cheerio, see you tomorrow perhaps," to Fred and dropped off.

As I stepped on to the boards to cross to the engine, the driver gave a toot and eased the train down towards me crossing over from the fast line to the slow as he did so. As he came by I jumped on to the step and climbed up into the cab. I had noted the number as it approached me - 48353 of 18B Westhouses. In the cab, apart from the driver, was a fireman who I recognised as one of our old hand passed fireman and at the boiler front - Reg Cordon, one of the fitters endeavouring midst clouds of steam to change or refit a new gauge glass. The driver, who turned out to be a Toton man, was looking back and as soon as the brake had cleared the junction, brought the train gently to a halt.

Our passed fireman got off, the driver saying thanks to him and away he went. When the fitter had repaired the glass to his satisfaction he gathered up his tools and got off also. He didn't look very pleased at the prospect of a long walk back to the shed in the rain, which had now started to fall. Sensing this, the drive whose name turned out to be Ted, said to him,

"Thanks mate, sorry you've got a walk but I had to clear the main."

As if to justify his remark, another freight train came clattering past just as he said it.

Now I could get to it. I had a look at the fire, which looked in need of attention and checked the water level by means of the newly fitted glass. This was out of sight above the top nut, which I was not happy about, as I liked to be able to see where it was.

"OK mate?" asked the driver, "What a day I'm having. My name's Ted by the way. From Toton and we're the Hasland to Water Orton. Shall we get going or do you want to get your breath back? Better have your name for the sheet as well. Do they call you Dave?" he asked.

When I told him, "Yes, among other things," he replied,

"Right then Dave, we'll get on shall we?"

So saying, he looked at the hand brake, which I wound off and with a toot on the whistle, dropped down the gear and eased the regulator off its face.

"See if you can see the guard mate, er Dave," he called. "Can't see a lot here at all. Too much steam about."

The piston gland on his side was blowing very badly and the one on my side wasn't much better. Still I managed to spot the guard waving and waved back, tooting as well for good measure.

"This engine's not of the calibre of my last trip on an 8," I reflected and set about to do something with the fire. By holding the shovel blade into the hole at different angles it's possible to see the condition of the fire bed as it deflects the cold secondary air over the grate. There were some bluish flames towards the front but the back didn't look too bad. I'll probably get a chance to clean the front end out a bit, I thought, when we get to Branston, as it must be clinkered up. Being on the block we are almost sure to stand a while, particularly if I have a word with the bobby when I go up to sign the book and of course mash some more tea.

Ted had been watching me out of the corner of his eye and said,

"Just keep your eye out Dave, while I have a look."

So I sat on the seat and, as there didn't seem to be anything in front before Branston, I linked up a couple of notches just for the hell of it, with the impetuousness of youth.

"I said Watch the road, not take over the job," Ted scalded but he had a grin on his face when he said it.

We're going to get along fine, I thought.

"Yes, you've got a bit of rubbish in there Davy my lad," he confirmed.

I remarked that I hoped to have a go at cleaning some of it out if we get a chance at Branston.

"Sounds a good idea to me," Ted answered. "This engine does a couple of trips before she does this job so the fire will be getting a bit dirty by now. My mate had to give it a rattle round at Wetmore yesterday but we weren't turned in there today. Bad luck for you that eh Dave."

By now I am, not very confidently, rubbing the brake, as we are getting nearer to Branston so Ted slips back into his seat. I look up at the gauge - 200 lb on it, 25 lbs down. "Don't start whittling again David," I told myself. "The honour of Burton is on your shoulders today."

As we draw to a halt, I wind on the brake and drop off to climb up into the box to see the bobby.

"Try not to smoke me out," he said. "You can have as long as you like. You've missed your path anyway now, with all that messing about down at the junction. You should be main line through here really. Mind you, think on! You've the tripper on the block behind you?"

While he was saying this I was wetting the tea and as I was leaving the box he asked,

"How's the fireman then. Is he hurt bad?"

I had to confess that I hadn't a clue and that I hadn't even found out yet what the circumstances were that put me on this particular footplate in the first place.

When I got back on the engine I found Ted with the pan in the box just about to try and lift up a lump of clinker out.

"That's two lumps out, Dave," he puffed, "Don't get upset, I left some in for you."

I grinned and took over then, after about 15 minutes of heaving and sweating, started spreading the good fire back over the grate. I wondered how Mick was faring back down the line on old 58160. Would he even realise what was required? Still, Fred would put him right, though I couldn't somehow see him doing any of it for him.

"Sit you down, I'll build it back up for you if you like," Ted offered. "Or have you got some fancy way of doing it yourself."

"I'm no expert," I replied. "This is only the second '8' I've ever been on."

I didn't like to say any more but was secretly quite pleased that he had offered and was willing to do it for me.

"I like to have a turn on the shovel now and again," said Ted, "'Ave to keep my hand in as it were?" And so, without any effort, he shot a charge around the box and then sat down.

"That should do for now," he puffed, "Don't want to put it out do we?"

Clouds of black smoke were now issuing from the chimney and I could hear the signalman's remarks echoing round my mind.

Ted knocked the blower on hard to lift some of it away.

97

"The bobby won't be very pleased with that lot," I said, going on to tell Ted what he had said to me earlier.

Ted replied, "There's one thing for sure, Dave. He won't be opening his window to complain."

I noticed some lumps appearing up the tender back so I picked up the coal pick and went into the tender to break them up. After splitting 4 or 5 quite big lumps, a mini avalanche started and I dashed out of the hole just in time, only to find that I had left the pick behind. Still I am bound to find it as we go along I console myself. First thing wrong today, I think. What will I do next?

"Bet you daren't go and tell the bobby we're ready to go," Ted challenged.

"Watch me. I can out run him," I answered.

"But can I?" Ted laughed in reply.

As I climbed down to go, the bobby who had been watching behind his closed windows, put his hand to his mouth and, pretending to cough, waved and turned away.

"I think he knows," I said, climbing back into the cab, relieved at not actually having to face him on his home territory as it were.

While we waited for the road to be set, having checked the boiler, which was now a more pleasing threequarters of a glass and noting the gauge now read 210 lbs, I decided to ask Ted to relate the events which led up to me having to be with him.

He told me that, as they approached Wetmore Bridge, his mate went to check the water level in the glass. As he did so the glass burst and scalding hot water and steam came jetting out between the hinge of the protector causing him to scald his face quite badly.

As he reeled away Ted threw his jacket over the glass and shut off the isolating cock, having already thrown the brake over. Shutting the regulator, he turned to his mate who was obviously in a bad way so he drove on to the station where he stopped in the platform to summon help. This was immediately forthcoming and the fireman was escorted off the footplate leaving Ted on his own with a train blocking the main line. He was just going to ask for a porter or someone to ride with him on the engine up to the Junction where he hoped to find another fireman, when the fireman off the station shunt engine, who was just coming out of the refreshment room with a fresh can of tea, weighing up the situation, volunteered to ride up to the sheds with him. A quick phone call from the station to the shed and the rest is history.

After hearing this I decided to shut off the other gauge frame on the assumption that it had probably been renewed at the same time as the one that had burst. Whatever anyone else thought, it made me feel better.

The fire was burning through nicely now and the gauge had gained another 5 lbs to read 215. I felt happy and just wanted the signal to come off so we could get started and I could begin to really build it up to my liking. The smoke had cleared by now and I was just debating whether to drop the damper to keep her quiet when, with that familiar rattle, the signal pulled off and we were right away again. Only down the slow and onto the block it is true but on the move never the less. There was one train in front of us, another off the Leicester branch and we followed him down until he came to stand at the end of the block at Barton and Walton Station.

"What time did you come on this morning, Dave?" Ted asked.

"5.10" I replied.

"5.00 myself," Ted added, "Reckon we'll be on overtime today, before we even get to Barton at this rate. We usually work back with this engine and get relieved at Trent. Nine hours booked job. That's when everything goes to plan. Do you like a bit of overtime? 'Cause it looks like you're going to get some today."

"I've never had the chance of any yet," I answered, "But I am saving up for a motor bike!"

"Well, there you are then, Dave lad. Might make a front wheel today if we work the job through as booked. Depends on control of course." Ted mused.

With a lurch, the van in front set off so I eased off the tender brake again and we hissed our way down behind it to stop at the signal his train had just left.

Over to the box I went to be told we would be going after the Walsall passenger and that the bobby at Branston couldn't see out of his windows since some dirty so and so had sooted them up, after promising to do the opposite.

"It's my mate you want to see, not me," I replied, "He did it."

"That explains it then," laughed the bobby, "Tell him from me to stick to what he knows best." He then asked after the welfare of the unfortunate Toton fireman. I was now able to tell him what had happened.

News travelled fast on the railway and the genuine concern of all when something happened was typical of the comradeship shown throughout the system.

When I got back to the engine the rain had stopped only to turn to snow before we moved off.

"You're in luck now, Davy boy," said Ted, "If this lot starts to come and means it, you'll be able to buy the back wheel as well."

The starter alongside us for the main, came off, followed by the distant and as I looked back down the line a Stanier 2-6-2T came fussing by with three coaches in tow, to stop in the station platform in front of us. Nobody appeared to get on and nobody got off and with a toot, he steamed off into the snow, which had really decided to start falling with big flakes.

I lifted the damper, wedged the $^3/_4$ - $^7/_8$ spanner under the handle to stop it falling shut again and checking the water, waited for Ted to open the regulator so that I could put the exhaust injector on. Off came the peg, I wound off the brake and with a toot, Ted eased up the handle and with a couple of slips, 8353 chugged off across the points in a cloud of steam and out onto the mainline.

Now she was beginning to work hard for the first time since I had made her acquaintance. She began to show what a work-worn old girl she was. The motion was banging like mad and every time the big end passed the ends of the stroke the thump shook the whole engine. Steam was issuing from all sorts of places that

Mr Stanier had never intended and as I picked up the water feed prior to turning on the injector, the play in the drawgear between the engine and tender rivalled any cakewalk at any fairground in the world.

I decided to set the injector feed to a moderate rate but such things had been decided many months before by my predecessors, as it was seized solid in one position and that was that. As the months went by I discovered that this was the norm and an adjustable feed valve was only found on a new engine, like 8313 - which it had been my joy to fire two weeks previously.

Still, we're on this old lady now so, taking up the shovel, I set about charging her up, feeding in a bit more than normal to replace what was thrown out at Branston, 8353 seeming to like the boiler fed that way and maintaining just over threequarters of a glass all the while the regulator was open. I was firing to the chimney and slacking down after every charge, partly because I liked to keep things clean and dust free and partly because not all the fuel is ending up in the box, such are the antics 8353 is kicking up.

"Don't forget the troughs mate," called Ted. A quick look at the tank gauge showed about ½ a tank of water.

I went over to Ted and confessed that I hadn't dipped a scoop before.

"Now's your chance then," Ted replied, "I'll tell you when."

Looking forward through the steam, I spotted the troughs coming up and went over to the handle on the tender front and removed the safety chain.

"Right now," shouted Ted, and down I wound the handle as if my life depended on it. It was a bit stiff at first then suddenly went easy almost as if it had been taken out of my hand, as the pan entered the water and centrifugal force took over.

The gauge on the tender in front of me rose up rapidly to the top and 'whoosh', water came spurting out of the top of the gauge and straight in my face and neck.

"Lift her out, Dave," I heard Ted calling, as I came up for air - as it were.

"What is it about water and me?" I ask myself

Ted's method of driving is noticeably different from Albert's I observed. He only has the regulator half open and seems to use a longer cut off, where Albert was using full regulator and pulling her up short. Mind you, with an engine in the condition of 8353, she would probably be too rough if pulled up too much.

As far as I was concerned the firebox still required firing virtually constantly, whichever method was used.

The journey continued much as on my previous trip and the snow began falling heavier and heavier. When we arrived at Water Orton we had to wait while the platelayers cleared the points before we could get into the sidings, such was the quantity of snow coming down. I went up to the box to sign the book (Rule 55 - Protection of Train) and naturally took the can with me to make yet another brew. The bobby told me it had been snowing quite heavily there all day. I replied that it needed something there to brighten the place up! He had the last laugh though, for as I went to return to the engine I tripped over something lying hidden in the snow, and fell all my length, spilling the tea out of the can and loosing the lid. As I got up he leant out of his window and shouted,

"The company pays you to work, not play in the snow....."

He just managed to close the window in time as a well-aimed snowball hit the glass.

After loosening off the train we picked up the guard and wended our way down to Bromford Bridge, where we topped up the tank again, yours truly being very, very careful this time to avoid any stray jets of water. As I was by now very wet and feeling rather cold, I decided to have another go at the fire while Ted and the guard gave Control a ring. We still had to turn the engine but a 'Black 5' occupied the table just then and would do so for a long time it would appear, as it was part way round and stuck in the snow. The turntable at Bromford Bridge was outside and the well was easily half full up with the white stuff. The platelayers had just arrived and, armed with shovels, were starting to dig it out.

I used the last of my tea to make yet another brew in my now lidless can and was about to scrounge a mug to drink it out of when Ted and the guard returned from the phone.

"Good lad Dave, just what we need, a nice hot cup of tea, said Ted. "Half an hour we've been hanging about down there. Anyway, we're working our way back and I've arranged a relief for you at Burton," he announced. "Don't know when that will be, mind you"

I told him about the turntable and he replied,

"Well that's all we need. They needn't think we're working back tender first either! You'll be able to buy the whole bike by the time we get you home tonight. Pity you're not coming through to Toton," he laughed, "Then you could have had petrol in it as well!"

The guard thought he would put his two pennyworth in as well, so I finished my tea and went out to have a look at the engine. There were a couple of platelayers standing in front of the fire having a well-earned warm. By way of conversation I remarked that it's no fun being a platelayer in this weather!

"Oh, we don't mind this son," one of them replied, "Plenty of overtime while this lot's falling. Last for days this will."

"Rather you than me," I thought.

The turntable still hadn't moved so I went back to the cabin. We sat in there for another half hour or so, chatting to the resident Saltley disposing crew, the Derby men off the 'Class-5' with their guard and a lone Sheffield man who was supposed to be road learning.

"Learning 'em,!" he said, "I can't even see half of 'em!" Which brought a laugh, so desperate were we all to be cheered up.

After about another hour the phone rang and Control ordered us all to leave our engines in the care of Saltley men and that they would send the crew bus to take us to New Street station, there to make our way home on the cushions.

When I eventually got back to Burton Shed to sign off it was 6.50 pm. Harry Hemsley was on the window and when I asked him about signing on in the morning he said,

"Come after your 12 hours rest - say 7.00 am."

This I did, going across to relieve, in my turn, Mick Taylor, who was enjoying his second firing duty and none too pleased to see me as a result. I told him not to worry as his turn would count. What I did not tell him was that he was going disposing, which I should have been doing had it not been for Fred asking for someone with a bit more experience.

Ted Cross knew what Fred meant. He wanted someone he could trust to help him and that it was no reflection on Mick's abilities.

And just to keep the record straight, not one flake of snow had fallen in Burton, nor did so for weeks to come.

Chapter 7
Round the Houses and Down the Market

One of the fascinations of being a young fireman at Burton was the variety of small branch lines that wandered through the town. Some were operated almost exclusively by the respective brewery locomotives, partly on their own brewery owned tracks and otherwise on tracks maintained by British Railways – by way of inheritance from the Midland then LMS.

Indeed, the Bass 'Mainline' from their town centre brewery to the Shobnall based Bottling, Malting and Cooperage premises, ran for over 80% of its distance on BR lines and likewise, in the opposite direction, to the Dixie and Horninglow sidings areas and from their own loco sheds towards and around the Hay Branch, was also operated over BR tracks and controlled by BR signalboxes and men/women.

Whilst BR engines did run regularly over some of these lines, others only saw a visit from a BR engine working a ballast or other maintenance train.

One such duty I was involved in entailed signing on at 12.45 one Sunday afternoon and walking through the town to New Street No.1 Box with my mate for the day - Bernard Davies, to relieve the early crew on a Permanent Way maintenance train. The gang were renewing a set of points and a short section of line that ran by the General Hospital. The windows of the hospital wards overlooked the scene of activity and no doubt provided much needed relief and entertainment for the convalescent patients, who were watching the activities with great interest.

To my surprise, the engine on the job was one of our old ex MR Class 2F 0-6-0's, the only occasion I can ever recall seeing a tender engine anywhere near this location. The reason being that a tank engine would not have sufficient water capacity to enable it to complete a full day's work without having to top up its supply.

We climbed aboard old 58186, to find the set we were relieving ready to go. I forget who they were now, after all these years, but I do remember the fireman emphasising the need to avoid excessive smoke and blowing off in view of the rather sensitive location at which we found ourselves.

I had a look round and found the fire damped down with the damper shut, a full glass of water and about 110 lbs on the clock. The tank gauge showed just over half full and to confirm this in my mind, I climbed over the tender to the back to check the level by looking in the tank itself. As the gauge was indeed reading correctly, I got down and had a look at what the P.W. men were doing.

They had a turnout laid out like a giant Airfix kit and were assembling it chair by chair and rail by rail into its location. On enquiring, the ganger told me that we wouldn't be required to move for at least two hours so I returned to the cab to pass the information on to Bernard.

"They've only moved twice all day, so the early men said," Bernard replied. "Might as well go up to the box and have a chat with the bobby. Bet he's bored to death with nothing to do but work out his overtime."

So off to the box we went and were soon involved in a game of dominoes with the signalman and the telegraph man making up the four. He was waiting to re-connect and test the turnout when the installation was completed.

The afternoon dragged on with numerous games of dominoes played and cans of tea consumed. Just after 4 o'clock the ganger called up and asked us to move back about ten yards. Bernard said he would go and see to it, so I relaxed in the corner of the box and watched the world go by. After ten minutes or so it occurred to me that I hadn't heard the sound of any movement outside, so I got up to see if anything was amiss. There was Bernard with the dart in his hand, poking away in the firebox. I got up and ran along, getting up into the cab to find about 60 lbs showing on the gauge and the fire almost out.

Burton (New Street No. 2) signalbox. Photo: Authors Collection.

"Don't worry lad," Bernard puffed, seeing the look of alarm on my face, "Soon have things right again. We'd got ourselves too comfortable up there."

"Go and get yourself a cup of tea, we'll only be a few minutes," he shouted down to the ganger who had reappeared by the engine steps.

"I'm sorry if we're working you too hard that you can't keep up," was the ganger's sarcastic reply.

Bernard's answer to that is unprintable.

In less than ten minutes the gauge was showing a healthy 100 lbs, so I informed the ganger that we were ready. We made the move, which brought the bolster wagon at the rear of the train perilously close to the Duke Street crossing gates. Bernard explained to me that he could probably have started the move with just the 60 lbs steam but didn't feel confident about stopping with such a restricted space to work in.

"They wouldn't have liked me to go through the gates, would they," he reasoned, "And they haven't got a bobby in that box."

As only about 300 yards separated the two boxes of Duke Street and New Street No.1, with both controlling level crossings, you will appreciate the need for caution. Within that stretch, a turnout - the one under renewal - led towards the Bass boiler house and a second one led the other way into the hospital boiler house. Moving wagons into this second location being the only other occasion when a BR engine had need to travel over this section of line, other than maintenance trains such as the one we were on. The Bond End trip engine, one of Burton's stud of 0-4-0's, normally performed this duty. Otherwise, all traffic was to and from Bass premises and worked by their engines.

The fire was beginning to burn through nicely now, thanks in the main to Bernard's ministrations, so I fed a round into the box; my first time with a shovel in my hand after nearly five hours on duty; and knocking on the injector, topped up the boiler again, slacking down the footboards as I did so. About 7 o'clock, with the job all straightened up, we set off back towards the sidings at the back of the station to dispose of our train. We ran across New Street crossing and then waited for the bobby, who had to shut the box after closing the gates, then walk past us to Park Street No.1 Box to do the same. Then James Street (no level crossing here), Uxbridge Street, Anglesey Road (known as Dale Street), to Wellington Street Junction, the same procedure with the bobby riding with us between the last three named places as they were further apart.

At Wellington Street we bid him farewell and, reversing, propelled the train up to Leicester Junction. Reversing again we then headed off down the slow line towards Burton Station. Opposite the platform we again halted then reversed

No. 41516 ex works in LMS days. On which the author went to the market.
Photo: Authors Collection.

the whole train across all running lines to the other slow line for the opposite (Southbound) direction. Here, our guard secured the train and uncoupled us. We re-crossed the running lines and awaited a path back up the main line to Leicester Junction. Here we again reversed and ran 'wrong line' down the slow, to re-couple onto our load at the other end. These we then propelled into the P.W. Sidings adjacent to the station prior to running back to Leicester Junction and going onto the shed, with just enough time left to put 58186 away. All in all, an interesting day and in some ways unique in the way it was worked.

It was to be nearly 12 months before I again ventured down into town on an engine, when I found myself booked for two days, again with Bernard, on the early turn 105 Target, the Bond End Tripper. Our engine was Johnson 0-4-0 ST number 41516. This engine was certainly the smallest one on the London Midland Region, if not British Railways entirely, having a tractive effort of just over 8,000 lbs.

Signing on at 5.20 am, we prepared the engine and coaled her up. She had two small coal bunkers, one on each side of the firebox and great care had to be taken when coaling so as not to damage the fittings on the firebox top, of which the whistle was the most vulnerable. The firebox was of the round-top type and a set of Salter safety valves controlled the steam pressure which lifted at 140 lbs. She had cylinders of 13" diameter and 20" stroke, driving a pair of 3' 10" wheels. A piece of bent steel sheet formed a front and roof for the open-backed cab, giving the engine an appearance of great antiquity, which of course she actually had, having been built in 1883. Facilities such as seats and the like were non-existent. Indeed, no provision at all had been provided for the driver and fireman who struggled to even find enough room on the spartan footplate to work at all.

This job took you over just about every level crossing on the southern half of the town and, so proud did one feel astride this old lady, that you hoped you were not seen by anyone you knew.

Belling off the shed at twenty past six, we run out of the yard en-route to Shobnall Sidings. As we pass an 8F, standing on the slow line at the gantry, its fireman, standing on the tender back as he fills her tank, cannot believe what he is seeing and nearly falls off - trying to get a better view. He shouts some ribald comment which is blown away by the wind. I shout back that any fool can fire an 'eight' but you should try turning the key on this thing.

41516 has a flat, deep grate and Bernard suggests a moderate fire of even thickness and level over the box. I was glad that I had brought my gloves as I soon abandoned the shovel in favour of firing by hand. I found another thing that had to be watched was the water level, which soon dropped when working hard and the tiny injectors were painfully slow at putting it back again.

Having collected half a dozen wagons, including two tankers, we were joined on the footplate by our guard and, as if it wasn't crowded enough, he was followed by a travelling shunter as well.

"I'll start issuing tickets," I think but reflect that there wouldn't be enough elbow room left for me to clip them.

We set off out of Shobnall Sidings and across Wellington Street to drop down under the main Derby – Bristol line. Bernard keeps steam on and pulls the gear up a couple of notches as we charge down the bank to give us a run up the other side to Dale Street Box. The bobby has the gates open for us and we rattle across, to stop with our little train just clear. The shunter and guard drop off and in no time are calling us back to enable us to position the two fuel tank wagons at the discharge point in the wharf there. I take the opportunity to spread another few pieces of coal around the diminutive firebox while our passengers are busy and am pleased to see that our half mile dash hasn't winded our poor old 1516, as she still has 130 lbs on the clock. However, by the time the water level has recovered, we have lost another 10 lbs.

Deely 0-4-0T No. 41536 shunts Moor Street Wharf. Photo: P. Webb

"This isn't going to be any picnic," I tell myself. "I'll have to watch her like a hawk."

Bernard, as if reading my thoughts, says, "Don't worry about it Dave. This old girl will plod on with 80 on the clock." With that, he took his hat of and hung it over the gauge.

"That's solved that," he said.

Our guard appears by the cab and says to Bernard, "We've got two empties down the dock, so leave these here," meaning the four wagons still attached to the tanks.

"We'll pull them out, stick them on front of these, then pull the lot over the gate, shove the new three in their place and right away!"

When the gates open, Bernard does the shunters bidding and, in no time at all, we are again sitting in the wharf behind the gate while the traffic clears.

One of Worthington's little Planet diesels draws up at the gates on the far side with a train of ten or twelve wagons for Shobnall. These engines are even smaller than 1516 but their low gearing allows them to pull quite prodigious loads for their size.

Soon the gates open yet again and the Planet sets off at a gallop to gain momentum for the climb up to Wellington Street. One of Bass's smart, red 0-4-0's charges across in the opposite direction with a long train of vans and open wagons in tow. Then the dolly drops off and away we go, in their wake.

As we cross the road I notice one of my old teachers, Ken Stokes, sitting astride his cycle, waiting for us to pass before the gates are opened again for the road. I pop the whistle and give him a wave.

"Take a hundred lines, Fleming," he grins, "I must not …" the remainder of the text is lost as we steam away. I toy with the idea of actually writing them and giving him them the next day then decide its too much trouble. A grand chap, Ken Stokes, who made Geography interesting and a joy to learn.

A line up of four of Worthington Brewery's planet Locomotives. Photo: Authors Collection.

We run our three empties and one full wagon across Uxbridge Street and onto Bond End line. There we leave the three empties and propel the full coal wagon back across the crossing and into Everard's brewery. Here we shunt a couple of empties out and position the full one for unloading. No beer is transported by rail from this brewery which is a satellite of the main concern based at Leicester, although some raw materials are received by rail from time to time.

It's worth mentioning that the daily brew from this brewery was collected and transported to Leicester by road in a Sentinel steam lorry right up to and including the time of my footplate days during the early 50's.

Bernard, the guard and the shunter all disappear into the brewery allowance room, "To try one," as they put it. "You're not old enough," I'm informed. "But not to worry, we'll drink yours for you."

I feel much better for that, not liking waste, I don't think!

The 'sampling' over with, we dragged our couple of empties back over the level crossing to join the three already there. We then ran round them and, when re-united, proceeded to push them down and over Branston Road level crossing and into Bond End Wharf itself.

There was a raft of wagons loaded with timber planks standing alongside a dock servicing the Midland Joinery works. As the planks were longer than the wagons, the planks were loaded at an angle, overhanging the rear end boards and hanging above each following wagon with a match wagon at the rear for the last overhang. There were twelve of these wagons and Bernard told me that the Shobnall Jocko usually brought them down, along with other traffic for this wharf.

We collected a van containing cabbages and another of potatoes in exchange for our empties and ran back as far as Uxbridge Street crossing, propelling them round to the left towards James Street Junction and headed towards Park Street No.1 only to branch off sharply to the right. Bernard sent me up to the James Street Box to collect the staff keys. We then proceeded very cautiously along a single line which came to a curve round to the left arriving at Park Street No.2 Gates. There was no signalbox here and the shunter inserted the staff key into a small ground frame to unlock the gate mechanism. The guard and shunter then pushed the gates open across the road, which incidentally was the main route out of Burton - as indeed was Branston Road. Bernard trundled 1516 and our two vans across the road, stopping to wait for the shunter and guard to go in front and open the gates across New Street at No.2 Box. Here the lever frame and gate gear were housed in a Midland Railway designed signalbox. Our shunter unlocked a second side gate, climbed the steps up to the signalbox, unlocked this and after ringing the bell, wound the handle to close the gates across the road and lock them in position. Bernard popped the whistle and over the crossing we went. The vans were pushed round to the right, behind a warehouse and left for unloading by the market agent. This in effect, brought fresh produce by rail to within 200 yards of the town market.

It was possible to carry straight on across the town, crossing Station Street to join the Wothington's system but it was never used when I was on the turn. The last time I saw those gates in operation, except for the demolition train, was just after the war.

Arrival behind the warehouse signalled the occasion for another quick pint and as soon as the shunter joined us, Bernard, the guard and he, partook in another 'walkabout.'

"Many round the market?" I asked, when they returned.

"Don't know, son," the shunter answered, "But the Market Hotel was pretty crowded."

"Where do you mash on this job?" was my next question. Only to be met with peals of laughter.

"Mash? Tea, you mean," laughed the guard. "We don't bother on this job. I forgot about you. Sorry about that. Nip up to Uxbridge Street Box when we get there. We'll wait for you. Oh! And here – I've brought you a packet of crisps."

One phrase kept going through my mind, "We'll wait for you."

"This is a railway we're running, not a bus trip," I thought, "Although I suppose today's job is like a mystery tour!"

Having reversed the actions of our outward journey, we soon found ourselves back at Uxbridge Street again.

"Tell him to turn us down the Bond," said Bernard, as I got off.

"You want to make a can of tea, lad?" asked the signalman when I gave him Bernard's message. "When you get back, tell him there's two loads of malt for Walker Street just come down the Bond. That'll bring a smile to their faces," he added.

So I walked back to the engine, complete with my can of tea and passed on the message to Bernard.

"Wondered why you was walking," he said, "We would have picked you up at the box you know!"

"Come on then, let's get to it," the shunter interrupted.

So, back down to Bond End we went for the two vans of malt. Our shunter had them hooked on and Bernard was whistling for the road almost before the bobby had got the gates closed following our arrival.

Soon we were on the way back, only to have to wait for two trains from James Street Junction bound for Shobnall, one headed by a Bass diesel and the other by another Worthington Planet. Although Worthington had a fleet of steam engines, they were rarely seen over this side of town, all their Shobnall bound trains being in charge of these Planets.

Then it was our turn and we were away, over the crossing and down the line to stop by yet another siding. Soon we were pushing our two vans around the very sharp curve into Atkinson's Maltings. There was an empty van and wagon waiting to be collected, so Bernard dropped 41516 onto these and the shunter coupled up.

"Shouldn't be long, lad. Get your tea," says he, dropping down to join his two partners in crime, whereupon the trio disappear into the Maltings and leave me to it.

I have a lid of tea and a couple of sandwiches. The crisps go down well also.

Having fed the inner man, I turned my attentions to the fire. I got the special short dart from the tank top which, incidentally, we had filled down at Bond End earlier, and I had a poke around in the fire. There didn't seem to be any clinker worth the mention in there so I added a few knobs around the grate and shut the door. Dropping down the side, I had a look at the ashpan. This was one advantage of a four-wheeler. Looking underneath from the rear of the engine allowed a clear view inside. It looked a bit choked up so, getting the rake down, I pulled the spent ash out onto the ballast. 41516 lifted her valves, so I decided she had liked this little bit of attention. Back up in the cab, I closed the damper, opened the doors and on with the injector. The old lady quietened down and she and I settled down to await the return of the magnificent three. As we stood there the inevitable rain started to fall.

"That's all we need," I thought. I dropped down off the engine again and fished Bernard's big, railway issue raincoat from the locker and put it on. It was soon driving in and hissing off the firebox front in little spurts of steam. After about ten minutes the rain eased off to a steady drizzle and the three wise men returned.

"Come on a bit heavy – that, lad. We'd 'ave got drowned if we'd come back then, so we stopped to have another. Only thing to do, don't you think?" quotes our shunter with a grin.

"Right then, are we all ready, gentlemen?" asks the guard. "OK then," he continues, "Right away – Leicester Junction!"

Off we went, dropping our shunter off at Dale Street, before following a line which curved sharply away to the left behind the box. As we dropped our two empty wagons off in the junction sidings, our relief came up and I was pleased to hand over 1516 with a clean-ish fire, empty ashpan and 140 lbs on the gauge.

As we arrived back at the shed I gave Bernard his mac. It was only then that he realised I had got it on. He, at least, was wet both inside and out.

The following day we followed a similar pattern, only this time on 41523 which, although similar in appearance, was a larger and stronger engine altogether.

The Dallow Lane job was another turn which had its moments. I was 'red inked' for a five day stint on this duty with a rather cantankerous old driver whom I shall call Charlie P. (not his real name) who lived nearby my home. We had enjoyed a strained relationship for years, since I had accidentally broken one of the panes in his front bay window during a vigorous game of street football. Any old engine seemed to find its way onto this job, like a 2F or 3F, or a 1F or 3F tank.

On the Monday and Tuesday we had a Class 2F 0-6-0 number 58305, which still retained its original Kirtley half cab, yet had been fitted with a Belpaire boiler, steam sanding gear and vacuum brake. The seat on my side was all complete and with the sun shining on a fine September afternoon, I was quite looking forward to the outing.

The coal on the tender consisted, amongst other things, of some very large lumps which would need attention from the coal pick before they could be used. One of the first duties in the afternoon was to shunt the Allsop Sidings. These were situated along the ex LNWR Burton avoiding line. The two signalboxes, all the cabins, weighbridges, wharves, etc. were typically LNW, as were any of the original signals that survived. Traffic for Shobnall maltings, Yeoman, Cherry and Curtis maltings, J.B.Kind's timber yard, Dallow Coal Wharf and Hallam's, were all sorted here.

Ex MR Class 1F 0-6-0T No. 41839. Photo: P. Webb

As we ran up and down the 'main line' shunting rafts of wagons about, we were passing what we local lads called the Co-op Field; so named because, in the days of horse drawn coal, bread and milk delivery vehicles, the horses were turned out into the field for well earned rests at the end of each day. Indeed, until the middle 1950's a few horses were still in use.

Now! This field divided the back gardens of Shobnall Street from the railway upon which we were now shunting and Charlie's garden was one of them. To my surprise, he said to me, "Chuck a couple of those lumps off will you and pop them in my coalhouse."

I couldn't believe I was hearing this but I was and, as they say, I did. After all, he was the driver and his word is law. This went on all week until, by Thursday, his little coalhouse was full. On Friday we had number 41839, an ex MR Class 1F 0-6-0T, also fitted with a Kirtley cab. She also had some rather large coal in her bunker, which threatened to block the shovelling plate when they worked their way down.

"I know a good place for them," I thought. Our coalhouse.. So, when we passed the appropriate place, I heaved two big lumps off onto the track side. Charlie P. slammed on the brake and brought 41839 to a shuddering halt.

"Some coal has just fell off the engine, fireman," he says.

"I know that," I answered. "I've just thrown it there."

"Get it back up here," he commands.

"What!" I exclaimed, "I've filled your *** coalhouse and now I'm going to fill ours."

"Get that coal back on the engine," he repeats and has the audacity to add, "Do you know how much the Company pays out for coal each year?"

An argument ensued with all the old animosity coming to the fore.

"This engine doesn't move until you do," was his concluding remark.

So down I got and heaved both lumps back onto the footplate. Revenge is now foremost in my mind.

"How can I get even with the old devil?" I ask myself, my thoughts being focussed on this one goal.

"It's got to be today because it's Friday," I realise. Then it came to me!

Later in the day, it was the custom to propel two rafts of wagons up to Stretton Junction. Although the LNWR had laid the line with double track, the one line was now used as a long siding, with the other line becoming bi-directional and operated with a staff. It was the practice to try and get both these rafts of wagons up to the Junction in one go and thereby gain the best part of an hour, before the next part of the turn, for oneself. Charlie was a bit of a footplate chef and usually spent some considerable time practicing his culinary skills during this hour or so obtained.

The trick was to marshal both lots of wagons together and haul them down towards the bridge at Shobnall, stopping short of the dip to get under it. Then, having raised a good head of steam, whistle the bobby in Allsop's Sidings Box who, in his turn, would waggle the signal on the other line (the one we were not on) to let the driver know that the way was clear all the way through into the sidings at Stretton Junction. All Hell is then let loose as a flat out attempt is made to push 80 empties or so up the bank, collecting the staff from the bobby as you thunder past his box. I had managed to grab it every time that week, not I might add, without some anxiety but resolved to drop it this time.

"No cooking for you tonight, Charlie," I decided.

As we had as smaller engine than usual, we might not get up anyway, I reasoned but I had no intention of leaving it to chance.

In due time, we collected up our huge train.

"Not so many tonight," our guard tells Charlie, as he climbs aboard.

"How many?" I ask.

"51." He answers.

I grin to myself, "If we had only one on, you still wouldn't go straight through."

"Ah – revenge is sweet!" I reflect.

So I do my bit, building up a huge fire and old 41839 blows her head off with the full 150 lbs on the clock. Charlie P. nods in approval.

"She's not as big as we've had all week," he remarks, "But you've more than made up for it, it would seem."

So saying, he reaches up and pops the whistle.

"Enjoy it while you can, you old buzzard," I think, as we roar away with full regulator and gear.

Charlie eases the handle and pulls the lever up a notch or two then slams the handle right across. Old 41839 is bombing along valiantly and I throw another round in the hole. We are coming up to the box now, faster if anything, than we have been all week. A quick glance at Charlie P. to see the smug look he is wearing when everything is going to plan, then I reach out and grasp the tablet off the bobby as cleanly as I have done all week. Without a second thought, I open my fingers and watch as it falls from my grasp to go bouncing off into the undergrowth alongside the track.

"Blast! I've dropped it, Charlie," I call.

A look of horror crosses his face as he reaches for the handle, snatches the regulator shut and spins the steam brake open.

With a shudder and a terrific snatch, old 41839 comes to a halt. I'm off the engine and running back to try and find the missing staff. I've a fair idea where it went but of course you don't stop a train of that length and weight in a few yards. The bobby joined me in the search.

Where the author dropped the tablet. The bushes extended further along the fence at that time. Note the signalbox beyond the water tower. Photo: P. Webb

"I thought you'd got it clean, lad," he said. "Mind you, he was shifting tonight!"

I couldn't trust myself to answer so I said nothing. The guard got off and went up the line to check his train. The bobby told me he had sent the message, 'Train running away on right line,' in case a coupling had parted and part of the train had broken free.

"What had I started?" I asked myself and began to worry a bit about the outcome of my actions. In the cold light of day it did seem a bit petty and childish.

The bobby found the staff after a good twenty minutes then of course, we had to wait for the return of the guard.

"Are you keeping it?" I enquired of the signalman.

"If the train's still together, you keep it," he replied.

The guard eventually returned to report that everything was alright, to my intense relief, so we started the whole saga again.

As we struggled over the top of the bank at the bridge over Horninglow Road, a look across at Charlie P. brought an answering glare, which would have struck me down on the spot had his apparent thoughts been realised.

By the time we had put our train away, there was precious little time left for eating and Charlie only managed to fry a quick egg that he ate between two rounds of bread. As the yolk dribbled down his chin, it was all I could do to avoid laughing. Never had my cheese and pickle sandwiches tasted so good.

Charlie P. retired that winter so our paths never crossed again. Not at work, at least. Sad to relate, he only enjoyed retirement for a short time before he passed away. I wonder if he managed to burn all that coal that cost the Company so much.

Chapter 8

On the Main Line with a Vengeance

Whitsun Bank Holiday Saturday morning 1953, found me sitting in the mess room with Charlie Wadsworth on 7 am. Control Relief. The whole of the previous week had been one of glorious sunshine with temperatures in the 70's and this day bore promise of being the same.

These were the post war boom times for the railways, with full employment and reasonable monetary reward for ones effort. Most people managed a holiday with their families and as ownership of the motor car was still uncommon, the usual way to journey for that holiday was by public transport, the railways getting the lion's share of the business.

Charlie reached into his overall pocket and pulled out his watch.

"Twenty to nine, Dave," he said, "At this rate we won't be getting a job at all, It'll be put a couple away and home to mother. Just you see if I'm not right!" he added.

Hardly had he spoken when in came Ron Harrison the foreman's runner.

"Here you are Charlie," he greeted us, "Ted says, will you away up the station and relieve the Sheffield – Torquay. They've Grimethorpe men on it and he don't sign past Burton. It's due at 9.25 and it'll save another stop here for the swap over. 73015 on it. Anyway, it's all down on this," he added, thrusting a piece of paper towards my Mate.

"Only to Saltley anyroad," he added.

"I've only got the lad with me you know. Does Ted realise that?" asks Charlie.

"There's only you to send, Charlie," Ron replied, "The 8 o'clock men were late off yesterday and won't be here in time and the 9 o'clock set would be cutting it a bit fine," he explained.

"Alright then but on his head be it. Come on son; tell your dad this will cost him a pint. More than one if you let me down, mind," Charlie grumbled.

And so started an association which was to last until Charlie's sad demise. Until that moment I was unaware that he knew my father but it transpired they both used the same pub and had many a shuffle of dominoes together.

With that rather discouraging remark, I gathered up my bag and jacket and followed him out of the mess room. As we walked up the path to the station, Charlie asked me if I had ever been on a Standard 5 before. I had to admit that I hadn't, although I'd had a good look round a couple that had been on the shed.

"That makes you the expert then," he said, "Can't say that I've ever been near one before. Still, I expect it's the same as a black-un. Don't suppose you've been on one of them either, have you?"

"No, I've not," I admitted, "But I have had a few trips on an 8."

"Treat it like that then," Charlie advised, "And if that don't work we'll think of something else."

Feeling much better by Charlie's remarks and less on my own, as it were, I perked up and felt quite important as we walked by the Moor Street crossing gates, with the usual array of train-spotters all looking enviously at us. At least, so I thought. When we stepped onto the platform, the station was alive with passengers. There must have been well over a hundred, all loaded down with suitcases, the children jumping about with excitement, clutching buckets and spades.

"Blimey! They'll never get all them on," Charley remarked, "It's already called at Chesterfield and Derby, according to this paper and we've got another stop at Tamworth as well!"

BR standard Class '5' No. 73015 leaves Burton with a train for the north. She looked a lot cleaner when the author fired her to Gloucester. Photo: P. Webb

9.25 came and went with no sign of our train. A freight rattled through, so it must be well behind time I reasoned, although the 'goods' was pegged for the slow line at Leicester Junction, the only time incidentally, I ever saw that distant pulled off.

"Pop down to the Inspector to see what you can find out," Charlie requested.

So off I went. Bob Gilman, good old unflappable Bob, was the Inspector in charge.

"Twenty minutes late at Chesterfield. Not heard from Derby yet," he replied to my enquiry. "Think we'll have to hang another on the back for all this lot," he went on, "I've got the Jocko in the bay with it ready now."

I thanked him for the information and returned to Charlie.

"Did he leave Sheffield right time?" he questioned me. "If it did then he's in trouble and that means we're in trouble," he qualified.

"But if the loco's duff, won't he change it at Derby? They've usually got plenty there," I reasoned.

"He might, if they've got owt but then again he's done with it when he gets here aint he." Charlie mused.

"Just have to wait and see, won't we." I said and leaned back on the bench to enjoy the sun and the sit-down while I could. Probably won't have much time to take it easy when we do get going, I decided.

Eventually, 73015 and her train ran in, all of 35 minutes late. My opposite number, obviously another passed cleaner and even younger then myself, staggered off the footplate and collapsed onto the bench we had just vacated.

"Is it that bad?" I asked him.

"Worse, mate. She's a b….." he pointed in reply.

The garrulous old driver told my Mate that we had eleven on and if he never saw another Standard in his life it wouldn't be too soon.

I climbed aboard, put my traps in the tender cupboard and looked up at the gauge. 160lbs. I couldn't believe my eyes. These Standards are pressured to 225 lbs, as are Black-5's and 8F's. Opening the firebox door, I thought the bulb had gone, so dark it was in there. The only saving grace was a full glass of water.

"I'm just dropping off to check the dampers," I called to Charlie and slid down the steps on the left hand side. The front one was about half open and the rear one was shut tight.

"That's not helping things a lot," I think to myself.

Now! The dampers on all Standards are controlled by a pair of brass wheels, through the centre of which runs a square thread. Until you are familiar with these engines, it's a problem to decide which way to turn what to open and close them. Later on I discovered that on some engines an arrow and a legend 'open and shut' was inscribed into the brass. This engine had no such refinement.

Climbing back into the cab, I decided to close the front damper, fully open the back one and give the hopper doors a gentle shake as well. Whilst I'm busy doing all this, Charlie has killed the brake in readiness for our extra coach to be added. This will make twelve in all and the recommended load for a Class 5 engine, over the Derby Bristol line, is ten. So Charlie could ask for a hooker-on. Bob Gilman, accompanied by the guard, a Sheffield man, came up to give Charlie the load and ask if he wanted a pilot. The guard also informed us that we were now over 40 minutes late. Charlie, ever philosophical, received all this information very calmly and decided to take the lot unassisted. When I pointed out the state of the boiler and fire he just shrugged and said, "Leave it to me, son. I'll soon have that lot burnt through. Just do what Uncle Charlie says and we'll be alright. Besides, we'll be here another half hour waiting for a hooker-on."

Turning to Bob, he said, "I'll see how we go to Tamworth so give Saltley a bell just in case. Get in your van and let's get on with it," he added, this time to the guard, then to me,

"When I tell you, give the fire a good rousing with the dart. In the meantime sit on your seat and lean over the side. Look like an old hand when we go by the shed - for them devil's benefit."

Looking back, I get the 'right away' from our guard and give Charlie a nod. With a blast on the chime whistle, Charlie pulls the regulator handle out towards him and 73015 strains to move its twelve coaches out of the platform and up the 1 in 60 towards Moor Street Bridge. With the sands open and full gear, Charlie pulls the handle out even more until the small valve is right open and on to the main.

Our Standard gets to grips and the blast from her chimney is a joy to hear as she climbs up the slope and heads over the bridge to drop down towards Leicester Junction. As we pass by the end of the shed, still in full gear and regulator, I can see the faces at the mess room window and give them a wave, trying to convey the picture of a man in total control of his job. If only it were true!

"Right lad, get that dart going," Charlie's voice shouts across to disrupt my daydreaming.

I get up to do his bidding as he eases the regulator and winds the gear back to link up the valve travel. The fire is now burning bright and after levelling it out, I withdraw the dart, now red hot, and stow it back in the rack. It's no easy matter manoeuvring this hot piece of bar, nearly ten foot long, out of the fire and into the tender but 73015 rides like a coach and makes the task a lot easier.

Charlie has a quick look in the box and suggests I fill the back corners and under the door, then, "Fire her like an eight," he advises. The gauge is now above the 200 lbs mark but the thrapesing Charlie has given her has pulled the water level down to about half a glass. Slipping the exhaust injector on, I set it for a medium feed then charge another round into the box. The Five is bombing along now and, remembering she is fitted with a speedometer, I glance up at it to find we are doing nearly 60 mph as we run through Barton and Walton Station.

Strewth! Are we this far already? I think, amazed so, picking up the shovel, I get down to it again. In all my time to come later, with Charlie, I never knew him to thrash an engine again like he did 73015 on that first half mile out of Burton Station. In fact there were times when I had to ask him to open up a bit more to get a decent blast and draw on the fire. A true professional and a gentleman to boot!

Soon Charlie was shutting off and dropping the gear down to the drifting position, about 45 per cent cut off, prior to stopping at Tamworth. As he did so the safety valves lifted to unleash 225 lbs of steam, created by my efforts, into the atmosphere. Wasteful but nevertheless, satisfying. I eased the blower and opened the doors. The damper involved more effort to close, being very stiff to wind so I left it as it was. The exhaust injector had changed over to live steam with hardly a blip.

When we stopped in Tamworth High Level, the station foreman came up to ask if we would need the pilot at Saltley. Charlie said no but did say that there would be a 'banker' required up Camp Hill. The foreman then said that the Control wanted to know if he signed for Gloucester and would he continue to there.

Charlie looked across at me and asked,

"What do you think, mate?"

"I'm game if you are," I replied.

"OK then," Charlie answered and, turning to the foreman said by way of explanation, "It's all on his back you see!"

"You'll get a new guard at Saltley as well, driver," said the foreman, "This chap doesn't go to Gloucester."

Our guard is giving the 'right away' so off we go again, not without a little anxiety on my part. Saltley is barely 40 miles from Burton but goodness knows how far Gloucester is - and with Camp Hill Bank to climb as well! Then there's the Lickey, of course! This is becoming quite an adventure for yours truly.

I'm firing to the chimney with a constant rhythm. 73015 is fresh off shops, having been recently 'soled and heeled' and is, to all intents, brand new. The pressure is rock steady at 225 lbs and the injector is maintaining the water nicely at just over threequarters of a glass. The heat of the fire and my efforts, combined with the hot sunny day, are keeping my shirt wet. I have long since discarded my jacket and hat and the sweat is running down my face in torrents. Risking a couple of minutes on the seat, I notice that we are running down the fast line, new ground to me, as on all my previous visits to Birmingham we have gone round via Coleshill and Water Orton.

Rejoining the old line at Whitacre Junction I remember the time when we ran away down the bank from Arley Tunnel when the steam brake pipe fractured between the engine and tender on our 8F. We clattered through here then, completely out of control with only the tender handbrake and, hopefully the guard's brake, to try and stop our full coal train. The driver on the Jubilee-hauled express had the peg thrown against him that day. Thank goodness he managed to stop in time. But, thankfully no such occurrence today, as we sped across the junction at nearly 70 mph. Charlie shuts off steam again for the Saltley stop, where our guard will leave us and the 'banker' will come up behind.

Washwood Heath and Bromford Bridge are passed. Charlie whistles for the 'banker' and as we run past Duddeston Road, I see a 3F with clouds of smoke gushing from its funnel and her fireman working like a Trojan. She is fitted with a Fowler tender so I know her to be 43435 as it's the only 3F as far as I am aware to be attached to one.

As we stop, the valves lift again. At least the banking crew will be able to see that we are doing our bit. Charlie exchanged waves with the new guard and a crow from the 3F was answered by our chime whistle as he again pulls out our Standard regulator and we set forth to attack Camp Hill Bank. As we passed Saltley Loco Sheds the gradient increased to about 1 in 100. A quick glance forwards showed both home and distant signals off. Charlie drops the gear another couple of notches as we swing to the left at Landor Street Junction. The line then swings round the other way and the gradient here increases to about 1 in 60 as we climb under the line from New Street to London. What sort of a hill do they have to climb to get over us? I wonder. As the full weight of the train comes onto the 1 in 60 I feel a slight check in our movements and a slowing of the blast from the chimney. 73015 is not overstressed as Charlie drags the gear down a bit more. She is still on the first valve and as the gradient eases slightly a quickening of the beat is heard. Looking back between firing as we round the right hand curve, I detect not one but two plumes of smoke thundering away behind us. No wonder we are climbing so quickly and well. We pass Bordesley Junction where a connection drops down to join the ex GWR.

Approaching Camp Hill Box, Charlie blows another tune on our chime whistle,

"Might as well have a push all the way," he shouts, "This old lady has got to get to Bristol. All they've got to do is drop back down at Duddeston Road."

As we passed the box the bobby was waving his flags about and Charlie gave him a wave. Another quick glance showed the rearmost engine dropping back, leaving just the one burst of smoke and exhaust behind the last coach. Having passed the box the bank flattened out to about 1 in 300 for a pace before steepening again to 1 in 100 as we leave the embankment to enter a cutting. On, through Moseley Tunnel and out the other side to enter Kings Heath Station. Another blast on our chime whistle to thank the bank men and we're on our own again, accelerating towards Kings Norton and Blackwell. The shovel hasn't been out of my hand since we picked up the banker at Duddeston Road and Charlie, sensing my feeling of tiredness, shouted across to leave it for a bit and sit down to enjoy the ride down the bank.

If I had expected Charlie to let our engine have its head I was wrong as, with steam off, he kept rubbing the brake to drop down at about 35 to 40 mph. Still faster than any other descent I have ever made but then, that was with a loose coupled goods train. The water in the tender tank was down to about 1500 gallons now, despite having filled the tank at Tamworth, the amount when full on our Standard being 4725 gallons. Charlie said there would be enough to carry through to Gloucester, where we could fill the tank from the crane at the platform end.

Ashchurch came and went followed by Cheltenham with our speed touching the high 70's in places. As we neared Gloucester the GWR line came in alongside and ran parallel for the last two or three miles. It gave us great pleasure to over-take one of their Moguls with six coaches only in tow. But could we count it as a triumph for the LMS when on a BR Standard Class 5? Then again, she was a Blackie with refinements.

Running into Gloucester, I was all cleared up with a nice clean cab, no spillage on the floor, a bright fire and just under a full glass of water. As we stopped I knocked the injector off and was rewarded with those valves opening again to indicate maximum steam pressure. Two old hands got aboard and I felt proud to say to the fireman, who must have been 30 if he was a day and probably a passed man, that she was a good-un. If they hadn't been there I would have willingly gone through to Bristol and what is more, Charlie knew the way.

Sitting in the refreshment room eating my snap and drinking a well earned mug of tea, care of the tea urn 'OCS,' Charlie made a remark to me that made me feel ten feet tall, tired though I was.

"You've done well, lad," he said.

Just four words but the George Cross couldn't have made me more proud.

We had pulled back twelve minutes of the late running we had inherited from the Grimethorpe men at Burton as well!

"Why do you think that other fireman had got into such a mess, Charlie," I asked.

"Well, you see lad, there are drivers and drivers and some of them forget that they had to learn as well. There's no substitute for experience and it's up to the driver to pass it on. Still, he'll have to fill in the 'please explain' report, not me. I expect he'll blame the fireman but those who read it will know the full truth, don't you forget." And with that he got up and went to ring control.

"Do you feel like a bit more work?" he asked when he got back.

"Yes," I answered although in reality I was tired out.

"Right then. 3315 with a load of empties for Bromsgrove then light engine Burton. How's that suit you?" he announced.

Charlie was renowned for not being able to say No to Control, who made sure he always had work to do. He also liked the money, as indeed did I. What a team! But would my stamina match my enthusiasm?

Soon we were trundling our 40 odd empties back towards Bromsgrove, whence we had come. The GWR was getting its own back and overtaking us in droves but who cared! 43315 was a Derby engine and in surprisingly good nick for one of theirs.

"Probably not had her long," said Charlie when I remarked about it.

As she still had a complete seat on the fireman's side, he was probably right. Relaxing upon it, I reflected on the labour intensive journey down, in comparison to this gentle stroll back. Still! I knew which I preferred. Now I had experienced express work I hankered for more. Flashing the odd round about the box every few minutes and with the injector gurgling away merrily, I had plenty of time to enjoy the scenery. We were turned inside at Cheltenham, Ashchurch and goodness knows where else, to allow an endless procession of scheduled and extra passenger trains to pass us. At their heads were everything from Jubilees and Class 5's to Crabs and in one case an 8F. Compounds on semi fasts, 2P's and 4F's on locals. Even a cheeky 4F on another train of empties passed us.

Before we left Ashchurch we were on overtime and with 70 miles to go before we reached Burton, it was going to be a long day. We eventually arrived at Bromsgrove where we backed out train into the cripple sidings by the wagon repair yard, under the direction of our guard as Charlie didn't know the lay-out there. Here, Control ordered us to leave 3315 on the shed and travel back on the cushions. Apparently, traffic was so heavy around Birmingham that a path couldn't be found for a light engine.

"Bet some of them kids are on the beach now, digging like mad," said Charlie as we sat on Bromsgrove Station waiting for a ride to New Street. There was nowhere to mash on the station and although the signalbox was on the platform, the bobby, unlike the majority of his kind, wouldn't let me have any boiling water. I daren't nip back to the shed as we hadn't a clue what time the next train was due. The porter knew but, what with his accent and his stutter, we couldn't understand what he said.

Eventually an asthmatic old 4F wheezed in with three coaches in tow and we climbed aboard the first coach to occupy the front compartment as was the custom with footplate-men. There were two other crews already in residence, one of which I though I recognised.

"Aren't you the two who relieved us at Gloucester on 73015?" I asked.

"We most certainly are," the fireman replied, "Saltley men," he added.

"But I thought you were Gloucester men," I answered.

"No. That's all we've done today. Down to Gloucester on the cushions, then Bristol and back to Gloucester again on the cushions. Should have worked back from there but they caped the job so here we are," he explained. "Good work if you can get it."

A bump at the rear of the train announced the arrival of the banker and, after an exchange of whistles, the old 4F and the banker got the train in motion and up the bank. The Lickey is a long drag and by what I could hear, the banker seemed to be doing most of the work. I'd have loved to have got up and dropped the window to watch and hear the spectacle and if Charlie and I had been the only ones present I probably would have done but not in front of the other four. Be casual and pretend it was an every day event, which it probably was for them but not for me.

We arrived in New Street, having called at every station bar Blackwell, on the way. A few quick strides and we were aboard an express for Burton, arriving there in time to book off at 9.50 pm. After 14 hours and 50 minutes on duty. More asleep than awake, my trusty old bike carried me home where I slept through 'till about mid-day on the Whit Sunday.

Signing on for 5.30 am on the Bank Holiday Monday, I eagerly waited to discover what duty would come my way. Would it be another passenger turn as on the Saturday? There were plenty of extras about. Imagine my chagrin to be sent to the LNER Yard to take the place of the Eastern Region fireman who hadn't turned in, presumably finding the Bank Holiday attractions more tempting. Old faithful 3F-T number 47464 was again the engine. I was surprised to find that the job was running at all on that day and, sufficient to say, it was very quiet with only one train in and out, off the Eastern, that being in charge of J6 number 64215. Her fireman told me she was one of Colwick's real old nails and only fit for freight work. He mentioned, casual like, that he had been to Skegness on the Saturday with a K3. Not to be outdone, I truthfully said that I'd been on the Sheffield to Torquay, but conveniently forgot to mention that we got off at Gloucester.

So bored did I become with the lack of action that morning, that I adorned the tank sides of 47464 with the legend 'LNER' with a piece of chalk obtained from the shunters' cabin. Just to complete the picture, I changed the first 4 to a 6. It amused me to see that the adornment lasted for some considerable time, until the vagaries of dirt and weather finally faded and washed it away. If this was vandalism, I stand guilty as charged!

However, at the end of this turn I was pleased to see that I was booked, on the Tuesday, on loan to Toton.

"How do I get there" I asked.

"Please yourself," was the reply. "Just be there for six. Either on the train, on your bike or walk it."

Apparently, 2 hours, by the day, was paid extra for this loan period. I decided to give my 250 BSA a run out and go on that. One of our gang had been there the previous week, when he had two turns on a steam Jocko, one on a diesel and one on a Tripper.

So it was with great anticipation that I set forth at the unlikely time of a quarter to five, for Long Eaton. My geography went a little astray on that first morning and I actually arrived about 10 minutes late, having got lost and fortunately meeting another fireman walking to work there. I asked for directions and we arrived together, my guide giving directions from the pillion seat.

Introduced to my mate for the day by the remark, "Are you the Burton fireman?" I soon found myself standing on Trent Station awaiting the arrival of the York – Bescot steel train which we were to relieve.

My mate's name was Alf who was a passed fireman of about 35 years of age, and very tall which was emphasised by his very slim build. As we chatted, he naturally asked me what sort of experience I had. Had I ever been on an Austerity before? I said that I hadn't been out with one but had been on a few of them in the shed yard.

"Well. Today's your chance," he announced, "We've got one, when it turns up."

WD 'Austerity' 2-8-0 'Rough Old Plodders'. Photo: P. Groom

Eventually, that well known clanging noise assailed our ears as a cloud of steam appeared and, enveloped within, hove 90606 of York 50A. As we stepped on board, the fireman made an elaborate gesture and showed me his seat.

"Sit thee-sen down me-mon," he announced in a broad Yorkshire accent, "And mek tha most on it. It'll be tha last chance thee'll have," he declared, or something similar, adding, "Er's a rough-un an t'pick-up don't work either." (Austerities are not fitted with water pick-up apparatus).

I looked round to see a nice, clean footplate and a full glass of water with 195 lbs on the gauge. The firehole door was shut and the blower hard on.

"Typical old wreck," Alf commented. "Better fill the tank before we go any further. Give her a chance to come round as well."

So, up on the tender back I climb and drop the bag in the hole. Alf turns the water on and the inevitable leak catches me squarely in the stomach.

"It's going to be one of those sort of days again, is it" I reflect. Wet before we start. Our eight wheeled tender had a water capacity of 5,000 gallons when full. Whilst up on the back I had a look at what passed for coal in the bunker to find it was predominantly briquettes.

"Yes. It really is going to be a day of days alright!"

Back on the footplate I notice the clock is now showing 220 lbs, although I did not know at that time this was to be the only occasion in our acquaintance that it would read that high, 180 to 200 being more the norm.

The guard came up and gave Alf the load, which I think was 18 bogie bolsters and a brake, equal to 42 wagons. With a familiar clatter, the signal pulled off as our guard was walking back to the van. When he arrived I exchanged waves and gave Alf the tip. He popped the whistle and, dropping the gear down, gave the regulator a pull to ease our load of steel away and out of Trent Station.

Another surprise greeted me as I opened the firehole door. Where were the smokeplate and the mouthpiece shield? Blast it! Why hadn't I looked in there before we moved off! What with filling the tank and breaking briquettes in half, I just hadn't had time. No wonder that Yorkshire fireman had been so flippant. I fired a charge round the box as I would an 8F and shut the door again. What about all that cold air hitting the tubeplate? Better tell Alf about it, though what he can do about it now is nothing, I supposed.

"You often find that on these old things," he answered, "And the leaking tubes to go with them as well," he added. "At least it gives you a big hole to fire through."

Another thing I hadn't done, which I usually do on taking over an engine, was to check the dampers. Which one was which? I'll have to ask Alf, I decided. He'll think I'm really hopeless. Still, can't be helped. He soon put me right and, as it happened, I had opened the correct one.

The water was now in sight in the glass so I put my injector on. The Austerities may not have a lot going for them but let it be said, the injectors were brilliant. Alf had got 90606 pounding along now and the ride could only be described as atrocious. He was standing up as sitting down was too uncomfortable to even contemplate. There was as much steam coming out of the glands and goodness knows where else, as was going up the chimney and every joint and bearing of the motion was thumping and banging like a school band on an off day. Every time the big ends came round to the ends of their stroke it was just like a big hammer striking you in a very personal place and they came round very quickly when attached to 4' 8" diameter wheels.

We clanged and bashed our way through Weston and Barrow on Trent under clear signals, only to get a caution at Alreston, finally coming to a complete stop at Stenson Junction.

Our train of steel was very heavy and the Austerity brakes didn't seem to be of the calibre of an 8F so Alf had to show extreme skill to keep our train under control over the undulating course from Trent. Despite my best efforts, 90606 came to a stand at Stenson with 160 lbs on the clock.

"Why won't she steam?" I wonder. "It's the 4F battle all over again."

Alf tells me that all Austerities are fickle steamers and a challenge to most firemen. Describing my firing methods, he confirmed that I was doing all the right things. I decided to get down and clear the ashpan of some of its contents. It certainly seemed to be quite full. This discharging of ashes on the permanent way was not encouraged and one had to avoid starting a fire on the sleepers. Alf wasn't too keen on the idea but had to admit that it had its merits.

"Don't go mad," he said, "Only just skim the surface."

When I got back into the cab he was busy prising a lump of clinker free of the bars.

"Get some of this out and we might do better," he puffs.

Between us me manage to lift four big pieces out of the grate and spread the remaining good fire over the area. A sprinkle of fuel on the top and we're as ready as we'll ever be. Judging by the piles of dead clinker at the side of the line, we are not the first to do a spot of fire cleaning here. Just to encourage us in our labour, I notice the gauge still reading only 170 lbs. At least it hasn't lost any more, which must mean something. I hope. Another charge round the box and, with the blower on full, the needle starts its slow journey up the scale. As it makes 200 lbs the signal drops and we are faced with the 1 in 200 up to Repton and Willington Station.

As we struggle to get our load of steel on the move and up the gradient, the foundations of Willington Power Station and its complex of sidings are being laid down on our left, whilst on our right a three coach local stopper runs off the North Stafford to join the Midland main line with a service from Crewe to Derby. At its head is a Class 5, newly out-shopped and running-in on this line which joins these two rival works of the old LMS Railway.

With me firing like fury and Alf pounding away with the cut off and regulator, we crest the top of the bank in Repton and Willington Station then start the descent to Burton. Steam pressure is still reading 195 lbs so perhaps our efforts at Stenson were worthwhile after all. We are signalled main-line through Clay Mills and Wetmore, only to be turned down the slow line and on to the block at Horninglow Bridge.

The bobby has his flags out again and indicating two trains ahead of us. Looking ahead I can see the tripper in front, as we draw up behind the last wagon with its tail lamp hanging on the drawhook. We make our way slowly behind him in the queue until at last we are standing at the starter by the station exit, prior to the climb over Moor Street Bridge again.

Ex GCR 'Robinson' 2-8-0. Photo: P. Groom

Funny thing is, here we are at Burton and I haven't seen a single person that I know, with the exception of the bobby at Horninglow Bridge Box. An even funnier thing was due to occur however, for when we arrived at Leicester Junction a set of Bescot men stepped on board to relieve us. Here I was, less than a mile from home and I had to travel back to Toton to collect my motor bike. Alf found this quite amusing and our guard pointed out that, whilst it might be a bit of a bind, I should be grateful for one thing: If it wasn't the day after Bank Holiday, we would be working back and not riding on the cushions.

So it proved to be the following day when we had 90730, which carried no shed plate at all and was an even worse specimen than 90606 if such a thing were possible. We worked back to Toton with 43969 of 16A and a load of empties.

On the third day our intrepid Yorkshiremen turned up with another challenge in the shape of 63621, an ex Great Central Class 04.

"What do I do with this thing?" I ask our comic fireman.

"Just chuck it in t'ole lad. It'll sort out its sen," he replied, "Yer Mam cud do it."

He then demonstrated the pull-out injectors to me and left us to it.

"Bet you've not been on one of these before, have you?" Alf enquired. "Neither have I," he added when I said I hadn't. "We're both starting equal then," he concluded.

In these days of diesel and electric traction, when a driver has to have days and weeks of training on a particular class of locomotive before he is considered competent to drive it, it's interesting to reflect that, in steam days, whatever kind of engine came their way, the drivers and also the firemen, were expected to climb aboard and work it whether they were familiar with it or not.

Our guard, who by the way, I discovered was named Horace, informed us as usual of the train make-up and weight adding that, although he hadn't a loading for the engine, presumed it must be alright as it had come all the way from York.

Having filled the tank and had a good look round our strange steed, we got the tip from the guard and set forth on our journey once more. The fire looked decidedly healthier than on the previous two days and I was pleased to note the needle on the gauge at 180 lbs. Opening the damper prior to firing a few shovel-fulls into the box caused the 04 to open her safety valves, which was a rewarding sound, particularly as I hadn't yet done anything except lift the damper handle.

63621 plodded off down the line towards Weston-on-Trent with no apparent effort and soon settled down to a steady 25 miles per hour, up hill and down dale, no faster and no slower, no matter what Alf did to her. And so we trundled on, with half regulator and about 40 per cent cut off, for mile after mile. For my part, I kept the back corners filled and just rolled the rest in over the door, finding my adviser correct in saying, "It'll sort out its sen,"

When we got relieved at Leicester Junction, the same Bescot driver had what seemed to me a very young and inexperienced fireman with him that day.

"They're ganging up on me today good and proper," he said as he climbed aboard.

"My mate's not turned up and, as if it's not enough having to bring him up with me, I've got to contend with this thing as well."

I quickly took the lad aside and put him right about our engine.

"You'll have no bother with it," I reassured him, "She's a doddle."

To my amazement, we had 43969 back again as on the previous day so she hadn't been idle overnight either.

My fourth and last day was sadly not with Alf, with whom I had got on well and taken quite a liking to, but with some crotchety old devil on an old 2F, 0-6-0, tripping about to and from Calverton Colliery or some such place. 58173 was the engine and was in quite good nick with no blows from the glands or anywhere else, its only fault, apart from the driver, being a sticking clack which required much clouting of the clack-box top during the course of the day to make it re-seat after using the injector.

Another few weeks passed and I again found myself out on loan, this time to Derby. As I had to sign on there at 7.30 am. It was convenient to catch the 6.59 stopper out of the Tutbury Jinnie Bay at Burton. This train, which only ran as far as Derby, was part of a Leicester engine diagram and conveyed the workers to Rolls Royce from Burton and Repton and Willington, stopping specially at

Peartree and Normanton Station for this purpose. It could have just about any engine at its head from a Class 2P or 3P 4-4-0, through a 4F to a Class 5 although a Compound was the usual engine on the job.

Wondering what task was in store for me, I walked across the tracks to Derby (4 Shed) and reported to the running foreman there. Hopefully it would be to the North or Nottingham or possibly Crewe; all, places that I had not yet been to. Probably shunting at Chadd, I mused or maybe St Mary's. But – No,

"4023," said the foreman. "She's outside. You're with Jack Marsden. Chadd - Water Orton. He's out there already."

I groaned inwardly. Over the old familiar ground again. Still! Can't be helped.

"Bit of a busman's holiday for you, this job," laughed Jack as I climbed aboard. "Bet you thought you was off to London or Manchester or something like that didn't you?"

"I had hoped for something different," I had to admit.

"Still! If you can't take a joke you shouldn't have joined," Jack joked. "I've got the tools and put a bit on for you so there's only the sand boxes to fill and we're away," he continued.

He pointed me in the direction of the sand store and off I went to carry out the task, luckily finding a couple of buckets on the way. I soon had them filled and tramped back to our engine.

44023 stood at the head of a long line of engines and, naturally, the sand was stored at the opposite end of the shed yard. Three trips later, all six boxes were filled to my satisfaction and, after a quick look in the smokebox, I was ready to go.

We ran round to Chaddesden Sidings, which was a vast complex laid down by the Midland Railway before the turn of the century. Row upon row of wagons and vans filled the area. Who would have thought then, in 1953, that in less than 20 years it would all be swept away and the site become an out-of-town retail complex. Such is the way of progress but is it really progress?

I had visited these sidings many times before, on trip workings from Burton and in consequence, was able to play my part with very little instruction as we ran down on to our train. Ernie, our guard, gave us the load; full train for a Class 4F; consisting mainly of coal but with a bogie bolster, carrying a transformer, at the rear. Jack thought this would be better behind the engine so, after a word with the yard inspector and Control, this was duly arranged with us doing our own shunting. Eventually we were away, by now nearly 40 minutes late and soon found ourselves standing opposite platform 6 at Derby Station, awaiting a chance to cross the junction at Derby South and continue along the old Birmingham to Derby Junction Railway line towards Peartree and on to Burton.

The day continued uneventfully and, after having delivered our train to Water Orton, we ran light to Saltley Loco, where we left 44023 on the pit. Then, it was in the crew bus to New Street and back on the cushions. I followed Jack and Ernie onto the train at New Street without a second thought, only to find in due course, as we sped through the platform, that it wasn't scheduled to stop at Burton. It must have been the only train of the day that didn't, much to the amusement of Jack, Ernie and another Derby crew who were in the compartment with us.

The following day saw much the same pattern of working, this time with 43955, another of Derby's Class 4F's, but I made sure of my return train, riding back on the following stopper. On reflection, it probably took as long on this as it did the previous day on the express to Derby then back from there to Burton. However, the trains were run for the benefit of the public, not us railwaymen or so we were led to believe.

Reporting to Derby on the third day, the foreman informed me that I wasn't supposed to be there.

"Didn't they tell you at Burton or here yesterday?" he asked.

"No," I answered quite truthfully. I didn't like to admit that I hadn't been to either place to find out.

"Better go with Jack again, then. I can use his mate for something else. He'll like that as he loves to finish early," the foreman decided. "But don't forget, you're back at Burton tomorrow."

So Jack and I had another trip together, this time on 44317, an ex shopper that had just been soled and heeled. I think she was a Bedford engine, 15D at that time. When we arrived at Water Orton, instead of taking her on to Saltley Loco, we ran down to Bromford Bridge to turn and then came back, light engine, coupled to a Garratt and ran via Toton, where we left her in the pit. From there we ran back to Derby with another 4F whose number I haven't recorded, which was heading for the shops. The contrast between the two engines, experienced on the same day, was unbelievable with 44317 riding like a coach and this last one running and sounding like it had got square wheels. Jack was pleased to make two hours overtime and we went over to the Railwaymans' Institute, across the road from the station, where he bought me a pint and shook hands before we parted.

Reporting for duty at Burton the next morning, to work on the Shobnall Jocko with 41878, gave me plenty of time to recall the events of the previous few weeks. The trip out on 73015 was to be the first of only three turns I ever had on an express working and I only went out on loan again once more.

This was also to Derby, for one week, signing on at 8.30 at night. An epidemic of influenza was rife and people were literally dropping like flies all over the place. Every career and occupation was affected, the railway being no exception. Mini promotions, if only temporary, came the way of us surviving passed cleaners who found ourselves firing on jobs normally coming our way only in emergencies.

Signing on at Derby on the Monday night, I was sent out to St. Mary's as second man on a 350 hp diesel shunter, number 12006, a jackshaft drive fitted engine allocated to Toton which was running in and on test following a visit to the works. My driver, who I think was called Cyril, told me that Derby hadn't any diesel shunters of their own but managed to cover its shunting turns with ex works engines most of the time with substituted steam engines always available when required.

A very boring evening ensued, the only good point being the ability to mash without getting off the engine, except to obtain the water. However, Cyril was organised on this point, having a gallon container of water to hand in the cab. I gathered, from what the shunters told me, that the second man usually took a share of the driving duties but there were no moves to teach me how to do it, willing though I was to learn. In fact, from just watching Cyril operating the controls, I felt sure I could have driven 12006 without any trouble. If ever there was a case for single manning, it was on these diesels but it had to have a second man, partly from local agreements and partly because it worked a tripper across to Chadd and back during each turn of duty when it growled along at 15 pmh, its maximum speed.

On returning to the shed to sign off just after 4.00 am the following morning, to my excitement and amazement, the foreman asked me if I would like to do a lodging turn the following night, signing on at 6.30 pm.

"Yes," I answered, without a second thought, discovering I was to be the fireman on a fitted freight which we relieved at Chaddesden, where it was booked for examination. Tuesday night saw me arriving at 4 Shed just after 6.00 pm. Looking down the sheet, I found my driver's name and alongside, the legend – 'Burton man.' They could at least have written my name in, I thought. About 6.15, a driver entered the lobby and signed on. The foreman's clerk gave me a nod and I stepped forward to introduce myself.

"Mr. Palmer?" I asked, "I'm Dave Fleming and I believe I'm your mate tonight."

He reached for my hand and shook it firmly.

"Jack Palmer's the name," he answered, "Pleased to meet you. I believe you've not been lodging out before. Does your mam know I'm keeping you out all night?" He joked, his eyes twinkling as a big grin creased across his face.

"I'm going to be alright with him," I think to myself.

"Ever been on a Five before?" the inevitable question. "You do look a bit young to be out at night, if you don't mind me saying so. Still, don't worry, your uncle Jack will put you right."

"I've had a Standard to Gloucester with twelve on and we did alright," I replied. "Otherwise, the nearest to it is an Eight," I added.

Jack replied, "We had a new Five one night, last time I was on this job. Not a bad engine I thought. Better than some of these Trafford Black 5's any-road, not that that's very hard I can tell you. Right load of rubbish some of them are."

We had arrived alongside a 4F and Jack said, "Up you get then, we're cadging a lift. You didn't think we were going to walk it all the way did you?"

The 4F driver seemed to have been waiting for us to arrive, for no sooner were we aboard than he moved off. His fireman was a bit intrigued to see me with Jack, on one of the top link jobs at Derby and asked my how I came to be there. I told him what had happened and said it was quite a surprise to me too.

"You'll be alright with Jack," he said, "You might have been with the Mongolian Butcher. Then you'd have known it. Eats cleaners for breakfast he does. You need an excavator to fire for that mad b…"

"Who's the Mongolian Butcher?" I asked.

"Les Folwell," he informed me. "If you're ever booked with him, go sick because you will afterwards anyway. He'll have you burn more coal to Leicester than Jack will to London," he advised, adding, "Yes. You have no trouble dropping off to sleep after you've had a trip with the Mongol."

So the conversation continued and in no time at all we were pulling into Chaddesdon Sidings complex.

Acknowledging to the driver our thanks for the lift, we dropped off the 4F and crossed over to our train. At its head stood a grimy Stanier Black 5, not the BR Standard I had hoped for. 44817 was a London engine, Cricklewood (14A) based I think, or Kentish Town (14B). The Trafford Park fireman, quite an old hand, in his middle 20's, said she was a 'good-un.'

"Tha'll not nod off though, tha knows. Gland's blowing bad this side. That'll keep thee awake!" he grinned.

The footplate was immaculate, belying the outside appearance and with a nice hot fire, full glass and 220 lbs on the clock, he couldn't have handed her over in better condition.

"Your guard's not shown up yet," he informed me, "And my dad don't go past here."

"Your dad?" I asked.

"Aye. The guard's me old man. Started on't Midland he did. Retires at Christmas. We 'af-ter ge 'im a good ride or I get it in the neck when 'e gets me 'ome," he explained.

Just then 'Dad' arrived by the engine and had a word with the Trafford Park man. Apparently the Chaddesden guard still hadn't arrived so he gave Jack the loading and went off with his son and the driver to catch their working back to Manchester.

With a roar, 44817 lifted her valves so I dropped the damper and opened the doors.

"Not a good start, this, lad," Jack stated. "We'll miss our road if he don't come soon. Not like him to be late."

"Perhaps he's got the flu as well, like your mate," I said.

"Could be. I'm going over to see the inspector to find out what's going on," Jack replied and dropped down the side to disappear down the yard.

A good 20 minutes elapsed before Jack returned with a shunter. He climbed up onto the footplate and stepped across to kill the brake.

"Wind her off, mate," he called to me, nodding to the tender handbrake.

I carried out his bidding and he reversed the engine, easing up to squeeze the coupling. The shunter slipped between, uncoupled and unpiped the brake.

"Caped, mate," Jack announced. "No guard. The only one they've got won't come off his booked jobs. Mind you, I don't blame him. He'd not come prepared for lodging. So we're light to the shed, then a passenger to London. I suggested we went light engine all the way as she's one of theirs but Control said "No" so there we are."

Back to the shed we went, to leave 44817 on the pit.

"Glad I've not got to put her away. Not with that big fire on." I said to my mate when he came out of the lobby after telling the foreman what was going on.

"No one will," he replied. "She's off to Bristol now. Just had a failure in the station. Been a godsend she has. Never rains but what it pours."

As we walked over to the station to await our ride to London, she came out behind us and backed down onto the train standing engineless in platform 6. The two crews exchanged footplates, the Derby men taking up residence on another Class 5 standing in number 5 Bay. She had a ring of brass filings all round the hub and over the spokes of her right rear coupled wheel and blue smoke was drifting out into the night sky. The heat was shimmering in the air and could be felt at least six feet away. If we'd had a toasting fork to hand we could have browned a few slices of bread by it.

Handing me the pep pipe nozzle through the window, the fireman shouted for me to spray the axlebox with water, which I did. Clouds of steam ensued, though whether it did much good, in truth I have no idea. Another set of men came to join us from 4 Shed. The driver, a heavily built man with his engineman's hat pulled well down over his eyes, walked up towards out little party.

"Hello Jack," he greeted my mate, in a gruff voice, "What you doing here?"

"We've been Caped, Les," Jack replied. "Guard's not turned up. Got the flu or something and the Trafford guard don't sign past here."

"B....y guards. Who needs 'em anyway," Les growled back. "Still, you won't have me breathing down your neck tonight, will you!" he added.

"Les... Les?" I thought. Could this be the infamous 'Mongolian Butcher'? Come to think of it, he did look a bit Russian in appearance.

His fireman was having a laugh with my pep pipe pal.

"Is your mate Les Folwell?" I asked him.

"Yes, he most certainly is," he answered, "Why? Do you know him or do you know of him?"

Putting his two pennyworth in, our friend on the hot box Class 5 said, "This nice young Burton man is riding down with you tonight Brian. Perhaps he'll give you a spell to Leicester if you ask him nicely. Better ask him now though, you'll not have any breath left later." He no doubt felt quite safe, sitting up in his cab, leaning out of the side window,

Just then our train came bustling in on platform 4, to stop with the water crane nicely alongside the filler. I nipped up onto the tender back and dropped the bag in, making sure there were no kinks in it before shouting to Brian to turn it on.

"Chuck us your shovel up. I'll push some coal forward for you," I called to the Midland fireman.

"Not for me you won't, but you'll need all you can get with your mate," he answered, throwing it up to me.

"I'm not with him. I'm just giving his mate a hand," I shouted back.

"Good on you, pal. You're about full up. I'm off now. See you around," he called back.

"Off," I yelled to Brian and, lifting the bag out, swung the arm clear and climbed back down onto the platform to rejoin Brian.

"There's no lid," I informed him.

"That's the least of my worries," he answered, "Thanks for your help. See you at Pancras."

Picking up my traps, I joined Jack in the front compartment of the leading coach.

"Thought you was stopping on to give young Brian a hand," he greeted me, "Sort of took pity on him – like."

"It was suggested," I replied.

"Take no notice of that idle so and so," he laughed. "He'd run a mile if it was said to him," referring to the hot box fireman.

With a blast on the whistle, we were on our way. I hadn't had time to notice our engine, except the tender that is, which was filthy and could have been attached to any of Stanier's masterpieces. However, the three-cylinder beat of a Jubilee was soon in evidence as I settled back in my seat to enjoy the ride.

Having only been over the road to Leicester from Derby once before and then in the opposite direction, I hadn't a clue where we were. Jack was nodding into his newspaper as I peered out of the window to view the countryside in the gathering darkness of the August evening. After braking hard and running into Leicester Midland, Jack sits up sharply from his doze.

"Leicester, Jack," I tell him, "I'll just go and give Brian a hand. Shovel some coal forward or something."

"Right. Good lad. He needs all the help he can get with that b...er," he commented.

Brian was up on the tender back and Les was just turning on the water. I jumped onto the footplate, grabbed a shovel and climbed up to shovel some more coal forward. The tender was less than half full and I wondered if it would last out to London. Brian is back on the footplate now and slinging coal in the box with his bare hands. His face is bright red and running with sweat.

The 'Mongolian Butcher' shouts, "Are you staying in there or what, you young devil?"

I'm off like a shot, back up to the compartment and safety, with Jack. We now have a set of Wellingborough men and their guard with us for company as well. The fireman, an old hand, promptly falls asleep.

"Somebody's been working hard," I remarked.

"Who? My mate?" asks the Wellingborough driver. "He goes to sleep waiting for the lights to change – and that's on his bike, coming to work!"

45655, 'Keith,' is pounding away, just the other side of the coach end.

"Does this bloke ever pull her up?" he questions my mate. "I'm glad I'm not his fireman."

"He does lay into them a bit," Jack confesses.

"Now! Tired Tim there, really would have something to get his head down for if he was firing for him. The man's insane. How many firemen has he got on there anyway?" our Wellingborough friend enquires.

"Just the one," Jack replies, "And my mate gives him a hand at stops, don't you Dave?"

I nodded. What a close call I'd had. I could just as easily have been booked with him as with Jack but then, we've only come light-engine from Chadd to Derby Shed. Who knows what he's like out on the line. Perhaps all mainline men are like this. The Derby ones anyway!

As we thrashed through Great Bowden I recalled that, only six weeks ago, I was there, playing cricket for Byrkley Street Chapel Methodists, an annual fixture. A tradition of so long standing that no one could remember how it had all begun. The exhaust from our Jubilee was so loud and constant it was impossible to tell whether we were climbing up a bank or running down the other side. Water suddenly came bursting in through the open top light window, to fall on our sleeping beauty. He never even stirred, let alone woke up.

"The scoop works, then," Jack commented.

"It's a form of sickness, sleeping like that," answered our Wellingborough guard. "I've read about it somewhere."

"Well, you've got more time to read than most of us, lolling about in that van of yours," his driver remarked.

And so the conversation went, drifting from guard's duties to sleeping sickness, through mad engine drivers to goodness knows what else.

We run into Wellingborough and I again get up to do my bit. Brian and I are both in the tender this time, heaving coal forwards from right at the back.

"Do you think you'll have enough?" I ask him.

"When it's gone, that mad sod is the next thing to burn," he pants. "When you've used it, that's that. Not my worry. Let him sort it."

"Go and have a minute," I tell him. "I'll shift this lot for you."

'Keith' lifts her valves and Les slips the injector on to quieten her down and save steam.

"Come on lad, back you go," he shouts to me. I need no further bidding and am out of the bunker, through the cab and onto the platform in a trice. As I run past the Wellingborough men on the platform and step into the coach, the driver remarks to 'Tired Tim' "Now there's a fireman for you, you" the remainder of his comments lost in the shriek of 45655's whistle as the 'Mongolian Butcher' sets her in motion for her final ordeal to London.

Arriving in St. Pancras, I go up to the cab and peer into the tender. There is no coal of any sort to be seen. The gauge is down to 190 lbs and Brian is sat on his seat, slumped over the side, too worn out to care. Les is down on the ground, going round inspecting the engine for hot bearings etc.

"Shall I run the rake through the fire for you?" I ask Brian.

"Please yourself. I couldn't care less. If we aint got enough to get us to the shed, hard luck," he answers.

Jack made no comment but the expression on his face said it all.

Les, 'The Butcher' climbed back into the cab and seeing Jack, said, "Three minutes early eh! Pretty good! We were a couple of minutes late away at Wellingborough you know!"

"Are you coming then, Dave?" asked Jack, "We're at Cricklewood you know, not Kentish Town, like these two."

As we walked off down the platform to catch the stopper, he said that he had to leave before he said something he shouldn't.

"Are they lodging>" I enquired.

To my surprise, Jack said, "No. They work the newspapers back as far as Leicester, then on the cushions to home."

"What are we on, then?" the obvious question I then ask.

"6.55 semi-fast in the morning," he answers, "Prep' the engine and bring her down to the station. Then away. Stop at Luton, Bedford, Wellingborough, Leicester, Loughborough and Derby. Train goes on to Sheffield. Usually we have the same engine back that we bring down but not tomorrow, obviously."

Down at the lodge, we have our supper and then, after a wash up, we turn in. A shunter is bashing about outside all night long and I cannot get to sleep, no matter how I try. Whoever is in the next cubicle is snoring fit to wake the dead, to make matters worse. The fact that I have done very little doesn't help either. I must have nodded off eventually for the steward had to wake me in the morning.

Jack is already in the mess room, tucking in to egg, bacon and fried bread when I walk in.

"Get yourself a good breakfast, lad," he tells me. "Just sign the book. You'll need more than sandwiches going back."

Apparently, the price normally gets stopped out of your wages but mine never was. Some clerk at Derby is probably still trying to find my name on their staff strength… but it was very tasty!

We strolled down to the shed and consulted the train board, to find 45009 marked up for us. Collecting the tools and lamps was not such an easy task. All the spanners that you rarely, if ever, use were in the bucket. The $^3/_4$ x $^7/_8$ key and the gauge frame key were not.

"Here we go again," I think

I spot a fireman taking a set of tools into the stores and waylay him.

"Here. Have the lot," he remarks and dumps them on the shed floor at my feet.

I gather them all up and carry them to our engine. The shovel looks better than the one we've got for a start.

"Starting a Stores of your own," laughs Jack.

We only want a dart now and we're complete. Now for the sands. Where are the sand buckets? It was an unwritten law in all the sheds that, when you have finished with them you leave them on the end of the turntable where everyone can see them so naturally, that was the last place to find them. The six boxes on a Class 5 are quite large and take a lot of sand, maybe two or even three buckets each. I spy another fireman with two buckets and trail him around until he's finished with them. Snatching them up, I am busy back and forth between the dryer and our engine, each load weighing about 50 odd lbs each. I only put one bucket-full in each of the back boxes. In my turn I am also being stalked for their possession. Are these the only two buckets in the entire depot? Surely not! All this scavenging about is causing me to neglect the fire. Whilst on my prowl I have spotted some broken firebrick so 'borrowing' the shed sweeper's barrow, I fetch a load to spread over the bars as is my fashion when able, no matter what class of engine I'm on. Preparing an engine in the hour allowed is quite enough to keep one busy, without the need of searching around for equipment and in a strange depot as well.

Stanier Class '5' 4-6-0. No vices with these engines. Photo: K. Fairey

In time, I get the table and we move out of the shed to top up the tank; our last task before setting out and running down to our train standing in St. Pancras. You are discouraged from blowing off or making smoke in the station area and should you do so, are very quickly remonstrated by the station inspector.

Our Class 5, number 45009 was a long way from home, being a Carlisle engine. The guard came up to give us our load.

"Eight on for 290 tons. Stop at Luton, Bedford, etc, etc," he told Jack and noted down his name. He was a London man and working his rest day, he informed us.

"Bully for you, mate," Jack retorted as he went away.

The fire looked a bit dead but I knew that when we got going it would soon brighten up to become white hot. With all but a full glass and 220 lbs on the clock, I was ready as I ever would be. Open the damper, fire a charge round the box and up with the flap, half close the doors, watch the smoke at the chimney top. When it clears, do it all again.

The exhaust injector keeps flying off and is becoming a nuisance. Usually it's a case of: put it on and forget it. I decide to use the left hand live steam injector as well, to help maintain the water level. This means that, although the left injector can't maintain the level on its own, at least it gives me time to fiddle around with the other one. I tell Jack about it.

"Do your best," he answers, "If you need me to ease up, just say so."

Do your best! I reflect. What else does he think I'm doing! Still. I don't suppose he means it as it comes out. When Jack shuts off for Luton the thing flies off and, having corrected it, when he opens up again it repeats itself. This proved to be the pattern of events all the way to Derby. Every time the position of the regulator was altered, off would fly the injector. Jack mentioned the trouble to the relieving driver, a Millhouses man, when he stepped on at Derby.

"Why didn't you fail the blasted thing, then?" he asked.

Jack's face was a picture when he got off.

"Drivers!" he scorned to me as we walked off, "Not fit to drive sheep some of them."

As we came out of the lobby after signing off, Jack shook my hand again.

"You're alright, kid," he said, "See you tomorrow night."

Alas. On signing-on the next night, his regular mate had reported back so I became a spare man, finding myself on Station Pilot duties with a grumpy old mate on a Class 2P 4-4-0, number 40404, one of Derby's finest. But I could laugh at his grouching and groaning for after all, wasn't I being paid lodging allowance and mileage money for just trundling up and down and round the station all night, aboard a cloud of steam with a Class 2 in the middle of it!

My third express run was with Charlie Wadsworth, on a rambler's excursion to Malvern, aboard 45062 but that's another story.

Chapter 9

On the Leicester Passenger

Until the Beeching cuts, Burton was situated on a railway cross-roads and had lines radiating to all four main points of the compass, the busiest lines being North to Derby, from where it was possible to divert to Nottingham, Manchester, Sheffield and York; or South to Birmingham, with onward connections to Gloucester and Bristol, diverting to Walsall, Wolverhampton and South Wales. Over to the West it was possible to reach Crewe and North Wales or indeed Scotland via the West Coast Mainline; all these being accessible from Tutbury on the Derby – Crewe line. Alternatively, a journey to the East was achieved by way of the Leicester Line, giving access to the East Coast and London. A regular passenger service was operated over all four lines, some trains running through and calling at the town with others starting and terminating here.

The pull-and-push service to Tutbury, known locally as the Tutbury Jinnie, maintained the westerly connection, with through expresses and local services serving the North and South directions. Journeys eastwards to Leicester were of the all-stations, stopper variety and these trains were divided up for operating purposes, between Burton and Leicester Depots.

I fired a number of turns on the local service between these two towns, a distance of some 32 miles with ten stops, eleven stations being served in all, the average journey time for these trains being 1 hour 10 minutes. Running through the South Derbyshire and Leicestershire coalfields, the line was subject to numerous speed restrictions, these all contributing to the average journey speed of between 30 and 40 miles per hour.

A trip along this line which was and still is, full of interest both historically and industrially, would not be out of place at this juncture so I will describe a typical turn on the 6.03am. departure from Burton, although the outcome wasn't at all typical.

Signing on at, I seem to recall 5.20 am, we look at the board and see that we have 40633 and she is stabled somewhere in the New Shed as 'NS' is chalked beside her number. My driver is Cyril Parnham, one of the regular passenger link drivers and a deputy foreman to boot. He is none too happy having me, a Passed Cleaner, booked to him in place of his regular mate and says as much to Bert Sinclair the running foreman.

Having received this boost to my confidence, I accompany him to our engine, which is standing one pit round from the doorhole, all prepared and ready to go. I had prepared the engine, usually a Class 2P, for this turn a number of times in the past and had worked the job once before with Harold Wildgust, on 40526 but I wasn't going to tell Cyril that piece of information. Not after his comment in the lobby in front of all and sundry. Let him worry for a bit!

After putting my gear away in the tender locker, I have a quick look round and see that we have what appears to be some decent coal in the tender. The tank is full, according to the gauge but I nip over the back and visually check through the filler hole. Just over 100 lbs on the clock, water out of sight above the top nut and a lump of fire just inside the door with bare bars under the arch. I quickly spread the fire over the grate, gradually adding more coal as I do so. I had actually been on the depot since just before 5.00 am, as was my normal practice when on these types of jobs but had gone straight to the engine and had a go at the fire before I signed on.

Cyril had a quick look round our steed and shouted for me to try the sands. 40633, being an LMS built engine (actually built for the SDJR in 1929), was fitted with four 'leading sands' pipes as opposed to the two fitted to MR built examples. These presumably operated OK as he shouted, "Right. Off," and climbed back on board.

LMS Class 28 4-4-0 No. 40633. Note the dabeg pump fitted on the front left side framing. Photo: W. Garbett

"I'll just have a look in the smokebox," I say to him, "Then I'm ready."

"Be quick about it then," he answers, "Then get the table."

I do as he bids and in no time at all we are turned and running out of the shed doorhole. I notice that Cyril has lit the lamps. As 40633 runs past me in the yard, he leans over the cab side to ask if we need any water.

"About 200 gallons down," I shout back so he pulls up at the water crane.

I scramble up the tender back and drop the bag in. In less time than it takes to tell, the tank is overflowing and Cyril winds the supply off. I can't believe it! With the exception of my feet, I am still dry!! I toss the bag out and shut the lid. Back on the footplate the pressure is rising nicely. These LMS engines are pressured to 180 lbs psi, as against 160 lbs on the Midland ones. They are both fitted with the G-7S boiler, in common with the Class 4F's but unlike the latter, they steam more freely on the Class 2P's for some reason.

We reach the top of the yard and before pulling over the points to allow us access to the 'belling out' peg, I change the red shades round for running down to the station. Cyril says nothing but I am prepared to bet that he would have done, had I not done it. Reaching the peg (signal), I press the plunger to alert the signalman in Leicester Junction Box and tell him that we are 40633 for the 6.03 Leicester Passenger.

Now! To say that I am not delighted to be on 40633, would be a lie, as she is fitted with a Dabeg Feed water heater, one of only two engines in her class to be so treated, if not in the whole country (the other engine being 40653). I had been very intrigued with this piece of apparatus, which stood large and proud on the left hand front framing, alongside the smokebox. The idea was to pre-heat the feed water by means of exhaust steam, prior to it being forced into the boiler by a ram operated by an eccentric driven off the left hand coupled wheel. As she was fitted with only one live steam injector, with which to maintain the boiler, without a second and usually exhaust injector as on conventional engines, I reasoned that this pump would have to be given a try. When asked about it some time before, my guide and mentor – George Wallace, had told me that some drivers didn't like it being used and that indeed, you could get along quite nicely with the live steam injector only, with the three coach loads normally used for local passenger work in this area. He did, of course, tell me how to work it as well and I couldn't wait to try it. However, as the water was still above the top nut, I would have to be patient for a bit longer.

Running by the Burton Station South Signalbox, under the caution of the 'calling on' signal, we stopped beyond the box by the Ind Coope Bottling Stores to await the road back across to the Down Main, where we would halt over Moor Street Bridge prior to backing down onto our train.

"Shall I change the red shades again," I enquired.

"No, leave it. He knows where we are. Besides which, we are still showing a red light to anyone who runs by on to us," Cyril answered.

A short parcel train ran in to the platform from the south and once he was clear, the road was set for us and getting the dolly, we ran out across the Up Main onto the bridge then backed down onto our train standing in the Leicester or South Bay Platform.

As we had run up from the shed I had been adding more fuel to the fire. My ministrations had raised the clock until it now read 170 lbs psi so I dropped the damper to avoid lifting the valves. The shunter was on hand to couple us onto three coaches forming our train, closely watched by Cyril.

"Turn the steam on," he announced as he climbed back onto the footplate. More of an order than a request.

Opening the stop plug with the ³/₄" spanner to admit steam to the system, I gave it a minute then adjusted the regulator to read 50 lbs on the CW (Carriage Warning) gauge. Dropping onto the platform, I went to the front of the engine and lifted the lamp off the lower bracket and reached up to position it onto the top bracket below the chimney, removing the red shade at the same time, to denote our new role of 'Stopping Passenger Train.' Collecting the other lamp from the tender, I rejoined Cyril in the cab. Looking back down the stock, I was pleased to see steam issuing from the rear and other places not originally intended by the designer.

Whilst all this is going on a Birmingham bound train passes in the adjacent mainline platform, with a Class 5 at its head. Frank Rigby, our guard comes up to give Cyril the details of the train.

"Three coaches, equal to 105 tons. Call at Gresley, Moira, Ashby, Swannington, Coalville; miss out Bardon Hill, stop at Bagworth, Desford, Kirby Muxloe and Leicester. We shall be at least two minutes late leaving. See you at Leicester," all in one long monotone.

Cyril exchanged a few more words with Frank as, with a blast on its hooter, the Class 5 heaves its six coaches away over the Moor Street hump.

"We're next, lad," Cyril calls over his shoulder as the bay starter pulls off and Frank blows his whistle.

With an answering toot, Cyril yanks open the regulator of 40633 and we are on the move. As I open the damper she gives a slight slip of her 6' 9" drivers as they cross the points to follow in the wake of the Class 5. As we curve right to join the main line proper, I look back to see our three coaches following obediently behind. I shoot three nice shovels full down each side with one more in each corner and another under the door. Up with the flap and close the doors, leaving just a small gap between.

Between firing this charge I glance up to see all signals clear at Leicester Junction for a good run up the bank. Having shut off for the junction, which has a 20 mph speed restriction on it when turning up the branch, Cyril opens up when the train is clear to charge up the 1 in 200 past Birmingham Curve Junction Box and over Branston Road to level out on the Stapenhill Viaduct over the Trent.

The water is well down in the glass now even though I have had the live steam injector on. 40633 is not riding at all badly when compared to her Midland Railway 7' 0" sisters. At least I have been able to fire her OK so far without throwing half the coal around the cab. With the water reading half a glass I decide to ask Cyril if I can try the pump. The steam gauge is nicely reading 175 lbs and the fire is white hot so now seems the right time. Cyril has got her with the regulator just on the main valve and about 40 per cent cut off.

"Please yourself, lad. You're the fireman," he answers, "Do you know what to do?"

"I think so," I shout back.

So, making sure the tender feed is open, I shut off the live steam injector, push down the water lever and ease open the steam valve. 40633 is hammering along now and just about to pass Bretby Junction Box. This is the only stretch between Burton and Leicester that isn't subject to a speed restriction and our 2P is taking full advantage of it, touching over 60 miles per hour as she climbs ever upwards with our light train. I am now having difficulty keeping my feet and the thought crossed my mind as to how those Nor-West firemen managed when I saw the 2P's flying through Lichfield Low Level on the front of a Jubilee or Royal Scott on a London bound express in my train numbering days.

Despite my wandering mind and cake-walk stance, I am avidly watching the gauge glass to see if the pump is doing its job - and isn't it just! The water is fairly leaping up the glass so I ease back the water flow to try and slow it down a bit. After a bit of fiddling about I seem to achieve the desired feed. Another quick round into the box onto my neglected fire, with half the fuel missing the hole altogether and I sit down to view the scene.

Cyril beckons me across to his side and points towards the front of the engine and the Dabeg pump. Everything has disappeared in a cloud of steam and it is only the speed we are travelling, blowing it down, that allows Cyril to see where we're going.

"Shall I shut it off, then?" I shout to him, trying to converse over the banging and rattling of our mount.

"I think you'd better, don't you?" he shouts back in reply.

I comply with his request, somewhat reluctantly, as I am quite impressed with its performance. After all, hotting up the water before injecting it into the boiler has got to be a good idea. So - on with the live steam injector and a quick squirt round with the pep pipe to lay the dust and coal spillage.

We are now dropping down into Gresley Station so Cyril shuts off, drops the gear down a bit into drift and we run under the road bridge which, having suffered badly from subsidence, is packed up at each side with baulks of timber and into the station, the original brick built platform of which has subsided to nearly track level, coming to a stop at a replacement, timber built, platform beyond. I take the opportunity to fire another round into the box while we stand as, although it's considered bad practice to do so, at least it all goes in the hole whilst 40633 is stationary.

No. 40633 emerges from Gresley tunnel with a train for Leicester. Photo: Authors Collection.

Whilst I had been playing with the Dabeg pump we had passed Swadlincote Junction where the Swad' to Woodville Loop left our main line to the left passing Cadley Hill Colliery and on to Swadlincote Station and Woodville, rejoining the main line at Woodville Junction. Then Coton Park Sidings and Box; soon to become a reception area for open-cast coal; before passing Bonas's and the Netherseal Colliery Branch coming in from behind Gresley Box as described in the 'Overseal Tripper' chapter 4.

After no more than a minute or so Frank is giving Cyril the 'right away' and off we go again to climb out of the station towards Gresley Tunnel (623 yards long). The climb got ever more severe as the years progressed with subsidence from the colliery workings each side. The Midland Railway had purchased the mineral rights below the tunnel, to preserve it from the effects of subsidence, for an alleged £10,000 ion 1861, a fortune in those days, followed, it is rumoured, by a further £6,000 in 1885; both sums to the Marquis of Hastings.

40633 is working hard again as she burst out of the other side and the one injector is having a job to keep the boiler fed. I toy with the idea of putting the pump on again but decide to leave it for a while as it will soon replenish the level if it gets dangerously low. Cyril's a bit heavy handed with his driving methods I tell myself as I feed another round into the box only to be knocked off balance as we cross the junction with the Woodville line as just mentioned earlier. Here there are a maze of points and crossings with Woodville Junction Sidings to our right and the Woodville line coming in on our left.

Then we are steaming under Spring Cottage Bridge with Moira West Junction leading off to the right actually under the bridge arch itself while another line shoots off to the left into Rawdon Colliery. Here the Nuneaton line, a joint venture between those two old rivals, the Midland and London and North Western, turns south to head towards Nuneaton and the LNW London to Crewe and the North main line, passing Donisthorpe, Measham Collieries, Shackerstone, Market Bosworth and so on, to Nuneaton - Abbey Street. We however, continue to climb straight ahead towards Moira East Junction which forms a triangle with the Nuneaton line at Moira South Junction. Nestling inside the triangle can be seen Overseal Loco, sub-shed to Burton and originally another joint construction between the Midland and LNWR, the former building the shed and the latter the combined water tank and coal stage.

As we stop in Moira Station, 40633 blows off, despite the injector being on so I am well pleased with my efforts. Passed Cleaner I might be but at least I can make the old girl steam. Mid you! Cyril's heavy handed driving helps as it gives a good pull on the fire and draws the heat generated through the tubes to further superheat the steam in the superheater elements.

As we are standing and the injector is beginning to make some headway in the rather depleted boiler, the valves soon shut as the cool water pulls the temperature down a little. We have just over threequarters of a glass and I am contemplating shutting it off when Frank gives the 'right away' and off we go again. The gradient out of here is slightly less severe but still a climb, though 40633 makes light work of it. A Coalville 8F rattles by in the opposite direction with a full load of coal, probably for Hams Hall Power Station. I wonder if she will carry straight on and go via Birmingham Curve and Branston or swing left at

Moira East to travel down the Nuneaton line to get there. Probably via Branston, I decide, because there is another line linking Coalville with Shackerstone if she were routed the Nuneaton way. Another charge around the box before she gets into her stride and we are slowing down for more speed restrictions caused by the pits subsidence of the North Leicestershire Coalfield,

The market town of Ashby is our next stop. As we run into the station the branch line to Melbourne and Derby runs in on our left from behind the signalbox. This line ran through to Derby by way of Worthington, Melbourne and Tonge and Breedon into Normanton where it joined the Derby line near Peartree and Normanton Station. Interestingly, the War Department took over part of the line during the Second World War to train some of the sappers in the art of railway working. Ashby-de-la-Zouch, to give it its correct name, was also the terminus of the Burton and Ashby Light Railway, a street tramcar enterprise, also owned and operated by the Midland Railway and running in competition to the railway and in consequence, itself. Operating from 1906 to 1927, one of the few obvious traces of its existence is visible in the station yard where a section of track at its terminus point is still in-situ in the forecourt.

Ashby, one of the two major towns on the branch, warranted a slightly longer stop than the other stations and when we received the 'right away', 40633 was simmering very nicely at the safety valves with my favoured threequarters of a glass of water bobbing in the gauge and a nice hot fire to boot. Being left hand drive, unlike her Midland sisters, Cyril was able to receive all the 'right-aways' himself as, with one deft movement, he popped the whistle and yanked the lever open. Our 2P strode off up the 1 in 565 out of the station with no effort at all. By now, of course, it was fully daylight and I resolved to extinguish the lamps at Coalville, if I had time. The line runs on an embankment for the first half mile or so before crossing the A50, where the climb stiffens to an average of 1 in 160 before dropping down to enter Swannington Station. The level crossing gates at the far end of the platform were open, ready for our departure though, of course, we were well clear of them as we stopped at the platform. Leaving the station, the line actually dropped away at about 1 in 240 for the first few hundred yards, one only three places on the whole journey eastwards where this happens. Soon we are approaching Mantle Lane West where the most historic part of the branch joins from the left hand side, that of the Swannington Incline, dating back to 1833 and the head part of the Leicester and Swannington Railway.

This incline was worked by a stationary steam engine which hauled the wagons from the colliery at the bottom, by a steel rope, up the 1 in 17 gradient to the exchange sidings at the top. In the early sixties this magnificent winding engine was dismantled and removed to the National Railway Museum at York, where it can be seen operating on compressed air at frequent intervals throughout the day. The task of removal was entrusted to the Burton Breakdown Gang and I am proud and privileged to have been included in the team, though not a regular breakdown gang member.

At Mantle Lane West the line continues its upwards climb with a vengeance, averaging 1 in 120 into Coalville Town Station. Mantle Lane East Box is passed and as we run into the station the loco shed throat is passed on the left at the platform end. Cyril makes a gentle approach as the crossing gates at the far end of the station are closed. We are allowed four minutes here so I dash up into the tender back and drop the bag in to top up the tank. Cyril turns the water on and 1,000 gallons are quickly fed into the tender. As Cyril closes the valve, I glance across towards the shed prior to throwing the bag out. An ex MR Class 2F 0-6-0 is on the turntable, which was sighted just the other side of the platform wall. Coalville always had an allocation of these 2F's, primarily to work the Leicester (West Bridge) Branch, as they were the largest engines permitted to pass through the Glenfield Tunnel, this line of course, being the other end of the Leicester and Swannington Railway.

The gates are now open and with the starter and the back peg off, Cyril is looking for the 'right away.' Frank obliges and we are off again. A flick of the sand valve control to check any slipping of 40633's 6' 9" wheels and we are roaring away up the bank to pass Whitwick and Snibston Colliery Sidings guarded by Coalville No.1 Signalbox. 40633 is getting into her stride again, just on the main valve and pulled up to about 35 per cent cut-off. As I turn to feed another round into the white hot fire she lurches and bounces from side to side as we cross Coalville Junction where the single track cord to Shackerstone on the Moira West to Nuneaton line leads off the branch to the right. I am thrown off my feet and go sprawling across the footplate. Instinctively I hold on to the shovel with one hand as I put out my other to save myself, only to grasp the injection steam pipe and burn my palm. Cursing and uttering words my mother never knew, I scramble back to my feet. These 2P's are notoriously rough to ride on but 40633 hadn't been too bad until then. Cyril looked across, being made aware of my predicament by the clout the shovel had given to his leg.

"Always a bit rough, that crossing, lad," he remarked.

"Why didn't he say something, then?" I thought.

Wrapping my hand with my handkerchief, I pick up the shovel and after a glance forwards to see a nice, clear, point-free track ahead, carefully and painfully add more fuel to the fire. The most hard-worked live steam injector in the country is losing its battle to maintain the boiler and is down to just below a quarter of a glass, with the needle following it back round the clock and just passing 150 lbs in the wrong direction. Out of the corner of my eye, I catch a glimpse of an old banner type signal, followed by a level crossing. Bardon Hill, the banner signal controlling movements in and out of the nearby quarry. In another mile our upward climb is going to change from a 1 in 200 rise to a 1 in 76 fall. As we reach the summit of the incline at 565 feet we pass Ellistown Colliery Sidings Box.

"And where will the water level be then?" I ask myself, "On with the water pump and never mind Cyril."

Kicking open the tender feed, I push the water lever down and open the steam valve. After a few moments the level begins to rise in the glass so I knock off the injector. Grabbing the shovel next, I feed another round into the firebox, letting the glass fill to the top before knocking off the pump. I then note that the steam is still holding at about 145 PSI.

My hand hurts like hell but I have no time to bother with it as we crest the summit and Cyril shuts off to coast by Ibstock Sidings and come to a stop alongside Bagworth and Ellistown Station platform. I take the advantage of a stable and stationary position to incline my shovel and examine the fire. I note that it's getting a bit thick under the arch so down with the rake to pull some of it back. None of the Midland engines seem to like anything but a thin fire under the arch, I have discovered, but with the wild gyrations of the 2P's they seem to shake some forward and down there. Cyril notices my actions and, glancing up at the somewhat depleted pressure on the gauge, asks me if everything is alright.

"Yes. Nothing I can't handle," I reply, sincerely hoping that I am doing the right thing.

"Off we go then," he answers, toots the whistle and away we go again.

I pull the, now very hot, rake out of the fire and after a quick glance to make sure no bridges are coming up, wrestle it round and back on top of the tender. Another round into the fire and a check on the water level, which is now just over half a glass with the altered and now downward angle of our engine. So, on with the injector again as we rattle down the 1 in 70 average gradient past the Nailstone and Bagworth Colliery Sidings, the latter also fed by an incline similar but not as severe as the one at Swannington. On, past Desford Colliery Sidings and Box, to arrive in Desford Station.

This station, along with the previous one at Bagworth and that of Swannington, are those where the start is downhill. Today however, the bobby has his red flag out of his box window as we move away across the level crossing. Cyril pulls up by the box with the train still across the road. The bobby informs us that platelayers are working on the crossover at Desford Junction where the Leicester (West Bridge) line leads off to the left. Actually it carries straight on, with us curving off round to the right. This is also the start of another climb as far as Kirby Muxloe Station.

We move off down to the junction, only about ½ of a mile away, where Cyril shuts off and slows down to a walking pace to cross the track where the platelayers are working. I give a blast on the whistle and receive an answering wave from the lookout. All the gang stand clear as we crawl past. I am totally amazed and surprised to see that every single one of the platelayers is a woman. They all wave to me as we pass, only to move straight back out of sight and onto the job as our three coaches clear the line.

As I look across to give Cyril the tip that we are clear, 40633 lifts her valves and blows off hard. Not from the sight of those females I hasten to add, merely that my little performance with the rake has certainly paid off. If only my hand didn't hurt so much I would be a happy little fireman. Interestingly, Desford Station, like many more, is some considerable distance from Desford itself, being closer to the village of Newton Unthank.

The valves soon shut again as Cyril opens up for the steady climb to Kirby Muxloe and after slipping on the injector, I steel myself to fire another round. The 'T' piece across the top of the handle is red with my blood when I have finished and push it back onto the tender shovelling plate. Sitting down on my capacious seat, I unwrap my soaked handkerchief and examine my palm. What a mess! One big blister, which has burst and is bleeding profusely. What am I going to do now? I wonder.

Just then, out of the corner of my eye, I notice Cyril close the regulator for the next stop. Kirby Muxloe level crossing gates appear and we are running into this delightful station, quite the most picturesque on the branch. Somewhere over to the left are the ruins of Kirby Castle, though not, as far as I am aware, visible from the train. But I am not interested in the scenery today. Pain directs my attention in one very self centred direction, I'm afraid. Cyril glances across and, seeing my obvious distress, asks what the trouble is.

"Good God, lad," he exclaims, when he sees my hand, "What have you done?"

He quickly jumps off the engine and fetches Frank, our guard, up onto the footplate. Fortunately, Frank is a qualified First Aider, secretary of the local Burton Railway St. Johns Ambulance Section, no less. Weighing up the situation very quickly, he dashes back to his van to collect his first aid gear and applies a substantial dressing to my injured hand. The Station Master, puzzled at the delay in our departure, comes up to the engine and, seeing the situation, offers to wire for a relief fireman at Leicester.

"I'll be alright," I rashly reply, with the bravado of youth.

"Well, if you're sure," Cyril intercedes, "We'd better get cracking."

Frank goes back to his van with a parting comment sounding like, "You're a silly fool," or something similar and away we went.

A check on the water level shows a full glass, no doubt because the injector has been on all the while we have been standing at Kirby Muxloe, so I knock it off with my good hand. The clock is beginning to drop back as we climb the last mile before starting the last and final descent into Leicester itself. Until now I have been firing from the right hand side of the cab, with 40633 being a left hand drive engine so I decide to try a round from the left hand (driver's) side for a change to see if that is any better for my injured hand. Folding a pad out of a sponge cloth with which to hold the shaft, I feed another eight shovels full onto the fire.

As we run over the summit of this last climb, Cyril eases our engine slightly as he pulls the handle back onto the small valve and winds back the reverser. I slip the injector back on as our full glass of water has become ½ a glass, now that 40633 is facing downhill. The clock seems fixed on 170 lbs PSI, for which I am eternally grateful, so I sit down again to enjoy the ride. Soon we are crossing the viaduct over the River Stour and the outskirts of the city are spread all around. The Gas Works is on the right with the Electricity Power Station virtually opposite. Not the most salubrious part of the metropolis, it would appear. The old Great Central line is crossed next, with the Leicester (Great Central) Motive Power Depot just below us on the left as we pass by on the embankment. I always paused from my labours at this point to see what was on the shed. Usually something of interest and this day I am not disappointed. Two B17 'Footballers' are standing in the yard, one resplendent still in LNER light green, along with a B1, a couple of K3's and assorted 0-6-0 tender tank classes. I always hoped to see an A3 Pacific, of which Leicester (GC) had two or three but was never lucky enough.

Across Saffron Lane Bridge, which crosses this wide thoroughfare on the skew, with the gasworks previously mentioned immediately beyond and we are approaching Saffron Lane Junction. Here the line splits with the right hand cord heading for Knighton South Junction and the left for Knighton North and Leicester which we are taking. The left hand curve is only 22 chains and has a permanent speed restriction of 15 mph imposed upon it.

I manage another round into the box as we squeal round this curve with the flanges of the wheels grinding away at the rails. A quick clean round with the pep pipe follows as we run into Leicester Midland Station to stop with 40633's chimney just clear of the Great Central overbridge which spans the station platforms. Normally, on nearing the end of a journey, the fireman would run the fire down prior to it going on the shed but on this turn we were relieved by Leicester men who worked our engine and stock forward as another train to, I think, Peterborough and Ely.

"Not this thing again," the fireman commented as he climbed aboard, "It's criminal sending it out with one injector," he added.

"Why, what's wrong with the pump?" I answered.

"Everything!" was the terse reply. "If you ever get it to work, you can't see where you're going."

I had to concede that he had a point there. Years later, when I was fitting, I had many attempts at making it steam tight, without much success. In later life, after I had long left the Railway service and 40633 had made her last journey to the scrap-yard, I became aware of several different jointing compounds and materials that would have guaranteed a successful result but alas, too late for the old lady and her Dabeg Pump.

We gathered up our traps and made our way to the crew rest room on platform 1, where Frank had another look at my hand. He cleaned it up beautifully and put another dressing on it, courtesy of the local first aid box. He advised me to go to the hospital when we got back to Burton, which I promised to do. Having had our break we made our way to platform 3 to await the arrival of our return working, which I see from my notes was hauled by ex LMS Compound No. 41072 of Kettering (15B). The fireman on the engine looked to be as old as my father and had everything in apple pie order with a big fire, full pressure, an immaculate footplate and the water in the glass just below the top nut. The only thing missing was the wood on the fireman's seat, a rather small piece of plywood lying over part of the resultant hole in substitute.

"Sorry about the seat, mate," he apologised, "It were on last week when we had her. Some thieving swine has swiped it since."

Nothing unusual about that, I thought, though I could never understand why it happened. Surely not by footplate-men, I reasoned, with the resultant inconvenience and discomfort it caused. But then again, you can never tell what some people get up to, let alone understand it.

Shutting the damper to keep her quiet while we waited in the station, under penalty of death if the valves lifted, I was just admiring a group of young ladies on the opposite platform, when another fireman stepped up onto the footplate.

"Come to relieve your mate," he announced to Cyril.

Cyril looked across at me before he welcomed him aboard.

"The young hero there says he doesn't need relief but as you're here you'd better stay, particularly on one of these. He'll never reach the front of the box in his state."

The firebox of a Compound with its G9S boiler was certainly quite a bit longer than the G7S on 40633 but I was a bit annoyed as I had, up until then, never fired one. Perhaps Cyril's right, I reasoned. You get no medals for carrying on. I later learned that Frank had told the Station Master at Kirby Muxloe to ignore me and wire for a fresh fireman and here he was. Another young Passed Cleaner like myself. It reminded me of my own first trip to Birmingham, the circumstances of which were in some ways similar although in that instance, the injuries were more serious.

"Better go and keep Frank company then lad," Cyril addressed me so I gathered up my belongings and left the cab. Cyril didn't suffer fools gladly. Goodness knows what was really going through his mind. Two amateur firemen in one day! One thing was certain, I decided, no matter what happened steam-wise, it wasn't likely he would take up the shovel or offer advice. Not that I had had trouble with 40633 on the way here but how about my compadré on the way back? Still! Not my problem now, I tell myself as I settle into Frank's seat in the brake-van. But I was still annoyed as I had been marked up (red inked) for this job for three days and this was only day one. No chance of that now I supposed.

As for the return journey, once round the Saffron Lane Junction the branch is an unremitting climb, apart from the dip through Kirby Muxloe to Desford Junction, where the ladies were still packing ballast, until Ellistown is reached, then virtually downhill all the way to Burton. 41072 made light of most of it with her five-coach load, though she did lose her feet getting away from Bagworth on the 1 in 76 there. Should you be wondering, the Leicester Passed Cleaner appeared to cope with the vagaries of 41072 quite well, so far as could be judged from within the brake-van.

On arriving back at the shed an accident report had to be completed, mainly it would appear, for Control's benefit, to cover the six minutes late arrival in Leicester. There was no sick pay in those days and if you didn't work you had no money. Bert Sinclair, the Running Foreman, was well aware of this, of course and told me to come to work as usual the next day, if agreeable at the hospital and he would find me something to do.

I duly turned up bright and early the next morning with my hand all wrapped up like an Egyptian Mummy, a pair of gloves in my pocket just in case I had to go firing. Eventually, I found myself riding to Derby Works on a dead engine, an S&DJR Class 7F 2-8-0, whose number I haven't recorded, along with another colleague on a diesel shunter, both being towed by an equally run down 4F.

The following day I went on duty at 3.00 am to do some 'calling up' and generally run errands with the third day much the same. After a second week of light duties my doctor declared my hand fit for action and, although sore for a while, it did not give me any more trouble.

Compared with her older ex Midland sisters, 40633 always seemed a more lively and stronger engine altogether. I felt that the slightly smaller wheel diameter of 6' 9" compared with 7' 0?" of the Midland engines, to be the reason. Later, when an apprentice with Les Bull, we carried out a valve and piston examination (ME6) and I was surprised to discover that she was fitted with double heads to the piston valves. These appeared to be so arranged to allow earlier steam admission to the cylinders along with a more controlled exhaust. Les wasn't really sure himself as he hadn't come across it before either. During my time in the Works at Derby on the Valve and Piston (V&P) Section, I only came across it once more, also on an ex SDJR, LMS built 4-4-0; I think it was 40631.

Fowler Class 4 2-6-4T. No. 42333, Burton's No. 42336 never looked dirty like this. Photo: Authors Collection.

Another engine that I fired on two occasions, on the Leicester, was Fowler Class-4, 2-6-4 Tank number 42336. This engine was the complete master of the job and a run on her was like a day out. She rode like a coach and, although a bit hot in the summer months, was extremely cosy in the winter. Very sure footed and with a Compound type G9S boiler and firebox, pressed to 200 lbs per square inch, she played with her train. Her only vice, if it could be called one, was that on the return run, once clear of Gresley and the subsidence restrictions, given her head, she would roll like a battleship as the low level of water in her depleted tanks sloshed about when she wound herself up to almost 70 mph down through Coton Park and Bretby Junction before braking over Stapenhill Viaduct for Birmingham Curve and Leicester Junction. All this fun and being paid for it as well! No wonder I was reluctant to give it up the footplate for an apprenticeship! However, you soon came down to earth when you arrived on the ashpit and had to put her away. The cab did seem a bit restrictive in size then, compared with a tender engine.

Most drivers and firemen preferred these early Fowler engines to the later Stanier and Fairburn examples, good engines though they were. Truly a credit to Henry Fowler's design team. It just goes to show that some things can hardly be improved on. Yes, the old 2300's only needed a drop grate and perhaps a few more baffles in the tank to make them perfect engines!

Whilst on the subject of the Leicester Branch Passengers, another incident comes to mind which occurred when working the 7.08 turn with Charlie Wadsworth on 40436. We were bowling along the fast stretch and had just lurched across Swadlincote Junction when Charlie called out in alarm and, closing the regulator, made a strong brake application. I looked out, only to see some geese flying up off the track immediately in front of us as we bore down upon them.

"Did we miss them, mate," he called as he opened up again.

"Don't know but I think so," I replied. However, some white feathers started to flutter by the cab from the front of the engine so perhaps we didn't miss them all, I thought.

By now we were running into Gresley Station. As we stopped, I jumped off and ran to the front of the engine, there to find a rather sick and bedraggled goose partly wedged under the smoke-box and front framing. He viewed me with a malevolent eye and hissed angrily as I approached him. Now, let it be said that I had had a few nasty experiences with geese before, as a child, on my uncle's smallholding so I retired accordingly and reported back to Charlie. Charlie, being of sterner stuff than yours truly and never knowingly looking a gift horse in the mouth, quickly grabbed the firing shovel and nipped off, just as the guard was blowing the 'right away.' Seconds later Charlie was back with the goose under his arm, very much dispatched into the land of Morpheus, no doubt with the aid of the shovel blade. A toot on the whistle and we were roaring away out of the platform and into Gresley Tunnel.

"Here, mate," Charlie called, "Put a good-un on and watch the road while I pluck and dress this little beauty."

Up the bank we roared with yours truly at the controls and Charlie sending clouds of feathers flying round the cab like snowflakes. As I shut off for the Moira stop, Charlie took over to bring us nicely to a stand at the platform. I quickly fed another couple of rounds into the fire and, as Charlie went back to his plucking, I acknowledged the 'right away' and got our train in motion again. The same routine was observed at Ashby and Swannington so that, when we arrived at Coalville, all was completed, with only the smell of burnt feathers and offal to give the game away. A big smile on Charlie's face and a happy temporary driver (me) completed the picture.

"Pity it's only Tuesday," Charlie observed, "Be nice for the week-end would that. Still, I expect it will keep. Wouldn't like to come for Sunday dinner by any chance?" he added.

I declined the offer but then! it hadn't eyeballed him like it had me! It couldn't have! It never had the time!!

Chapter 10

A New Beginning

The first Saturday of September, 1953, saw me signing on at 5.30 am to prepare and work the Station Shunt with Horace Pritchard on Midland Class 1P 0-4-4 Tank number 58087. The fireman on the job was usually a Passed Man as all three regular drivers were elected members of the town council and it was not unusual for them to attend council meetings for the odd hour during the morning. Thus, in their absence, their driving work was carried out by the Passed Firemen with the Shunter acting as Second Man - and all done with the approval of the Railway Authorities. Presumably the regular fireman was required for driving duties on that late summer Saturday morning, hence the substitute – yours truly.

As we made a few gentle movements around the station's environs, our duties were tinged with not a little sadness on my part as this duty marked my last firing turn for, on the following Monday morning, I was to take up my position as an apprentice fitter, as agreed when I started two years and one week earlier.

Horace was very interested in my career progress and, by way of a parting gift, allowed me to do some of the driving during the morning, providing of course, that I did the firing as well.

Our first task was to attach the returning stores van to the rear of a Birmingham to Derby Local for onward dispatch back to the works, Horace of course, being at the controls this time, my turn only coming later. Another job was to collect an extra coach from the sidings and stand with it in the dock alongside the North Bay prior to adding it to the Sheffield – Torquay - shades of my own turn on this summer extra with Charlie Wadsworth on 73015.

W.H. Smiths had a distribution centre in the old station yard and frequently received a couple of vans of papers and magazines which were shunted next to the old cattle dock for their attention. They were hauled out and taken across to the Derby Street Wharf Sidings for onward dispatch later in the morning - then with myself at the controls.

58087 was one of the three of her class allocated to Burton for this duty and the pull and push service to Tutbury, the third engine being a spare to cover boiler washouts, exams, repairs and the like. The other two engines were 58080 and 58058, the latter only being used on the pull and push service as a last resort due to her rather run down condition compared with her two sisters. All three engines were fitted with screw reversing gear as befitted a passenger locomotive and had quite a good turn of speed, 70 mph not being an uncommon performance when on passenger duties. They steamed quite freely as well, in common with all Johnson designed locomotives. Therefore, a quiet meander across from one side of the mainline to the other, with two parcel vans in tow, was hardly likely to extend 58087's capabilities but nevertheless was quite enjoyable to me in my temporary role as driver.

Horace, to be fair, although watching my every move, never said a word to me during the whole operation, for which I was eternally grateful and did much to instil confidence in my abilities. His career in local government progressed a pace, with him becoming mayor and later an alderman of the borough. A further honour was to have a home for the elderly named after him, thereby carrying his name into perpetuity.

Come 12.30, we returned to the shed, just in time to put 58087 away as there was no requirement for an engine down at the station on a Saturday afternoon.

Ex MR Class 1P 0-4-4T No. 58080, sister engine of the last engine the author officially fired. Photo: Authors Collection.

So ended my footplate career and it was with some anxiety that I presented myself at the shed on the following Monday morning, at 7.30 am, reporting to Mr. Jack Hodgson, the foreman fitter. As I entered the foreman fitter's office, situated in the South-East corner of the Old Shed, I must have appeared to all therein as yet another cleaner coming for instructions. There were fitters, boilersmiths, tubers and their respective mates all awaiting their daily instructions and work cards. In the back corner opposite the stove, a typical railway heater of quite grand proportions considering the area it had to warm, was situated the Shop Officeman's desk, presided over by one – Stan Hoult. He had started his railway career on the footplate at Derby but, following an accident which left him with a permanent limp, performed the duties of Shop Officeman with great efficiency and not a little humour. He was, I would guess, in his early thirties when I first made his acquaintance. It was Stan who first greeted me and made me feel welcome in my new environment.

After much discussion and not a little swearing and cursing, the assembled artisans wandered out of the office and into the shed to take up their allotted tasks or, more likely, mash a cup of tea, leaving just the three of us still in its confines.

"Whats thou want then?" Mr. Hodgson asked as he turned to me, "Tha'll find plenty to clean up at the Drop Pit tha noes," his broad Lancashire accent ringing clearly across the room. At first glance, his slightly stooped, thin, almost frail figure, topped by a fairly small head, the face of which was rather angular; indeed Mr. Punch like; did not either impress me or command my respect. I was soon to discover otherwise!

"This isn't a cleaner. Leastways, not any more," chipped in Stan, "This is our new apprentice." "Am I right?" he asked, turning to me.

I confirmed that this was indeed the case, forming the opinion as I did so, that my new boss was not aware of my appointment at all.

"Better send him with Joe, then," he flustered. At least, I thought that was what he said as, truth to tell, I hadn't so far understood hardly a word he had uttered.

"Come on then," said Stan, "I'll take you to him and introduce you. At least he will be on the job, unlike some I could name."

I followed him out into the shed and, turning through the dividing wall into the New Shed, we walked over to Class 3F number 43256, an old friend from my days on the Trippers. A big, friendly man and a smaller, thinner man were just arriving at the engine as we did so. The smaller one had a Hessian sack over his shoulder which he dumped with a crash onto the engine framing. It was indeed, an old bolt bag and was now doing duty as a means of carrying tools, a function it had performed for some considerable time judging by the dirt and grease ingrained upon it.

"What are you doing out here, Stan?" Joe greeted him with a grin, "You mind you don't get lost!"

"Get lost yourself," Stan replied, "I've brought you a little helper. Meet Dave, our new apprentice."

As I was at least a head higher than Stan, indeed taller than all three of them, I thought the 'little helper' remark somewhat inappropriate but I knew it was all part of the fun.

"This gentleman is Joe Benson, fitter extraordinaire and the good looking one behind is his mate – Gerald Love," Stan continued, "Look after them and they'll look after you."

With that he turned on his heels and left me to get acquainted with my new workmates and the job which I had set my heart on doing when first I started on the railway two exciting and fulfilling years earlier.

After the usual greetings, Joe produced the 'X' Repair Card and explained what we were about to do. On the front of the card; an amber piece of stationery of approximately A4 size; a long line of pre-printed jobs were listed. These were universal and all embracing for every class of locomotive on the railway and, as such, not by any means applying to any one loco in its entirety. In fact, with familiarity and practice, the only thing normally read on the front of the card was the engine number. However, this could not be said for the back of the card as here were listed all the jobs and reports that had been gathered from drivers' reports since the engine's previous 'X' Exam, mainly jobs that could only be done when the engine wasn't in steam. Also all the defects, major and minor, trivial and unimportant, that the examining fitter had found during his pre-'X' repair examination. A typical 'steam' job would be changing injector steam valve stop cocks, as these closed off the delivery pipes into the boilers. This would incidentally, also involve re-cutting the seat upon which the stop cock plug closed. The same applied to the steam supply valve for the injector as well. The regulator valve gland would also usually require packing, as would the large and small ejector valve glands. Other, 'non-steam' tasks could include: securing various motion nuts and bolts, like eccentric sheaves and rod nuts, slidebars and blocks, big and little end nuts, bolts and wedges, siderod gradient pins, sanding gear and brake gear; all requiring the fitter's attention.

Whilst all this was going on, the boilerwashers would empty the boiler, remove all the washout plugs and thoroughly wash our all the sediment and scale therein, poking into nooks and crannies around the firebox water spaces with long thin brass wires to dislodge the more awkward pieces from their remote corners. This task completed, the boilersmith would examine the inside of the water spaces with a long wire on the end of which was fashioned a piece of oil soaked waste which, when lit, illuminated the inner recesses of the firebox sides, corners and crown. This inspection might reveal a broken stay or a leaking smoke tube, all of which would have to be attended to before the engine could again be steamed and released to traffic.

If a boiler smoke tube required renewal, it might be necessary to remove the blastpipe or main steam pipe in the smokebox, to afford access for the work to be done by the tubers. On superheater fitted engines, there was naturally, a need for the fitters to remove some of the superheater elements before access to the flu tubes was made available. But, I digress...

All these tasks and more, were to come my way during the coming months and years. At least I knew my way around the engines, even if I didn't know much about what made them tick. I had resolved to keep what little knowledge I had gleaned, to myself and start again in apparent ignorance with a clean slate, as it were, and learn from there. One of my uncles, who had been in engineering all his life, gave me some very good advice which has stuck with me throughout my life and which, in turn, I have passed on to all the subsequent apprentices it has been my good fortune and joy to work with over the years. It was: never to be a 'know-all' and say, "I know that," whenever anyone tries to explain or show or tell you anything. Always show an interest, even if you do know already for, sooner or later you will discover something that you didn't know before. If you keep saying, "I know, I know," people will not bother to tell or show you anything and in consequence, you will finish up knowing very little. Furthermore, for my own part, I would add that one can learn from anyone and everyone, however great or humble their background or occupation.

Joe went to great pains to show and explain the methods of diagnosis and repair of the various parts of the different engines that we came into contact with over the next few weeks. He was the son of the redoubtable running foreman, of the same name, who had struck fear and trepidation into the hearts of us, as young cleaners and who was destined to continue so, with us as apprentices.

One of Joe junior's passionate interests was First Aid and he was a very keen and active member of the St. John's Ambulance Service, as was his wife, Marion. He was naturally, also a member of the local Railway Ambulance Team and in no time at all, had recruited yours truly as a member as well. We used to meet and practice in a room alongside the railway, just to the north of the station and adjacent to W.H. Smiths warehouse, the scene, in fact, of my last footplate duty. The Honorary Secretary was Frank Rigby, a passenger guard with whom I already had a passing acquaintance as the reader will be aware.

Joe's apprenticeship had been served in Derby Loco Works and in consequence, his knowledge of the steam engine was second to none. Not, that is to say, that the other fitters with whom I subsequently worked were of less ability by any means.

Gerald Love, I was soon to discover, was a very gentle man and a devout Catholic. I never once heard him say a word against anyone at all or blaspheme either, for that matter. Very early in our association, I discovered that he sold lottery cards in aid of the local Catholic Church funds. As Joe was one of his customers, I asked what they were about and if I might purchase one. Such was the calibre of this man that he had never pressed me to buy one as he knew that, as an apprentice, my income was not very high. Indeed, after my firing wages, they were abysmally low. He explained to me that the tickets were sixpence each (2¹/₂ new pence) and contained within the sealed ticket, two letters. If those two letters were the same as the first and last letters of the headline in the Saturday edition of the local newspaper, The Burton Mail, then you won £2, a princely sum, especially to an apprentice, in 1953. I decided to buy two tickets and low and behold, to my utter surprise and disbelief, I won the £2 with one of them. Needless to say, I never ever won again and must have paid back the £2 many times over but nevertheless, I enjoyed the winnings that week.

My mother had sent me out to work every day with a mashing made up of a portion of tea and sugar sufficient for one brew-up, in an old mint sauce jar, ever since I had started work. This had always been of acceptable strength when brewed in my own can, leastways it suited me - and all the gannets that always appeared to scrounge a cup whenever anyone mashed. As I was now the third member of the Joe and Gerald team and sharing their tea during the mid morning and afternoon breaks, which were always taken in the cab of the engine they were working on; unlike most other fitters who took theirs in the fitters' hut; I dutifully handed over my mashing to Gerald, having had the offer to do the honours; a task I quite expected to have to perform; turned down by him. He apparently didn't approve of the two ingredients being together in the same receptacle, nor the proportions either for, on returning the jar for a refill to my mother that night, to her disgust and my amusement, a note was found therein reading: "Dear Mrs, Fleming, Please moisten the spoon when putting the tea in," meaning naturally, that an extra amount of tea was required. However, my mother, bless her, was quick to point out that if the spoon was damp the tea would stick to it and we would finish up with less tea in the jar, not more. I couldn't decide whether or not she was serious as she kept very po-faced when she explained it but, as she had a good sense of humour, I presumed she was joking after all. Needless to say, another jar was produced and I ever after, took two of them to work, one containing the tea and the other, sugar.

My notes tell me that this first week saw our little gang on the Tuesday, working on 43652, another 3F, again doing 'X' repairs and on Wednesday through to the end of the week with a Class 4F number 44436 carrying out a Number Six (ME6) mileage exam. This was a complete overhaul of all the running gear and involved the removal of the connecting and coupling rods, removing the respective bushes for re-metalling, in the case of those of the coupling rod and the big end brasses and the renewal of the little end bearing bush. While all this was going on the valves and pistons were also removed for the renewal of their rings.

Before these last two items could be extracted, a certain amount of preparatory work had to be carried out. First the front framing work had to be unbolted and removed. This revealed the two cylinder covers and steam chest covers. Approximately three dozen $^7/_8$" of an inch nuts secured each of these cylinder covers which, when removed, were threaded onto a length of spun yarn in order of removal to ensure correct replacement. When all the fastenings were removed the cylinder covers were lifted off by the use of a set of rope pulleys attached and hung from the smokebox door handrail. Then, using the smokebox door as a crane jib, the covers were swung aside and lowered to the ground one at a time. Before the pistons could be removed, the crosshead had to be parted from the tail rod and the gland cover and packing rings removed. Parting this crosshead was always something of a lottery. Sometimes the operation could take hours, though it was usually achieved in minutes, at least on the older, inside motion engines like the Midland designs of 2F, 3F, 4F, 1P and 2P Classes; both tender and tank types.

These were fitted with draw cotters which, when inserted through the slots in the crosshead and tail rod, drew, as the name implies, these two parts together before being hammered home. But, we are concerned with the opposite action of parting these two components so, having knocked out the draw cotter, a hardened steel 'button' was inserted through the hole in the front of the tail rod. A pre-formed, half-moon piece (which incidentally fitted all the Midland engines quoted, thanks to that Company's standardisation policy) was fitted into the back of the crosshead fork, followed by a keeper plate to hold the button in place. Between this plate and the half-moon, a wedge was inserted which, when hammered well home with half a dozen or so blows with a sledgehammer, would usually break the tapered joint and allow the crosshead to be removed, the usual result being the whole assembly of crosshead, wedge, half-moon, plate and button falling to the pit floor in five separate parts. With the gland cover and packing rings removed the piston was then ready for removal. The piston head was eased out of the cylinder with the pulley blocks attached by a sling around the piston head nut. The lift was transferred behind the head around the piston rod and the whole assembly removed with the aid of the smokebox door 'crane' as with the cylinder covers earlier.

The piston valves were dealt with in a similar way, the crossheads being parted with a mini version of the main crosshead gear, a cold chisel invariably being used as a wedge. Some fitters had an arrangement of shaped pieces to insert through the slot of the valve draw cotter which, when correctly fitted, achieved the same result. Indeed, with the later Stanier and BR Standard locos with outside valve gear of the Walschearts variety, this was the only way to do it.

Having parted the crosshead, the valve was then wound out of the steam chest by means of the reversing gear. These valves, particularly on Class 4F's were quite stiff to remove, more so if the engine had been stood in the shed for a while and the steam chest had become cold, allowing the carbon build-up to set hard. It was the normally accepted practice when carrying out the mileage exams to remove the valves first to avoid this trouble. Indeed, such was this a prevalent problem with the 4F's that, in later years when I was involved in mileage exams myself, I endeavoured to identify the next engine to be examined and, if a 4F, arrange with the running foreman to allocate a job for it which finished during the early morning so I could remove these valves while the steam chest and valves were still hot. Otherwise, whilst reasonable efforts generally managed to extract the offending valves, it was not uncommon to spend a day or more on this operation, with copious amounts of paraffin soaking its way between the valve and liners and oil or paraffin soaked rags burning merrily away, all in an attempt to soften the carbon holding the valves captive.

However, moving on from this digression, once the valves were free, the back and front guide bushes were removed for re-metalling. The valve gear pins and bushes were next examined for wear, along with the eccentrics. Whereas the valve gear pins and bushes were usually within acceptable tolerances for wear, the eccentrics not infrequently required removal for re-metalling also. Any coupling and connecting rod bushes requiring attention were loaded onto a trolley and transported to the Fitting and Blacksmiths Shops. In the latter, stood the water hydraulic press. On this ancient contraption all these bushes were pressed out, with water spurting out from numerous sources and in all directions soaking all and sundry in the vicinity. The tighter the bushes, the more effort was involved to generate enough pressure and as a result, the wetter became the 'unfortunate' - pumping the handle, usually me, whilst an apprentice. And to think that I had thought my days of regular soakings with things concerning water had finished when I left the footplate and the recalcitrant tank fillers!

With all these various bushes, brasses, slide blocks and eccentrics safely in the hands of Charley Tovey, the Coppersmith; a character in his own right; to be re-metalled then machined down to size in the Fitting Shop next door, we return to the engine where the fun continues. Having removed all the old rings from the valve heads, the heads themselves have to be de-coked before the new rings are fitted. Likewise the piston heads and the portage in the steam chests.

Two more tasks are still awaiting attention. The drawgear; front, rear and intermediate; are one of those items. To check the intermediate draw gear it is necessary to squeeze the engine and tender together to compress the buffer gear and release the tension on the drawbar. A large clamp was provided on the shed for this purpose. The other and much preferred method, when possible, was to scotch the engine or tighten the tender handbrake, dependant on which way round the engine was stabled, then push the two together by use of a convenient engine in steam, thereby taking the load off the drawbar, enabling the tender end pin to be knocked up and withdrawn. Once parted, the engine or tender was drawn away and the intermediate drawgear and buffers examined for wear and possible renewal. Fastidious firemen, like my previous self, constantly hosing down the footboards with the pep pipe, tended to cause the drawbar pin to rust solid, particularly at the engine end, resulting in many hours jiggery-pokery before its removal was achieved, not helped by its relative inaccessibility from below the cab, its lower half being above the steam brake cylinder.

Whilst these two units were apart the intermediate hoses for the steam brake, vacuum brake and water feed were also examined, along with the carriage warming hoses, if fitted. These were removed in any case during the summer and sent to the Works for refurbishment, only being refitted at the onset of winter. Although, after all these years, I forget the precise dates, these were laid down by the railway authorities and had nothing whatever to do with the weather bureau. Incidentally, vacuum and carriage warming hoses, or 'bags' as they were known to railwaymen, along with the gauge clocks for the same, were the only items of equipment that were standard throughout the total British Railways system, on both the locomotive and the carriage and wagon departments, irrespective of which constituent company they had originated. As a matter of interest, on the side of these vacuum and CW hoses was a red rubber patch with the numbers 1 to 12 marked on them. A second set with the number 0 to 10 was included. The idea was that, when a new 'bag' was fitted, the person concerned removed the two relevant numbers to indicate the month and year it was done, i.e. 4 from the first set for April and 5 and 7 for 1957 from the second set. A good idea if every-one did it but of course, like all such things, it was not always done.

When all things appertaining to the engine and tender connections had been checked and changed as necessary, another fun-filled task awaited the unsuspecting apprentice; the checking and cleaning of the inside of the tender tank water spaces. A washout drain plug was fitted into the tank bottom which had to be removed to empty the tank. Opening the tender water valve would drain out most of the water via the intermediate water bags (hoses) but the last inch or so still warranted removal of the plug. This task completed, having received a sleeve-full of sludgy water down your arm whilst unscrewing the plug, a small dustpan (of the guards variety) and a bucket was obtained and down through the tank top filling hole you went with your paraffin flare lamp in one hand to light your way and the bucket and dustpan, together with a ⅝" spanner, in the other, to crab walk and dig your way through to the front of the tank. Normally, about three buckets full of sludge would be shovelled off the bottom of the tank before you reached the front where, in about an eighteen inch high space beneath the shovelling-plate, would be found two filter plates behind which were the tender water feed valves. The filter plates had to be removed for cleaning and to allow access for the feed valves and their operating linkage to be examined. The plates were thoughtfully secured by brass set pins, thereby preventing them rusting and seizing up in this wet environment. The ⅝" spanner soon had them removed and the plates freed. These filter plates were very necessary to prevent foreign objects entering the water valves and either blocking them or, in the case of more solid items like lumps of coal and wood, jamming them in an open or closed position.

During the course of my career, many things were found in the tender tanks, from the obvious sludge, coal and wood, to rags, firemen's caps, or jackets and sadly on one occasion, three drowned kittens. I bet they didn't jump in on their own either, poor things! The odd fish was not unknown, sometimes still alive and flapping about in the dregs of water left in the bottom. These usually lived on for a few more days in a jam jar in the fitters' hut until either the wrong diet or the lack of oxygen in the smoke laden air, both from the locos and the fitters' fags and pipes, saw them succumb to their inevitable end inside the shed cat.

Occasionally, large quantities of coal would be found beneath the filling hole, silent testament to some lazy preparing fireman who couldn't find the energy or sufficient interest to replace the lid after filling the tank and before going under the coal hopper. Presumable these sorts left the lids off their dustbins at home as well, for both actions are similar and require much the same amount of effort. Little details like these used to annoy me when I was on the footplate. Like: hooking up the front coupling out of the way and chaining back the CW bag. They both took only a moment to do and, to my mind, made things tidier and look that much better, apart from keeping things safer.

Joe had a doctrine that he would never ask anyone to do something that he wasn't prepared to do himself. So, into the tank we both went, with Gerald waiting on the top to receive full buckets of dross etc. and filter plates. When we emerged with the job completed, filter plates back in and incidentally, a new level float fitted, yours truly's overalls had changed from a well washed blue to a dark and very damp brown. Joe's on the other hand, apart from the odd smudge, looked as if they had never seen the inside of a tank for many a long day – and he had done most of the work!

General view of No. 2 (Newshed) the 'Bugut' with its door open can just be glimpsed through the 2nd arch on the back wall. Photo: Authors Collection.

The following week Joe and Gerald were on nights and I found myself with Les Bull and his mate Joe Marsland. They had just finished their night shift, which I gathered came round every third week. Les had been one of Joe's apprentices and held rather strong views on the abilities of some of his fellow artisans. There was no doubting his skills and knowledge, however and very early on I came to the conclusion that he and Joe were the two best fitters on the repair gang. His mate Joe Marsland was one of three brothers working at the depot. Charlie was a driver, whom I vaguely recollected having fired with on one occasion and only to Chaddesdon and back with a Class 3F. No trouble on that trip but then, with a 3F you usually had a good trip, provided you kept the fire thin at the front under the arch, thickening back to the door and not forgetting the back corners of course. The other brother, Dave, was also a mate and was the complete opposite of the others. Whereas they were tall and thin with angular features, Dave was short and stocky with a round face. I never heard Joe or Charlie swear but Dave's profanities were numerous and duplicated in nearly every sentence. However, although I only worked with him occasionally, I found him to be a great guy who would not let you down.

The first week with Les and Joe introduced me to the vagaries of life in the 'Bug Ut' as the fitters' cabin was known. This cabin, constructed in the north-east corner of No.1 (Old) Shed, was about the size of a large garden shed and was the official abode of the Shed Fitter. It was to here that recalcitrant drivers sent timid firemen with requests for the fitter's assistance on ailing engines. I know from experience how intimidating it could be to open the door and after reeling back from the blast of heat emanating therein, to be faced with a sea of faces, none very friendly and try to decide to which one you address your request.

"Wadder you want?" more a threat then a question, would growl from the far corner of the cabin where, from his high stool by the desk, the Shed Fitter ruled his eight hour kingdom.

"C.. Could someone c.. come and look at the brake on number 'so and so' (or whatever the problem was) p.. please," the fireman would hesitantly ask before beating a hasty retreat.

"Go and have a look, mate," to one of the fitters, would be the normal result of the exchange or on the rare occasion the Shed-man going himself.

There were three examining or shed fitters, working the three shift system of 6am-2pm, 2pm-10pm and 10pm-6am thus providing cover around the clock, six days per week with Sunday afternoon being the only eight hour period not covered. To enable them to have time off the Saturday and Sunday 6am-2pm turn was covered by the day fitters in turn though usually the 6am-2pm Shed-man covered one or sometimes both turns on overtime. When I first started, these fitters were Reg Corden who we have already met, changing a gauge glass on the Toton 8F whose mate was Tommy Ross. Then there were the Fern brothers: Jack and George, fitter and mate respectively. The third pair were Geoff German and his mate Cyril Barclay. I had met these two previously on that infamous day when we set out for Birmingham Gas Works with 51217, so I knew what a chalk and cheese pair they were. These three pairs, all excellent steam men, were so different, one to another, that they really need a chapter each.

The cabin itself measured roughly ten feet by twelve. Along half of one of the longer sides, which was fully glazed on its top half, was a desk that had originally run the full length of the shed but had subsequently been crudely sawn off to half its length, the removed section replaced by a bench. Two rough pieces of wood now supported the end of the remaining desk and it was from here, perched upon his high stool, the Shed-man conducted his shift, as already described. Behind him in the opposite corner was a coal fired stove of the type found in guards brake vans. A superheater flue tube on end formed the chimney which disappeared through the cabin roof some eight feet above. This stove was usually white hot along with the first foot or so of the chimney which softened to a dull red as it passed through the hut roof to continue upwards some eight or ten feet before discharging smoke and sparks into the shed proper, thereby making its own contribution to the smoke-laden atmosphere which was the norm most days inside the Running Shed.

Imagine, if you can, the humidity created on a wet or snowy day when upwards of fifteen or twenty wet coats were all hanging up to dry, with most of their owners sitting around on the benches, drinking tea, smoking and arguing out the latest subject under discussion. It defies description. Sufficient to say that oxygen was fighting a losing battle to keep all the occupants and the fire supplied with the fire seeming to take the major share.

But, how I grew to love it! Every single subject under the sun was avidly debated, from the whereabouts of the various pubs, past and present, in the town, through governmental policies (especially around voting days), to what would be the best bet on the card for the current race meeting. Football, cricket, boxing and the like all had a regular airing as with any group of men anywhere when thrown together. Even the railway got a mention now and again.

I remember the number and locations of level crossings in the town being a subject to get a review from time to time, usually after one or more vociferous members had had a long delay at one or the other of them. There were over thirty sets of these gates in the town so you can imagine the arguments ensuing regarding their number, especially as, during the discussions, no one ever wrote anything down but tried to remember them all in their heads as they counted. In the afternoons, the fact that some had visited the pub during the lunch time did little to help matters either.

I was happy to just sit quietly and listen as I drank my tea and munched my sandwich; usually beef dripping or occasionally cheese; vary rarely joining in. After all, I thought, why pay good money to go and see a variety show when there was much better entertainment here for free. Nothing I had ever experienced until then had matched these discussions and arguments that raged in the relief cabins and fitters huts of the railway at that time.

The fitters and their mates were not the only occupants of the 'Bug Ut' either. Four tubers and a boilersmith also inhabited those confines along with three other apprentices as well as myself. All this camaraderie was broken up most mornings by the arrival of our redoubtable foreman who would burst through the door about a quarter past eight with the comment "Now, come on gentle-men, 'ave you no jobs to be going to?" his broad Lancashire accent grating against the eardrums, particularly on a cold and frosty morning when the temperature seemed to drop 100 degrees and probably did when leaving the cabin. And so we would all troop out into the cold shed to open up the icy cold steel lockers to extract the equally chilly tools required for our daily toils and amble off to commence our allotted tasks.

On that second week, my first of many with Les Bull and Joe Marsland, I see that we had a normal X Repairs day on 42756 on Monday, followed by a No.2 Mileage Exam and X Repairs on Tuesday and Wednesday on 58080; one of the Tutbury Jinnie engines and sister to the engine I had on my last footplate turn; followed by another Crab, No. 42763, from which we removed the blast pipe; a dirty sooty job; to enable the tubers to gain access to some of the lower smoke tubes that required renewal. Friday saw us on another X Repair, this time on 4F number 44100.

This ended my first month of duty as an apprentice and very enjoyable and instructive it had been too.

Chapter 11

Forward and Onward

So the weeks went on with various fitters having the pleasure of my company, as it were.

'Talcum Malcolm' was one from whom I very soon attained a degree of confidence in my abilities, which far outweighed my knowledge. Frank, to give him his proper name, should never have been a fitter, at least not on anything as grimy as a railway engine, as he had an aversion to getting dirty. Thus after his very quick training course, I was usually presented with the repair card and left to get on with it while Frank occupied his time between some personal project of his own and the current debate under discussion in the 'Bug Ut'.

Frank always smelt nice, looked clean and neat, with his shoes highly polished. Smudges of dirt on his overalls were almost unknown and on his hands and face never. Nevertheless, his knowledge of the steam engine was legion and only surpassed by his ability to pass on that knowledge from a safe distance to yours truly whilst I did the actual work.

A typical week with Frank that I have noted from my diary very early on during my training shows five different engines, all for washout and X repairs as follows: -

Class 3F 'Jocko' No. 47464 on Monday, with 41536 Tuesday, 47643 Wednesday, 43709 Thursday and on Friday 43188 to round the week off.

This trust in my ability did untold good for my confidence and with Frank having a quick check around each day afterwards, no harm was done. If I wasn't sure what to do or felt that something was a bit beyond my knowledge at that time I only had to ask and Frank would immediately come to my aid with advice as I have described. He later left the railway to take up a position as maintenance man at a small company in town whose main business was that of making beer drip mats. This proved to be just as dirty as railway engines with the added disadvantage, to one of Franks demeanour, of printing ink stains which didn't wash off very easily but had to wear off once on the finger ends.

Before long he managed to obtain a position in local government in the architects department where the lifestyle and mode of dress, a lounge suit, was more in keeping with his ideal. However, let it be said that I enjoyed working with, or should I say for, Frank and we remained good friends until his sad demise at quite an early age.

Between us we rebuilt St Chads Church Boy Scouts Troop, which was in decline when we took it over. I believe it is still going on from strength to strength to this day and I like to think that it owes it's continued success to the input that Frank and, to a lesser extent myself, put in to it.

Quite a number of fitters did not have a Mate working with them, this position being filled by apprentices to a certain degree. Another fitter with whom I spent many weeks was Jack Turner. Jack was fast approaching sixty years of age when I first made his acquaintance. His health was deteriorating along with his strength. A constant worrier, he would whittle and ponder about even the most basic tasks. Totally unjustifiably in my view as he really knew his job. A bag of nerves was Jack, who would jump at the slightest thing. Although an obvious target for leg-pulls and pranks, he was never or rarely the victim of such capers, as his general demeanour and age commanded respect. I was quite fond of the old chap and enjoyed working with him.

One particular incident I call to mind was when we were carrying out repairs on a Class 4F, which was stabled on the pit next to the New Shed doorhole. Amongst the various jobs listed was that of fitting a new water pickup scoop pan under the tender tank, the original one having been damaged, possibly on a crossing or set of points. Jack went underneath to start removing the damaged pan, whilst I collected a replacement from the stores. As I returned I was just in time to hear a cry of alarm from below the 4F and see Jack come dashing out, hotly followed by a stoat. It was difficult to tell which was the most scared, the stoat or Jack!!

The author as an apprentice enjoys a mug of tea sitting in his 'firebrick armchair'.
Photo: Authors Collection.

Another occasion was with another 4F, actually on the same pit. One of the driving axlebox springs was broken and in consequence required changing; quite a task in the shed, calling for considerable skill and not a little strength as well. The method used required the engine to be jacked up until the spring became free in its hangers. With the driving axle this involved jacking it up until the leading wheel on the affected side became clear of the rail before the weight in turn came off the driving spring. Then with a board spanning the pit and a bit of packing under the spring buckle it was only neces-sary to knock the three securing pins out to release the old spring, which invariably clattered down onto the floor of the pit below. The process was then reversed with the new spring on the board and a bit of adjustment with the jack to enable the three pins to be replaced, securing cotters in place - down with the jack and the job was done. About 1½ to 2 hours maximum. But not with Jack. He was constantly worrying that the jack would not hold up, or else the spring wouldn't fit or even worse that the whole engine would fall over and slip into the pit. But he was a real gentleman in every sense of the word, so all I could do was smile and reassure him that everything would be all right.

Another elderly character was Arthur Taylor. Of short, stocky build, he must have been in his sixties and was reputedly even older. He considered himself the 'Mileage Exam' king and when the foreman gave him easier jobs in deference to his age he was soon in the office complaining and wanting to know when his next No. 6 Exam was going to be. Arthur was never happier than when he had a big sledgehammer in his hand. Inevitably his enthusiasm was encouraged as a plentiful supply of engines was usually coming up for examinations! The inside motion ex MR engines were his speciality and he could have all the various parts stripped down and into the fitting and turning shop in double quick time. It was when he was putting it all back together that the fun started. On more than one occasion he had been known to put the left hand piston in the right hand cylinder and visa versa having replaced all the covers and secured all the seventy odd nuts around the circumference only to find that the crossheads would not fit as the draw cotters were sloped the wrong way. His Mate George Bosworth, 'Bozzy' by nickname, a dour ex army infantry man, lost no time at all doing a tour of the shed to relate to his confidants the latest faux par. But Arthur continued to dash along in his own inimitable way, dropping clanger after clanger. But let it be said, he knew a few tricks not in the book, which achieved results that I would have thought impossible.

One example of this type of impossibility was on yet another 4F, which had run a side rod bush hot. The white metal bearing had fused and run out and the brass bush itself had caused the actual crankshaft surface to corrugate so that it had the appearance of a round corrugated iron sheet, albeit rather a small one. My thoughts on seeing the crankpin was that the wheel would have to come out and be sent to the Shops for the crankpin damage to be rectified and said as much to him. "Not a chance!" Arthur replied. "You watch and learn."

This I was more than happy to do, naturally. Arthur had the remetalled bush machined to the tightest fit possible to go on the journal and, with liberal amounts of oil applied, literally hammered the side rod and bush onto the crankpin. A quick visit to see the running foreman to arrange to keep the 4F on short jobs for a week and hey presto, when removed and examined seven or eight days later, the crankpin was as smooth and as good as new. Another re-metalling of the bush, followed by machining to the correct clearances and the engine was released to traffic in the normal way. "And you won't find that in any book!" was Arthur's comment.

His oversize overalls and short legs combined to cause the seat of his attire to hang rather loosely and low around his nether regions, earning him the nickname 'Dragarse', shortened usually to 'Drag'! When he retired, allegedly at 65 years of age, it was rumoured that he was in fact nearer 70 than he would have you believe. It came as no surprise to me to learn that he had secured a position at a local factory performing some basic repetitive function on piecework and at the same time giving his fellow and much younger workmates a run for their money.

If Arthur cut his hand or finger or the like, he would not run to the First Aid man for a plaster or other such like treatment. He would plunge the offending digit or appendage into the nearest patch of grease and grime until it stopped bleeding then carry on. Anyone else would have suffered from blood poisoning or dermatitis but not him. You may search the 'Lancet' from cover to cover but Arthur's treatments and cures will be conspicuous by their absence.

A stalwart member of the 'Bug Ut' forum and one of the main voices in any debate whatever the subject; Arthur's alleged claim to fame was helping to build the Sydney Harbour Bridge. In fact the story was that Arthur had the help while building it, not the other way round, culminating in fitting the final and, naturally golden, rivet to complete the same. And no prizes for guessing who knocked it in and hammered it over! Whether or not it was true the story was told with great conviction and on more than one occasion let it be said.

Arthur, needless to say, like some of the other fitters, had been employed elsewhere prior to coming onto the Railway and, in common with most other itinerants, had been directed there during the war. Jack Turner had indeed been a soldier in the First World War, a fact that played no small part in the condition of his health in later years.

Ernie Thompson, another of this elite band of war directed fitters, was without question the preferred mate to be with in my early days. He, like Frank, would give you free reign to do all or most of the work although to, be fair, he did do his share as well. His wife did not enjoy very good health and, as she had not usually risen out of bed when he left for work, he had cultivated the habit of nipping back home, only about five or six minutes walk away, in the middle of the morning, usually around half past ten or so, to check on her health etc. On the way back he would call in the 'Coopers Arms' public house for a 'Livener' which meant in reality that once he had gone at - say 10:30 a.m. he rarely returned until after dinner at 1:30 pm. Very early on in our association, I realised that our recalcitrant foreman., Jack Hodgson was very aware of these morning jaunts; but could never really be sure of Ernie's whereabouts during the time of his absence. "Where's yer mate?" his Lancashire accent would grate in my ears with the enquiry as to Ernie's whereabouts, day after day.

I soon became an accomplished liar on Ernie's behalf, whilst trying to conceal his actual location from 'Hodgy'. "I think he's gone to the stores. Did you not pass him?" I would reply, or possibly the Fitting Shop or cabin, or tool cupboard or even the toilet would be substituted. "Isn't he underneath" was another ploy used from time to time. "I've just heard him hammering something not two minutes ago" I would further qualify the lie. Off he would go in whatever direction I had indicated. "How can he be so gullible?" I asked myself. Then, when he was out of sight, I would sneak off myself to the "Coopers" to find Ernie and tell him that the foreman was looking for him. Ernie would make some suitable but unprintable remark, buy me a half of bitter and carry on with his game of dominoes. So honour was satisfied. Ernie was happy that his wife was OK, I enjoyed my half pint and at the end of the day, 'Hodgy' got his engine with all the repairs completed; so everyone was happy.

Towards the end of my first year on the tools another fitter made his appearance back at the shed - one Johnny Webb, who had just completed his National Service in the R.A.F. He had joined up expecting to do an eighteen-month stint only to have it extended to two years just prior to his demobilisation owing to a National Emergency at the time. He was naturally not very pleased about this turn of events, particularly as his engineering skills had only been stretched to the challenge of assembling standard W.D. beds for the duration of his service. Johnny was an excellent tradesman and another of Joe Benson's protégés. His return coincided with the allocation of five Reidinger Valve fitted Crabs from Saltley in exchange for a number of our Walschearts fitted Standard Crabs, but more of them later.

As previously mentioned, other residents of the 'Bug Hut' included tubers and a boilersmith. The tubers were four in number, working in two teams. Bill Chadderton, known as 'Chaddy'; Johnny Sloane 'Sloany'; Ernie 'Brigham' Young and Maurice Percy, known as 'Mogs'. 'Chaddy' and 'Mogs' usually made up one team, with 'Sloany and 'Brigham' the other. Their duties consisted of repairs and replacements to both small smoke tubes and large superheater flue tubes. In addition they erected brick arches and later on, when they came in, refractory concrete arches as well.

Johnny Sloane, an Irishman of great energy and small stature, was a fairly young chap who, in common with many of his race, had been injected with a gramophone needle at birth, set at high speed and consequently chatted away incessantly and rapidly all day long. His mate Ernie Young, his direct opposite, was elderly, tall and a quiet sort of chap, of immense strength, which far belayed his appearance.

Burtons Brakedown crane. Photo: P. Webb

If, as occurred from time to time, a big end bolt or, more often a Stanier type solid crosshead, was over-tight and would not come apart, everyone in the shed would come and have a go in turn with the sledge. When Ernie tried and the offending article still would not break then you really did know that you were in trouble. Although he probably weighed only about 13 stone, he had the ability and flare to apply every single ounce of his weight behind every blow.

Johnny and Ernie worked well together and never to my knowledge had any disagreements. Indeed, to us apprentices, Johnny was like a big brother whereas

Ernie was like a father to us all. Chaddy and Mogs had a different arrangement whereby, once the job was in hand, in the mornings Mogs would disappear round to the lodge where he was courting the daughter and Chaddy would continue on his own until dinnertime when, following a visit to the 'Forest Gate', he would go to sleep in the 'Bug Ut' under the examiners desk in the afternoon while Mogs carried on where he had left off. Another of Chaddy's jobs was that of 'van man' on the breakdown train. His duties entailed looking after the riding van and tool van. These he continued to devote a whole day to, every week. Let it be said that they were never found wanting, with all the equipment to hand and in working order, packing available and riding van clean, victualled and watered. The crane, when it was included in the make up, was also kept fuelled and watered and in light steam, this being a joint responsibility with Sam McBride, who always drove it when available.

The crane, incidentally, originated on the Caledonian Railway and dated from I think 1886. It's lifting capacity was a useful 15 tons, ideal for most vans and wagons currently in use at the time.

Of the two boilersmiths, the chargehand Colin 'Dusty' Miller resided in the office with the Foreman fitter. The other one, Arnold Eaglefield, 'Arnie' to his friends, was a man in his middle fifties, typical of his breed, being quite hard of hearing, the result of a lifetime of boilermaking with it's constant hammering and riveting in a time when ear protection was unheard of and if it were, no doubt frowned upon by it's contemporaries. His eyesight was not all that good either, and he wore spectacles with very deep lenses. A very quiet person who I always felt a little sorry for as he seemed enclosed in his own world, no doubt as a result of his impaired hearing. But a thoroughly nice chap nevertheless. He spent all his working day changing broken firebox waterspace stays, both side and roof, the latter caulked and nutted, the former either riveted or as the roof stays, caulked and nutted also, depending on the class and type of engine. Examination and changing of lead plugs, that important piece of equipment in the roof of the firebox, was also the boilersmith's forte.

'Dusty' the chargehand boilersmith also shared some of his work, but quite a lot of his time was taken up in examinations following boiler wash outs, and paperwork. In later years, when a number of Mr Staniers Class 5's, 8F's and 'Jubilees' were allocated to the shed, it became the custom to give the boiler a water test prior to washouts when the pressure was boosted up to between 250 and 280 PSI. He would take perverse delight then in crawling around in the back of the smokebox looking for superheater element joint leaks, so that he could book them and clearly make a very dirty job for some unfortunate fitter or other.

When I was fitting I always tried to be present when this inspection was being made to the engine I was working on so I could see the leaks for myself. They often never showed up until well above the boilers working steam pressure of 225 PSI so I invariably treated the reports with the contempt they deserved and ignored them. They were usually only a very slight dribble anyhow. If there had been a serious blow affecting the performance of the engine, as I knew from my own footplate experience, then the driver would have reported it anyway and it would already have been entered on the card. The water test then would, of course, reveal which ones were at fault. I hope the reader will not be alarmed by this somewhat cavalier attitude for, let it be said, if I thought the leak required attention then it most certainly got it, even if it meant the engine being stopped for a week or more; not unknown with jobs of this nature.

I was only too aware, from my firing days, of the effects of steam blows in the smokebox, be they from superheater elements, main steampipes or whatever. Apart from the steam losses incurred, the detrimental effect to the creation of a partial vacuum therein affected the draw on the fire and pull of the heat so produced through the boiler tubes. Hence my comments about drivers' reports. In a nutshell – if no reports, then no problem.

The gauge frame fitter was one Harry Buggins. On permanent light duties, Harry had found his niche in the order of things by virtue of his job. His very essential and vital task consisted solely of the inspection and maintenance of the boiler gauge frames. He carried out 3 - 5 and 7 - 9 week examinations on all Burton engines. I am not quite sure just precisely what the difference was between the two exams, but one of the most important features was to ensure a clear passage through the top and bottom of the gauge frames to the water spaces above the firebox, thereby eliminating the risk of a false reading. The outcome of a false reading as to the water level in the boiler and over the firebox has been well documented before. Probably the most well known example being the Coronation Class Pacific during the war, crewed by a Passed Fireman and Cleaner which dropped it's plugs due to the firebox crown becoming uncovered whilst showing over half a glass of water in the frame, due to the bottom waterways being blocked with scale; an error which the unfortunate crew paid for with their lives. The attention that Harry gave to his duties ensured that this precise fault would never befall a 17B plated engine.

Harry's brother Jack was a driver at Burton with Jack's son Bob being a fireman at the time.

Of the two chargehand fitters, Ernie Gaskell was on days and Sam Hardy on nights. Ernie also carried out gauge frame exams along with Harry, as well as attending to his chargehand duties, which were not very exacting except when the Foreman was absent; when he stepped into his shoes and performed the duties in his place.

Sam Hardy, known on the shed and throughout the district as 'The Black Abbott', was a formidable character and quite the antithesis of Ernie who was of a quiet and retiring nature. Sam led his night shifts from the front and struck the fear of God into all who crossed him or disagreed with his methods and points of view. His house was at the top of our street, so I was perhaps more aware of his ways than most, prior to meeting him. His son, David, became an apprentice at the shed soon after I returned from my two years National Service. Sam, by this time on days, was covering for the Foreman who was on long term sickness by then. He used to rant and rave at the poor lad, as I was well aware, for many a long day. To the fitters however, it was something new and unknown and some of them were not long in saying so either, so disgusted were they of his attitude to his son, who had all the appearance of a nervous wreck. A bully Sam certainly was!!

His work methods were typical of the man. His talent for bending the rules was only exceeded by his ability to talk his way out of it when things went wrong. He was once called to question by the District Motive Power Superintendent himself when observed attempting to re-rail a 'Crab' of some 70 Tons with Burton's 15 Ton lift crane, only to remark that he was assisting the operation with jacks!! He later moved onto Foreman fitter at Wolverhampton Oxley, where no doubt, the Western Region wondered what had hit them.

Ernie's son Wally was the oldest hand apprentice when I started and had gone to Derby for his twelve-month stint in the Works the week previous. I was obviously aware of who he was from my cleaning days but did not make his acquaintance until the full year had elapsed. He was of stocky build with very blond, wavy hair. For some reason, which I never discovered, the Foreman did not like Wally at all. In consequence, contrary to normal practice, when he returned to the shed after his year at the Derby Works, he carried on as an apprentice right up until his twenty-first birthday. The usual thing being for the returning apprentice to be used as a fitter in his own right, and paid the same as well. This was certainly the case in my own experience and with the other apprentices as well. So, not only did Wally have to wait until he came out of his time before he worked on his own, but his pocket was heavily hit as well.

I always got on very well with him myself, although it is only fair to say that his mouth was often in gear before his brain as it were. His girlfriend, later to become his wife, had parents who owned one of the better class fish and chip shops in the town. I must confess to passing through a period of envy on that score for a while. To the extent of enquiring as whether or not his girl friend had a younger sister. Not that I was enamoured by his fiancé myself, but I was very partial to the products of her parents shop.

Next in line of seniority of the apprentices were Johnny Slater and Tony Marshall. Both had started about the same time and we got on really well, socialising together away from work with our current girl friends. Johnny had a flair for buying and selling, and it was seldom that he hadn't got some 'bargain' or other on offer.

On completing his National Service, he very soon left to take up a new career selling 'Corona Mineral Waters'. Within two years he was the top salesman, at least in his area if not the country so his progress through the company was assured. We kept in touch for a number of years, with his wife Elizabeth and my wife becoming very good friends. However, as our paths were moving in different directions, we eventually drifted apart and the last I heard of him he had a flourishing Off Licence and general grocery business. His father was Harold Slater who had to suffer my firing misdemeanours with a 4F on the Overseal Trippers.

Tony and I, on the other hand, did not see eye to eye on things in our early days, with us finally coming to blows one hot summer afternoon. All I can recall of it now was trying to avoid rolling into a puddle of dirty water during our contretemps. One thing was for sure however, it cleared the air, incidentally providing some entertainment for the rest of the staff at the time, with the two of us better respecting each other and becoming friends afterwards.

Now I was back in the shed environs all the time it wasn't long before our redoubtable shed shunter, George Terrington, searched me out again to run his bets for him whilst he was on his holidays. One driver, I recall, did a very complicated bet during one of these periods, involving seven or eight different horses at three different race meetings. He went to great pains explaining it all to me before presenting me with his stake money, which consisted of a ten shilling note; a princely amount in those days and nearly a quarter of my weekly wage. I only listened with half an ear, telling myself that the whole thing was far too complicated to have a chance of winning. However, along with the other sixpence each way and 'bob' roll-ups and the like, I duly trotted off to the Bookie's, making a special point of bringing this particular wager to his notice. He, for his part, hummed and harred for a while and then decided to accept it. "Don't give much for it's chances," was one of his contemptuous remarks. "Mind you, it would cost us a packet if it did come up," he observed. And so it proved to be! The winnings were presented to me in a sealed envelope so I am not sure of the amount. Sufficient to say, my commission, at sixpence (2½p) in the pound, was paid in paper money that week. As the driver wasn't on duty when I returned to the shed with his winnings I enquired of his home address and took it round at dinner time. I didn't want the responsibility of it and was glad to hand it over.

He invited me down the garden and into his shed before he opened the envelope and checked its contents. "What Her don't know, won't do her any harm." He commented in justification for his actions. A big smile creased his face as he handed me a £1 note and a cabbage, "for your mother," as he put it. I quickly pocketed the £1 and walked back down the path, openly displaying the cabbage for his wife's benefit. Very nice if you can pull it off, I reflected to myself, but how many times has it all gone wrong? I wondered. George just smiled when I told him about it. How many pounds in commission has he earned in his time?, I mused.

George was based at the top of the loco yard in a building, the origins of which, when first built, has always intrigued me. Its main function, in the fifties, was to act as a base and relief cabin for goods guards, a shunter's (George's) cabin and a workshop for the shed joiner.

This latter post was filled by one James Wallah when I first started at Burton Sheds. Jim, as he was known, was an ex brewery drayman or lorry delivery man and could reputedly down 14 pints of beer a day without any apparent impairment of his ability. I had known of Jim for many years having attended school with his daughter throughout my primary and junior years. His main duties consisted of repairing and replacing the footboards of the various engines on allocation to the depot, these naturally being very susceptible to damage by fire and hot coals, as one would imagine. Any other items around the shed and its environs manufactured from wood also received the attention of the shed joiner; it being more convenient to utilise his talents than secure the services of the Company's civil engineering department. Jim's official status was that of fitter's mate, as was his successor Frank Parker. We shall meet Frank later on when doing my stint on the Wheel Drop Plant.

On Frank's retirement, one Charlie Lester took up the reins. Charlie, also employed as a fitter's mate, was in truth a Time Served Carpenter and very proud of it. The quality of his work was soon apparent to the local shed hierarchy, who lost no time in requesting production of various articles to utilise this new found talent in their midst. To watch him work was a joy to behold. The obvious love for the material of his trade apparent in every stroke of his plane and chip of his chisel.

When my wife and I were contemplating marriage our early abode was to be the front room of my parent's home with the hallowed front room being our daytime residence and my bedroom for the nights. Now! the front room window had never been opened in my living memory and one had to be quick with the wedge to open the ones upstairs otherwise bruised fingers and blackened nails were the outcome. All that was required was a repair to the sash cords but as, until just prior to our wedding, the property had been rented (incidentally, from my Great Uncle), these repairs had not been carried out, the landlord, in common with most of his ilk, being reluctant to fund the operation. As neither my father or myself knew how to put these faults right, I sought the advice of Charlie.

"I'll come and show you," he said and duly called round one evening for the demonstration. Sure enough, in no time at all, the front room windows were running up and down the sash as efficiently as the day they were made. The look in my mother's face was a picture, so delighted was she at the result of Charlie's labours.

Inevitably, tea and cakes were produced and, following general conversation, it was discovered that Charlie's wife had delivered our milk during and, for a period after, the war, the delivery being made by the milkman, or I should say maid, by pony and trap with churns of milk aboard, out of which gallon jugs were filled for dispensing, at the door step, by pint and half pint measures into the customer's receptacles. And never a drop spilled I might add.

Charlie then looked on while I carried out the repairs to our bedroom window. I have repaired many a broken sash cord since, both for others and ourselves but not once without bringing Charlie to mind.

Charlie's talents did not stop there. After we were married he invited my wife and I to his little terraced house one evening where, to our surprise, we saw within his living room, he had installed a complete chapel organ including all the pipes. And he proved to be an accomplished organist as well.

Another dubious distinction to sit on his family's shoulders was that of being bombed out during the war; one of only five families in Burton to be so unfortunate, luckily at least in Charlie's case, without loss of life.

The nickname 'Wag' was applied to Charlie so when his son, also Charlie, started as an apprentice he, naturally, became known as 'Little wag,' or 'Wag Junior.'

Not all the fitters were resident in the 'Bug Ut' by any means. Another small group of characters were based, for want of a better word, in the machine shop. Of these, the most outstanding were Sam McBride and Jimmy Mullett. Sam, a Lowlands Scotsman and proud of it, was another draughtee, directed to railway work during the war; having previously been a resident of Burton by reason of being employed by the Scotch Foundry in the town. Sam's talents were legion, particularly when out with the breakdown gang, of which he was undisputed leader; the foreman aside.

Partial to a pint of Marston's, followed, in common with many of his race, by a whisky chaser; his favoured hostelry was The Forest Gate which was just on the far side of the Moor Street Bridge at the bottom of the slope from the level crossing next door to the Tin (Elam) Church previously mentioned; both buildings catering for the good of the soul, dependent on the participant's point of view.

Jimmy Mullett was an ex North Stafford man, born and bred; also a regular patron of the Moor Street hostelry. He had the misfortune to suffer from a stammer that got progressively more pronounced in coincidence with his liquor intake, which was quite prolific; so much that, after a good dinnertime session, he would become completely impossible to understand and as a result any conversations in the afternoon were reduced to a series of swear words, his ability to impart never appeared to be impaired. He had, I believe, served his time in the Stoke Works of the old 'Knotty', being transferred to Burton, as was the way in those days, at a later date. Here he sampled the local product with dire consequences. Some said, rather unkindly I thought, that he only came to Burton because he couldn't get the words out to refuse.

Jimmy's skills in locomotive management and repair were second to none and he could time a set of valves with the best of them, provided of course that it was before dinnertime. Also a member of the breakdown gang, Jim drove the crane when Sam wasn't available; which, I understand, caused a few anxious moments for the other members of the gang. Jim's Mate in the early days of my apprenticeship was Jim Carvell with Sid Booth mating Sam McBride.

I had very little to do with Mr. Carvell who was well into his sixties when I made his acquaintance. Of Sid, more later.

The other fitter resident in the machine shop was Dennis Hickin. Dennis was a young man who had recently finished his National Service, and was the apprentice immediately before Johnny Webb. I think I only worked with Dennis two or three times at the most and when I returned from my twelve month stint in the Works at Derby he had left to take up employment elsewhere; with the Coal Board I believe.

When Joe Carvell retired, Sam's brother John McBride secured employment in his place and, naturally, in no time was mating his kinsman.

During the course of the day, when not in the machine shop, they would all gather for their mid morning break in the far corner of the new (No.2) Shed where the firebricks were stored. The gently curved shapes of these bricks lent themselves to some imaginative uses and it wasn't long before our intrepid gang had fashioned some very comfortable armchairs with a few old bolt sacks for a bit of padding.

Back in the machine shop all the work created by the Mileage Exams and Wheel Drop Plant kept the machinist very busy. This person, who's name I cannot recall, performed wonders with the ancient machines at his disposal. A large and a small lathe, planing machine, grindstone and pedestal drill made up the machinery, arranged around the sides of the room with a marking out table in the centre. All of these were of great antiquity, rumoured to have been purchased by the Midland Railway from Noah when he had finished using them for completed the Ark!! Originally belt driven from an overhead line shaft, the brackets for which were still in position on the wall, they had all been fitted with electric motors by the time I arrived on the scene.

When the various axleboxes, bushes, slide blocks, crossheads and big ends brasses, eccentric sheaves and the like, not forgetting valve guide sleeves, piston packings and sundry pins and fastenings, his time was certainly full. In all of these labours our machinist was assisted by one – Ted Gopsall. Ted was another character I wish I had been able to get to know better. He had a sense of humour all of his own and his dry wit was unique to himself. As an example, one thing sticks in my mind whenever I think about him. It was the custom, whenever a meeting of the staff was called by the Union representative to discuss some grievance or other, to hold it in the machine shop. All effected parties would attend and, after hearing the arguments for and against from both sides, the floor would be thrown open for general discussion and debate. When everyone had had his say the steward would ask if anyone else had anything to add before putting the matter to the vote. At this point, much to the amusement of us apprentices I might add, Ted would stand up and always guaranteed to say, "Well brothers, it's clear to me that summat needs to be done about summat." In spite of or in consequence of this, the vote would be made by a show of hands and we would all return to work. How I wish I had known Ted for longer before he retired.

Another story concerning Ted was related to me on more than one occasion. Apparently, this occurred one winter's night during the war. Ted was working until six o'clock at night and on checking off, fell in beside one of the Running Foreman, also going home, who lived four doors away from Ted. On reaching the foreman's house, Ted wished him good night and continued the few paces to his own door. The foreman happened to look round - only to see in the moonlight that Ted had a huge lump of coal under his arm! The foreman shook his head and thanked The Lord that they hadn't met any Railway Police; a not unknown occurrence by any means. They would both have been for the high jump for who would have believed that the unfortunate foreman would be unaware of Ted's illicit burden!!

Before the various parts coming for attention in the machine shop could be turned or planed they first had to be re-metalled by the coppersmith – the redoubtable Charlie Tovey. Mr.Tovey was yet another character in a shed full of them. However, sad to say, his sense of humour and general attitude to life did not endear him to many. He was the only person in my entire experience who always wore his overalls with the top button fastened all the time, which, with his bulbous neck protruding above the collar, gave the appearance of him being constantly strangled. I could understand the need for such precautions whilst re-metalling, when a splash of hot metal down the front of your attire could prove quite exciting, but not all the time.

Promptly at 11 o'clock every morning Charles would stop whatever he was doing and, putting on his coat, would proceed at a sedate pace down the path to the Forest Gate for his beer. He made no secret of it and, unlike others, who crept away by various routes and times to different hostelries, strode off without any attempt at concealment. Jack Hodgson, our foreman, was very much aware of

Charles's perambulations but Jack's numerous remonstrations with him made no difference. Jack did not push the point too far as he knew he would have great difficulty replacing Charles, if at all. Charles was, of course, aware of this and made the excuse that if he was still working at a proper coppersmith's he would have had his beer supplied and paid for by the firm; a local tradition that I believe was practiced elsewhere in the town. There was no question that Charles Tovey was very good at his job. I personally never knew of one single instance when the white metal parted from it's fused surface once applied by him; which was more than could be said for some of the items so treated at the Derby Works. Following his daily jaunts to 'The Gate' he would always return on time to continue his work and scowl at all and sundry until knocking-off time. He also had a sense of humour all of his own; the type of thing amusing him being, for instance, when presenting him with a broken steam sand supply pipe for repair and asking him for a replacement, he would give you one of an opposite hand to the one you asked for, although he could have just as easily given you a correct one, knowing full well it would be difficult or impossible to fit.

Charles shared the shop with Bill Dunkerley the tinsmith, who he appeared to like and a succession of blacksmiths who he positively hated. They, unlike the tinsmith, made a lot of noise with their anvil hammering and, of course, also generated a lot of heat with the hearth. I quite enjoyed a bit of blacksmithing myself, finding the exact science of metal heating and fusion fascinating. This, needless to say, did not place me in a good light with Charles either.

When setting valves on inside motion engines fitted with Stephensons valve gear or link motion, as it was officially known; if the valve travel had to be altered, this was done by either drawing out, to lengthen the stroke of the eccentric or jumping, to shorten the same, if the reverse was required. This, of course, required the hearth to be lit and heat generated, to enable the appropriate eccentrics to be so treated. This, along with the inevitable pools of water from the leaky press, was a constant source of annoyance to Charles.

Bob Ferraby, the last blacksmith we had, an ex Army farrier and a master of his art, was well aware of Charles' disapproval and hostility so, having failed to make his peace with him, annoyed Charles further by hammering twice when once would do and tapping the anvil between blows in an apparent, thoroughly professional although somewhat unnecessary manner. Additionally, asking Charles to help by giving a blow, when Bob was using a former leaving him no hands free for the hammer, nearly gave Charles apoplexy, procuring a curt reminder, as if one were required, that he was a coppersmith and a tradesman, not a blacksmith's striker, the last point being emphasised with a sneer. Little Bill Dunkerley would take up the hammer and oblige with Bob smiling to himself, as Charles looked on, glaring as usual.

Bill, the tinsmith, was a real gentleman and the exact opposite to his contemporary Charles. He would do anything he could to be of help to anyone. His main duty was the repair and maintenance of engine and guard lamps. These latter were quite an elaborate affair with a swivel incorporated in the design allowing three different aspects, one red, one green and one white, to be shown whilst being held; being lit by oil, in common with those of the engine. Guards, being human, liked to keep their own lamp and in consequence, were always prevailing upon Bill's good nature to put right any faults occurring in their own 'personal' ones.

Now! It's no secret that guards and goods guards in particular, by the nature of their job, were occasionally given the odd present by appreciative local station staff and shunters or the like, for services rendered. It was not unknown therefore, for some of this fare to find it's way into Bill's workshop by way of thanks from the occasional guard. The odd rabbit, cabbage, bag of fruit for example. Charles viewed all this through jaundiced eyes, as he had never been known to do anyone a favour in my experience. But Bill by his very nature, would always share this generosity with Charles, such was his way. Bill had a shop and so could always be relied on to supply the odd packet of cigarettes, box of matches and the like. He even ran a 'tick' account, with participating clients settling up on paydays.

Some days Charles would be even more cantankerous than usual, giving a professional opinion about some aspect of coppersmithing, which naturally, nobody could argue with. He often complained that the apparatus at his disposal precluded him from repairing the larger pipes, as he could not get them hot enough to braze. This necessitated an occasional journey to the Derby Works, a task often for one or possibly two of the apprentices, if the job was urgent. One such trip that stands out in my mind was with a broken tender steamheat supply pipe, which ran underneath the full length of the tender. It was from an old Midland Class 2P and was in two almost equal halves when we took it to the Works for repair. Down to the station we went, each carrying one half and on the arrival of the train, dumped them into the brakevan, then sat back in the next compartment to enjoy the journey. Collecting our pipes on arrival at Derby we duly carried them over the bridge to the Works and into the coppersmith's for the repair.

"Charlie havin' a black-un on 'im again" was the usual greeting from the shop foreman on our arrival, his notoriety having spread to Derby we were amused to learn. "Come back for it dinner time," he would add and so we would go for a stroll around the Works to try and seek out Wally who was doing his twelve months there. All straightforward so far. Dinnertime arrived and we made our way back to the coppersmith's shop for our steam heater pipe. There it lay – all thirty feet of it! We looked at each other, both having the same thoughts. "We shall have some fun with this on the way back!" We didn't realise the half of it!

First we had to get it over the bridge to the station and once there, over the station footbridge to the opposite platform 4 and 6. The Works Bridge was fairly easy but we weren't very popular with the Works staff dashing back in the opposite direction after their meal break. On the station platform we had to weave around parcel barrows and the travelling public to reach the station footbridge where we found that, having climbed the stairs with our burden, it was too long to negotiate the corner at the top. So – back down again to have a re-think. A GPO porter came along, driving one of those little tractors towing a train of parcel barrows loaded, in part, with parcel bags. Johnny Slater flagged him down and asked him if he was going to platform 4 and 6. He was so we prevailed upon him to take our pipe and us with him. John climbed on the first barrow and I on one three or four back and thus, holding the pipe between us, set off down the ramp to negotiate the tunnel under the station. The postman took it very slowly and with the widest of sweeps round the bends we duly arrived safely on platform 4 and 6.

Thanking him profusely we walked to the south end of the platform to await our train. It duly arrived and proved to be a Newcastle – Bristol Express made up of the then brand new BR Standard Mark 1 stock. At least, the front brake was. These brakes had a corridor along the side with the parcel section divided by a wire mesh screen; not like the open van style LMS stock we were used to. To make matters worse, this parcel section was full to the roof with mailbags and locked up. There was nothing else for it but to thread our pipe down the corridor alongside. This we attempted to do but even with both double doors open, geometry came into play and proved that the 30 odd feet long copper pipe would not thread down a 4-foot wide gangway via a seven-foot opening (coach measurements guessed at!) While all this had been going on the fireman had topped up the tank, the passengers had all alighted or boarded and the guard was standing behind us; not too pleased with our performance. In frustration, I gave the pipe an almighty kick and it sprung into the brake. The guard slammed the doors as we scurried in after the pipe and, at a blast of the guard's whistle; we were away – 3 minutes late and all down to us.

"What are we going to do at Burton to get it out?" I wondered. "Don't worry, we'll think of something," Johnny reassured me. I wish I were so confident I thought, having visions of travelling to Birmingham with the blasted thing or even, Heaven forbid, Bristol. Twelve minutes elapsed and we were running into Burton station. "Two minutes we've got here," the guard informed us testily, "Make sure you don't hold us up any more." A threat more than a statement and we were left in no doubt he meant it. We dived off the train as it stopped, wrenched open the doors and pulled the pipe for all we were worth. We managed to yank the end out just past the door edge when Johnny trapped two of his fingers between. Yelling and swearing, we pulled all the more but to no avail. My earlier fears seemed justified. A glance down the platform showed the station inspector giving the 'right away' to the guard, whose presence behind us was becoming quite unnerving. "You've not heard the last of this," he threatened, "Kick it back in and let's get them doors shut." "No way!" Johnny retorted, his fingers throbbing with pain, "Get a hold of it and give us a pull instead of just bellyaching!" The fireman, looking back for the 'right away' signal and seeing our plight, got down from the footplate and came to see what was going on. He immediately lent a hand and, with the three of us pulling and the guard kicking it from inside, the pipe came free. Slam! – Slam! Went the doors and, with a blast on the whistle, the Class 5 heaved the train away up the slope over Moor Street and on towards Birmingham; the guard leaning out of the window shouting something indecipherable back at us.

"I think we've upset him," Johnny remarked as we hoisted our pipe, now with a distinct bend, onto our shoulders, walking it back down the path to the shed. When we arrived, the fitter whose task it was to replace it under the old 2P's tender remarked about the bend at the one end. "I wonder why they didn't straighten that out," he commented, "It's going to be awkward to put back like that." Johnny and I looked at each other and said nothing.

Nothing more officially was heard by us of the incident but one of the office girls confided that the shed master had received a letter from the traffic office about the delay to the 12.45 ex Derby, Newcastle to Bristol train of five minutes in total, charged to the Motor Power Department and the complaint had been mentioned to our foreman. Sufficient to say that, so far as I am aware, no further items of any length were ever sent by passenger train again but always had to wait for transport in the stores van overnight.

I used to enjoy my trips to the Derby Works, one of the frequent reasons being to collect the new piston and valve rings for use on engines undergoing Mileage Exams as, being brittle, they often got damaged and broken; sent in the stores van which would visit possibly four different sheds in a night and contain innumerable heavy items such as locomotive springs, sets of motion, i.e. connecting and coupling rods, crossheads and the like, along with boiler fittings, injectors and so on. On arrival at the Works one reported to the Progress Clerk in his office who, in the fullness of time, would lead a string of lads from various depots around the Works collecting various items for each individual. Yet another 'Charlie', the abuse that man; who always reminded me of Winston Churchill; took, on our behalf, day after day was disgusting, yet I never heard him be anything but polite in return. Always saying, "Thank you," to the various issuers each and every time on his rounds. What would the real Winston have said? I often wondered. But then, who would have dared argue with that great man in the first place!

Whereas most of the time these jaunts were to Derby I did go on two occasions to Horwich near Bolton, once for a 'Crab' whistle and the other, a part for a Reidinger valve gear rotary drive. Getting there was quite a marathon entailing changing trains at Manchester and Bolton, the latter to catch the one coach shuttle to the Works. I unfortunately never went to Crewe, much as I would have liked to, though I did once make the trip to Colwick near Nottingham, then an Eastern Region Shed, to procure some parting tackle and a big end cap nut for a J39. This entailed catching a bus for the last part of the journey from Nottingham to the depot, but more of that later.

Many were the pranks we apprentices got up to during our working day. One such occurrence came about when a van was shunted into the shed for the onward dispatch of dried sand to possibly Overseal or Horninglow, the loading of which I had been involved on more than one occasion when a cleaner. Not now of course, as an apprentice. In one of the dim corners of this van lay a box, by now long past the sell by date, of fish. It was just beginning to make it's presence known by it's increasingly ripe smell. The cleaner's chargehand, by then George Edwards, or 'Twinkletoes' as he was known, owing to his rather small size of shoes, was going to dispose of this box in the usual way, into the firebox of the nearest engine in steam. This we volunteered to do for him and he accepted but not before removing one of the larger specimens, a Haddock, Wally declared. He should know, we reasoned, with his chip shop connections. After careful observation, we seized our moment, dashing into 'Hodgy' the foreman's office and placing it on a ledge in the darker recesses of the wall under his desk. There it lay for over a week, smelling stronger and stronger by the day and being slowly cooked into the bargain by the not inconsiderable heat of the nearby office stove. One of the unfortunate outcomes of this enterprise was to bring Hodgy out into the shed more frequently than usual, not endearing us to our colleagues one little bit. Poor old Stan Hoult endured the smell longer than most until, in desperation, he implored us to remove it whilst he kept Hodgy out of the way on some pretext or other. Stan of course knew what and where it was all the time but never let on, pretending not to have discovered it's presence either. A good lad was Stan and a hero to have put up with it for so long.

Just prior to my commencement as an apprentice Les Bull got married. His wife was a Gresley girl and, as was quite usual in those days, their early-married days were spent living in and sharing the bride's parent's home. This entailed a daily return trip by train from Gresley to the Works. Whilst the train times were comfortably scheduled allowing him plenty of time for his journey into Burton for his 8 a.m. check-in time, the same could not be said of the return trip. His aim was to catch the 5.12 p.m. out of Burton station if possible, saving him over an hour wait for the 6.20 p.m. alternative. To expedite this aim Les had his cycle positioned by the shed doorhole. Following check off, he would dash round the shed and leap aboard his bike, pedalling furiously down the path into Wellington Street where his sister would be waiting at her front door to relieve him of it before he dashed off on foot to the station. We watched this circus act for many evenings until one bright sunny afternoon temptation got the better of us.

The 'Crab' for the 6,50 London was standing all prepared on the long corner pit down towards the 'Bug Ut' and under the shear legs. We thought it would be a good idea to hoist Les's bike onto the back of the tender and from there, hang it on the hook of the shear legs hoist. This we duly did, retiring to the 'Bug Ut' to await events. We did not finish our time until 5.30 so we were in no hurry to depart. Hardly had we completed our plan when, to our chagrin, the crew climbed aboard the Crab, drove off the pit and out of the shed, leaving Les's cycle hanging some twenty feet or so in the air. The sun shining through the roof illuminated the bike, casting its shadow onto the off-white whitewashed wall dividing the two sheds, above, appropriately, the shadow board. In due course Les came charging round the table-hole, dashing towards the doorway, arms outstretched to grab his bike handlebars prior to leaping on and pedalling away in his normal smooth and well practiced manner. But not that night. The bike being absent from it's usual place, he crashed into the wall, falling in a heap half way through the door. Scrambling up he stared about, not having time to be angry, just nonplussed, crying, "Where's my bike?" and yelling, "I'll miss my train!"

"Perhaps it's gone without you" one wag suggested unsympathetically. Calming down from his initial panic and realising he was not going to be a passenger on the 5.12 that evening, he started to look around. It took maybe three minutes for him to notice the outline of his trusty steed etched in the sunlight on the wall, a further minute to discover its exact location then no time at all to see our faces pressed against the 'Bug Ut' window. With the intuition of a mastermind he put two and two together, concluding, in a further millisecond of time who the perpetrators of the crime were; so fast in fact that we were lucky to scramble out of the hut before he got at us.

"OK then, where's the ladder?" he asked us, his remark suitably embellished with certain unprintable invectives. Now! Ladders were a rare commodity in a loco shed, at least ones long enough to reach the 'Lesmobile'. Just in time to save the moment a 4F rumbled onto the turntable. Our little gang dashed over to persuade the driver to stable his engine under the shear legs.

"Gaffer won't like it put there," he commented, "He likes to keep the long pits for the big engines." "We know that," we answered, "But Les would like his bike back." Our saviour looked up to see the machine suspended and, having a good laugh, obliged us by backing down to allow the tender to occupy the position recently vacated by the Crab.

We gave Les a wide berth for the next few days but he soon got his own back on us by threading our jackets along the handrail of a 3F, stopped for boiler and firebox repairs which had some lagging removed to allow some new stays to be riveted over on the outside. On replacing the lagging and then the handrail the opportunity was too good for him to miss. After first threading the sleeves of our coats along the rail, he hammered home, really well, the taper pins securing the rail then riveted the ends over for good measure. We put in some unpaid overtime that night before we managed to retrieve our attire; I can tell you. So, honour was satisfied and life continued nice and peacefully, at least until the next time …

A few months after the cycle incident Les and his wife purchased a house in Burton, in the next street to where I lived. To meet the mortgage requirements certain repairs to the house had to be carried out within a set period of time; 3 months I think. Nothing exceptionally serious but nevertheless time consuming. One of these tasks was the painting of the house on the outside and, feeling I had the experience, having just helped my father paint our own abode, I duly volunteered my services to Les. Between us we burnt off the old paintwork, primed, undercoated and glossed the whole house. It looked a picture when we had finished, putting the street to shame. The woodwork in a pleasant shade of brown with the stonework cream, after the fashion of the day. Even this painting work was not without incident when his small son, then about 15 months old, assisted me by plunging his arm into the paint tin covering his previously pristine, white angora wool cardigan to one with a brown sleeve, his hand and forearm to match. I fortunately managed to prevent him from testing his taste buds by blocking the next move to his mouth, much to his disgust.

One of the anomalies to catch out the unwary, particularly strangers, was the differing diameters of the two turntables. The one in the No.2 Shed, the most convenient for engines entering just for the purpose of turning, was 55 feet, whereas the old No.1 Shed table was 2 feet longer at 57 feet diameter. One outcome of this was that Jubilees with 4,000 gallon Stanier tenders could only use the Old Shed, whereas those with the similar looking Stanier 3,500 gallon tenders could use both; as indeed could the Fowler fitted varieties. Another and more surprising instance was with the last batch of Class 5's, modified by Ivatt, which had a slightly longer engine wheelbase and modified intermediate drawgear combining to extend the overall wheelbase just those few inches to prevent them from fitting onto the New Shed turntable. Leicester had a couple of these later Class 5's, numbered in the 4466X series and they would sometimes turn up with the late afternoon local which came on the shed to turn and have it's tank filled prior to returning about 6.20, about an hour and ten minutes being allowed between it's arrival at Burton station and it's return departure time.

Imagine the crew's surprise when, having turned older members of the Class earlier in the week, albeit a tight fit, they found that the engine they were blessed with that night was just too long to fit. A few gentle shunts back and forth usually occurred before they were convinced, then they were forced to make a mad dash back to the yard and reverse back, through the congestion usually present, to gain access to the other turntable in the Old Shed; all the while the clock ticking relentlessly towards departure time from the station. The charade played out before us apprentices, with the firemen running back and forth up and down the table not believing what they were seeing, always provided a little amusement before we relented and let them in on the cause of the problem that they were obviously unaware of beforehand. I believe the Leicester LDC had an agreement draughted barring this batch of engines from that particular working as the delays caused by having to gain access to the Old Shed table was leading to real risks of late starts for the return working.

Around 1960, three BR Class 9F's were allocated to Burton. These, naturally, would not fit either table so maintenance and boiler washing out presented a problem. Boiler washing was done in the New Shed doorhole, effectively blocking access to the roundhouse whilst this was being done. Also, any maintenance requiring access below the engine had also to be done in the same location, though naturally not at the same time. The inconveniences of these arrangements were considerable, so much so that arrangements were soon made to exchange these locomotives with Stanier Class 8F's; Toton scraping their barrel to find a selection of run down specimens with which to effect the exchange. Operational considerations had also to be taken into account, thus the duties for which the 9F's were allocated went with them, the lesser duties commissioned to the alternative power being substituted. Before the change an alternative was suggested that the pit directly opposite the running-in road be extended through the wall to accommodate the new engines but the idea was rejected as too costly. Perhaps, if they had asked him, Jack Pullman may have made the hole in the wall for them thus reducing the brickwork alteration costs by 50%. Sorry Jack! Only joking!

My next move, apprentice-wise, was up onto the Drop Pit, as will be seen in the next chapter…

Chapter 12

Up the Drop Pit

The 'Drop Pit', or Wheel Drop Pit to give it's correct name, was situated in the loco yard on the South side of the No.1 (Old Shed). Installed in the 1930's as part of the LMS Locomotive Depot modernisation plan, instigated prior to the second world war, it's completion was the only significant improvement at the depot; with the sole exception of electric lighting in six designated 'concentration pits' in the No.2 (New) Shed; the proposed modern coaling plant being cancelled presumably by the impending hostilities.

It was the normal practice at the time to base two sets of artisans on the Drop Pit, working days and nights, week and week about.

Tommy Turner was the fitter on days on my first morning up there along with his mate Frank Parker, who I have briefly mentioned earlier. Both these two characters had worked together for a number of years and were well set in their ways. The introduction of a third person, namely me, was something for which they were unprepared, though it had obviously occurred several times before. I was immediately aware of the remark, "You'll enjoy that, I don't think," made by my fellow apprentices when they heard 'Hodgy' telling me to go up there on that first morning. However, I resolved to make the best of it. After all – I had faced 'Cock' Ford and lived to tell the tale so what the hell!

Tommy was a local town councillor and also owned a shop, selling general and green grocery on Calais Road, quite near to where one of my aunts lived; who, incidentally, wouldn't dream of shopping there except in desperation, preferring to use a rival establishment further along the road. I therefore resolved to refrain from mentioning my relationship when in his company. He always wore an extremely ancient and heavily grease encrusted flat cap from beneath which sprouted a mop of straggly, grey hair. At the end of my first day in his company I was amused to discover, when he removed the cap and exchanged it for a more seemly replacement to travel home in, that this straggly fringe of grey was the only hair he possessed, the remainder of his head being bald. An ex North Stafford man, he had learned his trade in Stoke Workshop and his skill and knowledge of the steam engine were without question.

Although a labour councillor, his leaning towards the extreme ranks of communism was very real, becoming apparent as the weeks went by. I soon decided however that, come the day, Tommy saw himself not as a common serf but a commissar. He was treasurer of the local Burton Artisans Sick Club, to which we all paid sixpence (2½p) per week, receiving in return, if ill for more than two weeks, the princely sum of £2 per week for a limited period of time. Whilst this may not appear to be very much by today's standards, it was significant all those years ago when a skilled man earned only four or five pounds a week and there was no company sick pay, only the government scheme. When a man had a family to provide for with rent and rates or even a mortgage to find, that £2 was a considerable help. A couple of years or so after I had made his acquaintance, Tom and his family decided to emigrate to Canada, coincidental with his re-election to the council. He decided not to stand for his ward but, being then asked to serve as the next Town Mayor, put his emigration plans on hold agreeing to stand again. However, he did no canvassing nor hold any meetings in support of his stand and, come the Election Day, failed to retain his seat. He then made local history, albeit infamously, by becoming the first and I think the only mayor of the borough who was not an elected member of the Council at the same time.

Following his term of office as Mayor his emigration plans were revived and, in consequence, he left the service. As I knew where he lived I was asked by 'Hodgy' to call and collect the books and bank papers for the sick club from him. I cycled to his very palatial bungalow and was amazed to have the door opened in answer to my ring by a maid complete with black dress and white apron. "You should preach communism!" I reflected, "You're more Conservative than Winston Churchill!!"

An ex MR Class 2P 4-4-0 is stabled on the drop pit road as a 3F receives attention inside. Photo: Authors Collection.

Tommy's mate – Frank Parker, was a nice quiet chap who left Tom to get on with things, helping out and doing all that was required without, hardly, a word being said. A real good mate was Frank. He came to work on his old faithful cycle and was rarely seen, on or off the premises, without it. Some said that he even went to bed on it, though I imagine Mrs. Parker would have had something to say about that. All that swarf on the sheets indeed!

The Drop Pit itself consisted of a pit, some twenty feet or so deep in which was mounted a hydraulic ram on top of which was the all-important table. On each long side of this table a cast steel bridge piece some three feet in height was mounted, atop of which was a running rail. These two cast bridge pieces were so arranged as to give a running line gauge to match the standard track gauge of 4' 8½" The table was approximately 10 feet long.

When lowered down the hole a pair of girders were so arranged by chains and counterweights to move into position when the table was roughly ten feet into it's descent, enabling a continuity of the running line to be maintained when they moved into position. This, of course, enabled the engine under repair to be drawn off after the wheels and axles had been removed; and, of course, conversely, for the engine to be re-positioned for re-wheeling on completion of repairs. As the hydraulics system used water as it's power medium it was essential that it never froze up. Consequently, a very large cast iron stove was provided in the centre of the corrugated iron clad, steel framed shed, which housed the plant. Naturally, being on a railway premises with an inexhaustible supply of fuel, this stove never ever in my memory, went out - winter and summer alike - and in consequence attracted a considerable number of visitors throughout the 24-hour day (though, of course, not so many when Tommy Turner was on).

The hydraulics themselves were pressurised by a triple expansion pump, which looked somewhat like a small single direction steam engine, with the pumping action to the three cylinders being applied through connecting rods complete with big and little ends and crossheads. The drive shaft was powered, via a wide and long canvas drive-belt, by an ancient electric motor dated 1933. Sadly, after all those years, I have forgotten the names of the manufacturers of both the pump and the motor but the pump at least deserved a place in a museum – even then. I can still hear it's rattling clatter in my mind's ear as it free-wheeled, with it's note changing to a heavy thump – thump as the pressure was applied to the lift table. Marvellous, happy, happy times. Will we ever see their like again? Sadly, probably not.

The building itself, in common with the rest of the entire shed premises, was lit by gas. At some point in time an extension pipe had been run down one of the supporting columns and to that a gas ring was attached, it's main function being to boil the water to mash the inevitable cup of tea. A simple matter you might think. To fill a kettle with water, place it on the ring, wait for it to boil and then mash the tea in whatever receptacle you favoured. Wrong! Or at least not where Tom was concerned. He had a small saucepan into which a measured amount of water was poured. This was placed upon the ring and, as it was hotted up, a china teapot was produced. When the water approached boiling point, closely watched by Tommy, it's contents were poured into this pot, which was then placed carefully aside, a clean hand cloth having been folded and positioned on top of the metal bench to receive it. Another measured amount of water was added to the saucepan and the boiling process re-commenced. After an adjudged period of time the china teapot, now nicely warmed, was emptied of it's contents and two precise measures of tea leaves were placed therein. At the exact moment the water in the saucepan came to the boil (no sooner and certainly not later) it's contents were poured into the pot and onto the tea leaves. A teaspoon was produced and the pot contents were stirred so many times one-way and an equal amount of times the other. It was then left to stand for, naturally, an exactly calculated period of time before being poured into Tommy's china cup complete with saucer and Frank's old earthenware mug, each containing, of course, an exact amount of milk. Another minute or so would elapse before Frank was handed his mug. Tom would then sit down with cup and saucer in hand, raise the cup to his lips, take a sip and declare with a smile of pleasure and satisfaction, "Excellent. Perfect." Thank goodness neither of them took sugar. I don't think I could have stood for any more. This ritual was carried out twice a day, every day, with Frank patiently sitting by the stove and puffing away at his pipe. No offer of a cup was ever made to me or, so far as I could ascertain, anyone else either. I took to mashing with the boiler-washers who had made their own 'brick-arch' furniture outside the sandhole with a duplicate suite inside the shed for cold, wet inclement days. Tommy would describe this tea making ritual in great detail and the explanation would be carried out with as much conviction as when explaining some detail or information about the workings of the Drop Pit and engines thereon.

Tommy and Frank's opposite numbers on the other shift, I was to meet the following week. The fitter, (another Tom) Marshall, was a Londoner of indeterminate background; another wartime directed fitter although he had served a period of time in the RAF. He had always got a car for sale and sometimes turned up in a different one two or three times in the same week. He had a name as a bit of a wide boy, a reputation for which he seemed inordinately proud. A completely laid-back character, he was easy going and the complete opposite of his namesake on the other shift. His mate, Les Wilshee, a stocky chap sporting a Ronald Coleman moustache, was a happy type who liked nothing better than a yarn or a good story. He was, however, a little deaf and did not always hear precisely what was said so, in consequence, sometimes came out with the wrong replies; which added to the fun. Life was one big laugh with these two in contrast to their counterparts who nearly bored a teenager to sleep. With the Turner – Parker team it was very obvious that Tommy was in charge but with these two it was near impossible to tell.

When a locomotive ran an axlebox hot a certain amount of work had to be done before the engine could be positioned over the Drop Pit table. If a coupled wheel axlebox was in need of repair, as was usually the case, any motion involved had first to be removed. With inside motion engines, usually of the six wheel, three axle variety ex Midland and LMS vintage, the coupling rods were removed complete but with outside motion engines if the trailing axleboxes were the ones affected then only the side rod gradient pins were knocked out and the rear section of the coupling rod removed. Indeed, though not always the case, on Black 5s it was the trailing boxes that ran hot most. The reader may recall that this was the case with the Class 5 at Derby on the occasion of my loan to that shed when a Passed Cleaner. That engine found it's way to Burton for repair, as did most engines suffering from this fault in the district.

The removal of the gradient pin called for careful positioning of the engine to enable the said pin to pass between the spokes of the wheel. First the securing cotters and nuts were removed, and then a request was made to the running foreman for a driver and engine to assist in the operation. This was frequently my old mate Dickie Smith. An engine in steam would be coupled up and the loco under repair gently moved until the desired position was arrived at. The pin on the one side would be removed and then the process was repeated for the other side. The same situation applied, of course, even if all the motion had to be removed. Then, the little end gudgeon pin had to be so set to pass out of the crosshead and through the spokes behind, with the added need of the big end being at the bottom position of the driving wheel at the same time. This applied, of course, whenever a side of motion was taken down in the shed as well. Once this was completed we would ask the driver to push the engine over the outside pit to complete the stripping of other items, which would impede the removal of the axle; for instance, sand pipes, brake rods, cylinder drain cock control rods (known to us as taprods) and other ancillary fittings like exhaust injector steam supply pipes (a job and a half in themselves). If the weather was bad, i.e. snowing or raining, we would have the engine pushed straight over the table and remove all these other bits and pieces under cover but it was a lot more convenient to carry out these jobs outside if possible.

An unidentified Class 4F stands on the sandhole road with its leading axle removed. Photo: D. Chance.

Having got the engine onto the Drop Pit with the affected axles/wheels positioned centrally on the table, another factor had to be considered before starting removal of that axle – (wheelset or set of wheels). Whereas a Class 5, 8F or Jubilee, and the like, could be towed around the yard with any pair of wheels removed, the same could not be said of an 0-6-0 tender engine. If, for instance, a leading pair of wheels was removed from a class 4F, then the unsupported weight of the cylinder block would cause the engine to dip down and lift the trailing wheels partly off the rails, with the inevitable result of a derailment when being shunted about. To counteract this possibility the table was first lifted up above the rail as high as the pump could manage (usually about 2 to 3 inches). Whilst this condition was maintained, pieces of steel plate packing were inserted between the centre axlebox tops and the frame; also over the drawbar between the engine and tender, usually at the engine end. This latter packing helped to utilise the weight of the tender to hold the back end down as it was supported by the middle axle. If a trailing set had to be removed, the same packing was applied to the centre axle with the drawbar packing being inserted under the bar to enable the tender to hold the back end of the loco up. The centre axle when affected needed no such packing as the loco was obviously adequately carried by the leading and trailing wheels.

Deeley 0-4-0T No. 41536 stands on the drop pit through road note the bogie and wooden packing supporting the rear end. Photo: Authors Collection.

With an 0-6-0 or 0-4-0 tank engine even more care was required as, without a leading or trailing axle the 0-6-0 became very unstable and an 0-4-0 would fall straight down the hole after it's wheels. To overcome this a four wheel bogie was used. This was positioned under the engine's buffer beam and strong, heavy wooden packing was used to make up the space, when the engine was lifted as previously described. Then, with the wheels removed, the loco was pushed gently back through the rear of the drop pit until clear of the stripping ground; there to stay until ready for re-wheeling. Not for them the constant journeys up and down the yard as various engines were needed for rewheeling, or even wagons of sand for unloading into the sand drier; for the sandhole road adjacent to the Drop Pit was the preferred storage siding for the wheeldrop engines.

All these problems overcome, we now get down to the business of actually removing the wheelset. By now all that was usually required was for the spring pins to be knocked out, the horn stays unbolted and any oil pipes disconnected. As the weight came off the springs with the lowering of the table and the springs were finally loose, the fitter would be ready to give them a shake and, if free to move, punch out the pins from each end. If a spoke looked to be in the way of any of these pins, all the weight would be lowered off the wheels so that the mate could turn them with the aid of a long bar.

Having removed the spring pins, the weight would be slightly applied again to lift the axleboxes off the horn stays so they could be unbolted. These stays joined the two halves of the frame together below the gap into which the axleboxes were inserted. With these stays removed or unbolted as the case may be, the oil pipes were dismantled and the wheels were ready for removal. These were partly lowered to ensure that they were free to come out and not sticking up in the horns. The fitter would then scotch them firmly in place and climb out prior to the table with the wheels being lowered to the bottom of the hole. With the side rails now out and locked in place, the engine was ready to be drawn outside and clear of the table. When this had been done the wheels were raised to rail level, un-scotched and pushed out to the rear of the plant to be stripped down.

A primary consideration at this stage was to endeavour to establish precisely the cause of the casualty (hot box) in order to: (a) complete the casualty report and (b) rectify the fault to prevent it's recurrence when repaired and back in traffic. With this in mind at was the usual practice to strip down the offending axlebox first. This, in theory, was but a matter of 15 to 20 minutes work but, as with all things, could take considerably longer. With everything on that side of the axle having been extremely hot, causing white metal to melt and run down to fuse everything together in the wrong place, plus the distortion, which went hand in hand with anything made of steel when overheated, you can imagine the problems arising.

The first thing to be done was to remove the spring. This would be hanging by it's centre pin from the spring hanger. A few sharp blows on it's suspension pin with a hammer and long punch usually saw it fall away onto the ground, from where it was man-handled out of the way. Next came the spring hanger itself. This was usually retained by a long pin of some 3 to 4 inches in diameter which passed through the bottom of both sides of the axlebox cheeks and the underkeep, the centre spring buckle being retained within the underside of this keep. Now here was where the fun could begin, if the melted metal from the bearing and axlebox sides had run in amongst this assembly. When this pin was removed, only the two side pins securing the underkeep to the axlebox remained to be knocked out, again a problem from time to time. The oil snub was removed from the box top for further examination and the axlebox finally removed. What a mess was guaranteed to be revealed then! An axlebox brass completely devoid of bearing metal and very discoloured. "Was this ever brass?" one wondered. The axle itself would be burnt blue and invariably badly scored. It only then remained to remove the other axlebox assembly (the good side) and assess what work, if any, was required to that while it was stripped down.

The causes of hot boxes were many and varied, usually but not always related to the breakdown of the lubricating system. A broken supply pipe or hose was a common cause with mechanical lubricator faults a close second. Another fault was the underkeep being full of water instead of oil. Indeed, one of the standard checks on the X repair card was to drain the underkeep of water and refill with oil. A very dirty and unpleasantly awkward task, which I suspect, was not carried out with the enthusiasm it warranted in a good many cases. A drain plug to facilitate the operation was fitted to the underkeep on all modern engines but not on many of their older, more ancient sisters. Dirt in the oil pipe was another not infrequent find. The oil snub on the axlebox top contained a non return valve and small filter. This filter was often blocked with sludge and occasionally the non return valve spring broken. Sometimes the underkeep pad on the hot box side was found to be just a bit of bent and bare, tangled metal, devoid of any padding. All evidence of this nature had to be retained for the casualty inspector to see when he compiled his report.

These inspectors only appeared when traffic delays had occurred following the breakdown of the affected locomotive. When they did, they usually took the form of a young and somewhat inexperienced individual whose knowledge of his subject was somewhat lacking. Patently obvious when faced with the likes of the two Tommys, in particular Tommy Turner who, if they said a word out of place, spent the next half hour or so putting them right in no uncertain manner. And they never got a cup of tea either!!

The horn stays were refitted to bridge the gap left by the removal of the axles to maintain the frame's strength, prior to the loco being hauled away for storage whilst repairs were carried out. They were usually stored in the sandhole road alongside the Drop Pit as stated earlier. This was most convenient, as in the fullness of time the lubricating system of the loco itself would have to be examined.

An LMS Hughes Class '5' 2-6-0 No. 42890. Photo: P. Groom.

A classic example of a hot bearing being caused other than by lubrication supply breakdown, occurred to the Class 6P Jubilee No. 45717 'Dauntless' which was just being run-in following a general overhaul at the Crewe Works. Diagrammed to work a Crewe to Derby Class B passenger train, this engine ran a hot box on the driving coupled axle during the journey. The driver also reported the valves out of beat on arrival at Derby. A fresh engine was found to take over the return working and the Jubilee was dispatched to the shed. In no time at all word of this mishap had got to the Works, where they immediately wanted it in the Shops, "To make a proper job of it," as it were; such was the rivalry between the two establishments of Derby and Crewe. But the DMPS would have none of it and 45717 was dispatched to Burton into the tender care of yours truly, by then out of my time and one of the fitters employed at the Drop Pit.

On stripping out the offending axle I could not initially find anything wrong with the oil system to have caused the bearing to overheat. Indeed, when the flexible hose to the axlebox was removed, oil poured out of the feed pipe from the lubricator and, when stripped down, the oil snub was clean and in perfect working order; as one would expect with a newly out-shopped engine. So what had caused the bearing to overheat? Further investigation revealed that the eccentric sheave for the Walschearts valve gear to the middle cylinder had worked loose, presumably because of poor initial assembly, causing the middle cylinder to receive excessive amounts of steam by comparison with the two outside ones. This had caused undue stresses on the axle causing the axlebox to overheat. For an engine that had been in traffic for some time this would possibly not have happened but, as everything was tight and new (apart from the sheave), something had to give. No wonder the valves were out of beat! The axle, boxes and eccentric were all sent to Derby Works for correction; from where, no doubt, a number of cynical letters and phone calls to Crewe emanated.

Another engine, one of our Crabs No. 42756, gave me a headache for a while. She ran a driving axlebox hot and, following the usual procedures, was refitted and returned to traffic, after a few days on local work, as was the normal practice. To my surprise and embarrassment, on her first main line run on the London beer train no less, she ran the same box hot again and had to be replaced at Wellingborough. Hodgy was none too pleased and lost no time in telling me so, as was his right, to my eternal shame. Now! 42756, being a Horwich built engine, was fitted with a Wakefield mechanical lubricator instead of the more usual Silvertown variety and I, in common with some of the other fitters, was not over fond of them, considering them to be unreliable. As I had already cleaned out and tested the one fitted so far as possible, I suggested that a refurbished one be ordered from Horwich as a replacement but our redoubtable foreman would hear none of it. "There's nowt wrong wi't' one that's on," he declared, "It's thee 'at's not fitted it reet," his accent jarring in my ears. My apologies to any Lancashire readers but his version really could wind you up.

Thus suitably chastised, I went through everything again with a fine toothed comb, so to speak, but could find nothing to cause the overheating. On the return of the axlebox and wheels from Horwich Works I invited Hodgy up to the Drop Pit to witness the assembly which he declined to do, though he did have a quick look and witnessed the oil flowing from the open end of the oilfeed pipes when pumped. Not that there was any back pressure to overcome then, of course, because the axles were not even connected up let alone running down the line with a full train in tow. Never had underkeep pads been soaked in oil as much before refitting as those two. New snubs and hoses were fitted and tested, as were the oilways in the bearings themselves. Both springs were also renewed and the engine was rebuilt with as much care as was possible.

"There's only one thing left that I can't check on now," I remarked as I notified Hodgy she was now ready for traffic again, "And that's the axle weights." "Now tha's talking daft!" was his answer. I had a word with the running foreman and asked if, after a few days running in on local work, he could find something less demanding than the London or Bristol beer train for her to make her mainline debut. "We'll send her on the Rowsley. How would that suit," he suggested. "Worth a try," I thought. Thus the scene was set. Come the day, she made it to Rowsley so no failure in traffic occurred but she did overheat the offending box again. Back she came in disgrace with Hodgy by now going up the wall and the shed Master, Mr. Lewis, also getting in on the act.

"You're lucky you haven't got a No.1 form," he exclaimed. However, he was a much more reasonable man to talk with than our foreman and had been a fitter himself in his earlier days; not that our foreman hadn't of course. I explained my misgivings regarding Wakefield lubricators and also my suspicions about the axle weights. Having spent a month of my Work's year as an apprentice out on the weighbridge and test pits over at Derby Four Shed, the colloquial term for Derby MPD, I felt that I knew a little of what I was talking about. The upshot was that when 42756 was re-assembled for the third time she was sent light engine to Derby to be weighed and I went with her. She was found to be carrying nearly four tons more than her designed weight on the problematic axlebox with the other five boxes being variously heavy or light accordingly. Only the pony truck was anywhere near correct.

Having the acquaintance of Jack the weighbridge fitter, he wrote down the various amounts by which each axle spring hanger would have to be stretched or shortened, then bid me luck. Unlike the engines he dealt with, which were all new off Shops with their hanger pins free, our Crab had been in traffic some considerable time and as a result, some of the top hanger pins had seized in the frames. However, my mate George and I persevered and removed each one in turn to either jump or draw it as required, in the blacksmith's fire, to attain the required length; much to the disapproval of Charlie Tovey, our coppersmith, and the delight of blacksmith Bob, who never believed in using one hammer blow when two would do. Needless to say 42756 went back into traffic complete with new lubricators which she may or may not have needed and soon gained a reputation for a smooth ride with never as much as a warm bearing again.

To get back to my apprentice days, as mentioned earlier, Tommy Turner emigrated to Canada and his place was taken by Johnny Webb, then recently back from doing his National Service in the R.A.F. Also, as previously mentioned, Jim Wallah transferred to the OMD (Outdoor Machinery Department) and Frank Parker moved, complete with bicycle, to the top of the yard to take his place as shed chippie. This left Johnny and me on the Drop Pit together with Johnny "borrowing" a mate when on the night shift, until a replacement could be recruited.

About this time, five of our Crabs were exchanged with the 5 unique class members fitted with the Reidinger valve gear. This gear had been recently applied to these engines in place of the Lentz gear previously carried. The reason for the exchange was, I believe, given as lack of maintenance staff at Saltley where they were previously based, depriving them of the more individual attention they required. So we were lumbered with them. Of the five locos numbered 42818, 42822, 42824, 42825 and 42829, one – 42824, was in Horwich Works at the time of transfer and did not arrive for several weeks after her sisters had made a bad name for themselves with their Burton crews. But, more of them later...

One of the jobs that confront the steam artisans from time to time is that of spring changing. I have already described the process involved in changing a locomotive spring, on a 4F with Jack Turner, who incidentally, for some reason, was always known in the shed as 'Schonkie.' As you will have seen, it was quite an involved process with considerable muscle power involved; and that only with a relatively small engine – a Midland type 0-6-0. Imagine the effort involved to change one on, say, a Black 5 or an 8F. On the Drop Pit however, it was a totally different story. Half an hour's job on average barring snags, whatever the class of engine. I have on more than one occasion changed one on a Crab, due to depart on one of the beer trains to Bristol or London, in 20 minutes, with the help of my regular mate George on the table handles; the main fun on this job being to position the affected wheel in the centre of the table without a balance weight in the way of the removal of one of the three pins.

A trial setting was first attempted by the driver easing his charge onto the table to see how things were. If lucky and all the pins were accessible, then the hand brake was secured and the job of changing the broken spring was undertaken. However, sods law being what it is, invariably one or more of the pins were behind a balance weight. The engine was then reversed out to stand clear of the plant. Here the driver would attempt to make the engine wheels slip to achieve a different position when it was brought back onto the table. To assist the slip we sometimes first oiled the rails. Having noted it's position before the start, it was surprising how often the wheels stopped in a similar position afterwards, no matter how vigorously the wheels had spun. My old Mate 'Dickie' Smith or Jack Lewis or another of my old drivers – Jack Pullman would invariably be the driver as these three were permanent shed men, having been taken off the main line for reasons of health or failing eyesight. Jack Pullman used to joke that he could slip to an inch but it was only a joke, unfortunately and it was not unheard of for five or six attempts to be made before achieving the desired position. Only when the axle in question was positioned correctly in the centre of the table could the job be carried out, as any off centre position would run the risk of bending the ram beneath the table due to an unbalanced lift. One task associated with Drop Pit work was the actual repairs to the affected axle journal. In most cases it required machining, which involved turning and buffing on the wheel lathe, which was situated in the far corner of the Old Shed, outside the machine shop door. This meant pushing the affected wheelset into the shed. Firstly one had to push them back through the pit, across the table and out the other side to continue in totally the opposite direction for about four or five engine lengths to clear the spring points of the Drop Pit road. Once on the move along the slightly down grade, having got the wheels in motion - came the need to stop them. With the average ex Midland engine coupled wheelset or pony and tender sets, their control was quite reasonable but a pair off a Crab, Class 5 or the like or even a 2P or Compound was a different story. These larger engine wheels with their bigger balance weights took a lot of effort to start rolling and then to stop them when on the move was something else entirely. One of the fears was that they would de-rail themselves while racing along free and unconfined from the locomotive from which they had found their unaccustomed liberty. Having safely reached a point clear of the spring points protecting the Drop Pit, we then had to reverse our progress and push the errant wheels around a double curve, in doing so crossing the sets of points converging lines from the ashpit and the coal stage, before entering the shed and onto the turntable. Pushing a wheelset along a straight piece of track is one thing but around a curve is quite another entity, particularly with our Crab and Class 5 wheels and the like. There the risk of derailment was greater, as the wheels demonstrated an aversion to going round corners, much preferring to go straight on. As the balance weights passed over the top centres the turning rate increased and as this impetus was alternatively from one side then the other, they were soon off the road if you were not very careful. Judicious use of pinch bars however, carefully controlled their tendency to twist and derail.

Of course, another hazard was ever present whilst rolling the wheels in or out of the shed brought you in conflict with engine movements about the yard. On more than one occasion I was confronted with an engine coming out of the shed and had to reverse up the ashpit road to allow it to pass. Most drivers were quite understanding and would give way to us it being much easier to reverse an engine than stop and reverse a set of wheels.

One dark rainy morning I had quite a spectacular collision with a set of Crab driving wheels and a 4F emerging from the shed. Being unable to stop their progress in time, my Mate and I jumped quickly out of the way and left them to their fate. The impact was quite considerable with the 4F's buffer edges receiving quite noticeable indentation. The driver, a Saltley man, was quite surprised, to say the least, and quoted a few words not found in the Oxford Dictionary or any other dictionary for that matter. As his indignation was addressed to me, I was quick to point out that his fireman should have preceded him out of the shed to warn him of any dangers or obstructions, conveniently overlooking the fact that the same obligation also applied to me. But then, as an artisan, I wasn't to know that, not being subject to the rules applying to footplate staff. In no time at all, such was the noise of the crash, Bert Sindair, the running foreman, was on the scene along with the usual crown of onlookers, all snugly aware they were not involved and could therefore enjoy the drama laid out before them. To my amazement, the wheels were still on the lines and not derailed as I had expected so Bert, with the wisdom of Solomon, had the 4F reverse into the turntable whereupon I followed with the wheels and thus, with the aid of the vacuum tractor powered off the engine, was able to turn the table to the appropriate pit in the shed and run them off. The 4F fireman then turned the table back, enabling them to leave the shed for a second time, checking firstly that all was clear this time.

Bert went back to his office, no doubt relieved that all had turned out well for, if the wheelset had derailed, the consequent delays to engines coming out of that roundhouse would have been considerable. The audience melted away, no doubt to discuss the event in more detail and we carried on with the daily grind. The outcome of the furore was the instruction that before movements of wheels etc. about the loco yard and shed were carried out, the services of a driver must be secured, to act as conductor during the operation. This was dutifully carried out for a time until conveniently forgotten, mainly because there was often no driver available to perform the duty, causing intolerable delays when there was work was to be done. However, it should be said that, in the interests of safety, the movement of wheels was never or very rarely done during darkness or in foggy conditions.

Many and varied was the class of engine dealt with on the Burton Wheel Drop. A LNW Super D made me thank my lucky stars that the hot box was not on it's flangeless pair, as the problems that would create did not bear thinking about. Likewise, on the BR 9F, which also had no flanges on it's middle set of coupled wheels. Talking of 9F's, an amusing occurrence befell two of these engines and made my mate George and myself a lot of work into the bargain.

BR standard Class '9F' 2-10-0 No. 92185. Photo: P. Groom.

A wagon arrived from Crewe Works bringing a refurbished set of BR Standard tender wheels, fitted with the roller bearing axleboxes. These were duly unloaded and pushed out to the Drop Pit in the usual way. The two Class 9F's arrived and the instructions were for me to replace the wheelset on the one tender with the refurbished set as one wheel had a loose tyre, then to swap the complete tenders of the two engines as one was due Shops with a reasonable tender whereas the other 'good' engine had a bad tender. Thus keeping one engine in traffic, which would otherwise have to be shopped for tender repairs.

George and I, having wrestled with the rusty brake gear on the front end of the loose type tender, changed the axle as instructed. Then the fun began! On inspecting the second engine I discovered, to my chagrin, that the exchange couldn't take place. "Why?" you might well ask! It transpired that on the one engine the gangway doors were mounted off the engine cab but on the other, off the tender. Both tenders, I might add, being of the same type. This exchange would have resulted in the impossible situation of having one engine and tender with two sets of gangway doors and the other with none. With great delight I informed Hodgy of the situation. After a few incoherent remarks our worthy master decided to inform the Shopping Bureau and ask for their instructions. They came back with the surprising instruction, the purpose of which I have never understood, to change the other two wheel sets on the tenders, like for like and then send the engines on their merry way, one to traffic and the other to Crewe Works. So we finished up with a bad engine having a good tender with indifferent wheels in the Works and a, presumably, good engine having a bad tender with one good and two worn sets of wheels in traffic. So much for standardisation!

Preserved ex MR 'compound' Class 4P 4-4-0. Photo: E. Edwards.

Another prestigious customer, this time while I was an apprentice, to call on our skills on the Pit, was the preserved Midland Compound No.1000. She had run one of her coupled axles hot; I think it was the trailing axle. With such a VIP loco the inevitable, very junior, Works engineer arrived, complete with fitter and mate from the Derby Works. After all, this engine was far too elegant for our rough shed lads to work on. Tommy Marshall and Les were incumbent on days that week and outside on the sandhole road, with a like pair of wheels removed, stood one of 1000's slightly younger sisters. Hodgy lost no time in finding Tom and Les other employment in the shed, leaving the Derby men on the pit to get on with it. On returning to the Drop Pit for the inevitable cup of tea, mid morning, I was interested to note that, although the siderods were now removed, nothing else had been done. At lunchtime the injector stem supply pipe was in the process of being removed and the brake gear uncoupled.

"If you need to know owt, don't be afraid to ask," Tommy remarked, cockney accent to the fore. Our schoolboy engineer; he looked no older than me; replied that his men and indeed himself, knew all there was to know about Compounds and that they could manage very well thank you. The look on the Derby fitter's face as he said it, was a picture. "You smug so-and-so," it seemed to say, "On your head be it," I thought. By the end of the day, 1000 was still standing outside the plant when the Derby men and me went home. Imagine our surprise therefore, the next morning when we retuned, to find 1000 standing on the sandhole road behind the other class member, her wheels out and stripped at the back of the pit. It hadn't taken Tom and Frank long to see them off. They had even got the rods off a 3F outside, ready for us to move over the table for our morning's work as well. Our young engineer nearly had a fit when he arrived and went storming off to lodge his complaint with Hodgy, whilst the Derby men and we three had a good laugh over a cuppa at his expense.

Probably the most famous customer of all was the largest locomotive ever to run on a British Railway; namely the ex LNER Garratt number 69999. Having spent all her life banking up the Worsborough incline on the old Great Central in Yorkshire, the electrification of this line had made her redundant. Some bright spark on BR decided to send her to Bromsgrove for banking on the Lickey and the Eastern region, no doubt only too pleased to get rid of her; readily agreed. So, after settling up at Gorton Works, she set off on one of the longest journeys of her life, destination Bromsgrove. Not being fitted with mechanical lubrication, other than to her six cylinders and piston valves, the axleboxes had to rely on siphon feed to lubricate them from oilboxes by capillary action; much in the same way as the Midland 2F and 3F's and other Victorian designs. All very well up and down a four-mile bank but not a 60 or 70 mile trip down to Derby. Suffice to say that she managed to run no less than three axleboxes hot, thus arriving at Burton for attention. Two pairs of coupled wheels were affected, along with a pony truck box. I was not personally involved in any of the repairs, other than to help push wheels into the shed. She arrived in the summer of 1955 and, if I remember correctly, the repaired boxes and wheels were just arriving back from Gorton for refitting when I started my twelve months in the main Works at Derby in the September of that year.

Another stranger and one I did become involved with, was another LNER engine; this time an old Great Central, Robinson Class O4 2-8-0, looking to be not long off Shops judging by the slight shine still showing through the grime on her paintwork. She was fitted with axlebox wedges, a refinement not found on LMS engines. On re-wheeling the engine, I asked Tommy Marshall what to do with them. "Ow should I know," he answered, adding, with cockney logic, "If the wheels go in - forget it. If not hit it wi' the 'ammer." They did go in, with plenty of play, so I slacked off the locking pins and tapped them down until the clearance seemed about right to me. In later years I made the discovery that, with a bit of service and mileage under their belt, the biggest problem was keeping them tight let alone adjusted, they being just one more feature to add to the slap, bang and rattle of a typical goods engine in traffic.

Ex LNER 'Garratt' 2-8-8-2T No. 69999, Frank Parker on the left, Ernie Thompson right plus Frank's bike. Maurice Harper (a visitor) on framing. Photo: P. Webb.

When I had returned from my twelve months Shop experience I had a month on the Drop Pit, filling in as a result of the absence of Tom Turner, now departed for Canada. I remember one of the first engines to turn up was an ex LNER Class J39, No.64823, one of Colwick's finest. She had run her left driving axlebox hot. This meant that all the motion would have to be stripped down underneath. Don Oliver had knocked the siderods off overnight and positioned her on the table. The brake rods were also off so we went straight to it, disconnecting the eccentrics and big ends from the crank axle. The first thing we noticed was how much bigger and beefier everything was compared with one of our 4F's. One big end was set on the bottom centre ready for attack so George and I decided that we would start on that one. Having loosened the draw cotter and removed the nut from the taper bolts, which secure the big end strap to the connecting rod, they required knocking out. George optimistically passed me the cap nut that fitted all our Midland engines but, needless to say, it did not screw on, being too small. A few tentative blows to the end of the bolt proved to be of no avail as I expected so, "What to do now?" I wondered. These bolts were quite large and thus, I reasoned, would take some moving. Putting the locking nuts back on but leaving them loose to protect the bolt ends didn't work either as they were not deep enough to span the turned down end and still have a few threads in mesh on the bolt.

"Get the machinist to make a cap nut," I thought, so off I went with one of the nuts. He didn't seem very interested, pointing out in his defence, that he hadn't got a suitable tap for the thread nor any equipment to turn one either. I suggested that he might like the challenge of overcoming these little problems but his reply was unprintable. Another "good idea" hits the dust! On acquainting Hodgy with the state of play, he suggested disconnecting the little ends and dropping the wheels out with the con rods still connected. All very well, if possible, but they still had to be disconnected before the wheels could be pushed out of the shed.

The upshot was that Colwick was contacted effecting the promise to dispatch a cap nut forthwith. I wondered why they first wanted to know the engine number. Six months later I was to find out. George and I stripped out the eccentrics and sundry other bits and pieces and awaited the arrival of the cap nut. The redoubtable Hodgy, in the meantime, found us a nice, dirty smokebox job, removing a blast pipe from a Class 3F for the tubers to gain access for some replacement work. When the cap nut arrived, looking extremely battered and well worn, obviously some fitter's cast off, we set to with a will and soon had the offending bolts removed. The rest of the job was plain sailing and by the end of the day we had the wheelset and exleboxes loaded in a wagon for dispatch to Doncaster Works. When they returned I was working elsewhere in the shed and played no part in the re-assembly.

The author in the cab of the LNER garratt No. 69999. Photo: Authors Collection.

By now, as briefly mentioned earlier, Don Oliver had come onto the scene, having gained employment at the depot whilst I was away in the Shops at Derby. An ex Regular of the R.A.F., he had previously served his time on the Southern Railway at, I think, Ashford Works and, seeking re-employment, had managed to obtain a position in place of Tommy Marshall who had decided that selling cars was more lucrative and certainly more cleaner, than mending steam engines. Don, who had inherited both Tommy's job and his mate Les, soon proved to be a very good fitter, flying the Southern flag with great style.

Inevitably, with increasing inter-regional workings, more LNER types found their way into and through Burton, with B1's, various 2-8-0's and J39's being the commonest, although K2.s and K3's also put in an occasional appearance. The first victim of this increasing presence was another J39, also with a hot driving axle, a malady that I was to learn they often suffered. This time the casualty was a Lincoln engine No.64728. Don was soon round the shed looking for me to borrow the cap nut, which I was only too happy to lend him. Imagine our consternation therefore, when half an hour or so later, he was back with it saying it didn't fit. Although I didn't doubt his word, I felt honour bound to go and have a try myself but, sure enough, it wouldn't even look at it, the bolt ends on this particular engine being too big to even allow the cap nut to pass over them let alone screw up the threads.

Once again Colwick was contacted and a cleaner was dispatched to "borrow" one on this occasion. It transpired that there were three different sizes of bolt fitted to this class of engine, dependant on when they were built. So much for LNER standardisation! I gleaned the information that nearly 300 of the class were built so, as far as we at Burton were concerned, that made 300 "One Offs."

War Department engines were also moved by rail from depot to depot and on two occasions they came to grief in the Burton area. One was an 0-6-0T of the type built in great quantities during the war and later of the LNER J94 type. The other was a beautiful little Peckett 0-4-0ST, both, needless to say, being immaculately turned out and spotlessly clean. The former was travelling under it's own steam accompanied by an army sapper who was no doubt pondering on his fate as a result, with the Peckett being towed dead with her rods off in a freight train. Her worthy caretaker had a better excuse as he was unable to attract the attention of the train's crew to his plight, or so he maintained. As both these incidents occurring after my own stint in Her Majesty's Forces, I had a certain sympathy for them both.

On each occasion the Royal Engineers duly sent a lieutenant to take charge, a sergeant to give the orders and two sappers to do the actual work, these worthies being billeted at the TA Centre in the town, the officer, of course, staying in a local hotel!! After giving them a "crash course" on the operation of the Drop Pit we left them to it; and very well they did too.

One other little feature comes to mind about the Drop Pit. When the need to remove a complete bogie from, say a Compound or Class 2P was required, the overall wheelbase precluded them from fitting onto the Drop Pit table without standing foul of the running lines each side. To cater for this situation four removable sections, some 12 inches long, were provided at the point of entry where the running road met the table lines. When these were removed the overhang of the bogie wheels cleared the truncated running lines and were thus able to be lowered into the well in the usual way. When the bogie unit was extracted from the well and pushed out to the stripping area a most obnoxious scenario was revealed. With the majority of the area within the frames being full of an oily, swarfy gunge within which was hidden two leaf springs on their sides and also, I think four, coil springs (between them providing side control and weight bearing), whenever the bogie was removed everything therein, whether broken or not, was renewed. As I only ever worked on one bogie set I cannot now recall just how everything went together but I believe the leaf springs lying back to back provided the side control whilst the coil springs took the suspension weight by means of a cradle onto the four bogie axlebox tops.

Incidentally, the reader may be interested to know that all the Class 2P, 3P and Compound locomotives had leaf springs under the trailing couple axles as is the norm with most engines on railways worldwide but they also had two coil springs to provide suspension under the leading or driving coupled axles. I was told that this arrangement was adopted as there was insufficient room to fit the more usual leaf springs, although there seemed ample room to me. Whatever the reason, these coil springs were forever breaking and no doubt constituted, in no small way, to the very lively ride that was the footplatemen's lot when aboard these machines.

Ex MR 3F 0-6-0 No. 43249 stands in the No.1 (old) shed, note the hoist and steelwork above boiler for handling wheelsets. The wheellathe was behind the tender. Photo: Authors Collection.

Following a spell of inclement weather the well of the Drop Pit acted as a natural sump and in consequence flooded to such an extent that the table would, in effect, float when lowered, thus not reaching it's lowest intended point. When this situation occurred the need to pump out the water was paramount. This was achieved in a rather novel way. A large T shaped piece of pipe had been fashioned, many years previously, presumably by some former Drop Pit fitter. The long upright of the T was lowered into the sump of the well situated in it's North corner. The cross piece was fitted with a piece of flexible hose at each end. One end of the hose was connected to the ejector steam supply outlet at the side of the boiler just beneath the ejector box, the connecting steam supply pipe between the two having first been removed (a finger burning task in itself).

When the large ejector was operated, a jet of steam passed down the flexible hose, across the T piece to blow out of the flexible hose on the other side and away, clear of the plant. The vacuum thus created in the upright, by the steam passing across the top, drawing the flood water up and away, blasting out with the steam, through the flexible hose. Once the system had settled down the small ejector was brought into operation and the large one closed down, to maintain an economy of steam. Dependant on the amount of water to be disposed of, half an hour to an hour was usually enough to pump the system dry. The one necessity to success was the availability of an ex Midland vacuum braked engine lake a Class 2, 3 or 4 or, of course, an LMS version of the same. A Crab was also suitable, having the same type of Gresham and Craven ejectors.

When I returned from Overseal, these suitable engines were getting thin on the ground so it was decided by the powers that be to install an electric pump to perform this function. Being the Railway of course, going as ever for the cheapest option, the pump was installed at ground level, with a length of pipe descending into the sump, which first had to be primed before suction could be achieved. This often took at least half an hour to do and when the system was finally operating, it was considerably slower than the method it replaced. And they call that progress!

An alternative, suggested by Don Oliver, utilising the original pipework with the flexible connection being attached to the tube-blower cock at the side of all Stanier and, I think, BR Standard engines, was not taken up, though I think that would have been very simple to adapt and quicker to get into operation, and of course, cheaper to apply.

Enough said about the Drop Pit I think

Chapter 13

The Reidinger Crabs

Burton's allocation of Class 5 Crab 2-6-0's in the fifties averaged ten to twelve class members and into this elite group of well maintained engines, the top of the shop in the shed's total of one hundred or so, came these five locos.

They soon found themselves at the head of express freight trains conveying the local produce to London, Bristol and Leeds, a far cry from the local trippers on which they had spent their years at Saltley, both before and after adoption from Lentz to Reidinger Gear. In no time at all they were falling apart all over the system. Whilst not, in most cases, complete failures, they would find themselves being replaced by more reliable power, following bouts of late running through time lost by these engines' inability to stay the course. Eventually they would make their way back on some less demanding working or other, only to be refitted to face the gambit once again.

Their inability to climb the banks without losing time was a feature they shared with their remote cousins the Caprotti Class 5's, but whereas the Caprotti's would run like the wind down the other side, these Crabs, like their Walschearts sisters, were not particularly speed machines.

Into all this chaos arrived 42824 fresh from Horwich Works after a general overhaul and gleaming in a shiny new coat of black paint lined out in mixed traffic livery. Following a boiler wash out she was kept on local work pending the arrival of George Fisher from Derby Technical and Research Department. As 42824 was stabled on the Sandhole Road, nice and handy for the Drop Pit, Johnny Webb was given the job of assisting Mr. Fisher with some modifications that he wished to carry out. He explained to us that, unlike the other four engines, 42824 was fitted with Vernier adjustable cams and it was with various different settings of these that he wished to experiment.

Hodgy came on the scene to find me another job but George Fisher overruled him saying that he thought an apprentice might benefit from staying to assist with the task. A sentiment with which I heartily agreed, though I kept the thought to myself of course. He also suggested that perhaps some of the other apprentices might join us as well. A suggestion that, needless to say, Hodgy chose to ignore.

Johnny confided in me that he had handed in his notice and would be leaving the Railway at the end of that week. He had the rest of that week off for holidays due and as a result Les Bull took his place the following day. I was to meet up with Johnny again later when I took up other employment at Drakelow Power Station.

The arrival on the scene of Les Bull was to prove most fortuitous, both for him and myself for, as a result of the knowledge gained whilst working with George Fisher; we acquired the reputation of 'Reidinger experts.' Not a title to sit easily on anyone's shoulders. But I digress! On with 42824's Vernier adjustable cams:

204

Reidinger valve gear fitted Hughes 'Crab' No. 42824. Photo: E. Edwards.

With both cam boxes removed the top covers were taken off to reveal the shafts and cams within. It was clearly obvious that the selection of steam engine spanners with which we earned our daily crust were totally unsuitable for use therein. So, while George and Les enjoyed a cup of the inevitable tea, I cycled home to "borrow" my dad's set of car repair tools; a rather superfluous set of equipment as he didn't have a car; but then who did in our station of life in the 1950's? This equipment included such items as circlip pliers and a few sockets with a ratchet, all of which proved their worth during the course of the next few days.

Bemoaning the rather constricted size of the cam box; of necessity because of the need to fit in the space between the valve chests of the original Lentz cylinder casting which naturally miniaturised the cams and shaft somewhat more than ideal; we set about removing the two shafts, which carried the valve operating cams. These were so arranged as to open the two inlet and exhaust valves in sequence, coincidental with the piston stroke, to admit and discharge steam at each end of the cylinder, as with any normal engine.

In a standard box the shafts and cams were all cast and machined out of one piece of steel. On the ones fitted to 42824 the cams were keyed onto their respective shafts to facilitate easier removal for adjustments to be carried out. The lobes of these cams were in turn splined onto the cam centres thereby enabling the lap and lead settings to be altered by selecting different positions of relativity when the lobes were re-assembled. To further avoid errors in re-assembly, all the centre splines were numbered, with one of the lobe splines marked on each lobe as well. Thus, having noted the original positions, it was just a matter of refitting the lobes to the new numbers designated. Of course all this takes a lot longer to do than it does to write about and it was three days, all in glorious sunshine, before we were in a position to retune the engine, prior to having it steamed and tested. This re-tuning procedure had to be undertaken whenever the shafts of the rotary drive were disconnected, such as for instance when repairs necessitating removal of connecting and coupling rods was required, even if the loco itself was not moved, as the cams inside the box invariably "relaxed" when disconnected, as any open inlet valves would endeavour to try to close with the spring pressure behind them, thus pushing onto and turning their respective cams, however slightly.

The twin faced valves resembled large cotton bobbins. There were four valves to each cylinder, two inlet and two exhaust, one of each for the forwards and backwards stroke of the piston. The exhaust valves were held on their seats by a steam jet with the inlet valves having compression coil spring to perform the same function. This steam jet to the exhaust valves only operated when the regulator was open and in consequence, allowed the valves to fall open when coasting with the regulator closed, thus eliminating any back pressure in the cylinders. When fitting these valves to the steam chest a specified clearance was laid down of so many thousandths of an inch between the end of the valve rod and the cam follower when against the back of the cam. I have forgotten during the intervening years precisely what those clearances were but, suffice to say, as with the motor car, it was of paramount importance to get them exactly right if optimum performance was to be achieved by the locomotive.

All this and more we learned from George Fisher who, I would say without fear of contradiction, had forgotten more about a steam locomotive than most had ever known. His willingness to pass on this knowledge to anyone who showed an interest made him number one in my book; unlike most of his contemporaries who kept their information firmly under their hats. I sometimes thought that, in truth, some of this latter breed had little to tell anyway!

To time the engine or rather the cam box, the locomotive was first positioned with the big end on the side to be tuned, set on the bottom dead centre, with the rotary drive disconnected at the return crank. A circular plate on the end of the cam box was then removed and the rotary shaft turned until a marker on the end of the shaft lined up with the centre line of the cylinder. It was necessary to rotate the rotary shaft around it's normal axis of travel when going forwards, to take up any slack in the various gears and connections through which the drive movement passed, prior to actually turning the cam shaft. I think it was anti-clockwise but I am not sure now. When the required position was achieved, all that remained to be done was to connect the rotary shaft to the return crank and replace the cam plate. If the coupling holes did not line up on the return crank, the coupling plate itself was splined to enable a favourable position to be found.

All this completed and with all lagging replaced on the cylinder ends and sides, 42824 was lit up and arrangements were made for her to work the afternoon tripper to Chaddesden Sidings, Derby, the following day in order to assess her performance. George explained to us that the application of the Reidinger Valve Gear to these Crabs had been somewhat compromised by having to use the existing cylinder block and rotary drive of the Lentz gear, there not being room to fit a reverse travel shaft. Consequently any increase in performance achieved in the normal forwards direction by increasing the cam lead could only be done at the expense of performance when in reverse. So, whereas he was obviously interested in observing the normal forwards performance, he was mainly concerned with how she performed, with a Class 5 load, when in reverse.

The following day, with the weather still favourable, we joined the crew at the shed outlet to journey down to New Dixie sidings and pick up our train. I was amused to find that our driver was Charlie "Green light" Smith ("Mr. Caution" himself). George introduced himself and tried to explain what was required and what we wished to try and to find out. Charlie puffed away at his pipe and gave no indication whatsoever that he had either heard, or intended heeding to, any requests made. All he did was to point out that there were five people on the footplate instead of the stipulated maximum of four, so someone would have to get off. I knew that someone would be me so I volunteered to do the firing if that was agreeable to him. My old mate Ray Allsop, his fireman, was quite in favour of the suggestion but Charlie, true to form and ever cautious, would not agree. However, we trundled down to New Dixie to pick up our load. With a nod from Ray, I sprinkled a couple of rounds into the firebox, mainly for Charlie's benefit, but there was no sign of approval or otherwise from him.

At the sidings our guard joined us to report that, apart from his brake, he had only three wagons and an empty van, some 80 tons in total, adding that there were a few at Old Wetmore to collect also. So on we rolled down to Wetmore where, I think, eight more vehicles were added, bringing our total, including the brake, up to thirteen in all. Not even a Class 1 load never mind a pseudo Class 5? or even 6 as our re-set Crab was supposed to be.

Ray said to his mate, "I'll go in the brake then shall I" and, as Charlie didn't reply, shot off with a wink to me before Charlie could change his mind. I put another round on the fire but left the doors open to keep her quiet, winding the damper partly shut as well.

A raft of coal empties with a Garratt at it's head, eased past us on the slow and, when his brake van was clear, the bobby pulled off for us to follow him down the block to Clay Mills, flagging and indicating one in front of us as we passed his box, which lay between the North Stafford (LNER) Bridge and Wetmore Road Bridge; this location being the one that had afforded us with such excitement as children when we had first discovered the presence of the LNER in our town.

I wasn't sure if Charlie had noticed he had a new fireman so I resolved to keep a low profile until we were out mainline when released at Clay Mills; known as Clay Mills Junction; when it would be too late to do anything about it, at least until Sunny Hill. The Garratt must have got the road straight away as we ran gently up to Clay Mills Home and Starter without catching him up. After about ten minutes a Class 5 came pounding by with an express and in no time at all we got the road, to follow him. With the needle at around 175 lbs and a full glass of water, I just wound the damper open and left 42824 to it. Charlie opened the handle onto the first valve and, with a sharp slap, the valves slammed onto their faces and we were away. It was only a matter of moments to take up the slack of our short train before accelerating out onto the mainline bound for Derby, some ten minutes away.

Looking back as we rounded the curve off the slow line, I acknowledged the wave from Ray, playing at being a guard with a big grin all over his face, shouting, "Right away" to Charlie who just waved and continued to look out of the side of the cab as he linked the gear up to his satisfaction, completely ignoring George's request to use full regulator. "Mind you," I reflected, "Very few drivers, even the heavy handed ones, would use full regulator with our little train."

I still couldn't decide whether or not Charlie was aware of my presence as I shot another ten into the box. The water level was beginning to drop down the glass too so, slipping the exhaust injector on, I set the feed to "fine" and sat down to enjoy the ride. At least, with her being just out of Shops, I could adjust the rate of feed to the water, a situation that soon changed over the following months.

Approaching Repton and Willington the back'uns were off also in our favour, presumably because the Garratt had turned off for Toton at Stenson Junction and had not delayed the following Class 5. I noticed how much sharper was the blast, even with this light load, on 42824 compared with the Walschearts Crabs which I had fired before. This, of course, helped the draw on the fire and in no time the valves were blowing off. I opened the doors and just left the flap up in an endeavour to keep her quiet, easing the damper a little at the same time.

All this cafuffle caused Charlie to look round into the cab at me. A quick glance at the clock and glass, followed by an upward nod of his head to express his approval and he resumed his position, with his head over the side watching the road ahead. "Well, he knows I'm here now," I told myself, "If he didn't before."

I increased the feed on the water valve slightly but 42824 continued to blow off. We were still mainline through Sunnyhill and crossing over Chellaston Junction and into Peartree and Normanton Station when we had our first distant board against us only to come to a stand at London Road Junction alongside the end of the disused ticket platform. Having just quietened down, the valves now lifted again, much to Charlie's annoyance. Short of pulling a hole in the fire with the rake and blacking the back end in; both of which I was loathed to do, standing in the mainline; I could think of nothing else as the glass was now full as well. I had damped the dust down with the pep pipe as we ran through Peartree, being careful not to wet Charlie's highly polished boots and wetting Les's in the process.

A London bound express came punching out of platform 4 behind a grimy Millhouses Class 5. At the same time a local, working probably from Nottingham, came running in across the junction behind a Fairburn 2-6-4, to enter platform 2. Then, to my relief, our peg dropped off and our Crab snapped her valves shut as Charlie heaved up the handle to pull our tripper across to join the Derby Station avoiding line where, on reaching the far end, found the road set right round the corner to the right and into Chaddesden sidings. I hadn't touched the fire since that last round just after Clay Mills and we still had 170 lbs on the clock. With a full glass of water and a nice tidy footplate, I was well satisfied with myself, though Charlie probably had other ideas!

Ray climbed back on the footplate, only to be scowled at by "Greenlight" but, knowing Ray, he wouldn't be too bothered. He looked into the box and seemed to like what he saw, although I had only maintained a rather thin fire. "Do you want a couple of rounds putting on?" I asked him, as I expected, correctly as it turned out, I would be riding back to Burton with the guard in his van.

The inspector at Chadd', seeing a Class 5 engine turn up, when he was expecting the usual Class 2F, was quite happy to find us a full load to take back, much to George's delight. "Ray will need a bit more in the box to drag that lot to Burton," I thought, as I climbed up into the brakevan, which I recall was one of the old ex Midland six-wheeled variety with a single veranda. Judging by the drumming and barging which emanated from those six wheels when we got going, I guessed she had been out of Shops a long time and had slid a few miles into the bargain, so many were the flats on them.

42824 appeared to have quite a struggle lifting the full load round the bend out of Chaddesden and into Derby Station. As we waited on the goods road by the Works, it was interesting to look across at the various engines and tenders awaiting Shopping. Also, at the station end of the Works, was the Crane Shop, actually situated in part within the old original Midland roundhouse. I always found this to be an interesting place and usually managed a quick look inside whenever I had to go to the Works for some purpose or other. Not only were MPD breakdown cranes overhauled there but civil engineers cranes as well. Eventually our brakevan jerked into motion as 42824 struggled to start our heavy train, consisting, as our guard told me, of 65 wagons, equal to 72. A class 5 load for a Class 4 engine, or even a 3½ !!

From London Road junction, the old Birmingham and Derby Junction Railway climbs gradually, though not too severely, all the way to Repton and Willington Station, before falling slowly down to Burton along the Trent Valley. Our Crab felt every extra degree of the incline, hanging on her drawbar as she struggled manfully on past Leys Malleable Castings, Qualcast and Rolls Royce. Through Peartree Station once more to cross over Challaston Junction and onto the block joining the queue to Sunnyhill where the four-track section ends. No danger of 42824 lifting her valves on the return trip it would seem, no reflection on Ray's skills of course. I bet Charlie had to use full regulator as well, so George and Les would be pleased.

We slowly moved up the queue until our turn came for the 5 mile dash to Clay Mills and the return onto the down slow again, which extended right through Burton and beyond Barton and Walton. Not that we were aiming to travel that far with Old Dixie and New Wetmore sidings being quite far enough.

I had noticed the sky beginning to cloud over when we left Derby and as 42824 started away from Sunnyhill the first spots of rain started to fall. By the time we had crested the mini summit at Repton and Willington Station the rain was coming down in torrents, as is often the case when the weather breaks following a summer heat wave. It was most amusing, sitting in that rickety brake van in the dry and thinking of those four up at the front trying to keep out of the rain, difficult enough when travelling forwards let alone tender first as they were. Well done Charlie! making me ride in the van. I bet that, summer sunshine or not, he would have his mac' with him. How right I was, I noticed as I joined the other three "drowned rats" on the engine for the ride back to the shed. As with most summer squalls, the rain had gone over as quickly as it had come. It made a change for me to be the one to finish up dry, I reflected.

Charlie, incidentally, had booked 42824, "Weak in reverse," on the repair card. Surprise, surprise! She was tried on the 4.20 Bristol and the 4.40 London the next week, with an inspector riding with her. On the 4.40, where the Burton men were relieved at Wellingborough, one of their drivers said she was the "strongest of those useless camels he had been on."

I do not recall any more work being carried out on 42824 by way of further adjustments to the cam settings and can only assume that she spent the rest of her time, at least up until re-Shopping, running around as a Class 6 in foregear and a Class 4 when in reverse.

As all the available Burton Crabs were commandeered nearly every summer week-ends by Derby and Nottingham Sheds for working the myriad number of excursions, the norm during the fifties and early sixties, our Reidingers were often amongst their number. If one of the wandering Crabs failed away from home, it was invariably one of the Reidingers. At least four or five times every summer, Les would arrive at work on a Monday morning to find himself sent to rescue one of our failed protégés from some shed near or far.

Following the Whitsun holiday break of 1957, with it's usual plethora of rail-borne excursions from around the Midlands, at the head of which featured our famous, or should I say infamous five (apologies to Enid Blyton), no less than two of them had fallen by the wayside. One, I believe at Gloucester whilst endeavouring to reach Weston-Super-Mare and the other at Chester en-route to North Wales. Les was soon on his way to the latter and I was requested to attend the other although still an apprentice – albeit at 20 yrs old and being utilised in the role of fitter every day, having completed my year in the Derby Works. So, armed with the tools necessary which experience had proved to be required, courtesy of Dad's tool kit, I caught the next available train for Gloucester.

On arrival I presented myself to the foreman fitter who was obviously somewhat taken aback at my youthful countenance. "You'll want someone with you I expect," he commented. "Mick Rowledge would be nice," I answered, Mick having completed his time in the Works with me as well. "He's covering at Ashchurch," the foreman informed me; so I was introduced to another fairly young fitter in his twenties who I seem to recall was named Norman. The foreman went on to explain that 42818, for such was our ailing steed, had failed with valves blowing-through and loss of power. "They've got a bad name down here, these Caprotti Crabs. The 5's aren't too bad but you can keep those things up your end of the country," he added. Of course they would put in an appearance in that area from time to time on our Bristol beer trains, a regular Burton Crab working.

Norman and I wandered over to 42818, stabled dead in a far corner of the shed. As we went along I explained to him that this "valve blowing-through" symptom was quite common with these engines and now that she was cold, provided she hadn't broken a head, she would probably be all right again.

The driver had been of the opinion that the main trouble was in the left front valve as a more pronounced roar up the chimney had been indicated when the left cylinder was in a position to receive steam in that quarter. I suspected a broken valve and so it proved or, at least, a chip out of one of the seats. This necessitated a new valve head being fitted to the rod and the two valve seats lapping in. Whilst I was doing this Norman removed the steam chest covers from all the other six valves to check their condition as well. The right back exhaust valve was also chipped so Norman set about replacing that head also. The inlet valve in that position was also slightly chipped but, as I had only brought one spare of each with me, we put it back for further attention when it got back to Burton. Having shown Norman how to check the valve clearances and where to set the engine for the relevant valves to be clear of the back of the cams, I made my way home as, having not disconnected the drive, there was no need to go through the procedure of re-timing the cam boxes.

As already stated, the effect of valve blow-through was quite common with these engines and had, I gather, also occurred when fitted with the Lentz gear. Both Les and myself were of the opinion that the cause of this was differing expansion of the various metals involved in the valve make up. The main cylinder/steam chest block was made up of cast steel with manganese valve seats inserted, two to each valve. These were, of necessity, of two different diameters to allow the inner head of the valve bobbin to pass through the outer seat to reach the inside seat. The valve bobbin itself, made of a more refined quality alloy steel, had also two corresponding faces of different diameters to match the valve seats. Also, the bobbins were mounted on a carbon steel spindle. It is no wonder therefore; different metals having differing expansion rates; that all these various component parts, made of dissimilar types of steel, whilst all in harmony when assembled cold, would go increasingly awry as they increased in temperature.

In fairness to the actual Reidinger cam box itself, it should be said that, in my experience, of all the failures and faults suffered by the engines so fitted, only one was attributable to the cam box itself. On this occasion the box had lost all its oil and in consequence a bearing had collapsed and seized. On examination the box appeared to have suffered some minor collision damage, which had gone un-reported. This had cracked the casing of the cam box allowing the oil to seep away. The surrounding cylinder lagging had suffered damage at the same time. The engine concerned was 42825 and had failed, in this instance, at Newton Heath, Manchester, conveniently near to Bolton and Horwich Works. She was towed there for repair and subsequently returned to Burton, none the worse for her contretemps.

Soon after my return from National Service in the autumn of 1959, Joe Benson, by now fitter in charge at Overseal Sheds, attained a promotion to Derby and Les Bull was offered the position, which he accepted. This "first step" on the ladder of promotion was a valuable position, presenting all the problems of a large motive power depot, in miniature - as it were. Thus, it fell to yours truly to shoulder the burden of the Reidinger alone. The following two years saw me attending to our "flock" at Blackpool, Newton Heath (twice), Stockport, Nottingham, Leicester, Wellington and Cricklewood (twice). Most times I had to lodge in the engineman's hostels overnight with the exception of Nottingham. On every occasion, except the one at Newton Heath concerning the cam box as described above, the faults were with the valves breaking. Naturally, I was not the only fitter at Burton to become involved with these engines but I did experience the lion's share. With the possible exception of Wally Gaskell, I believe young Charlie Lester was the only other fitter to attend to one at a "foreign" depot.

I, in turn, followed Les Bull to Overseal following his later promotion but that, as they say, is another story, to be related in due course.

With the arrival of more Diesels on the Railway and the general run down of the steam locomotive fleet, the Reidingers were early candidates once the Crabs started to go, in common with most "odd-balls." Being placed in store during March 1962, they were officially withdrawn between May and July of that year and all had been cut up at Horwich by the end of November.

An interesting experiment, in which I am pleased to have been involved to such an extent. One can only wonder at the outcome had Mr. Reidinger been given full rein to convert, say, a Stanier Class 5 complete with purpose designed valve chests and cylinders. How, then, would it have compared with the Caprotti 5's so fitted?

The cam boxes, as a matter of interest, were manufactured by a company going by the name of Jameson. I cannot recall, after all the intervening years, their location.

Our five Crabs were not the only British Railway's loco's to enjoy (sic) the benefits of this valve gear, as the LNER (BR Eastern Region) applied Reidinger rotary valve gear to two of its Lentz gear D49 'Hunt' class as early as 1949, basing them at Leeds (Neville Hill) and Starbeck. One wonders how these two compared with the more numerous Lentz fitted engines, which they worked alongside. Did they have the valve problems, which befell their LMS cousins? Classified D49/2, they had both gone by the end of 1959. Probably a case of two more odd-balls within a class half composed of them, the Lentz gear engines being 39 in number.

In conclusion, whilst writing on this emotive subject, a particular incident comes to mind, which occurred during the re-timing of the engine following a No. 6 Mileage Exam. Naturally, the drive shafts and return cranks had been disconnected and removed to enable the coupling rods and connecting rods to be taken down for overhaul. On re-assembly therefore, the necessity to return the cam boxes was required prior to re-connection of the drive shafts.

Now! Hodgy was intrigued as to how this was done, being ignorant of the procedure and desirous to find out. But, being him, he was too proud to ask, especially a person of my junior years. Having had the engine set with the big end on the bottom centre, I had removed the end cover prior to marking the centre line on the casing end. Carrying out this operation ideally required something to stand on, such was the height of the steam chest and cam boxes on a Crab. The nearest thing handy was a bucket so, with the use of this item upside down, the necessary height was achieved. Just as I was stepping onto this rickety platform George uttered that common phrase, "Ey-up, Hodgy's coming." Ascending some eighteen inches or so off the ground, I was aware of his presence behind me. To hold the one-foot rule, in use as a straight edge, and positioning it in the precise place for marking out with my sharpened pencil, required both hands. Concentrating on my task and forgetting my precarious position atop the bucket, I could feel his breath on the back of my neck as he craned his head upwards to see what I was doing. Suddenly, the bucket rocked on the protruding hoops of the handle and I was obliged to step hastily backwards onto the floor, the instinct of self-preservation being highly charged in my mind. In doing so I came down rather heavily onto Hodgy's patent leather shoes with my steel plated boots loaded as they were at that time with my 13 stone : something body. I discovered, for the benefit of any scientifically minded readers, that the screams and invectives uttered from a Lancastrian soul are just the same as any other. To my chagrin, it transpired that the poor chap had suffered two broken toes and spent the next six weeks or so with one foot in plaster. I was the hero of the hour, to my eternal shame, but after only one week away he limped back to work to haunt us, me in particular, so my fame was short lived. A diet of smoke-box and tender-tank jobs came my way with increasing regularity over the next few months, George and I being first choice for these unenviable tasks every time.

But I didn't do it on purpose – honest !!

Chapter 14

In the Shops

The last week of August 1955 saw me being called into the office by the Chief Clerk to sign for my travel pass and receive a lecture as to its use, this being to permit me to travel to and from Derby once each day, Monday to Friday for the purpose of employment at the Main Locomotive Works. "Not for going "Clubbing" and drinking at the week-ends," that worthy was keen to point out. (As if I would !) This remark, from a person who I had never even seen smile, let alone laugh, did not surprise me in the slightest. After all, had he not quoted these pearls of wisdom to all of my predecessors in their turn.

Thus, the following Monday morning found yours truly on Burton station to catch the 6.59 a.m. to Derby. This train ran every weekday morning, its primary function being to convey the workers of Rolls Royce, calling at Repton and Willington to pick up and at Peartree and Normanton to drop them off; this latter station being but a short walk from the factory gates in Nightingale Road.

It left from the North or Jinnie Bay every morning, being the following duty of an earlier local from Leicester; who supplied the motive power. At the time in question this was usually a Bedford Compound, though 2P's, the odd Black 5 and the inevitable 4F, would appear on the front from time to time. Nineteen minutes were allowed for the journey to Derby including the two stops, a task which the regular Compound managed quite well, the Black 5's laughed at and the 4F's struggled to achieve, albeit with only three coaches.

Snugly settled in a corner seat, I was pleasantly surprised to find myself joined by one – Terry Pilkington. An old acquaintance from my schooldays who, it transpired, was an apprentice in the Derby carriage and wagon works. He quickly introduced me to his two mates so I was feeling quite at home with everything. Another two joined us at Willington and that set the pattern for the coming months. Arriving at Derby on time at 7.18 a.m. there was ample time to walk out of the station, around to Hulland Street to cross over the long footbridge which gave access to the Works.

Now! - The Works started at the peculiar time of 7.42 a.m. with two minutes allowance for clocking-on. If, after this extended time, you still hadn't arrived, you had to ask the section foreman if you could start. Using his discretion, this worthy either allowed you to stay, with subsequent adjustments to your wages or sent you home, depending on which side of the bed he had got out of that particular morning. I, innocently, could not conceive how I could possibly be late with 25 minutes to get from the station to my place of work even though one did not clock-on at the gate but on the job which, dependant on where that was at the time, could be handily, just off the end of the bridge, like the Erecting Shop, or over the far side, such as the Boiler Shop. However, I hadn't allowed for the vagaries of the winter and the effect that adverse weather made to the timetable. Many were the occasions when our happy band were still on the platform of Burton Station waiting for the train to arrive from Leicester at the time we should have been clocking-on at Derby and even more occasions when I just made it after a pell-mell dash from a late running train.

The first time I was late was when working on the fitting benches in No. 9 Shop. Here were overhauled various steam fittings such as injector steam valves, sand valves, blowers, boiler gauge frames and the like. When I arrived, about ten minutes late, the foreman was nowhere to be seen so I sidled down to my bench to start work. The fitter with whom I was working told me not to start as they were on strike due to it being too cold. It seemed quite warm to me being used to the sub zero temperatures of the running shed in winter but, as an optimum temperature of, I think 55°F was the prescribed heat for a workshop and this hadn't been achieved on that particular morning, no one would start. I though to myself that, if they did something, they would soon warm up but I didn't think it prudent to say so.

The section foreman eventually spotted me and, being frustrated by the disruption to his production figures, vented his wrath upon my head, telling me that, as I was late, I couldn't start and must therefore go home. I protested loud and long at this juncture, pointing out that I had been on the Railway property since before 7 o'clock that morning and that I could hardly be held to blame for the late running of the train – but to no avail and back home I went. To say that I was annoyed would be a gross understatement but there was nothing I could do. I had swiftly learned that, in the Works, apprentices were the lowest of the low, with "shed lads," as we were known, just a little below that level.

However, I digress. On that first morning, having reported to the Works office, together with the other first arrivals, we were given forms to complete with such information as, name and address, schooling, etc. I was one of thirteen in number and it was explained that we would rotate around twelve sections on a monthly basis, each one of us having to miss out one section. Seven of those monthly sections were to be spent in the Erecting Shop (No. 8 Shop), three in the Fitting Shop (No. 9), two in the Boiler Shop, with the remaining one in the Diesel Shop, which I missed.

Following these formalities, seven of us were escorted to the Erecting Shop where I was placed on the injector section. Here, were fitted the injectors and associated pipework together with the sanding gear. I soon discovered that the Erecting Shop fitters preferred to have the "shed lads" with them rather than the works apprentices as we were more used to the type of work carried out there, having, as they say, done it all before whilst in the shed.

"Just bolt the pipework up hand tight," my Mate soon told me. As I was tightening up everything with a spanner, being my normal practice. On querying his comment he replied, "We haven't got time for such fancy things. We've only got eight hours to do two engines. Besides Jack'll soon nip 'em up on steam test." Towards the end of my twelve months at Derby I was to become all too aware of the consequences of that last remark as will be seen later.

With a frugal organisation like the Railway, most of the pipework and associated nuts and flanges were second hand, having been refurbished in the Coppersmith's Shop, to where they were sent from the stripping pits. Here they would be cleaned, checked and repaired as necessary, then forwarded to us in the

Erecting Shop in sets; i.e. 4F with left hand exhaust injector, 3F or 4F Standard (both sides live steam), 3F Tank with CWS (Carriage Warning System), etc; for refitting to the appropriate engine. Occasionally, however, a replacement pipe for re-assembly would have had a new flange fitted which would require backing off before refitting.

Towards the end of my first week on the injectors section and indeed, in the Works itself, I was merrily filing away at one of these new flanges when none other than Mr. Brown, the Erection Shop foreman came along. His was no meagre position to hold in the Works as he was responsible for the entire Shop not just a small part of it. What would be called a Production Manager or something similar nowadays. Indeed the Shop's "Mr. Big." He stopped by my bench to observe my actions and asked, "What are you doing laddie?" In my innocence I thought he was showing an interest in an apprentice and commenced to explain that I was backing off this new flange and the reasons why, as any apprentice would.

"But what are you doing?" he repeated.

I looked puzzled and started to repeat my explanation when he bellowed,

"Where's the handle laddie, where's the handle?" indicating the file.

"I don't have one," I replied.

"Then don't file boy, don't file," he roared back.

"Stuff it then," I bellowed back throwing the offending file onto the bench where the tang embedded itself in the woodwork, the file quivering from the force of the throw.

"I've been to the stores and they wouldn't give me one," I added by way of explanation.

I should explain at this point that a file handle was an almost unheard of luxury in the running shed and was therefore guarded by the owner with great care. Enquiries as to how they were obtained were met with replies such as, "You'll get some when you go to the Derby Shop," or other similar evasive remarks. The Works storemen were obviously aware of this and, in consequence, were loathe to issue us with one (and I bet they only cost a few pence as well).

Mr. Brown was, quite naturally, incensed by such a reaction from an apprentice, let alone a mere shed lad and demanded to know my number. Not, you will note, my name. Within another half hour or so the section chargeman, who I seem to recall was named Castledine or similar, appeared at my side. To say he was very annoyed would be a gross understatement. He escorted me to that holy of holies, the Shop foreman's office where, despite apologising humbly and a few more grovels for good measure, I shortly found myself on the station awaiting the next train home, after a parting remark of, "Don't let me see your ugly face before next week and consider yourself lucky you still have a job." Which, all things considered, I now know to be correct but at the time with the arrogance of youth, I found it hard to take. I must confess to having a bit of a short fuse during my formative years and whilst basically rather placid and laid back, it didn't take a lot to set me off.

Around this time, during my early months at Derby, I met the girl who was to become my wife and still is I might add, forty years on.

The above incident aside, I enjoyed my time on the injectors in No. 8 Shop. The daily battle with the brake-men who were trying to feed their associated pipes down through the same gaps we used for our injectors; with motion men scrambling around the reversing gear; others fitting fire-doors and the like; all taking place on the footplates which, without the tender attached, were a very restricted area indeed; how no one ever fell off the back of the cabs I do not know but, as far as I am aware, this did not happen – no one ever did!

Whilst working in the Erecting Shop I noticed that alongside the one running track in No.1 bay was laid a third rail. This I recall Joe Benson telling me about when he was serving his time in the Works and helped to build some 2-6-4 tank engines for the 5' 3" gauge Northern Counties Committee in Northern Ireland, as the LMS (ex MR) operations were called in the Emerald Isles before nationalisation; after which it became part of the Ulster Transport Authority. I believe these tank engines acquired the nickname "Jeeps" but whether this was by the enthusiasts or the Irish railwaymen is not clear.

The final week of my two month stint in the injector department saw me working in the test house, which was actually part of the injector section in 9 Shop. Here all the injectors were tested after they had been overhauled. Unfortunately the whole Works went on strike for some reason or another on my second day and was not resolved until the Friday. Whereas the Shop apprentices were included in the dispute, our luckless band of shed lads were sent across to 4 Shed, as the Derby MPD was known, to be used as required by the foreman there, who couldn't believe his luck.

He formed us up into four gangs of three and set us to work on X repairs, of which he seemed to have a backlog. I had mated up with two other lads by this time and we together formed one of the teams. One was Mick Rowledge from Gloucester, who in later years became relief shed master at Burton while I was at Overseal. The other I recall was named Norman from Mansfield, whose surname I have unfortunately forgotten. At dinner times we would go to the 4 Shed canteen and have a natter about this and that over our sandwiches, occasionally followed by a walk around the shed.

One problem we had at this time, when endeavouring to repair the engines in our care, was that of tools. As I knew a couple of the Derby 4 Shed fitters, having previously been sent to work there on odd days from Burton, I had more success than most in borrowing some. However, after two days of this, the 4 Shed shop steward called a halt to our efforts, saying that it was a betrayal of our, or should I say, their brothers, over in the Works. So the rest of the week was spent wandering around the Works and Shed or even Derby itself on occasions. Were it not for having to clock on I needn't have attended at all but poor old Mick and Norman were both in lodgings and had no other choice.

On return to work at the end of the dispute, the Monday morning saw me transferred to No.9 Shop, the Fitting Shop and on to the boiler fitting section. Here I spent a month packing boiler gauge frames, overhauling clack boxes, sand and blower valves, blowdown valves, CW valves and the like. Initially I found this quite interesting but, after the first week or so, found the repetition boring and looked forward to whatever the next month would bring. It was towards the end of this month that the incident with the late arrival, described at the start of this chapter, occurred.

As if this section wasn't boring enough, I next had a week on machining. Very interesting you might say and so thought I until I was shown what was required of me. I was soon parting off pre-bored pieces of hexagon bar at $5/8$ intervals. This I did for three days and on the fourth day, commenced tapping out $5/8$ Whitworth threads by hand down the centre of them. This task was completed on the following Tuesday, after which I was transferred to the motion section and onto eccentrics and valve gear.

This was much more interesting, with all the various parts making up the Stephensons Link Motion and the Walschearts Gear, the fine quality of the finished rods and links of the latter being particularly admired. The machining standards of Stephensons gear was also high, contrasting greatly with the rough and ready appearance of the eccentric rods and sheaves; this being due to the need to smith the rods when altering the valve settings and the white metalling of the bearing surfaces of the sheaves. This also applied, of course, to the eccentric sheave of the inside motion fitted Walschearts valve engines although, in their case, the rods were not smithed but the valve heads adjusted. Presumably, when Stephensons motion is applied to an outside cylinder engine (i.e. Class 5 No. 44767) the valve heads were adjusted in this case also, judging by the finish of the eccentrics rods thereon but I had no personal knowledge of this myself and, in fact, never saw this unique Class 5 whilst in BR service. I had to wait until 1986 before I had the opportunity to do so, when my wife and I enjoyed a trip from Fort William to Mallaig and back behind her. Her driver commented on how much better she climbed the banks than the Walschearts engine (45407 was her partner that year) but wasn't so free down the other side, no doubt due to the characteristics of the different gear, one having constant lead and the other variable.

Fitting new die blocks to the expansion links and valve rods, refurbishing and pinning the various motion points and levers, etc. was all very absorbing to me. The old Stephensons rods were attached to the sheaves by two square-headed bolts, which were inserted through the sheave from the back prior to re-metalling. These gave the appearance of studs onto which the actual eccentric rod foot was placed, being secured by two castellated nuts. When tightened, a flat securing cotter was inserted through the slots in the end of the studs when the nut castellations and slots were lined up. This frequently didn't occur when first tightened and washers were then inserted between nut and foot to achieve this, a tray of washers of varying thicknesses being to hand for the purpose. The same method of bolt and castellated nut was used to secure the two halves of the eccentric together. When each set of motion was completed it was loaded onto a trolley for dispatch to the Erecting Shop.

Running down the centre of the gangway between the lines of the fitting benches was a single railway line, let into the floor with a corresponding rail some ten or twelve feet above. Between these two lines was a post crane, which was used to handle the heavier items under refurbishment. There were, I believe, two of these cranes to each gangway, each with a driver who, when called, knew exactly what was required of them, without hardly a word being said.

After a pleasant couple of weeks on the motion benches I was moved on to the coupling rod and connecting rod section. Here I fell foul of the authoritarian and restrictive practices rife in the Works and totally alien to a young shed lad. I had the temerity to operate one of those post cranes to lower a side rod from my bench in exchange for another, having waited a considerable time for the operator to turn up without avail. Apparently my actions had been observed by the section representative who, far from being on my side, reported the incident to the section foreman, without first saying even one word to me. The outcome was that not only was I reprimanded but the poor crane driver as well. This naturally, doing nothing whatsoever for my popularity. The fitter with whom I was working however, was more sympathetic. He summed it all up in one phrase, "Ignore 'em mate, you can't even trump in here without permission." Not quite the precise words but no doubt you get the idea.

The leading crank pin on some classes of engine did not allow sufficient clearance for a threaded end and nut to be used to secure the side rod without fouling the slide bars and crosshead. This problem was therefore overcome by adapting a split brass bearing held within an elongated enclosure strap complete with a small glut and draw cotter, after the fashion of an inside big end. Some of the Fowler Class 4, 2-6-4T's were so fitted, as indeed were all of his 2-6-2T Class 3's. The Fowler 0-6-0 dock tanks and the Deeley 0-4-0's were similarly treated. These required careful setting up, unlike bushed rods which, if bored correctly in the first place, had to be right when fitted to the rods, having been machined during manufacture to match the wheel centres of the class of engine in question. The split brasses however, by their very character of several component parts, gave scope for error to creep in and catch out the unwary.

The method therefore, was to assemble the whole bearing complete and then check the centres with a trammel from the bush at the other end of the rod. Any errors were then corrected, either by shimming behind the front brass and the strap-end if the centres were shown to be too long or, if not long enough, a small amount, consistent with requirements, was machined or filed off the rear of the brass. No work was done to the rear brass, although it was sometimes necessary to include a small shim (if in the running shed) or fit a larger draw cotter.

With the arrival onto the LMS scene of Mr. Stanier, the recessed nut and cup method was used when this restricted clearance problem arose but, true to the tradition of the Railway, most engines fitted with the split brass, front side-rod bearings remained the same to the end, clattering about the system and presenting constant problems for the shed staff. With the bushes fitted and oilways and felt pads inserted, the only other parts to renew were the gradient pin bushes. These required drilling through for an oilway and two small flutes gouged out to allow the oil to be distributed about the pin. These would have been re-ground as required down in the Wheelwright's Shop, or renewed if below limits, as indeed would the crankpins.

For some reason the return cranks and eccentrics of the Walschearts valve gear engines, if fitted with roller bearings, were also dealt with on this section. This included all the Stanier engines and the Fairburns, Ivatts and BR Standards as well. These were placed in the tender care of SKEFCO and TIMKEN fitters who worked under contract. The smell of hot whale oil in which they 'cooked' the bearing races prior to assembly, permeated the whole section and beyond. Soon after I returned to Burton after completing my 12 months stint in the Works, a new shop was developed, commensurate with the increasing application of roller bearings to axle boxes etc. and these 'specialists' moved there along with the eccentrics and whale oil, much to the delight of all around whose nasal juices had been tickled rather obnoxiously by it's smell for long enough.

Having done, as it were, the valve gear and side rods, etc., it only remained to do the valve, piston and crosshead section. Although three or four other fitters worked on this section, the shed lads were always assigned to the care of Wally, whose surname, sadly I cannot recall. Wally had rather large, staring eyes, which had a myriad of expressions, dependant on what was being discussed at the time. He was a sort of father confessor to us shed lads and was held in great affection by all who knew him. A single man of some forty years or so, he always maintained that there was no substitute for a good pint and a shuffle of dominoes or a game of snooker. This, of course, we all hotly disputed, being young and virile and very much into the pursuit of the female form.

As I filed away at some crosshead draw cotter or scraped carbon from a valve or piston groove, I was fascinated to hear some of the subjects on which Wally's advice was sought, by a number of my contemporaries. They would appear from some obscure corner of the Works and sidle up to Wally with some problem or other. His eyes would open up sometimes so much that I quite expected them to fall out of his face. One lad I recall, who shall remain nameless, had taken to joining his landlady in her bed with the inevitable result – fatherhood, just about coinciding with his departure from Derby to his depot. Wally's eyes that day, took on an appearance which I have never seen the like of ever again. I don't know precisely what advice was given but I did overhear the mention of the Foreign Legion. The story went, that her husband was away overseas, doing his National Service, somewhat late as he had previously been working down the pits and consequently exempt. His young wife, some six years older than our hero, was lonely and frustrated. I have often wondered since, how they fared and of the eventual outcome.

Overhauling piston valves involved thoroughly cleaning the heads of every last bit of carbon. They were firstly cleaned by boiling in some substance or other and it only remained to clean away the softened residue, particular attention being paid to the grooves and cylindrical surfaces. A piece of old valve ring proved to be the favourite tool for decarbonising the grooves, as I had experienced in the shed. When cleaned, the heads were refitted to the valve rod. These had a machined spindle at each end with a shouldered centre section. One end of the spindle was roughly twice the length of the other and had a taper on its end complete with a slot to receive the valve crosshead and its securing cotter. Towards the shouldered centre the spindle was slightly thicker in diameter to form the location beds for the two heads. Immediately before these thickened shoulders, the rod was threaded for the locking nuts. To facilitate installation into the valve steam chest, the one head was slightly smaller in diameter than the other on most classes of engine. On the spindle, the smaller head was fitted up to the shoulder from the crosshead end and, to achieve a precise location, fixed in position with the old shims and the use of a trammel specially made for the purpose. The nut at that end was then locked up tight, its position also precisely set up to enable the tapered pin, pre drilled in both nut and spindle, to be lined up and hammered home, again achieved by shimming washers. When satisfied with the position of the first head on the spindle, the other slightly larger head was fitted to the other, free end, another trammel being used between the two heads to define its precise location and again, the use of shimming washers, as before. All that then remained was for the rings, usually five or six to a head, to be fitted. These were located against brass pegs in the grooves to prevent them from turning in service, without which the gaps in the rings would snag in the valve ports and break off. Such was the precision with which the valve gear was constructed that, with care taken in the overhaul of the valves as described above, it could all be refitted to the engine without any other adjustments being necessary.

The happy month with Wally all soon came to an end and I was moved to the dreaded Boiler Shop, working on boiler mounting; with another Walter, this time named Bull and known to all as 'Watt.' I had a, probably inaccurate, theory about how he got this nickname, from the fact that every time anyone asked him a question he, without fail, replied, "What," before he answered. Mind you! He was quite hard of hearing, as indeed was apparently, everyone else working in that noisy place. This was of course before the days of the Factory Act and the Health and Safety Executive. Nobody, but nobody, wore ear protectors and conversations were held by means of lip reading amongst the regulars therein. Never mind the women in the Lancashire cotton mills, their lot was nothing compared with these lads.

The work itself was very absorbing and, truth to tell, after a couple of days there, one ceased to notice the noise. "What?" - I had probably gone deaf myself.

The job consisted of fitting all the boiler fitments back onto the repaired boiler. Some of those boilers had spent a considerable time out of service prior to their overhaul and in consequence, all the mounting faces were rusty. It was a race between the stud gang and us to see who would get a particular boiler first, with the former usually winning. These lads drilled out all the old studs, replacing them with new ones, which were then caulked round to make them steam-tight. We then had to 'face up' the mounting in between to receive each particular fitting. To achieve this, much rubbing with a small piece of file ensued, initially to remove the rust and finally, to level off the face. All boiler fittings, bar one, had to have face to face joints with no jointing sheeting in between, the exception to this rule being the blowdown valve, which we shall review later.

When, after much filing and emery-ing, causing very sore finger ends, the time came to try on the particular fitting, the face of which you had prepared and checked with a face plate earlier. A light smear of marking compound (a concoction of red lead and linseed oil) was first applied to the face of the fitting, which was then mounted onto the studs and tightened up solid. As access to these studs was not always easy to attain, a variety of spanners, bent and angled to suit each purpose, were used. The nuts were then released, the fitting removed and the boiler and fitting faces examined to see if an even touch had been achieved all round the joint. If so, the fitting was replaced and nutted up solid, otherwise more work was applied to the faces until the desired effect was attained. The skill in achieving this work came, of course, with experience, which we shed lads lacked but our mates, in my case 'Watt', had in plenty.

One important piece of boiler equipment, which I was not very keen on tackling, was the 'cat head' or regulator header. This was bolted onto the main steam pipe actually inside the boiler, a joint packing being used in this case. Having scrambled into the boiler through the dome with some difficulty, you find your feet resting on two longitudinal stays, which run the full length of the boiler and firebox, in effect bolting the whole boiler/firebox assembly together. Watt then passed me two pieces of flat bar with concave half circles at each end, each tied with a length of rope, the other end of which was secured to somewhere outside. A hammer followed, also on a piece of rope. The idea was to hammer these two pieces of bar between the longitudinal straps on each side of the dome thus spreading them apart and enabling me to get down low enough inside the boiler to reach the header pipe flange. Looking up and signalling to Watt that all was ready, he hauled the hammer out then beckoned the overhead crane driver to lower the header itself in. The small circle of light through which you have got to get out suddenly halves as the cat head comes down through the dome towards you. Now! I have never been a midget by any means, always being a bit "big for my age" as it were (OK then! Fat!), so I mouthed my concern to Watt who ignored me and lowered down a sack of nuts and bolts for me to get on with it. Having successfully bolted the header to the pipe flange, complete with joint packing (without dropping any), the sack was hauled out and two spanners were lowered in with which to tighten the bolts. This completed, Watt pulled the spanners back out and lowered the hammer back down. "Out you come," he shouts down, "And don't forget to knock them sprags out when your legs are clear." I am now in a crouching position with my head in the dome, regarding the details of the porting on the cat head, roughly an inch or so in front of my face, and reaching down, I swing blindly with the hammer at where I think the stretcher bars are until, with a twang, they both spring free. With the speed of light, Watt has them out of the hole and is tugging at the hammer. I hold on to this as he has already rattled my ears with the straps, which is bad enough, but a 4 lb hammer is something else entirely! "Leave it where it is while I get out," I commanded, adding as an afterthought, "That's if I can." "What! Course you can," Walt answers, "And don't be all day. We've got more work to do you know!" After a struggle I manage to get my arms and shoulders out followed by my nether regions. How delightful the racket sounded after spending an hour or so in there. Of course it was not unknown for riveting to take place while you were in there, a condition that was suffered and endured by the riveter's mate every day, and they were more than welcome to it, believe me!

With the cat head in place and secured, the next item to be fitted was the regulator operating rod. This passed from the boiler front (footplate) to the dome cat head. After the regulator valve had been fitted, it was connected by a linking arm, to a small bracket on the end of the operating rod. At the footplate end the stuffing box could now be affixed to the boiler front and the gland packed. In the stuffing box area the operating rod was sheathed with copper and this always required renewal when the engine was Shopped, whether or not the boiler was removed from the locomotive. To do this a new end was fitted to the rod. The blacksmiths welded these on by good old fashioned blacksmith welding over an open hearth.

To my mind, one of the best experiences of my time in boiler mounting were these visits to the Blacksmith's Shop to have these ends replaced. Here were true craftsmen, practising an art which could trace its skills back to the middle-ages (or probably even further by archaeologists). To watch the smith and his mate at work was a real joy. First of all the gland end of the old rod would be put in the fire with the new end being gently heated to one side. After a certain time, when the rod became cherry red, it would be withdrawn and the old end chopped off by the use of a large smith's chisel, the force being applied by a steam hammer. After further heating, the rod end would be fashioned into a wedge shape matching that already formed on the new end attachment. When both had been heated to a particular temperature, indicated by the brightness and redness of the metal, they were fused together to become an inseparable whole; a true measure of the expertise of the blacksmith's art. I have always been intrigued by the skills associated with the forge and can vouch for the expertise required to achieve a successful weld by use of the blacksmith's fire. A task I have attempted but only managed to accomplish on rare occasions and more by luck than skill. Truly an instance of that old adage of there being no substitute for practice and experience.

The final week of my time in this section was spent in the test house where the boilers were, first hydraulically and then steam, tested. Having connected the boiler up to the water supply, they were pressurised to a point far in excess of the designed working pressure. I forget just by how much this was but it was quite considerable, possibly as much as 50%. A detailed examination of the boiler and fittings was then made and any defects noted. These, of course, had to be rectified and the boiler re-tested before Jack, with whom I was working, would sign the certificate. If and when all was well the boiler was then steam tested, again in excess of the working pressure by some 50 lbs or so. To achieve this higher amount, a Royal Scot type parallel boiler with a working pressure of 250 lbs PSI was sited alongside the test house to supply the steam. Like any young fireman worth his salt, I had always aspired to try my skills on one of these engines or, of course, a Pacific. And surprise, surprise, the regular fireman was only too pleased to let me have a go.

Ted, as I seem to recall his name, was in his middle 50's and told me that the boiler in use was the second one that had occupied the position since he had been on the job. A system of forced air draughting was available to supplement the natural air flow through and over the fire, achieved by the use of the jet (blower) as there was obviously no exhaust steam action in the smoke box to help draw the fire as there would be out on the road. The output of this boiler was more than adequate to meet the needs of the ex MR boilers being tested and the

2-6-4T engine boilers, with their 200 lbs working pressure, as well. However, the Stanier type 2 boilers, found on the 8F's, Class 5's and Jubilees, with their 225 lbs boiler pressure, were something else. Whereas only relatively few 5's and Jubilees were Shopped at Derby, not the same could be said of the 8F's or indeed, latterly the BR Standard 5's. One wonders what type and size of boiler was used at Crewe to test the Royal Scot and Pacific boilers?!

During my time at Burton, I had seen a number of boiler certificates signed by 'Jack Crewe' and here I was, actually working with him. His notoriety belied his appearance, being a quite normal kind of chap with no real outstanding features, who just carried out his work with a quiet professionalism, explaining his actions and motives to me as he went along. He was a real pleasure to work with. A Shop apprentice shared my week in the test house and, like most of his fellow Shopmen, was totally afraid of steam. We were standing talking one day on the footplate during one of my 'firing' turns, when one of the boiler gauge glasses burst. I quickly threw a handy sack over the offending frame and shut the steam/water handle down to isolate the two halves of the frame. On looking round, the Shop lad was nowhere to be seen, not only having dropped off the footplate, as maybe any sensible person would have, but had run out of the Shop altogether. "I thought the boiler had blown up," he said, by way of explanation, on his return. By this time, Ted had fitted a new glass and all was well. I managed to get the 'Scot' to lift its valves a couple of times but I must confess to making more hard work of it than Ted, who could make it steam without even breaking into a sweat. But he had been at it for much longer than me. How would he perform out on the road though? I wondered, with the loco

A new BR standard Class '5' under construction No. 3 bay Derby works erecting shop. Photo: Authors Collection.

bouncing and rocking all over the place instead of on the rock steady platform which was the case here? Mentioning this to Jack, he suggested I should ask Ted myself but added that he used to be a fireman on the road before failing with his eyes, so I guessed he would have managed very well indeed and decided to keep the impertinent arrogance of my youth to myself.

My next move was on to 'New Work' back in No. 8, the Erecting Shop, again constructing BR Standard Class 5's, the particular engines under construction at the time being 73090 to 94. Although certain jobs were done on all five engines, the majority of the time on this section was spent on 73092, to which, I have always since maintained, I made a significant contribution. The fitter I was with, Alan by name (again the surname escapes me), was quite a young man, not long back from his stint in the forces, doing his National Service. On new work, all aspects of the job were tackled, not just a particular section as in the repair bays. 73092 already had her frames assembled and boiler fitted when I made her acquaintance but I did help to wheel her, going on to fit the brake gear, motion valves and pistons (the cylinders were fitted as the frames were assembled). Also the injectors, sanding gear and other parts like the lubricator and associated pipework. Obviously, some detail parts had already been added prior to the boiler being fitted as it was more convenient to do at that stage.

One day Alan went to the dentist and, in his absence, I fitted the left side piston gland and crosshead followed by the connecting rod and was just inserting the little end gudgeon pin when he returned. He wasn't quite as pleased with my enthusiasm as I was, particularly when he saw the 'hammer rash' around the end of the crosshead draw cotter. He had me spending the rest of the afternoon filing it all off. 'Hodgy' would have loved him, I thought. However, having checked all I had done, he mellowed a bit and when I had filed all the bruises off the crosshead cotter, nothing more was said. By the end of three weeks, 73090 and 91 had gone completely, with 73092 in the Paint Shop, 73093 and 94 well on the way to completion, and 73095, 6 and 7 taking their places.

The Paint Shop was another interesting place to visit. The odd small detail on 73091 and 2 required our presence there and what a fascinating place it was too. Our little gang of three: Mick, Norman and me (poetic, isn't it!) had, of course, looked in there on our occasional dinner time prowls but this was one place where visitors were not encouraged. Two of the more interesting attachments we fitted were the SC Plate and the Number plates on the smokebox doors, the SC of course, denoting that the smokebox contained self-cleaning screens and therefore did not require emptying during services between boiler washouts. In practice that did not prove to be true but that was the theory at least. The paint finish applied to these new locomotives was quite impressive. Most of the cladding and panel-work, like cylinder and boiler lagging, running plates and cabs, already had a pink primer applied before assembly and this was first touched up, after any putty application, filing and rubbing down had been done. A creamy green undercoat was next applied, followed by two coats of black, the first one being matt and the second, gloss. The number and emblem transfers were next applied, along with the 'mixed traffic' lining. Finally a coat of varnish sealed the whole finish. Along with the vermilion buffer beams and numbers picked out in white, the effect was startling. What a shame that the chances of that beautiful finish ever being cleaned was such a lottery, depending upon where the engine was allocated and even then, little chance of being to a standard deserving of the painters' efforts.

Talking of painters' talents, during my twelve months in the Works, one of the original LMS Mainline Diesels had an overhaul and re-paint. This time a move away from the original black livery with silver waistband and numbers was made, the locomotive returning to traffic in Brunswick green with an orange and black waistband, as per the standard British Railways Secondary Passenger livery; all this applied by hand in the usual way. However, in place of the then standard 'ferret and dartboard' emblem, the first example of what was to become the new corporate badge was applied; however, not as a transfer but hand painted. I feel privileged to have been there to see this artist, for such he was, at work.

LMS mainline diesel No. 10000. Photo: P. Groom.

Down at the bottom of the Paint Shop, two old stagers were stored. These were ex-Midland 'Spinner' 4-2-2 No. 118 (673) and 2-4-0 No. 158A. Part of the bay in which these two old ladies stood was partitioned off to give more room for the construction and overhaul of Diesel shunters of the 350 h.p. English Electric 0-6-0 type. Interestingly enough, examples of most, if not all, of the various pre-Nationalisation Companies' types were gravitating to Derby about this time. As well as the ex Southern mainline Diesels, including 10201 and 2, being present, examples of their version of diesel electric 0-6-0 shunters were to be seen, along with the LNER versions and, of course, LMS examples, both with and without jackshaft drive. Also the prototype and unique lightweight BOBO No. 10800. Add to this, various odd 0-4-0 and 0-6-0's made by Hunslet, Simplex, Fowler and the like, mostly originating from sleeper depots, creosote depots and other permanent way departments, it only remains to mention the most unusual and unique of them all: Colonel Fell's Diesel Mechanical No. 10100.

Of this last mentioned locomotive, parts of it were found in just about every shop and department in the Works, including the Boiler Shop. Just before I left the Works an announcement was made to the effect that British Railways had in fact purchased the engine from the Colonel. The story around the Works at the time was that the railway had to buy it, as they couldn't find all the bits to give it him back.

The 'Fell' diesel No. 10100. Photo: P. Groom.

As mentioned before, three and sometimes four of our little band of shed lads used to take our mid-day break over in the 4 Shed canteen. One of the characters to be observed there was one 'Batty' Sloane. Not his actual real name but near enough for the purpose of this litany and for those in the know to recognise. He was a labourer on the shed staff and quite an eccentric. We would be sitting together at one end of the tables when he would come in. One quick glance would immediately tell us his frame of mind. Usually he would walk in, order a mug of tea, sit down, extract a doorstep sandwich from old newspaper wrapping and eat it (the sandwich not the newspaper – he wasn't that daft), slurping his tea. However, on other days, he would enter with a glazed look in his eyes; then the fun would begin. Spotting some young cleaner or possibly visiting fireman from another depot, he would pounce forward, and produce from his pocket a piece of chalk with which he would proceed to draw a circle on the floor around his victim.

"Get out of that if you can. You can't can you?" he would taunt. The look in his eyes invariably made his victim stand still. Batty would then circle round and round him, muttering incoherent mumbo-jumbo. Some wit would whisper to the poor unfortunate to stand still if he knew what was good for him. Eventually Batty would pat the victim on the shoulder, the manic look would go from his eyes and he would say something like, "Welcome, friend," or "You're now one of us," or some other such nonsense. He would then sit down and eat his sandwich as if nothing had happened, leaving his victim to stand around in startled amazement. Naturally, he not being assisted or comforted by any of the watching regulars who, being used to the performance and in keeping with regular human behaviour, usually found amusement in the poor fellow's dilemma. I once saw one of his victims push him aside and step out of the circle drawn round him. Batty, with great strength, which belied his somewhat slight build, immediately picked him up and put him back inside the circle.

Another time, he would capture some other gullible person in a corner and flash a tin at him, the contents of which was never revealed, even though he kept opening and closing the lid. This, in fact, was my own experience with him during one of my first appearances in the canteen. Naturally, this somewhat strange behaviour did not go either unnoticed or without complaint to the management, who sent him, on more than one occasion, across to the station to see the Company doctor. When, as occurred more than once, someone accused him of being 'crackers' or 'round the bend' he would dive into his pocket and produce a letter, from that same company doctor, saying that he was of sound mind, etc. "Have you got one to say you are sane?" he would challenge his accuser. There was never a dull moment when Batty Sloane was around. We often discussed him and sometimes conjectured that it was all an act, until he had another session, then the look in his eyes gave us doubts again.

When I later went back to Derby on a Diesel course in 1961, I enquired after his whereabouts as he was obviously not around and I was told he had sadly, been knocked down and killed in a road accident.

Another character who sticks in my mind was a shed driver who never, or rarely, went out of the canteen, unless he was going home, his fireman doing all the work. His overalls were spotless and his shoes shone like a guardsman's.

To my surprise, following my month in the New Work Section, I was moved back onto New Work, this time on frames. Here the frames were flame cut, two at a time on the cutter, following a template. Once the basic frames had been cut they were separated and all drillings and openings individual to each side were made. All the flame cut edges had to be smoothed off and this is where yours truly came in again! A file was pressed into my hand with which to do this. "They must be joking," I thought. 40 odd feet of locomotive frame, some 1½" thick, two sides, top and bottom, with various shapes cut out, all requiring smoothing down. "Haven't they heard of a grinder," I wondered.

"You've a day to do the set," I was told.

"In your dreams," I thought, as I commenced filing.

My! Wasn't that steel hard stuff. After about 20 minutes of filing I had smoothed off about 6 or 8 inches of the frame and my arms were aching.

After about an hour or so of this drudge, the foreman came to my rescue, sending me to assist on another job. "Do you know where the Stone Pit is?" he asked. I replied in the affirmative and was then told to report to the foreman there where I would be told what was required. The Stone Pit was used for various purposes, not least of which was cutting up old locos for scrap. Also, ex-Works locomotives requiring further attention were often dealt with there as space inside the Erecting Shop was at a premium.

On arrival, on the far side of the Works at the Stone Pit, there, amongst a line of old engines, stood this nice, shiny black, ex-Works Class 8F. "That's got to be the job," I mused which proved to be correct, and what a job it proved to be! It transpired that, despite having passed both its hydraulic and steam tests before being fitted to the locomotive, it had failed quite spectacularly, out on the road on its test run. The superheater header casting had cracked between the mounting flange and the header itself thereby causing the steam to escape into the smokbox and out to the atmosphere instead of passing through the header, round the elements, back to the header and down into the cylinders, as the designers intended.

To gain access to the header, the first items to be removed were the chimney skirt and ejector pipe and ring. This the two fitters, with whom I was to work, had nearly completed when I arrived on the scene. A liberal amount of soot already adorned their persons and we had hardly started yet. So, while they started to remove the superheater elements, 24 in all, I made a start on the blower pipe and main steam pipes. All told it took the best part of that day to remove all the main elements and bits and pieces to leave us a 'clean' start (hardly the best term in a smokebox) the following morning at removing the header. Having cleaned myself up as best I could, I made my way across the station to catch my train home, this being the 6.00 p.m. local out of bay No.5 to Burton, calling at Peartree and Normanton then Repton and Willington, being laid on, as mentioned before, for the Rolls Royce workers, this time of course, to take them home.

The following day, after much struggling and cursing, the mounting flange was finally disconnected and the header left sitting on its two carrying brackets, one on each side of the smokebox. The crane came along with what resembles two telegraph poles, and could very well have been so, which were inserted into two of the top flue tubes in such a way that they just cleared the underside of the header. A set of rope blocks was then attached to a sling around the chimney of the engine in front of us, with the other end around the header. Then, after much heaving by everyone in sight, the header was hauled from its position at the top of the front tubeplate and onto the poles. To our delight, it just cleared the underside of the chimney, which we had thought might also have to be removed and thus, in next to no time, was being manoeuvred out through the smokebox doorway, for the crane to take away. Whilst all this had been going on, a new set of superheater elements had arrived. Not for the Shop fitters to spend hours cleaning up jointing surfaces, and suchlike, before anything could be put back. The main steam pipes etc. had also been taken away for refacing. All we had to do was to clean up the header flange connection face on the front tubeplate and, even here, contrary to normal practice, a jointing gasket was made to save having to remove the header a second time to check its seating. An idea with which I heartily agreed, not that it would have mattered if I hadn't. Replacement was therefore, a reversal of the removal, taking just under two more days to complete.

I was to visit this site again during my final weeks in the Shops, as we shall see later. Thus passed a week supposedly on the frames. It was with little enthusiasm that I reported back to the Frames Section chargeman the following Monday morning. "Somebody seems to have it in for you lad," he greeted me, "Filing frames and playing in dirty smokeboxes. Now they want you down the Tender Bay, in 8 Shop. Can't remember many shed lads going down there," he added.

"It can't be any worse than filing frames," I replied.

"A lot dirtier, though," he answered.

So, over into to the Erecting (No.8) Shop I went once more. The tenders were repaired and rebuilt at the opposite end of No.3 Bay to the New Works locomotive building. As I arrived there, Brenda, the Shop office girl, was just leaving with the usual bundle of cards and papers in her hand. We exchanged smiles and I reflected that the number of moves I was being given lately were, on their own, enough to keep her busy. As I mentioned earlier, every section in every shop and department in the Works had its own clocking on/off point and all payment papers, etc. were kept on the relevant section. Whilst the main section staff rarely changed positions, we Shop lads and apprentices were always on the move, which must have kept Brenda very busy indeed.

Soon I was crawling about inside an old Midland tender tank, fitting new water feed valves and linkage, along with the associated sieve screens and water level floats. These few tasks completed, this particular tender, destined to accompany an old 2 or 3F for the next few years, was completed.

The method of working in the Tender Section was more flexible than in the New Works area further along the same bay, everyone taking their turn on brake gear, draw gear, water pick-ups, tank gear, wheels, etc. Our next tender was of the Fowler/Deeley type, paired up with Compounds in the main, as indeed was this one. Just a bare frame greeted us, with the painters daubing over a quick coat of black. The brake shaft was replaced first, with new bushes of cast iron being fitted into the frames to carry it. This was followed by the brake cylinder and piston. This item came already built up but, for the record, it had two broad brass piston rings and was single acting, with the return stroke being achieved by a return spring. The short link connecting the piston rod to the main brake shaft was soon fitted and our attention turned to the water pick-up gear shaft. Whereas the main brake shaft spanned the full width of the space between the frames, the water pick-up shaft was only a short affair, roughly two feet long, bushed into the main frame above the brake shaft on the driver's side, this being on the right on ex Midland and early LMS engines, with the inbound end supported in a similar bush mounted on a special plate-like bracket bolted underneath and from the front drag box. Attention was next turned to the brake hangers and their hanging brackets, six in all, followed by the rear buffers.

The more of these items that could be completed before the tank was dropped into the frames the better, as it was so much more pleasant and convenient to work in the open as it were. When the tank arrived it was lowered into the frames onto wooden pads. The overhead crane held the tank just clear of the frame while the securing bolt holes were lined up by use of tommy bars and the bolts inserted. The tank was then levered down the final half an inch or so and the crane released. It was but a few minutes more to tighten down the bolts and make everything secure. It was then possible to attend to items like water feed pipes, which have to be fitted to the tank bottom with rubber joints, the other ends being on carrying brackets fixed under the front dragbox. It was also useful to refit the water pick-up trunk beneath the tank at this stage, before the tender was re-wheeled. Also the shaft from which the scoop itself was raised and lowered from beneath the tank. When re-wheeling was complete, all that remained was to fit the brake pull rods and cross rods, the water scoop, complete with pan, which had to be set at approximately two inches below rail level when lowered, and the operating arm. One other item, preferably fitted before re-wheeling, was the CWS train pipe, which ran underneath the full length of the tank from front to back, starting from a flexible connection at the front to the CWS valve on the rear buffer beam. With the hand brake and water pick-up columns and handles all connected, the rear and front draw gear fitted and the intermediate flexible pipes (bags in Railway jargon) renewed and replaced, the tender was ready to be re-united with the engine. Though tenders all carried their own numbers on a cast plate affixed to the rear of the tank, it was normal practice to keep the same tender paired to the same engine where possible, though this was all to change in later years. All the foregoing tender rebuild would invariably take only two to three days, depending on the number of men working on it, usually two with mates or apprentices, the latter usually being shop lads.

After two weeks of this, another move was forthcoming for me, this time only across the Shop to the Valve, Piston and Motion Assembly Section. Not far for Brenda to walk this time. I was teamed up with a chap named Ernie and his mate on this section, yet again the surnames escape me. Although I had a basic understanding of the mystics of valve setting, these two were to fine-tune my knowledge, as it were, for which I was eternally grateful. Our first engine, I recall, was a Class 2P, one of the LMS built, similar to our own Burton No.633 but without the Dabeg pump of course. I was also surprised to discover that she had only single head piston valves, unlike the Burton engine, which had double headed ones. A quick smear of oil over these heads and Ernie had them in their respective steam chests in double quick time. Likewise the pistons and covers, all with the aid of the overhead crane which had a small auxiliary unit as part of its gantry for this and other like uses where the main hook would be too cumbersome. Meanwhile, Ernie's mate, Eric and I were underneath, re-assembling all the various gear and such like. The previous shift had fitted the back covers and slide bars during the night, together with the weighbar shaft. These latter items were usually fitted before the boiler was placed in the frames but this particular engine had only come in for a 'sole and heel' job (intermediate repairs) so consequentially. Had not undergone a boiler lift. "I bet it was fun refitting those back covers," I thought. In the fullness of time I was to find out.

With all the valve gear assembled, the valves were then timed; with yours-truly turning those big 6' 9" driving wheels round by means of a pinch bar. The relative movement of each valve up and down the steam chest was marked with a trammel on both fore and back gear and compared with the marks made before connecting up, this initial movement being made against stops inserted in the front steam chest ports. There was no need to check the back ports as the valve heads were set true to each other on the valve rods as described earlier, when I was employed on the V and P benches in No. 9 Shop. As all was not as it should be, the eccentric rods were removed to enable them to be 'jumped', that is shortened or drawn (lengthened), at the blacksmith's, by the required amount, usually within the parameters of $\frac{1}{16}''$ to $\frac{1}{2}''$ either way. The skill and experience of Ernie and Eric was such that, at least during the month I was with them, these rods never had to return to the blacksmith's for a second visit. They were always right when tried over a second time.

Whilst waiting for the blacksmith to do his stuff, the crossheads were refitted and the connecting rods coupled up. These were then tried over, also to determine an equal stroke up and down the cylinders, with the free space at each end of the stroke checked against previous marks, made when the pistons were 'bumped' at each end of the cylinders before the connecting rods were coupled up. And you only get one guess as to who was wielding the pinch bar again.

With this engine completed to the satisfaction of my two mates, we moved on to our second engine of the day, a Fowler Class 4, 2-6-4 tank. We had been unable to fit the siderods onto the 2P, as the trailing wheels were still missing, as indeed was the bogie. However, all three sets of coupled wheels were in place on our 2-6-4, so it was decided to fit the coupling rods first. This engine, like so many of her sisters at the time, still retained her split front coupling rod bearings, to which Eric applied himself with singular determination, whilst Ernie and I fitted up the valve gear; Walschearts in this case, as against Stephensons on our previous Class 2P. Again with great aplomb, Ernie slipped the valves into the steam chest and, having squared up the valve guides by shimming, coupled the valve stems to the gear. By this time Eric was refitting the slidebars, again squaring them up by means of shims, true to a line passed through the centre line of the cylinder from a temporary bracket bolted across the front opening, passing down through the stuffing box and on to the big end crank. When set up to his liking, the line cord etc. was removed and the crossheads tried in the bars. The pistons were next inserted into the cylinders and, after all the stuffing box components and cover had been slid onto the rod, they were connected up to the crossheads and the pistons 'bumped' - as before with the 2P. It only remained for the engine to be gently pinch barred along the pit to check the piston clearances and valve events in both fore and back gears, as previously described, for everything to be found correct; myself, once again, providing the motive power whilst Ernie and Eric did the checking, one on each side. Knocking off time certainly came round quickly on this section. This set the pattern for the first two weeks, with a series of 4F, 3F, 2F and 2P's coming our way, intermingled with the odd shunter. We had so far avoided Compounds, which were reputed to be quite difficult and very much labour intensive, so much so that, when working on one, the daily output allocation for the team so employed was reduced from two engines to one and a half.

The second two weeks were to be on the night shift, the precise starting and finishing times of which I have quite forgotten, and we started the week with a vengeance on, yes you've guessed it! a dreaded Compound; one of the ex LMS version, all the Midland examples being withdrawn by then. It was especially noticeable when working on these engines, what large machines they were.

Much larger than 'a 2P with outside cylinders stuck on' as I once read someone describe them! With both inside and outside cylinders, slide valves and piston valves, all driven by three sets of Stephensons motion, giving no less than six eccentrics between the frames, along with the high pressure crank, big end and connecting rod, there was a lot of work to be done before we went home the next morning. And – would we also slip the coupling rods onto a couple of 4F's as well!

The Compound, like the 2P described earlier, was sitting on jacks with only the driving axle in place so all the motive power was, again, provided by me and the faithful pinch bar, between the spokes and against the frames. And didn't they take some turning! Three sets of valves meant three full turns forwards and three turns backwards. Then, being Stephensons gear, down with the eccentric rods for a trip to the blacksmith's for adjustment. While they were away we turned our attention to the pistons, cylinders and slidebars, with all the usual setting up procedure, assembly and 'bumping up', followed by the fitting of the connecting rods and trying over again. At least, only two turns sufficed this time. Attempting to turn those 6' 9" wheels and pull round three con rods attached to three pistons, two of 21" diameter and one of 19½," proved too much for me and Eric had to lend a hand. I could not forget either, that we still had the eccentric rods to refit and try over again when they came back. It was well past our break-time by now and we still were nowhere near finished. Two of the other fitters came by, "Come on Ern', time to get your head down," they taunted, "aint Eric pullin' his weight?" "Bl..dy Compounds," Ernie cursed, "Time they scrapped the blasted things altogether!"

Just then, the labourer returned with the eccentric rods. "Come on," our two teasers commiserated, "We'll give you a hand. Soon be done, then you can nod off."

"Some chance of that," Eric chipped in, "We've still got them side rods to chuck on yet."

"Blimey. Some folks are never satisfied. You finish this thing then and we'll see to the rods. Give some blokes a bit of a job and they just can't cope!" one joked over his shoulder as they wandered over to the first of the 4F's. Was I glad when we staggered into the chargeman's hut to enjoy the last hour in fitful slumber, seated on an upturned bucket in a corner. As I stood, bleary eyed, on platform 6 at Derby Station, waiting for my ride back home, I could still feel the base ring of that bucket on my posterior.

Always, seemingly, a long wait for my train, I reflected, whether on days or nights. A quick glance across towards the Works revealed two particular locomotives still present on the holding lines and sidings. One painted a rather dull and faded red, the other bright green with a slight sheen and tarnished brass-work. The red one, it was revealed on closer inspection, was of a rather unusual and almost unique 0-6-4-wheel arrangement, tank engine, bearing the name 'Cecil Raikes,' of the Mersey Railway. But, why was she there and what was to be her fate? The other one had a rather more interesting and dramatic background to convey. Withdrawn from Toton in the early months of 1955, as number 41966, the last survivor of the London, Tilbury and Southend Railway's 4-4-2 tank engines; the remaining members of this type being of LMS origin;

she had been taken into the Works and overhauled then out-shopped as LT&SR, number 80 'Thundersley', for the centenary of that railway later in that year. Now returned to Derby works for scrapping, the men on the stripping pits had refused to cut her up. Hence her presence in the holding sidings, awaiting a decision as to her future. History now tells us she is safely enfolded in the arms of the preservation movement and on display, at the time of writing, at the Bressingham Steam Museum. Her consort, 'Cecil Raikes' also escaped the cutter's torch but I now understand is in Liverpool Museum.

My second night and indeed the rest of the first week, passed without untoward incidents, our workloads invariably being completed comfortably in time to afford our little team a couple of hours or so 'rest of the eyes' so to speak.

Ex LTSR 4-4-2T No. 80 'Thundersley'. Photo: E. Edwards.

Week number two started off with one of Mr. Stanier's 3 cylinder, 2-6-4T's, "Another bummer to draw," as Eric described it. This engine was completely re-wheeled, as the side-rods had to go on first before the con-rods, as on all of Mr.S's outside cylinders masterpieces. Thus, when trying her over for piston clearance and valve setting, one lost count of the number of times Eric and I 'pinched' her bulk up and down the centre road of number 2 bay. As more bits were added through the night, with more pistons and valves to deal with, so she became harder to get moving, not helped by our increasing tiredness. Still, we survived to complete her, then finished the shift by refitting the siderods onto a 2P, which had had its remaining wheels fitted, just behind us, during the night. Thus, we had completed two engines for the attention of the Paint Shop the following day.

The following night we were allocated an 8F and, on completion, made a start on a second one, fitting both pistons and valves before getting our heads down, leaving the day shift to fit the motion, box up and do the trying over, etc. Night three saw us with yet another of the dreaded Compounds. We were also requested to have a go at fitting the valves in a Fowler Class-3, 2-6-2 Tank. Apparently the day shift had been tussling with these for quite some time without success. I should perhaps explain that, unlike the more modern engines, the piston valve heads on these engines were both the same diameter, rather than the back head slightly reduced in size, as earlier described. Thus, it was first necessary to compress the back head before passing it through the front steam chest instead of just pushing it through as with reduced head engines. This always aggravated the continued progress into the rear chest, as, at this stage, it was also time to compress and fit the front head to its steam chest as well. With the back head having passed through the free space between the two steam chests it was anybody's guess what was happening to the rings fitted to it. Ernie explained these difficulties to me and suggested I have a go at fitting one of the valves while he and Eric made a start on the Compound.

So, with the confidence of youth and armed with a lead hammer, I advanced upon No. 40026 with grim determination to succeed. After 20 minutes or so of tapping and nudging I had only managed to get one ring of one valve of the front head into its chest, mainly I felt, because of the rings on the back head having sprung out and fouled the edge of the ports instead of entering the back chest. I decided to use a bit of 'Steam Shed Technology.' Sneaking back into the cabin I found a couple of large brown envelopes, which I cut into strips about an inch wide. Back at the engine I pulled the valve back out, with some difficulty, as the back head was non too keen to come back through the front head either. Having eventually hauled it out, I eased the strips of brown paper under the rings at approximately 120-degree intervals and compressed them back into position in their grooves. The brown paper was sufficient to take up the free space between the grooves and rings, consequently holding them in compression. After a liberal smear of oil around the heads, the valve assembly was re-entered into the steam chest and two or three taps with the lead hammer on the rod end saw the valve 'home and dry.' The same procedure was repeated on the other side, all in all about an hours work. Once the engine was in steam the dry, superheated, high temperature steam would soon burn the paper away with no detriment to the valves at all.

Feeling very pleased with myself, I reported back to Ernie to ask him if he wanted me to connect the valves up to their crossheads and then fit the front steam chest covers on. Far from being pleased, he looked at his watch and with a quizzical look asked me, "Have you used brown paper on them rings?" "I know what you shed lads are like." Having confessed that I had, I was lectured on the folly of such a practice. He told me I was in the Shops now not in the shed and they didn't go in for bodging here but did things properly. "Still, seeing as how you've done it now, you might as well carry on and finish it," he reflected, warning "But let this be the last time. Don't do it again." So I went back and finished off 40026, telling myself that Ernie didn't want the hassle of wrestling with them either. All that remained was for the valves to be tried over and the job was done. The rest of the week passed by with no other major problems, culminating with 73001 on the last night. Needless to say, and I bet you've already guessed, my two nocturnal friends, Ernie and Eric, were nicknamed by all and sundry – Morecambe and Wise!

Whilst I had been 'enjoying' the night shift, Norman had been out on the weighbridge and steam testing with Jack. To my eternal delight, my next assignment saw me taking his place outside on the test or 'Pit' as it was known.·Jack proved to be a very down to earth character, whose aim in life seemed to be to get through it with the least trouble possible, culminating with a session in the back room of the Midland Hotel for the last hour of the morning opening hours. He constantly cursed his mentors in the Erecting Shop, whose 'finger tight' doctrine caused him a lot of unnecessary work. Frequent storming visits to see the Injector and Brake Section chargehands, during which much swearing and table thumping took place, were to no avail, spanner tightening of nuts and bolts being sacrificed in the name of 'bonus,' a share of which, let it be said, came Jack's way and, of course, into the tills of the Midland Hotel taproom.

Jack would climb aboard, say, an ex-Works 4F, all resplendent in its new, shiny, black paintwork with bright red buffer beam, just as she was making steam. With about 100 psi. on the clock, he would knock open the water valve then, turning to the steam valve, knock that open, to test the injector. A roaring sound would emit from beneath his feet as clouds of steam, under pressure, would blast out of every joint associated with it, blowing to high heaven and taking the jointing inserts out at the same time. Above all this noise, Jack could be heard cursing and 'Raising Cain,' calling down all manner of fates upon the '8 Shop' boys. At least, their finger tight policy meant that the replacing of the joints was, in general, not too onerous a task, although some of those associated with exhaust injectors could be a bit awkward. Needless to say, unlike in the sheds, an inexhaustible supply of ready-made joints was to hand, to make life easier but, I reflected, after a couple of days handling hot nuts and bolts, burning my fingers, life would have been a lot easier if the joints had been tightened up before the tests were carried out. The steam joints on the injector bodies were particularly vulnerable as they were made of asbestos which, once wet, simply disappeared. These were always replaced, by Jack, with jointing packings, as indeed was the practice in the Running Sheds. The water feed joints were of rubber and usually only required tightening up, as did the jointing gaskets of the delivery pipes.

As I used to arrive on the job by about 7.20 most mornings, I reasoned that, if I had a couple of spanners, I could tighten up most of these joints before any-thing happened, usually just after 8.00 each morning. On mentioning this idea to Jack, he was more than willing and prepared, to furnish me with a spare key to his tool cupboard, so keen and prepared in fact, that I realised I was by no means the first lad to come up with this wonderful 'time saving' scheme. Thus, I would get stuck in as soon as I had pulled on my overalls, nipping around the six or eight engines lined up for testing and weighing, each morning. If a new 73000 was amongst their number, I was instructed to leave it alone as there shouldn't be any loose joints on them. If Jack found any defects on them, a couple of men would be sent over from the Works to put them right. It is only fair to say that, during my month on the 'job' this requirement never occurred until my last week when the first of the Caprotti 5's, No. 73125, appeared. But more of that later...

I found out very quickly that, if more than two of the engines appearing on the Pit were fitted with exhaust injectors, I could not usually get round them all before the steam raiser or Jack got started, causing an increase in my workload of replacing the joints consequently ruined. Scrutiny of the timetable at Burton revealed a parcels train at 6.10 in the mornings so I enquired if I could use that to start at Derby earlier. Permission forthcoming, I did so and was able to comfortably complete all the engines (and have the tea made for the arrival of weighbridge staff) before any harm was done. My reward for this diligence was the occasional ride out on the test run to Spondon or Ambergate or around the triangle, as the Chaddesden Loop was known. This I naturally, always enjoyed, although it wasn't quite the novelty to me that it may have been to some, without with my footplate experience. I think that my 'firing' prowess quite surprised Jack, until one day our driver proved to be Jack Marsden, with whom, you may remember, I spent a pleasant week when on loan to Derby as a Passed Cleaner.

Most of the loco types allocated to Derby Shops appeared on the Pit for test and weighing during that month. As well as the usual ex-Midland and LMS 0-6-0 tender and tank types, there also appeared 8F's, 2-6-4T's of all types from Fowler, through Stanier, Fairburn and Ivatt, to the occasional Riddles BR variant of the 80000 Series, Compounds, 2P's, a couple of SDJR 2-8-0's, an 0-6-0 Fowler Dock Tank, a Deeley 0-4-0T and one of the 47000 Class, and, completing the list, one Stanier Class 5 and a Jubilee; these last two not normally Shopped at Derby. The odd Austerity was also being Shopped at Derby by now but none of these came my way.

Lest the impression be given that Jack's sole duty was to try the brakes, seals and injectors, nothing could be further from the truth. Valve testing was another duty, with Jack having to diagnose and correct the odd defective engine that skipped through the net, albeit a rare event. In fact almost everything, apart from boiler defects, came within his parameters and rarely was he found wanting. The 8F, with superheater header fracture, correctly diagnosed by him, was one such example, quite correctly referred back to the Shops, as described earlier.

I was surprised to find how few of the older fixed solid link engine types required adjustment to their springing when weighed, in complete contrast to the more modern adjustable screw link engines which rarely, if ever, got away without recourse to some energetic spannering on the part of the weighbridge staff. However, such was their skill and experience that, when adjustments were made, whether to solid or screwed hanger link types, it was virtually unknown for a second dose of treatment to be required upon reweighing.

The highlight of the whole month however, must go to the arrival, rather late in the fourth week, of 73125 as mentioned earlier. Having completed steam tests on its injectors, brakes and the like, the stage was set for testing of the valves. The engine, probably the first ever Caprotti Valves fitted locomotive to be built at Derby, attracted a considerable audience of works hierarchy, all being present to witness the first movement under its own power.

BR standard Class '5' 4-6-0 No. 73142 fitted with 'Caprotti' valve gear. Photo: P. Groom

With all the officials assembled, the driver - our old progenitor of the shed staff, he of the spotless overalls, shiny shoes and cap - indicated to his fireman to unwind the handbrake whilst he wound the new and very stiff reverser into forward gear. Then, with a long and loud blast of the whistle (what a shame BR had discontinued the chime whistle by then), he pulled the regulator handle towards him. 73125 stood still with all its eminent audience looking on, clouds of steam emitting with a roar from the cylinder drain cocks, then, just when it seemed that nothing more was about to happen, she lurched forwards nearly half a turn of her 6' 2" driving wheels before easing to a halt, only to return back from where she came from with hardly a pause and without the driver touching the reverser. Having completed nearly $\frac{1}{2}$ of a turn in this direction, she commenced a second forward movement before the driver closed the regulator and applied the brakes.

The reactions of the assembled multitude ranged from downright disgust and embarrassment, through amusement to manic hilarity, all dependent upon their positions in the pecking order of things. The New Work Chargehand's face was a picture best not described and with the redoubtable Mr. Brown, the '8 Shop' Foreman, bearing down upon him, could anyone wonder!

I noticed my old friend George Fisher form the Research and Development Department lurking in the background with a wry smile on his face. Sidling over to him, I made myself known and an impish smile crossed his face as he glanced at his watch. As he did so the factory hooter blew and suddenly all the assembled 'overall brigade' disappeared as if by magic, leaving the dark suited, Homburg hated officials to walk away, back to the Works with as much dignity as they could muster.

"Can you get your hands on a few tools?" George asked me.

I replied in the affirmative and when the crowds had dispersed, we went over to 73125. After uncoupling the carden shaft on the off-side, we turned it through a quarter of a turn and reconnected it.

"Now we'll see some puzzled faces after lunch," he said.

I should explain that the during construction, George and his department had offered assistance to the Works on what was a new project and procedure to them but it had been turned down with the usual inter-departmental arrogance at the time prevalent there and up to a point throughout the whole railway system. It was the MR-v-LNW, LMS-v-LNER, one works-v-another and so on, syndrome all over again.

George said, "This won't make it perfect. It will still need some fine tuning but at least it will keep going in whatever direction it's meant to go."

And so it proved to be. And all from an observation of relative wheel and piston position during that one movement. As I have penned before, George Fisher was without doubt, the finest steam locomotive engineer it was my good fortune to meet and it was a privilege to have known him.

When the New Work gang returned after dinner, armed with enough equipment to build another engine, the chargehand suggested that 73125 be tried in reverse before anything was done. Naturally, she trundled backwards without any trouble and returned obediently when wound into forward gear.

"Must have been just one of those things," I overheard him remark to his assembled gang.

How I wished to disillusion him but George, now very much absent, had sworn me to secrecy.

With only two weeks of my Shop time left, I felt sure that it would be into the Diesel Shop but this was not to be. To my amazement, if not disgust, it was back to the New Works Section yet again, by now of course, building the Caprotti 5's.

73127, 8 and 9 were on the stocks, the latter being little more than a frame. Unusually, two sets of 350 hp Diesel shunter frames were also being assembled there also, as the Diesel Shop was getting ever more crowded with shunter repairs together with the presence of 10001 and one of the SR main-line Diesels.

So it could be said that my works Diesel experience consisted of fitting brake hangers, buffering and spring gear, prior to the whole assembly being transported to No.10 (Diesel) Shop for the clever bits to be done.

Just to round off this interesting year, on the Tuesday of the very last week, paired off with Derek, another shed lad, we were once again on the Stone Pit, this time to lend our assistance with an ex Works 4F that had had a 'water bump' due to an excess of water in the cylinders, resulting in a cracked rear cylinder cover. This of course, required the complete strip down of the big end, connecting rod, crosshead, slide-blocks and bars on the affected side of the engine. Amazingly, only the piston rod had sustained any damage, apart from the back cover. We two were left to our own devices to strip it all down, ready for checking over and rectification by the works staff. A considerable part of the second day was spent in removing the piston which, with the rod being bent, had jammed and broken through the centre. Serious scoring of the cylinder bore had occurred so arrangements were made for the engine to go back into the Shops for the affected bore to be skimmed out but this in fact had not been done when we completed our stint in the Works at the end of that week.

With the last two days spent working on 73128 and 9, thus I bid the Shops goodbye, only to return the following day with my beautiful fiancé and her young niece and nephew, to visit the Works on the occasion of the Open Day and annual garden show.

Amongst the engines on show was the 'Lickey Banker' No. 58100, which had been withdrawn in May. She had been stabled alongside the 8F with the superheater header problem out on the stone-pit. Head to head with 9F No. 92079 while its headlight and associated equipment was transferred. Another old stager on display was the complete opposite of 58100, being Burton's old stalwart, No. 41516, also withdrawn and awaiting scrapping, but re-painted photographic grey on one side only, complete with 'Ferrett and Dartboard' BR emblem and standard style number in place of the LMS and large style number as displayed in service. Thus both the largest and smallest Midland Railway engines were displayed on the same day though, unfortunately, not together.

Young nephew Cliff enjoyed himself collecting and recording all the numbers, whilst his sister played the sophisticated young lady and my fiancé Judy and I were just happy to be together.

Then it was back to Burton on the Monday and a start with real work and responsibility.

I seem to recall that, on my last week at the Works, the journeys home were not without incident either. Our little band of lads would catch the 1800 hrs 'stopper' to Burton as mentioned earlier, being the return working of the 17.10 ex. Burton manned by Burton men. Knowing most of these crews, it was my habit to ride back in the cab with them occasionally, when allowed.

Every seven or so weeks the driver would be Harry Painter, for whom I had fired on a few occasions during my brief footplate career. Now and then he would let me 'have hold' between Peartree and Willington and this last week was no exception.

On the Monday we had one of the then new 84000 Class 2MT 2-6-2's which had just been allocated to Burton, primarily for working the pull and push service to Tutbury (The Tutbury Jinnie), a duty from which they had ousted the old Midland 0-4-4T's that had been on the task since the early thirties when they had replaced the old North Stafford Class B 2-4-0's in their turn.

These new BR Class 2's were in a class of their own and, compared to their predecessors, it was like stepping out of a Skoda into a BMW or Rolls Royce. As I had not been on one of these engines before I was content to study Harry's method of handling this engine, the ride of which, it must be said, was comparable with the coaches behind and of course, much more exciting. Having made a mental note of his driving and more importantly, where he shut off prior to braking for the Willington stop, I felt confident to have a go the next evening if I should be asked.

The following day however, our solitary Fowler 2-6-4T No. 42336 was on the job. This had been the regular engine in use for the last few months and one that I had handled on several occasions so, no problem there, I reasoned.

"Come on then," Harry said as we came to a stop in the Peartree platform. I needed no bidding and was soon looking back for the 'right away' as the hundred or so Rolls Royce workers climbed aboard.

Anticipating the guard's signal, I knock off the brake as the ejector starts to regain the 21" of vacuum and thus release the brake, as I had watched Harry do. The green flag waves and, with a toot on the whistle, I heave the regulator handle open. With a hearty roar up the chimney this fine, sure-footed engine fairly leaps away from the platform with its three-coach load, checking as I do that the starter signal is indeed still in the off position. After about ten chuffs up the chimney I start to wind back the reverser gradually until, with about 30 per cent cut-off and the regulator on the first valve, we are fairly bowling along.

All the signals ahead of us are off, 'back-ins' as well, as I whistle for the crossing at Sunnyhill. Approaching Stenson Junction where the freight line from Trent Junction comes in from the left, I shut off and start rubbing the brake for the Willington stop as we rattle across the pointwork. As we cross I notice that the distant under the North Stafford Junction Home, which is also the Willington Outer Home, is still in the on position so I am staring ahead to catch an early sighting of the Home as we pass over this second junction where the Stoke and Crewe Line turns off away to the right. As we come to a stand at the end of the platform, the distant under the starter at the end of the platform is on also, only to clear as we get the 'right away.' 42336 needs very little encouragement to start away again down the falling gradient towards Clay Mills and Burton.

"Take your time, Davey lad," Harry's voice comes from behind me. "Someone's not far in front of us. No point in catching him up."

The Section Distant is on as we reach it but clears just as we have passed it. The Clay Mills Outer Home is off with its distant also resolutely on as I shut off and let 42336 and her small train coast along, winding the reverser down to the 45 per cent cut off position for drifting. Another whistle for the Clay Mills crossing and Harry takes over again for the last two miles or so into Burton, now again under clear signals. As we overtake the goods, sidelined along the slow line on our left, I am amused to see an Austerity, cloaked in a cloud of steam, at its head. Harry blows a derisive whistle as we pass him and I observe that its fireman is a supporter of Winston Churchill, judging by the wave he gives in reply.

The Wednesday, I recall to the combined disgust of myself with Harry and his mate, had a 4F at its head, standing tender first in the south bay, platform 5. I turned the water on and off while the fireman gave the coal a good dousing with the water crane. He had rigged a sheet up as well, in an effort to make things more pleasant but I knew that a rough ride was about to be experienced no matter what was done.

"Don't feel you've got to come with us tonight," Harry said. "I'd ride in the coach if I were you."

So, feeling a bit guilty, I took his advice. His fireman, to his credit, offered to go in my place but I pretended not to hear him. 42336 was apparently in for boiler wash-out and it was anybody's guess where the BR Class 2's were.

On Thursday another unusual engine was on the job, this time a Class 5. She was also tender first back to Burton, being a Leeds engine and rostered to work the 20.25 Fitted Freight ex Burton to that destination later on in the evening, having been 'borrowed' for this little job in the meantime. Again we doused the coal down before I returned to the train. The 'Blackie' played with our train as indeed did our Fowler tank, in contrast to the 4F that had made hard work of it rattling and banging along and losing two minutes into the bargain.

It was therefore with trepidation that I descended the steps onto platform 4 and 6 and walked to the south bay No. 5. To my delight 42336 was back at its head and, contrary to norm, was chimney first to Burton. Had Harry made a special effort for my last day? I wondered; and so it transpired.

His regular fireman was absent and in his place was one of the old hand Passed Firemen who had driven up from Burton and was obviously planning to drive back judging by the great fire he was building up in the box. Harry beckoned me aboard and time ticked by as we waited to connect with the late running Manchester – London which eventually ran in some ten minutes late behind a Stanier Caprotti 5.

"No bloody wonder!" our Passed Fireman commented when he saw what was on the front. The Trafford Park men exchanged footplates with a Derby set as was usual and after topping up the tank together with some smart work by the station staff, got away without losing any more time.

The rain, which had been falling fairly lightly until now, really began to lash down in earnest as we got the 'right away'. Our Passed Fireman, who I think was named Eddie, soon had 42336 on the move some twelve minutes late out of the bay. He went like the bullet out of a gun under London Road Bridge and past the factories of Ley's Malleable Castings and Qualcast, only to have the back board on at the Osmaston Road Bridge and the Outer Home for Peartree and Normanton at danger.

"Damn and blast it! What are they playing at?" he cursed, as he gave the whistle a pull.

The bobby held a red flag out of the box and so we pulled forward to him where he told us we could enter the platform at caution as a goods train was standing just clear in front of us.

The Rolls Royce men and women were very pleased to see us as they stood huddled together on the exposed platform with rain dripping from peaks of caps and raincoats etc. As they climbed gratefully aboard, Eddie went back to the box to find out what was going on.

"Don't look like you're going to get a hold tonight Davey," was Harry's comment. "We should be in Burton by now."

Eddie came back with the guard and informed us that there was yet another train standing in front of the goods in front of us, destined for the Chellaston Branch but was unable to proceed as a car had crashed through a bridge onto the line ahead and its last few wagons and brake were still across the junction and blocking our path.

We stood in Peartree platform for over an hour before the goods in front moved off, eventually turning onto the slow line and on to Sunnyhill. Then it was our turn. Both boards came off together and with a quick glance back, Eddie popped the whistle, released the brake and heaved at the regulator handle, all in one swift, smooth movement. A faint cheer was heard as 42336 leapt forward, only to be drowned out by the bark of the exhaust as we sped away with our load. By now the Crewe line passengers, still left on the station, had decided to make their way home by other means barring a few stalwarts who, by now must have been saturated, their tempers not improved by being able to see their own train standing at the Inner Home Board about 50 yards off the platform end. Still! We three were alright; snuggled in our nice, warm cab.

On braking for Willington; our intrepid driver, I thought, leaving it rather late to shut off, having cleared Stenson Junction and the North Stafford before he did so; following a heavy brake application, we nearly over-ran the platform and stopped with the last coach just in at the far end , to my secret delight. As the train was made up of non-corridor stock, much shouting ensued to prevent the passengers in the first two coaches from alighting and making the six foot drop onto the ballast with the contentious risk of injury. When the rear coach-load had de-trained we set back into the platform to allow the rest of our passengers to alight.

"They wouldn't forget this night in a hurry," I reflected but one look at Harry's face and I kept my thoughts to myself.

A few swift negotiations with the signalman and we were on our way. I picked up the shovel and fed a round onto the fire, which was looking a little sad by this time with the gauge down around 165 lbs psi. A quick pull through with the pricker as we ran through Clay Mills saw us through to Burton, where the valves lifted to wish me farewell as I bade Harry and Eddie goodbye, climbing the steps some 75 minutes or so later than I should have done. Now it was my turn to get wet as I hurried down the station bridge to go home.

Chapter 15

On the Tools at Last

Reporting back to Burton the following Tuesday morning, Monday being the late summer bank holiday week-end, I was surprised to be sent with Harry Buggins on gauge frame exams. As previously described, these vital pieces of equipment were periodically examined; every three to five weeks to be precise. My expectations had been to take up tools in earnest as a fitter, as was the norm with apprentices when they returned from the Shops. However, no point in arguing about it, just get on and make the best of the situation. As we had both got the necessary equipment to do the job, we elected to do one engine each, both engines that day being old Midland Class 3F's.

The following day, however and for the rest of the week, we had a much more pleasant duty to perform: that of examining the private locos based at the various breweries around the town which had occasion, during the course of their duties, to travel over British Railways owned lines. With Bass & Co being the largest operator, with a number of both steam and diesel locomotives in its fleet, we or rather Harry, decided to start there.

We did a quick gauge frame exam between us first, on a 4F, and then collecting our bikes, we sallied forth. On arrival at the Bass Loco Sheds, off Guild Street, we firstly enjoyed a pint of Bass best bitter before yours truly got down to the task of examining the two engines there present. As all these engines had been measured many times before, it was only necessary to check the tyre

Bass & Co. brewery engine sheds. Photo: Authors Collection.

wear and flange thickness. Harry enjoyed his second pint and on learning that within the hour, two if not three or more locos would be arriving or passing, elected to hang on while he consumed a third pint. All told, during the day, meal breaks forgotten, we managed to see and check half of the Bass fleet and whereas I had been content to down just two pints during that time, Harry lost count and thoroughly enjoyed the experience. To demonstrate just how much, he rode his cycle somewhat erratically into the back of a corporation bus on the way back to the shed. Before leaving Bass's I had arranged with the foreman to have sight of the remaining engines which he promised to try and organise for the Friday.

Harry didn't turn up for work the following morning, his wife notifying Hodgy that he had a swollen knee. No doubt sustained when he fell off his bike following the contretemps with the bus. So I set off with a cleaner to hold the other end of the tape as it were, this time for Truman's Brewery in Derby Street.

As the cleaner hadn't got a cycle we decided to walk down the line as the brewery was just to the north of the station on the Up side and opposite the Ind Coope Brewery premises. Having crossed Moor Street Bridge and passed Burton Station South signalbox, we had to wait before crossing the line as the Bristol – Bradford express was bearing down upon us. As it passed I noticed that the spring on the rear tender axlebox was broken so I dashed back to the box to tell the bobby to hold him in the station while I had a look at it and also to ring the shed to send someone down with a spring clip and tools. This he undertook to do whilst the cleaner and I ran down the platform to see what we could do. However, as we got there the Station Inspector was having the engine uncoupled to be replaced by a 4F which was standing on a line of wagons on the Up Slow,

Bass No. 1 the brewery had eight engines like this one. Photo: Authors Collection.

much to the disgust of the express crew. They ran their Class 5 forwards into the Jinnie Bay and the 4F crew, having backed onto the express, changed footplates with them. To say that I was none too popular with the Bristol men on the express was an understatement. Still, the inspector promised them another, hopefully better engine at Derby and off they went, the poor old run down 4F sounding like a band practice on a bad night.

"Er's a rough old thing," the Westhouses fireman off the 4F confided in me, "Probably drop apart before her gets to Clay Mills," he added.

"Let's hope she gets past Stenson, then she's Derby's problem," I answered as I examined the spring.

The top plate had broken and half of the two plates below the break were missing, so there was no way this engine was going far without a replacement spring being fitted.

Just then, Geoff German, the Shed Fitter arrived and after the usual friendly greeting of, "What the b... ..ell 'ave you been up to now?" he had to agree with my diagnosis.

After consultation with Control, it was decided to temporarily fit the spring clip as best we could, utilise the '5' to move the goods train off the Up Slow line and into the Derby Street Wharf, then take her to the shed for repairs. Here the Westhouses men would be found another engine with which to continue their journey.

As an aftermath to this incident, about a month or so later, both the cleaner and I received a letter of thanks from Mr. Bramley, the DMPS, which I duly took home to show my parents and fiancé. Mother was very proud of her observant son and my Judy was impressed, whereas my dad, ever the dour, practical Scotsman, asked how many loaves of bread it would buy.

With all the excitement over, we continued on our way to the brewery to have a look at the Truman fleet. This consisted of two Peckett 0-4-0 Saddle Tanks, one in use and the other as standby. The service loco was just pulling a string of ale wagons out of the gate prior to propelling them down to Derby Street Wharf. We were told that this movement had been delayed whilst the shunting operation previously described had taken place and I could sense that further interference by British Railways was not very welcome. I explained that I only wanted to check the tyre wear plus a quick look at the spare loco.

"I'll get the tractor driver to pull it out for you," the 'worthy' we were talking to offered. "Would you like a beer while you're waiting?" he continued.

"Can a duck swim?" I thought. "Thank you very much," I said as we both took the proffered glasses of the amber nectar. Truman's was my favourite tipple so I was more than pleased to oblige him.

"Are you old enough to drink that?" I enquired of my young cleaner colleague, more as a joke than anything.

"I'm big enough so I must be!" he replied, shrewdly avoiding a complete answer.

One of the Trumans brewery pecketts ventures onto BR lines. Photo: P. Webb.

How could you argue with that, though it would take him all his time to be sixteen? From the expression on his face I presumed this was indeed his first pint ever but he downed it like a man and offered up his glass for a second. Our host however, declined to comply with his request, though, let it be said, I didn't refuse the offer of another.

After all that, the rear (driving) axle flanges were found to be right on the minimum for wear limits with the leading axle flanges not much better. The standby engine was also seriously worn down so I informed our host that BR would be contacting the brewery advising them of the urgent need for repairs. As he needed more convincing, I compared the flange wear as indicated by our gauge with that of a nearby wagon which, fortunately, was well within spec. (they weren't always) and thanking him for the drinks, we bid him farewell, heading back to the shed.

The Black '5' from the Bradford express was standing over the pit in the Old Shed which ran down to the 'Bug Ut.' I noticed a new spring lying on the floor by the tender. On reporting back to Hodgy about the Truman's engines flange condition, he said something that sounded like,

"When th'ave filled t' form in, get yon spring changed. They want 'er for't Bristol tha' noes."

"What's wrong with the shedman changing it then?" I asked, quite justifiably I thought, as he had got to examine it before it went out, as per the MP 11 schedule.

"Just get on wi it," he replied, "Thaa found yon so thaa can change un."

"He still loves me, then," I reflected as I collected the jack and a few tools.

I scotched the engine and checked that it was in mid gear; most important with an engine in steam as, if the regulator valve is blowing through, it is not unknown for pressure to build up and set the engine in motion, even with the drain cocks open. Having knocked out the split pins in the retaining collars and jacked up the left rear corner of the tender, it took but a few minutes to prise the spring off the top of the axlebox. Out of the corner of my eye I could see, through the window of the 'BugUt,' Geoff grinning as he held Court.

All I need now is someone to give me a 'chuck up' with the new spring, which weighs about 80 to 90 lbs and I know just the man for the job. And if he objects or moans, he takes his own clip off the old one as well!

I open the door and make my request. As he gets off his throne to comply, a wave of laughter ripples round the assembled multitude.

Marstons beautiful Hawthorn/Leslie No. 3. Photo: Authors Collection.

Have I achieved a small victory? I wonder, or had he earlier correctly forecast my request. To be honest I don't care either way. At least I have got him off his backside and out on the job. He helps me to refit the links and position the shoes. When I return from the Stores with the new split pins he has bedded the spring and lowered the jack. I climb back up onto the footplate and re-apply the handbrake.

"What's on the clock?" he calls up from the floor.

"About a hundred," I shout back, "I'll put a bit on if you like," I volunteer and picking up the shovel, proceed to feed the rather dead looking fire.

With the aid of the blower, the gauge is soon showing 160 lbs, enough to test the vacuum and injectors and thus ends another day.

Harry was back on duty the following day (Friday) ready for the second visit to Bass, his knee encased in a crepe bandage.

"I bet he wouldn't have been seen this side of next Monday had not Bass's been calling," I thought, as with much huffing and sucking of teeth, he pedalled off with me for the brewery again.

We managed to see all the remaining Bass engines but one, which was based up at Shobnall that day and we both also enjoyed another pint or so. We thanked the Bass foreman for his organisation and the beer. As we were due to go to Marston's, which is at Shobnall, the following week, I mentioned that I would catch the missing loco then.

Bass's steam locomotives fell into two groups, the main ones being of Neilson (Glasgow) or North British manufacture with two, No's 3 and 7, being very much rebuilt examples of the original Thorniwell and Warham (Burton) locos. It was one of these last two which was outstationed at Shobnall, No. 3 I think.

On the Monday morning, I spotted this engine by the Bass, Shobnall coal store on my way to work so, rather than make my number with Hodgy, I found Harry and, having helped him to do an exam on, I think a Crab, we cycled off to Marston's Brewery on Shobnall Road. Marston's had two engines, a beautiful Hawthorn Leslie 0-4-0 saddle tank of about 1924 and an almost new, locally built Baguley Diesel, reputedly built on the frames of the steamer's sister engine. Both of these locos were in excellent condition, mechanically and in appearance and, I might add, have both survived into preservation, with the Hawthorn Leslie recently re-located on the Foxfield Railway.

Naturally the Diesel was in use, with the steamer only used on the odd day when her consort was under maintenance. Having carried out our checks, I am sure you will be surprised to read that a couple of pints of Pedigree was produced and consumed with much appreciation by Harry and myself. After all, it would have been ill mannered to refuse and weren't we representatives of the Railway.

The Bass fleet at this time, as a matter of interest, contained only one Diesel engine, another local Baguley product dating back to 1939, of which I have quite strong childhood memories as it spent most of its early working life at Shobnall. However, on the occasion of this inspection, it was down at Guild Street under repair, which no doubt explained No. 3's presence at Shobnall.

On our way back from Marston's we enquired at the Bass sidings signalbox of its whereabouts. They were expecting us to call; such was the organisation of the Bass system.

"Sit down lads, she'll be along in a minute or two," the foreman informed us, "Would you like a beer while you're waiting?"

"That would be very nice," Harry replied, before the Bass foreman had hardly finished asking.

Four bottles were produced and the tops lifted off, before you could say knife. Not quite what we were expecting but still, as the saying goes, 'Needs Must when the Devil drives,' or possibly, 'Beggars can't be Choosers.'

Bass loco shunting at Shobnall. Photo: Authors Collection.

"This is the life!" I thought, "And still two breweries to go!"

As Harry was wobbling a bit on our way back, I suggested we walk and push our bikes, at least until we got off the road but Harry seemed to find walking even more difficult so back onto the saddle we climbed. Harry avoided all the cars and no buses appeared so all was well.

The following day, Hodgy beat me to the draw and gave me a 4F blast pipe to remove. These must rate as quite the worst blast pipes to remove, being of two legs with the rear one hard up against the tubeplate. Each leg was fastened down onto the valve chest by two, four holed flanges, which located on eight studs in the bottom of the smokebox. The securing nuts rarely came undone as a result of being subjected to the heat and conditions within the smokebox and in consequence, had to be chopped through with a hammer and chisel, not the pneumatic type found in the Shops but the muscle powered kind, as with most things in the shed environment. And, of course, there was the soot to contend with as well. No matter how well the smokebox was cleaned out, you still got dirty and, if you should graze a knuckle or two, almost impossible to avoid on these jobs, then – Boy! Did it sting!

The following day, I believe, saw me on X repairs and so on for the rest of the week. I never did get to Ind Coope & Allsopp's until years later, when I took up employment there but I did at least visit Worthington's to do an inspection on one later occasion.

Now integrated into the Fitters' Rota, I acquired Arthur Taylor's old mate, George Bosworth, 'Bozzy' to his friends and a more loyal mate could not be wished for.

We were soon engaged on the Mileage Examinations as described earlier, with the odd spell of X repairs, breakdowns, smokebox jobs and the like. I was as happy as Larry, having the work and responsibility and, as I had got engaged and contemplated marriage, the Trade Rate money was very welcome as well.

After a lot of pestering, I even managed to get some week-end work as well, which pleased George, as previously he had to tag on to anyone who hadn't got a mate, some of whom he didn't see eye to eye with.

One Saturday, just as we were about to knock off and go home, a message was received that one of the Jocko's had de-railed all wheels in the brickyard sidings just to the north of Shobnall Bridge on the Dallow Lane Branch. A scratch crew was called for to man the breakdown vans and I was naturally the first volunteer. As I had never been on a breakdown before I was interested to learn just exactly what went on and how it was done.

Once in the riding van a quick shuffle of dominoes was soon organised and, with hardly the first game over, we were at the scene of the derailment.

The procedure routinely followed on arrival at any derailment, I was soon to discover, followed a three-fold course. Firstly: to ascertain if anyone was trapped or hurt, secondly: determine if the derailment was fouling the main line or running roads and thirdly: where was the nearest pub.

As a negative answer fitted the first two criteria, the third one saw us all departing to the Mount Pleasant Inn or 'Bessie Bull's' as it was more commonly known locally, after a former legendary licencee who incidentally, was my great grandmother. The hostelry was both famous and unique in many ways. Being situated at the side of the Trent and Mersey Canal adjacent to the Shobnall Basin (formerly the beginning of a canal branch into Burton town), it was much used by canal people over the years together with the local population out for a stroll along the canal towpath, particularly during summer months. It served an excellent pint of Marstons, the beer being delivered by rail direct from the brewery nearby and slid down the embankment from the railway into the cellar which, being below canal level, maintained an even, cool temperature; most important for the keeping of beer; all year round. There was no form of pumping installed, each pint being drawn directly from the barrels, commonly described as: 'from the wood,' in the cellar just a couple of steps down from the bar servery, in quart jugs and served over the bar. Delicious! The best pint of Marstons around. At the time in question, the premises were presided over by Tom and Jack Bull, sons of the late 'Bessie,' I therefore, being their second cousin, though age-wise they were more like uncles.

However, with only half an hour to go before closing time, we were soon back at the siding and addressing the problem of the derailment. Not only had the engine derailed on a set of points within the brickyard but a wagon that it had in tow, was derailed by one set of wheels also. It was decided that George and myself would address the problem of re-railing the wagon, whilst the rest of the gang, with their considerable expertise, would attend to the engine.

Firstly, it was obvious that it would not be possible to uncouple the wagon from the engine as the coupling chains were pulled taut between them. This was soon remedied with the aid of the oxy-acetylene cutting torch burning through one of the links, making certain at the same time, that no one was trapped or injured when the two vehicles parted.

I noticed that our wagon was loaded with baulks of timber destined for J. B. Kinds, the timber merchants about half a mile up the line. This, added to the tare weight of the wagon, meant we would have to deal with about a twelve to fourteen ton lift. As the two wheels of the derailed axle were lying immediately alongside their respective rails, I thought that, if I jacked up on the headstock from both sides until the tread of one wheel was just above rail level and the other with the flange well above its rail, it would tilt over slightly and, with a nelson pushing on the higher wheel, would ease over to be lowered down onto the track. And so it proved to be.

With an empty wagon, it would have been possible in this situation to use only one jack, set at a slight angle, under the centre of the headstock to achieve the same result. The wheels would be dragged up the sides of the rails, sliding over when the wheel flange on the high side rose above its respective rail, the flange of the other, inner wheel preventing the wagon from sliding right across and derailing on the other side.

A 'nelson,' to the uninitiated, was a device, rather like a screw bottle jack with two claw-like hooks which slipped over the rail each side of the wheel, to create sideways movement when screwed against an object, in this case the wheel. Another contraption, incorporating a wire strap and ratchet for pulling, was called a 'sylvester'. Don't ask me why or how these names originated. Sufficient to say they were invaluable and both worked very well.

Having checked the gauging of the wheels on our wagon and pushed it clear of the points so that the platelayers could carry out repairs, long overdue by the look of them, we made ourselves useful, assisting with the re-railing of the Jocko.

All this activity had attracted a considerable crowd of sunny, summer afternoon strollers to view our administrations, from the bridge which carried Shobnall Road over the running lines. On arrival home some four hours later, my mother was not surprised or alarmed by my late arrival as my father had been amongst the onlookers from the bridge, having been drawn by curiosity, to view the proceedings whilst on his way home from work.

For my part, I was more than pleased, having earned a total of twelve hours pay at time and a half plus the breakdown allowance, increasing my income for the week by about fifty percent. A very welcome boost to our wedding fund.

After that it was back to the normal grind of mileage exams and X Repairs over the following weeks, interspersed with the occasional out of routine task like superheater elements, blastpipes and other unpleasant jobs within the smokebox.

One of these that sticks in my mind was the repairs to one of the main steam pipes on Crab number 42826. This was reported as blowing rather heavily at its bottom joint, where it joined the top of the cylinder casting extension. As all the soot and ash from the immediate area had been blown across to the opposite side of the smokebox, this seemed to confirm the case. The method of making a joint between the superheater header at the top and the cylinder extension at the bottom, was by two half coned rings, the flat side of each ring making a face to joint with the pipe flanges and the coned halves with the castings. These half cones enabled the vagaries of the pipes' shapes to make a steam tight joint with the two castings whilst also coping with expansion as well.

The two opposite ends of the pipe are at a ninety degree angle to each other, with the pipe following the contours of the smokebox, curving both round and down at the same time. A face to face joint is achieved following much lapping with grinding paste and the two flange ends with the flat side of the joint rings. The conical faces of the header and cylinder extension are cleaned up and, if not chipped and pitted, are then ready for reassembly. I have seen fitters lapping in these faces also but as one cannot be sure exactly where the cone is going to come into contact with its seat, it is a waste of time and indeed, can be detrimental to the steam tightness of the joint as any resultant grooves in the coned face can provide an escape route for the steam.

If the header and cylinder faces are damaged in any way, they can only be repaired, in the shed, with plastic metal, not the most ideal solution but the only one available to us. The actual flange plates are loose on the pipe and this alleviates the need to line everything up when refitting to the engine as, when these three-hole flange plates are placed over their respective connections, top and bottom with the cones in place between the casting and pipe ends, it only remains to wriggle the pipe about a bit as you tighten up, to virtually guarantee a steam tight result on completion; providing, of course, that the preparation procedure has been carried out as described. However, let it be said that the job is no push-over as the pipe itself must weigh in the region of 100 lbs or more. Not the most pleasant of tasks, as with all the jobs in the smokebox and one that takes at least three days to complete.

Another rather unpleasant little job that came my way while an apprentice working with Les Bull, was that of a smokebox regulator that was blowing through so badly that the driver refused to take the engine out, even light engine, back to its own depot. The engine concerned was a Stanier Crab number 42952; a Crewe South engine. These smokebox regulator valves, incorporated into the superheater header, were one of the less welcomed ideas that the great man brought with him when he left GWR to take up his position as CME of the LMS. Both his early Class 5 and 8F's also incorporated this idea, as did the Jubilees but whereas these latter engines soon lost this feature; commensurate with the increase in superheating of these engines; their original Achilles heel, the 5's and 8's so fitted, retained them for all time; the domes atop their boilers serving as steam collectors only.

Access to these regulator valves was through an inspection plate on the front of the superheater header. If any work was to be done therein it was also necessary to remove the chimney skirt and ejector ring and pipework as well. I have already mentioned the reluctance of any nuts and bolts to come undone within the smokebox so you can see that, along with the dirty, sooty conditions endured, by the time you eventually get a view of the offending valve Mr. Stanier's name was not at the top of any list of friends you might compile.

On the rear side of this cast metal inspection and access plate is cast the supporting boss for the regulator operating rod which adds to the fun when the time comes for reassembly.

On inspection, the pilot valve was found to be in two halves, having broken clean across the middle, thereby leaving the cylinders open to steam constantly. No wonder the driver refused to take it home. Apparently, 42952 had brought a semi-fitted freight down to the LNW yard at Horninglow and should have taken up its return working to Mold Junction early the next morning, its place no doubt being filled by one of our infamous Class 4F's.

Les had no recourse but to send the complete valve set to Crewe Works for repair, with yours truly volunteering to take it for him. Hodgy, needless to say, had other ideas and it was duly dispatched via the stores van to Derby for onward shipment to Crewe. Ten or twelve days later a replacement valve arrived, all wrapped up in a corrugated cardboard wrapping, ready for Les to lap in and reassemble; and an excellent job he made of it too. When back in steam, not a whisper of steam issued from the cylinder drain cocks. After a couple of days running about on the trippers, Bert Sinclair wrote it up for Leeds, fitted, whence it went, never to be seen again at Burton as far as I am aware.

Very soon after our wrestling match with the main steam pipe on 42826, another unusual job (at least for us) befell George and myself, again from the 'Western' Shed at Horninglow, a Super 'D' this time, with piston glands blowing very badly. 49034 had got herself badly lost as she was, at that time, a Patricroft (10C) engine.

Ernie Gaskell, who was standing in for Hodgy at the time, told me it was on the New Shed Ashpit and that I could have a look at her when the driver brought her down into the shed. To say that the glands were blowing was an understatement. The whole engine disappeared in a cloud of steam as soon as the regulator was opened, with the left hand (driver's) side being by far the worst of the two.

We turned 49034 off on a long pit and set her with both big ends on the back quarter to afford the most room to work on the glands. At least the regulator didn't blow through when closed, for which I was more than pleased as steam passing through the cylinders can be very hot indeed. Fetching our bag of tools, peels of animated laughter greeted our return to this alien LNWR monster in our midst, from our various colleagues scattered about the shed. Their grinning faces peering over the cab sides of their respective engines.

After checking that our 'D' was parked correctly in mid gear with the hand brake on, I firstly tied a piece of rope to the regulator handle and across to the cab side to prevent anyone opening it whilst I was working underneath between the motions. This was a standard procedure laid down in the rule book but often ignored by maintenance staff and cleaners alike, fortunately rarely with fatal results. As I said to George, "At least I would get killed legally."

On Midland engines the piston gland covers are secured, depending on the type of engine, by either one or two studs and nuts top and bottom of the slide bars and quite easy to secure or release. On this engine however, I discovered, on climbing up inside, that the covers were shaped like a cross with a stud and nut on each of the four extremities, nicely tucked between each sidebar, with very little room in which to manoeuvre the spanners, particularly the one furthest away and up against the inside of the frame. But, you manage and eventually the packing rings are revealed. These turned out to be similar to the cast iron packings as fitted to most superheater engines, Midland 4F's and 2P's etc. included but, being the LNWR, much larger of course. And, like the Midland and indeed LMS standard versions as well, the main rings had broken in half. So, no more progress on that gland until a replacement set was obtained and machined.

The fireman's (right hand) side gland however, had not disintegrated so I was able to file a small amount off the sliding half of the packing rings to reduce their diameter and allow them once more to grip around a piston rod, all but curing the steam leak in the process. This was the normal action taken on most engines of whatever pedigree.

I should perhaps explain at this point that, with the event of superheated boilers and their consequent higher and drier steam pressures, the traditional materials in use at the time to maintain a steam tight seal where the piston rod entered the cylinder, was found to be inadequate. Thus, the cast iron packing ring developed. This consisted of two halves with one half sliding into the other, both in turn held together by means of a large spring clip. A small gap was maintained between the two halves when clipped together around the piston rod. It was when this gap was eroded, by the thrusting action of the rod travelling to and fro within it, that the steam was able to pass between the packing and the rod. Hence, by filing away a small portion from the ends of the inner sliding half, the all important gap was remade and steam tightness maintained.

Two rings of packing were fitted to each gland, with the all important gaps set at ninety degrees to each other. A locating peg was fitted between the two sets of packing to maintain this setting, thus preventing the individual rings from turning and causing the gaps to come in line with each other and avoiding the consequent steam blow through the gap that would have been so created.

49034's broken set was past any form of repair so a replacement set was ordered from Crewe. The piston rod dimensions were also sent with the order as we naturally had no jig to fit it into for machining an unturned set.

The following week when the packing rings arrived, Hodgy was back in command, apparently none the better for his holiday. To heap more coals onto his troubled mind, Patricroft wired to say that 49034 was overdue a boiler washout and X Repairs which must be carried out straight away. A special coded message was available for this action; I think it was 'OHIO' although I'm not certain after all these years. Thus the message would read, "49034 OHIO." Terse and to the point. Hodgy's ears needed repacking; such was the steam issuing from them as he came round shouting,

"Dave! Dave! Get yon packing in and' get shut ot thing as quick as thee can. They sez yon's due - washout. Bloody cheek!"

At least, that's what it sounded like to us.

In no time at all a crew were aboard her and oiling round, to send her off for someone else to worry about. How he got away with such things amazed me as, these 'OHIO' telegrams meant what they said, not send it home or to some-one else's back yard.

I was by now of course, a fully paid up member of the 'Bug Ut Forum', taking part in the daily arguments and debates. Some of the characters therein have been mentioned before but the supply was by no means exhausted. One who immediately comes to mind is Cyril Barclay, now alas like so many others in this book, no longer with us, having moved on to that other great railway in the sky.

Cyril was of a very staid nature; rotund in the extreme and endearingly gullible. Another North Stafford man, he held the position of Grade 3 Fitter and mated Geoff German, one of the three shed-men. He lived with his son who by all accounts, led him a right dance. A regular patron of the Forest Gate amongst other hostelries, his liquid intake far exceeded that of food and in consequence, he was always interested in what your sandwich contained. This trend of course, made him easy prey to us apprentices, who lost no time in preparing special items for him to try.

One of our more successful offerings had its filling of a proprietary brand of cat food called Kit-e-Kat. Each of the artisan staff took it in turns to purchase a tin of food for the shed cat which in its turn showed its appreciation by keeping the Bug Ut vermin free. So, as you might imagine, it was but a short step to remove the cheese from a sandwich and substitute it with a spreading of Kit-e-Kat for the further delights of Cyril's taste buds.

On being proffered the said sandwich, Cyril ate it with great relish, so enjoying it that he enquired as to its variety so he could purchase a tin for his own and his son's tea. One of us offered to buy one for him and bring it to work for him the following day providing he had the money. The required, princely sum of one shilling (now 5p) was handed over and thus the stage was set for the following day's entertainment.

Kit-e-Kat had that fishy aroma that seems to appeal to the feline species and resembled mashed up pilchards in tomato sauce, which it may well have been for all I knew. The following day we managed to avoid Cyril until about nine o'clock when, with all assembled within the hut, we presented him with the brown paper bag containing the tin of cat food, ensuring as we did so that we had seats near the door for a quick exit.

Cyril, to the great amusement of all present, had brought with him several slices of bread with a knob of margarine, a tin opener and his penknife; a ferocious looking weapon; with which to prepare his feast. The look of anticipation on his face quickly changed to anger, tinged with nausea as, with a great roar, he chased us out into the shed, his vast bulk no match for our youthful caprices. The assembled multitude was in uproar as, convulsed with laughter, they viewed the proceedings with great amusement.

On another occasion, when arriving for work on the 2-10 afternoon shift, having 'dined' at the Forest Gate beforehand, we recommended that he chew some peppermints lest Hodgy detect the alcohol on his breath. Cyril's money was again proffered and one of us was soon back from the local shop with a bag of Mint Imperials. Having passed the contents round the gathered assembly, pieces of chalk were cut up and added to the remaining mints to make up the weight, as it were. Cyril proceeded to enjoy the bag of 'mints', chalk and all, with great delight, offering the bag round from time to time, all kindly refusing his offer telling him that his need was greater than theirs. Following so soon after the Kit-e-Kat episode, no one dared tell him of the mint-chalk mix and the resultant stomach upset was blamed on the beer consumed during the lunch time.

Cyril's brother, Percy, was the complete antithesis of him, being small and thin of stature and as far as I am aware, tea-total. Yet another 'Knotty' man, Percy was employed as a boiler-washer. Still, a character nevertheless but not one to be trifled with. One of his party pieces was to march round the edge of a door, saluting and turning his head as if to give the 'eyes right' in the manner of a line of soldiers.

During my National Service when, as a squad instructor, I was endeavouring to train some shambolic parade of men in the execution of a similar manoeuvre, I often compared in my mind their pathetic efforts with Percy's precision movements. But then, he had only to line himself up with the door, not ten or twelve uninterested 'squaddies' who didn't want to be there in the first place. Then, who could blame them - neither did I, come to think of it!

Percy's Mate was Jimmy Foy, a Southern Irishman of indeterminate background and a very loyal friend to boot. One day, one of our 3F's drew up on the Old Shed Ashpit for disposal and on opening the steambox door, one of the washout plugs was found to be blowing (leaking steam). Percy elected to try and tighten it up, a rather foolhardy thing to do but nevertheless one which had been known to meet with success in the past.

Armed with a box spanner and a bar, Percy and Jim climbed up onto the framing to see what they could do. With less than 60 lbs of steam on the clock, Percy felt confident of success. The box spanner arm was not quite long enough to be operated from outside the framing so he climbed just inside to get a better purchase on the bar. The next moment saw the washout plug come adrift and propelled by 60 lbs of steam pressure, fly some 100 yards or so down the yard, Percy being severely scalded in the process. Jim, without a thought for his personal safety, dived into the smokebox and hauled Percy out, thereby saving his life and getting his self quite seriously scalded as a result. Both were hospitalised for a considerable time before returning to work. We should not criticise Percy too strongly for his rather rash action as, being a true railwayman, his first thought, as with many more, was to try and keep the job going.

Dear old Cyril and Percy. What a fine pair they were. Both serving the old North Stafford Railway at the 'Knotty' Shed in Burton off Derby Street adjacent to the north end of the station, having been sent there, as was the way all those years ago, from Stoke. When the shed was closed they were transferred down the line to the Midland Shed, there to work out their days on the railway that they loved, though you would never have got either of them to admit it.

Lest anyone should think that all we saw in Cyril was a figure of fun, let it be said that we lads were all very fond of him and learnt an awful lot about railway engines and their ways, learning from his example, many little tricks to overcome their countless foibles. A fount of knowledge indeed! Many were the tales he would relate to us, particularly following a visit to the Forest Gate.

One story concerned the 'Michelin Tyre' railcar which was tried out, besides other places, on the Tutbury Jinnie, during the Thirties or 'before the war' as he would put it. Being handy for Derby and the nearest 'pull and push' service to the Works, the Jinnie was used on more than one occasion during its life as a test train for various innovations and developments in that particular field.

One such occasion that comes to mind was with a motor-fitted Fowler Class 3MT 2-6-2T, number 4005? Which ran for a week on this duty whilst testing the new BR version of pull and push gear, with which she was experimentally fitted, in place of the more usual LMS type then current on some members of the Class. The incomparable George Fisher was in charge of this series of tests which, I seem to recall, took place in 1952. I believe that Johnny Slater, then still an apprentice, accompanied him on this occasion, as I was privileged to do with the Reidinger Crabs some eighteen months or so later.

The Easter of 1957 saw my marriage to Judy, followed by a honeymoon in Bournemouth. Anticipating the inevitable leg pulls I would be subjected to, I delayed my announcement of the coming event for as long as I dare, until I was obliged to by the obtaining of a free pass for my new wife and I to travel down to Bournemouth. As this was a 'foreign' destination, being on the Southern Region, it was a requirement to give two clear weeks notice of ones requirements. Thus the secret was out. Many were the words of 'advice' proffered to me during the ensuing days, delivered in most instances with a malevolent grin upon the advisor's face and most, if not all of it, too detailed and intimate for these pages, especially as this is about railways and not matrimonial delicacies. Sufficient to say that over forty years later we are still together, despite or because of all the advice given.

Geoff German and Cyril were on the station to see us off as we caught the 15.39 Bristol train to change at Mangotsfield for the onward journey over the S&D to Bournemouth. Just as we were about to depart, Cyril thrust a bunch of clothes pegs into my hand, by way of an obscure present, which it transpired, he had purchased from a Gypsy in the Forest Gate (where else) earlier in the day. When, on my return to work, I thanked Cyril for his gift, Jack Turner was quite vehemently disgusted and indignant.

"You should be ashamed of yourself," I can still hear him complain to Cyril, "You disgusting man."

Was I missing something here? I wondered. Was there some more sinister meaning to the gift of clothes pegs? I have never found out but have often wondered.

Needless to say, the lads at the shed had made a collection for us to purchase a wedding present and as a result we were pleased to obtain, amongst other things, a set of saucepans and an ironing board, all of which saw valiant service for many years to come.

Hodgy, true to form, welcomed me back with yet another smokebox job. I sometimes thought he kept them somewhere in a special drawer, ready to produce on these occasions.

Another four months passed by in no time at all until, hidden amongst my 21st birthday cards, a small buff coloured envelope with OHMS (On Her

Majesty's Service) on it, dropped through the letterbox of my parent's front door where we were temporarily living. My National Service instructions were within, with an ominously single rail pass to Fleet, Hampshire and instructions to travel for two years service in the Royal Army Medical Corps. Not quite what an aspiring locomotive fitter would expect but no doubt influenced by my being a member of the St. John's Ambulance Brigade. Or would that be too logical for the Army? Probably!

Thus my railway career was put on hold, though I did change a gauge glass on one of out 84000's whilst riding back from Tutbury to Burton when going home on leave.

As soon as he heard of the forthcoming fate of his mate, George commenced to regale me with advice on how to go on in the service of the Queen. An old soldier himself, I was soon party to the secrets of 'bulling' boots, brasses and blanco. Did I want to know all that? I wondered. Wouldn't it be better to find out the hard way with my fellow conscripts? Still, he meant well and, truth to say, most of what he said did come in handy when I needed it.

One final, if unusual job that came my way during those final weeks before becoming a soldier of the Queen resulted in the withdrawal and scrapping of the locomotive concerned. Old Midland Class 2F 0-6-0 number 58130 was reported as getting no lubrication at all to the cylinders. As my Mate Bob Shrive had reported it, I knew that the report was genuine and not just a lack of lubrication due to some malfunction or misuse of the sight feed lubricator. The initial report was a deferred repair on the washout card.

Now! One can not test a sight feed lubricator without either the engine being in steam or alternatively with a compressed air supply and as we had neither, I did the next best thing going across to Leicester Junction and having a word with Bob when he arrived as he was fortuitously on the tripper that day. He was able to confirm, to my satisfaction, that the fault lay somewhere other than at the lubricator itself.

The delivery pipe for the atomised steam coursed its way along the side of the firebox and boiler beneath the lagging, as was the way with most Victorian Age engines. (Out of sight and out of mind). At least until things started going wrong. It reappeared from behind the lagging down the rear of the front tubeplate support to enter the steamchest at a point just above the left side inner top slidebar, where it was connected by means of a union nut and nipple.

Bob told me that Jack Fern, one of the shed fitters, had disconnected this union when he checked out the fault and truth to say, the copious amount of cylinder oil sprayed around the immediate area certainly seemed to confirm this fact; so everything seemed OK up to this point. A few gentle probings beyond the union nipple with a brass wire revealed, not surprisingly, a small hole lined with a carbonised deposit. This came to an abrupt halt after about two or three inches. After a few more stabbings into the hole, suddenly another eighteen or twenty inches plunged into and through the hole without too much effort. Further investigations found the business end of the wire poking up in the floor of the smokebox, courtesy of the boiler washer who felt it scratching his leg whilst he was removing the washout plug from the front tubeplate.

The floor of the smokebox is made up of firebricks mortared together with fire clay which, during the life of the engine between Shoppings, takes on the consistency of concrete and very hard concrete at that! No doubt as a result of the high temperatures to which it is subjected. Through this apparent solid mass, our piece of brass wire, some one eighth of an inch thick, had found its way. I realised that the channel through which the wire had passed could only have been cut out by a constant jet of steam wearing away the aggregate therein.

An hour of excavation with hammer and chisel in the small confines at the back of the smokebox in the left hand corner behind the blastpipe exposed the offending pipe. There, sure enough, was the hole whence all that atomised steam had escaped to soak into the surrounding firebrick, converting the latter into a carbonised mass not unlike the slatey coal that 58130 burnt daily as part of her normal diet, commensurate with the lowly duties on which she was employed.

Now the question arose as to what course of action was necessary to put things right. I guessed that further progress along the delivery pipe beyond the hole would be made up solid, otherwise at least some lubrication would have reached the cylinders and steamchest so before further excavations were pursued, I decided to acquaint Ernie Gaskell with the situation; Ernie being in temporary command as Hodgy was absent through sickness or holiday.

Having examined the problem for himself he then informed the Shedmaster, Mr. Smith, who in his turn, having checked out 58130's mileage card, proposed her for Shopping on a special, casual basis. All the remaining work on the X Card was abandoned, the boilerwasher put all his plugs back and thus 58130 stood, all forlorn, in her corner of the shed to await the decision as to her fate. Eventually, following a quick 'repair' by the boiler gang with a barrowful of aggregate over the hole in the smokebox floor and lubricated by the inevitable can of oil down the blastpipe, she groaned her last journey the twelve miles up the line to Derby Works where, as mentioned beginning of this narrative, she was withdrawn from service and cut up. This ended the life of another faithful, long serving Midland loco, all for the sake of a few pennyworth of copper pipe and a little effort.

Chapter 16

Fitter in My Own Right

Following two, quite pleasant if rather poverty stricken years of National Service, I reported back to the sheds on the second Monday of September 1959, ready to take up my duties as fitter, from where I had left off.

Having hung up my coat in the 'Bug Ut' and been welcomed back by my workmates, I made my way over to the foreman fitter's office and the redoubtable Johnny Hodgson. 'Hodgy,' true to form, handed me a report card then turned to the next man. No, "Pleased to see you back," or any other kind of greeting passed those Lancashire lips. But then, that would be too much to expect from him. At least, if I had learned nothing else from my army days, I had come to learn that not all Lancastrians were like him; quite the reverse in fact, some of my best mates having come from the 'Red Rose' county.

Stepping back outside into the shed, I was joined by my old faithful mate George who, it transpired, had guarded my tools and locker from prying hands for the period of my enforced absence. Showing him the card, it proved to be yet another from out of that secret drawer of Hodgy's: a smokebox job. Some superheater elements to be removed from a Class 8F no less!

This engine, number 48127, was a foreigner, stopped for the replacement of a badly leaking superheater flue tube. The tubers required eleven elements removing to provide access for the removal and replacement of the flue tube. The district boiler inspector had ordered the work to be done following an engine failure out on the line.

These elements proved to be the worst set that had been my questionable pleasure to remove. It became obvious very early into the job that these flue tubes had not been blown out in a very long time. How any air passed through them at all was a mystery. The spaces between the elements were solid with char and soot. Normally, once the bridge bar on the header is undone, the elements could be swung from side to side and pulled out without too much effort by one man alone. These could not be moved at all in any direction.

Ted Hodgetts, the tube blower (bobber), another of Burton's characters, was called over and he spent some considerable time with his steam lance and rods trying to make a way through but with little success. Eventually a wire strap from the breakdown van was acquired and secured by one end to one of the elements with the other end around the drawhook of another 8F. Following much huffing and slipping the offending element was withdrawn from the boiler. Needless to say, all this extreme treatment rendered the element of no further use other than as a donation to the scrap bin.

The tension on that wire strap before 48127 relinquished its hold on each element and the 'crack' when it did was something to behold. Naturally, the usual crowd of onlookers was assembled to witness the fun. Bets were laid as to where the Class 8 'tug' would finish up if the strap broke. I must admit that this did worry me somewhat, particularly as the store window and office door lay right in its path but as with many things, no mishaps occurred.

Hodgy's only comment was, "I hope tha knows what tha's doin!" thereby passing all onus onto me.

So, after struggling for nearly two days, the 8F solved the problem in half an hour, albeit scrapping the elements in the process. If I remember correctly only one element from the top row was able to be reused, out of the eleven removed.

Having restarted my railway career in such a spectacular and sooty fashion, life soon settled down to a normal routine of X repairs and mileage examinations.

Whereas the Burton allocation of engines had been formed by predominantly ex Midland and LMS built Midland types with the most modern engines being the Hughes 'Crabs' and 42336, a few Stanier types were beginning to filter in during the late fifties with three Class 8F's being allocated: numbers 48002, 48401 and 48547. These were joined later by 48182, 48332 and 48728 plus Class 5's 44811, 45238 and 45262. Also the first brand new engines arrived in the shape of Darlington built Ivatt Class 2's 46493 and 4 in August 1952. The BR Standard Class 2MT Tanks 84006, 7 and 8, arriving in August 1953, were the last new steam engines to wear the 17B plates, all future new build engines being Diesel powered.

Thus in 1959, coinciding with Hodgy's retirement through ill health, came the first of these locos in the form of 350 hp diesel electric shunters D3568, 69, 70, 71 and 72. These were soon joined by D3585, 86 and 87.

Initially these eight locos were fuelled and serviced at Derby, which managed to keep a number of our footplate staff happy, trundling back and forth with

English electric 350HP diesel shunter No. D3572 unfortunatley derailed at Horninglow. Photo: E. Edwards.

them for this purpose each weekend. As their maximum speed was only 15 mph, the problems of line occupation and time taken were major factors in seeking alternative measures to alleviate this situation.

Our new foreman Frank Pepper was a complete contrast to his predecessor, being young, communicative and Diesel trained. He came to us from Cockshute, Stoke on Trent, which was a purpose built Diesel depot dealing predominantly with Railcar Multiple Units.

Our shed fitters had had a number of calls to these units over the preceding months, usually down at the station, which is not the ideal location at which to learn how things work.

Fortunately, most faults seemed to be cured by topping up the engine oil levels and resetting the low oil level switch, this safety device having 'tripped out' and stopped the engines. It was also possible to isolate the drive in a defunct engine by means of a device something like a toasting fork with two hooked tines, which enabled the final drive dog clutch to be withdrawn and disconnected, thereby separating the engine and gearbox from the driven bogie. This action prevented further damage to the engine/gearbox assembly when on the move, as they would then be driven by the bogie instead of the reverse action as when functioning normally, the power coming from the engine on the bogie at the other end of the car. This procedure was resorted to when, as often happened, the fitter failed to restart the engine.

The drivers who unlike our fitters, had received training on their charges, rarely offered any help or advice regarding the cause or cure of these faults. Sometimes a unit would arrive in the station, running with one or even two engines isolated already. Each power car had two engines, one driving each of the two bogies, so a standard, three-car unit consisted of two power cars with a trailer (non-powered) car in between. If running in multiple (two or more three-car sets coupled together), two isolated engines could be coped with at the cost of some loss in acceleration but loss of a third engine made a noticeable difference and was the kiss of death to a single three-car set. On these occasions all the remaining active driven bogies had to be isolated and the station pilot called upon to power the train as a locomotive with a set of ordinary coaches.

Our BR Standard 84xxx 2-6-2's made more than one trip to Derby or Birmingham in this capacity, the accumulative time loss being added to when on the Birmingham run by the need to fill the tank at Tamworth as they were not fitted with water pick-up gear that would have enabled them to take advantage of the troughs at Haslough.

Other total failures were either replaced by a complete steam engine and stock or cancelled altogether, passengers travelling on by the next available service. The steam train replacements were usually on Leicester or Walsall workings where no back up mainline trains were available. Then a 2P or 4F would be the usual alternative power. These Diesels certainly created chaos to the rail system during the early days of their introduction.

However, now we had Frank Pepper leading us, whenever a fitter was required to attend an ailing railcar unit whilst he was on duty; effectively between 7.30 am and about 5.30 – 6.00 pm; he would accompany them to the station or wherever, to advise and assist. Our shed men learned an awful lot by this means.

Obviously this situation was far from ideal. Not only was it causing delays in traffic, it was belittling and not a little embarrassing to the fitter who through no fault of his own, had insufficient knowledge to deal with these units. Indeed, some of the fitters, when covering for the shed men, would refuse to attend them at all.

Frank Pepper sought to arrange an unofficial two-week course for some of us to attend at the new Derby Etches Park Diesel Depot. Naturally, as was only right and proper, the shed men were the first to go with Geoff German blazing the trail followed by Jack Fern and Les Bull, the latter having taken up the vacancy created by the sad and sudden death of Reg Corden while I was away in the Army. Then it was Wally Gaskell's turn followed by me.

Thus, one May morning in 1960, I found myself once more aboard the 6.59 am local from Burton to Derby. Etches Park had been purpose built for the repair and maintenance of Railcar Multiple Units. It had elevated tracks some three or four feet above the lower ground level, supported on concrete pillars every six or eight feet of their length. However, with typical Railway blinkered efficiency, although mainline Diesels were beginning to come on the scene by then and serviced therein, these raised tracks had not been constructed to carry their greater weight. Consequently, the pillars were all beginning to crack and in need of strengthening.

I was soon involved in exams on Crossley Diesels, Peaks and 350hp shunters. I forget the names of the fitter and mate with whom I spent this very interesting two weeks but sufficient to acknowledge the unstinting willingness of the pair to pass on as much knowledge and information to me as possible during the time available.

Crossley Co. BO 1200HP diesel No. D5705. Photo: P. Groom.

All these exams were based on engine hours run and were classified from A to F, the former being little more than a check and top up of the various oils, to the latter when both inlet and exhaust valves were changed, all filters renewed, oils changed and crankcase insides checked, i.e. main and con-rod bearings and crankshaft condition checked. Fuel injectors were removed, checked and overhauled and pumps calibrated. Drive belts were tensioned and vacuum exhausters together with numerous other items all receiving attention.

We had an interesting day out to St Mary's Goods Yard and Chaddesden, where two or three of these Class A or B exams were carried out 'on site' as it were, on the resident 350hp shunters.

Another little excursion to Derby Friargate, initially to attend to a multiple unit that had fallen by the wayside, also proved worthy of note. We were additionally instructed to check and run up the AC Railcars stabled there alongside the goods shed. Apparently these four wheeled units were under consideration for use somewhere on the ex LNER lines in the Derby/ Nottingham area but I believe it came to nothing, not surprisingly as they had been an abject failure due to unreliability and uncomfortable riding wherever they had been tried out before. They were eventually scrapped in 1963 at the Derby Carriage and Wagon Works.

The two Type 45's or Peaks as they were known then, were fitted with Stones Vapour Boilers to supply steam heating for the coaching stock when working passenger trains. These units were a constant source of trouble and many locomotive failures owed their demise to their malfunction. From what I can remember, they were fuelled by the same Diesel that powered the engine and were flash fired, the atomised fuel being sprayed across two electrodes which when charged, ignited the fuel charged air. I recall that the gap between these two electrodes was critical to the ignition being successful, rather like a spark plug in a motor car engine but, after all these years, I have forgotten precisely what the setting was.

The water supply was also rather complicated with necessary fail-safe controls to regulate the high and low levels. The locomotives were equipped with water pick-up apparatus with which to top up the header tank from lineside water troughs in precisely the same way as steam locomotives. A huge sigh of relief was heaved by all and sundry when all the mainline coaching stock was converted to electric heating but this only occurred many years later and the steam heating boilers were still in use when I left the railway service.

It is only fair to say that the diesel engines themselves, at least those of the Sulzer and English Electric varieties with which I came into contact most, were fairly reliable and seemed to chug on with a considerable amount of neglect commensurate with the ignorance of the steam trained maintenance staff charged with their care during those early days. We soon learned the little faults and foibles peculiar to the various classes and on the whole, coped very well.

The Type 2 Sulzers (later known as 24, 25, 26) were rather prone to over-heating when worked hard for any length of time, caused I believe by the radiator louver systems not opening up to allow enough cooling air to pass through. The 'quick cure' when out on the line, which was the usual scenario for the shed fitter, was to switch the water system over to by-pass, a lever for this purpose being located on the side of the header tank. If this did not work or as sometimes happened, some other fitter further up the line had already 'beat you to the draw' as it were, then 'Plan B' was resorted to.

This involved the fitter emerging from the engine room, after a suitable delay, back into the cab with much pursing of lips and head shaking and having thus attracted the attention of the driver and fireman thereon, would utter those immortal words,

"Sorry mate, I'll have to fail her. You'll have to have a steamer; we've got no Diesels here!!"

A look of horror would cross the fireman's face at this juncture and a pleading glance towards his Mate could hardly fail to melt any but the hardest of hearts of any driver. This worthy would ponder the situation for a few moments before putting on a brave face and heroically suggest that,

"Perhaps if we take it steady we'll be alright. After all we're only going to Derby."

The fitter, for his part, promises to advise the Control to find a relief and thus, honour satisfied, he quickly dismounts disappearing from sight around the nearest corner.

About the time I went to Etches Park I moved my tools up onto the Drop Pit where I took over from Wally who was going on the shed in place of Les Bull, Les having taken on the job of Fitter in Charge at Overseal in place of Joe Benson who had secured a salaried promotion to Derby.

No less than twenty-two engines were ranged about the shed and yard with wheels out when I took over, including a WD Austerity, two Black 5's, two 8F's and a Crab together with numerous of the ex Midland/LMS type 4F's, 3F's 2P's and the like. As the night shift had been discontinued there was now only one team on the pit and George and I were it. We were just beginning to make inroads into this backlog of locos when, on arriving one morning, a Black 5 was standing out on the pit road. A Crewe engine, she had run the usual trailing coupled axle hot whilst working the incoming Mold – Horninglow fitted freight.

Now! Much has already been written about life on the 'Droppit' including the time now being described but this particular Class 5 was different. She was fitted with roller bearings on all coupled wheels and these were virtually unknown to suffer the indignities of a hot axlebox.

The table was occupied by a 3F at the time which we had re-wheeled the previous day and apart from replacing the brake gear, she was ready to be pulled out for re-rodding and return to traffic; two to three hours work with any luck.

Frank Pepper informed us that a casualty inspector would be in attendance the following day to witness the removal of the axle so, with the 3F completed towards the end of the morning; we set about preparing 44762 for her stage performance.

As described previously, with a little judicious setting, it was possible to remove the coupling rod gradient pins and drop the trailing half of the rod thereby alleviating the need to strip down the complete motion and this we duly did. With the 5 positioned over the table the brake gear pull rod, cylinder taps control rod and, biggest of all, the exhaust injector steam supply pipe were all removed. The cotters were all knocked out of the under stays and thus the scene was set for the following day.

By 9.30am the next morning, there being no sign of the inspector, I decided to drop the wheels out and get on with it, as this was not the only engine requiring our attention, so, uncoupling the stays, I instructed George to lower away the table. The axle came down without any trouble so when they were nearly clear of the horns I scotched them and clambered out. George completed the lowering and with the bridge rails in place I went to ask for 44762 to be hauled clear of the pit.

This done we soon had the table up again and the wheels rolled clear onto the stripping area behind the pit. By now it was gone eleven o'clock and of the casualty inspector there was no sign. A pair of wheels for the Crab had just arrived from Horwich Works so we decided to unload them while we waited to see if indeed he would turn up. If he did, we could then use the wagon to send the Class 5's wheels back to Crewe or wherever. Otherwise it would be released to traffic to avoid a demurrage credit to the shed. This would then incur further delay in despatch of the wheels whilst another wagon was ordered; probably an extra day.

With the Crab wheels unloaded lunch time was upon us so we departed for a well earned dinner. On return I was pleased to see that our belated inspector had now arrived and was sitting, somewhat impatiently, by our never-cold fire awaiting our arrival.

Of fair complexion with large, staring eyes peering through horn rimmed spectacles, one hinge of which was in receipt of a temporary repair by the use of what appeared to be Elastoplast, he rose up to his full height of about five feet and five inches, as I approached. I estimated him to be of similar age to myself and of a quite aggressive nature, the latter trait proving to be obvious as soon as he opened his mouth.

"Mr. Fleming?" he questioned as his opening gambit. "I gave strict instructions that this engine wasn't to be touched until I was present. What have you to say about that?"

Now! As I may have mentioned before, in my younger days my temper could incline to being somewhat short and his opening words did little to 'lengthen' it. At this moment George returned from his repast and quickly weighing up the mood, tactfully placed himself between us.

"We start here at 8 o'clock in the morning," I answered, "And we have more than one engine to think about. While we're waiting for you, they're waiting too."

"Well, you should have waited 'till I got here," he retorted.

"We did wait, until nearly ten o'clock," I came back and so it went on until I said to George, "Come on mate, we've got work to do if he hasn't," and walked away.

If I hadn't, I'm sure I would have hit him and I think George knew it too. He still hadn't put his overalls on but he grabbed the tool bag and came anyway.

All that our foreman said the next day was to advise me to think before I spoke. A piece of advice that wouldn't have done any harm to the casualty inspector also, I thought.

It transpired that the inspector was an ex privileged apprentice from Crewe whose father held a fairly high position on the railway and in consequence, had delusions of grandeur far outweighing his experience. Tom Turner would have had him for breakfast I reflected.

Our paths were to cross again some three years or so later when, having applied for the position of foreman fitter at Rugby no less; with very little hope of securing the job; I attended the interview down at Euston. To my chagrin, our worthy no less, was present on the panel. As I entered the room our eyes met and an instant flash of recognition came from behind those glasses; now of the rimless variety and very expensive looking. Any hopes of getting the job, however slight before, went out of the window at that moment but at least I had had the experience of a free day out in London at the Company's expense.

Interestingly, the roller bearing boxes on 44762 were of the Cannon type, where the axle was enclosed within a cylindrical casing joining the two axleboxes together to form one unit.

In between all the work on the Drop Pit I was now also engaged in carrying out Hourly Exams on our 350 hp Diesel shunting locomotives. George hated this work and spent many hours over the course of our association, complaining to himself and rehearsing what he was going to say to the foreman in defence of his case although he never actually confronted the foreman with his complaints although I presume it gave him some consolation to air his grievances if only to himself and me.

George lived with his sister; neither of whom had ever married; in the ex parental home in Anglesey Road, some five or six minutes walk from work. Part of his routine when he got up in the morning before coming to work, was to prepare the vegetables for their dinner. Then, about eleven o'clock, he would disappear for a short time. Where had he been? He had nipped home to put the aforementioned veggies on to cook. Thus, when his sister in her turn, got home about mid-day, they were nearly ready for her to strain and serve for their meal when he returned home about a quarter of an hour or so later.

This routine was followed for years, even after the shed was closed and he had gained employment, still as a fitter's Mate, at the adjacent Lloyds Foundry until one day he was arrested by the Railway Police for trespassing. I would dearly love to have been present that day to have heard his reply when accosted. Dear George, did a fitter ever have a more loyal and sincere mate? I very much doubt it!

Soon, Wally and I were off together again on another course at Derby, to the Rolls Royce Engine School no less this time at Littleover. Our chief clerk, being of a devious nature, still would not trust us to attend of our own volition insisting that we attend the shed to check on and off every day before and after each visit. As we had to pay our own bus fare each way daily then present the tickets at the end of the week for reimbursement we argued that this was a needless ritual but he was adamant that we comply with his wishes so the railway company paid us an extra hour and ten minutes per day; walking time to and from the bus station to the shed; five hours and fifty minutes per week for each of us for what was in effect a ten minute cycle ride each way daily.

Burton had just been allocated a Rolls Royce powered Yorkshire Engine Company built 0-4-0 Diesel shunter, number D2859, to replace our ageing allocation of museum piece 0-4-0 steamers. As this locomotive was brand new the power unit was covered by a manufacturer's warranty and a requirement of the guarantee was that all servicing and maintenance should be carried out by an approved Rolls Royce trained fitter. Hence our attendance on this course.

The authors pride and joy Class 02-0-4-0 Diesel No. D2859 crosses Branston Road.
Photo: Authors Collection.

Travelling to Littleover on the Trent bus, we duly presented ourselves at the school which was situated in an old manor house of quite palatial appearance. Having signed in we attended a short reception to meet our fellow trainees before getting down to the business, as it were. We were ten in number, one of whom was Walter Capps, a fitter or possibly chargehand from the Bass Brewery, who I remembered vaguely from the alcoholic sojourns with Harry Buggins some three years or so before.

Our group soon buckled down to learning the intricacies of the Rolls Royce Oil Engine and in no time at all, it was time for lunch, courtesy of our hosts. Our instructors warned us that our group was very much in the minority as far as courses went, being the only oil engine course there, the majority of other courses concerning the aspects and foibles of the various jet engines then in production by the company.

And so we were to find. On entering the dining hall the scene was a mass of blue uniforms of various shades with air forces both military and civilian from all four corners of the globe represented interspersed with smart, up to the minute, working attire of a group of British Airways fitters and some other airline personnel. However, we were not intimidated or overawed; far from it. On each table were flagons of water and of cider, one per four guests. Being a group of ten our table had three of each thereon.

Our nearest neighbours were eight Iranian Air Force Officers whose religion forbade the drinking of alcohol and it took very little negotiation to exchange our three flagons of water for their two of cider. We consumed the contents with great enthusiasm whilst enjoying our meal, in effect half a jug-full each. Needless to say, not a lot of information was absorbed during the afternoons.

Pages and pages of notes were written and during the practical sessions the training engine was stripped right down, rebuilt, bled and run up. During the second week, I think on the Thursday, we were taken to the Rolls Royce Diesel Engine Plant situated in the Sentinel Works at Shrewsbury, where we were given a conducted tour of the Plant and further wined and dined in sumptuous style by our hosts. Truly a 'Rolls Royce' Job!!

On the last day we had to undertake a written exam followed by a short interview with the principal instructor. He then wished us all a fond farewell and our trio caught the next bus home, clothed in an aura of new knowledge.

Attending work the following (Saturday) morning, I was pleased to see that D2859 had indeed arrived during the week and was undergoing driver training with a Yorkshire Engine Company representative in attendance. As the driving had been undertaken whilst working the Bond End shunting turn, for which 2859 had been allocated, this worthy considered himself to have been rather more fortunate than some of his colleagues as this job still entailed calling at the various brewery outposts situated along the line, where customary hospitality was still forthcoming. My old mates Bernard Davies, Gilbert Atkins and Freddie Smith were the three drivers so trained with Bernard being the driver usually on the job.

My certificate of competence duly arrived but to my embarrassment, Wally failed to pass the exam. Not, I feel sure, for any lack of skill but because of the written exam and interview afterwards. Thus my Sunday morning work was assured for the next twelve months at least as I was the only person allowed to carry out any mechanical work or servicing upon this new loco. With a wife and new daughter to support, rent and rates to pay and all the other bills commensurate with married life, this was a more than welcome piece of good fortune to come my way. As with most things, this situation became a habit and I continued to look after D2859 right until I left the Company's service some four to five years later. I even worked my holidays around the servicing schedule to maintain this continuity of attendance. Never did another locomotive in British Railways service receive such TLC (tender loving care). When I left the railway, coincidentally D2859 also moved from Burton to join her consorts at Bank Hall where they performed their duties around the tight curves of the Liverpool dockside. No more TLC then for her then, I'll be bound. Her immediate sister, number D2860, can still be seen carrying out her duties at the National Rail Museum at York. I am sure that D2859 would have been a better choice but then, I am a little bit biased in my thinking.

She only let me down twice in the whole of her time at Burton. Firstly, when quite new, one Saturday lunch time, as my wife and I were settling down to watch the Boat Race between Oxford and Cambridge, Ernie Thompson appeared at our door. He was the duty shedman, standing in for the usual man who, as I explained earlier, had the Saturday 6 x 2 shift off if they so desired. It transpired that D2859 had been taken down to the wholesale market across New Street No.2 crossing and no doubt having completed the shunting duties there, Bernard the driver, had gone for his usual visit to the Market Hotel to check that all was alright, as was his way, (hic! hic!), shutting down 2859 before he did so. On his return, on trying to start her she would not turn over. I was informed that the starter motor was whirring round and some strange noises were coming from the engine compartment.

Ernie and I cycled down to the market, with myself knowing exactly where to find her form my previous experiences with 41516 and 41523 some years before. Bernard sat inside the cab looking completely dejected. For my part I was surprised to see him there, expecting him to be waiting in the pub.

"Hello Dave," he greeted me, "I haven't broken it, have 1" he asked.

I climbed up onto the framing and removed the left front door of the engine compartment. A quick look round revealed nothing obviously wrong.

"Just give her a quick flick over," I called to Bernard.

"Whoa, whoa. Off!" I shout, before anything had hardly happened as the starter motor was jumping about like a wild thing.

As soon as the ignition was switched off everything settled down again. The starter motor sat in a cradle to which it was attached by a hinged pin and further secured by a spring clip around the motor body. The somewhat flimsy hinge lugs had broken free of the casting, leaving only the spring clip holding the motor in place. When at rest the whole assembly resumed its proper position and appearance. Ernie and I tried to jam the starter motor in position with brake sticks and shunters' poles, persuaded by brute force but to no avail. Each time we tried to turn the 170 hp engine it kicked the starter out of mesh. I decided enough was enough, being afraid that all this brutal treatment would damage the starter ring on the engine flywheel and declared D2859 a 'failure.'

Now another problem confronted us. Here we were, in the heart of '4 wheel country' on a Saturday afternoon. Where were we going to find another engine to haul 2859 out? Both the steam engines back at the shed had been out of steam for many weeks and officially in store.

Bass! I thought. Was one of their engines still about that could haul us out?

I jumped onto my bike and pedalled off to Uxbridge Street Signalbox to ask the bobby if he could help us out. He confirmed that there was one last trip due out of Shobnall very soon and that he would ask the driver if he would oblige. The driver agreed and leaving his train on the line by the box, he took his engine round to James Street Junction whose bobby had already been acquainted with the situation and switched him round to the right whilst I hared back on my bike to obtain the Annett key to open the gates at Park Street and New Street and to obtain the necessary authorisation form from Bernard to allow the Bass engine down what was in effect a one-engine steam line with an engine already there ('In Steam' as the term was still used, although in reality a Diesel). So, if not for the first time, almost certainly the last, a Bass's engine travelled over the James Street branch. I cannot recall the number of the locomotive, if indeed I was ever aware of it and can only say that it was a blue painted Diesel.

Her driver pulled D2859 along the branch and shunted her onto the Bond End branch, from where the Shobnall Jocko was able to retrieve her later in the day. A new bracket was obtained overnight and was fitted by yours truly on the Sunday morning, all ready for work again on the Monday. The broken bracket was returned to Rolls Royce for examination as a result of which I understand an improved, more robustly constructed bracket was developed. Apparently this same mishap befell one of the Bass Sentinels and they received one of these modified brackets as a replacement.

Oh! And when I returned home on the Saturday afternoon, my wife Judy greeted me with the announcement,

"Oxford won! You owe me half a crown!"

I had my money on Cambridge so I was a loser there but the unexpected four hours at time and a half more than made up for the disappointment.

The other time when things went wrong actually occurred while I was away for a few days holiday. I had serviced and refuelled D2859 on the Sunday morning prior to going away and apparently all went well on the Monday although Bernard didn't think she was pulling too well towards the end of the shift and reported the fact. The shed fitter couldn't find anything wrong and thus she was booked out again for the following day. When Bernard started her up in the shed the engine ran alright but when put into 'drive' she wouldn't move at all no matter how hard he revved the engine.

I should explain that D2859 had no gearbox as such, only a change direction box, power being generated by the engine speed creating velocity through a torque converter. The Rolls Royce powered railcars used a similar method of propulsion with added refinements commensurate with the speeds they achieved and used a specially formulated grade of oil in the torque converter to drive them along. D2859 and her sisters, not being required to reach speeds in excess of 20 mph, used the diesel from the fuel tank to form a drive medium.

Unfortunately, the fuel with which she had been filled that Sunday morning was not quite as clean as it might have been and in consequence, some of the dirt had found its way down the supply feed to the converter, only to be arrested by the inline filter provided for just this very reason. The filter had become blocked, cutting off completely the diesel supply to the torque converter, thereby denying it the means of its propulsion; probably a ten minute job to put right if you knew what the problem was. Unfortunately no one available did, so the job had to be done with a six coupled Jocko, only going where it could get, which was not many places when on the Bond End job.

Two Rolls Royce trained fitters were summoned from Etches Park and these two worthies, to their credit, put it right in about an hour which, considering they were unfamiliar with this loco, was very good.

This filter was not included in the weekly servicing schedule, only requiring attention after about 200 hours of operation. However, I made a habit of checking it and cleaning it at least once a month after this incident although, fair to say, there was rarely anything trapped in it. Dirty filter trouble was also experienced with some of our other 350 hp shunters at about the same time, following refuelling from this same batch of diesel.

It was hardly surprising that a certain amount of dirt could be present in the fuel supply when one considers the refuelling method then current in the shed, which was crude in the extreme. Two old rail tankers, one of which had started life in the service of United Dairies and the other, whose background was a complete mystery, were positioned on the coal stage bank and the Diesel locomotives were parked on the coalroad beneath them. A fuel pipe was connected between a tanker and a loco. The inlet valves opened and thus the refuelling was carried out by gravity feed. "Simple" you might say. Yes but not ideal. Soon the coal stage bank became soaked with diesel which turned into obnoxious slurry, on which the refuelling pipes lay between each filling operation. This gunge soon found its way inside the pipes and consequently into the fuel tanks of the locomotives.

We, the fitters, soon got fed up with this situation and following discussions in the BugUt, came up with a much improved solution to the problem.

I should perhaps explain that the refuelling cock on a 350 hp Diesel shunter is situated beneath the fuel tank and whilst this is convenient for the man refuelling the locomotive to connect the pipe; it being about waist height; some method of pumping it into the tank is then required as, it being a well known fact, liquids will not flow upwards of their own volition. This is all very well at dedicated fuelling points but not at Burton where no such facility existed at the time. Hence the coal stage saga, using the force of gravity to achieve the desired result.

Our solution, though simple in context, worked very well in practice and went thus:

On the 350 hp shunters, two air reservoirs were situated beneath the front buffer beam. These were charged up to and maintained at 80 psi when the engine was running. A drain cock was fitted to each reservoir and one of the disposal duties of the driver on stabling his locomotive at the end of its daily duty was to open these cocks to discharge the remaining air along with any moisture therein. We reasoned that if we connected an air pipe from one of these drain cocks to the vent pipe on the top of the rail tanker, the pressure buildup therein when the diesel engine was running, would push the diesel fuel out of the bottom connection and in turn, into the loco fuel tank via the connecting pipe, in the same way that a fuel pump would.

Suitable fittings were obtained and an oxyacetylene pipe adapted to act as the air connection. The following weekend the idea was put to the test and found to work most effectively. One shunter stood ticking over to maintain the air pressure whilst her consorts in their turn were topped up.

Out shedmaster, Mr. Lewis, was most impressed and soon organised a rotor for a fireman to oversee the fuelling operation thus releasing a fitter to perform the duties for which he was employed, i.e. that of maintenance.

All went well for many weeks to come, the fitter's only involvement being to set up the air line first thing in the morning and remove it when the refuelling operations were completed. When an engine arrived for refuelling, the fireman connected up the fuel pipe, turned on the two valves on the tanker and the loco and then started up the 'air supply' Diesel loco. When the loco being refuelled was full, he just shut the 'air pump' Diesel loco down, closed the fuel cocks and disconnected the pipe. The process was then repeated for the next engine to be refuelled. If two shunters arrived back to back or, if you prefer, cab to cab, they could be refuelled each in their turn without the need to shut down the slave loco whilst changing over the fuel supply pipe, provided the cocks were first closed.

As with most things, familiarity bred contempt and the inevitable day arrived when it all went wrong. On this somewhat eventful morning, the fireman in command of the refuelling ritual, was a rather laid back character with a liking for 'bar sports' i.e. darts, cards and dominoes, etc. Having set up yet another shunter for refuelling; which was nearly empty and in consequence required about 500 gallons of diesel to fill its tank, in common with its sisters, holding some 585 gallons when full; our hero decided to retire to the canteen for half an hour whilst this operation ensued. There, he became embroiled in a game of cards which absorbed his attention to such an extent that he forgot all about what was going on behind the coal stage.

Things mechanical and inanimate, in that androidfree age, not having the power of thought built into them, tended to chug on and on and eventually, with the Diesel loco's tank being full, the system started to pressurise as the excess diesel fuel being of a denser consistency than the air it displaced, would not pass out of the vent on the tank's top quite as fast as the slave Diesel was pushing air into the supply tank. Eventually this excess pressure proved too much for the old tank which ruptured spectacularly, spraying its contents around the immediate area with a force that would have done credit to 'Old Glory' in Yellowstone Park.

"Talk yourself out of that one!" was the general thought of the assembled multitude which always seems to gather when such incidents occur, boding the question, "Where have they all come from on a Sunday morning?" all of them being, of course, smugly secure in the knowledge that it's nothing to do with them; a warm, comfortable feeling on such occasions.

Suitably chastised, following an interview with the DMPS at Derby, where he no doubt toed the line at the end of the red carpet, our hero whose identity will remain forever locked in my mind, went on to follow a successful career on the footplate and was driving HST 125's amongst other things when I last heard of him.

Of course, the secret of his identity is obviously shared by many more of his colleagues of the time who, I am sure, will also conveniently forget his name should they happen to read this litany and so be reminded.

Casualties out on the line, where the locomotive is completely immobilised and unable to be moved without the attention of the fitting/breakdown staff, other than derailments, are comparatively rare although not unknown.

The 4F's in particular had a nasty habit of shearing off a driving siderod crankpin with the resultant contortions of the siderods requiring the fitters' attendance before the engine could be moved again. Contrary to popular belief, the footplate crew rarely if ever made any attempts to effect any repairs themselves though, to be fair, they were hardly equipped to achieve many miracles with the meagre and cumbersome toolkit with which the engine was supplied.

An unusual casualty befell one of our Crabs, No.42763, at Wychnor when working the return Bristol – Burton ale train one dinnertime. As she was approaching the junction, having just crossed the long viaduct over the Trent floodplain, the left hand expansion link of the Walshearts valve gear fractured at the top and bottom of its crescent, causing the eccentric on that side to fall and dig into the ballast and the left hand valve to shoot forwards in the steam chest. The driver said that the resultant noise up the chimney was something he had no desire to hear again.

I was an apprentice at the time and would dearly have loved to accompany Joe Benson and Gerald when they went on a hastily arranged light engine to attend to the problem. However, Hodgy, true to form, wouldn't hear of it and I had to be content with being told about it on their return.

The 4F which served as their taxi to the scene was utilised to bring 42763's train back to Burton from the Wychnor Sidings where the Wychnor Jocko had placed it, whilst Joe and Gerald set about making the Crab safe to travel. This they did by removing all the damaged parts from the left hand valve gear, namely eccentric, expansion link, valve rod and lift link. The left hand valve was then centralised so that both inlet ports were closed and the anchor link between the crosshead and lower end of the combination lever disconnected and removed so that the valve would not move when the engine was travelling. This combination lever was tied, in its extreme forward position, to the cylinder, at a suitable point and thus, with the valve secured, 42763 was able to make her own way back to Burton, steaming on her right hand side only, care being taken by her driver not to stop with the right hand valve on a dead centre.

Another incident that occurred many months later, again on the Wychnor Viaduct near to where it crosses the river, concerned an 8F; not a Burton one; which pushed the left front cylinder cover out as a result of the piston head becoming detached from the rod. Our breakdown gang were nearby, attending to a derailment in Wychnor Sidings at the time so were directed to the scene in double quick time. Very little damage had been done, other than to the cylinder cover and piston so all that was required was to remove the eccentric and connecting rod, knock out the big end bush to take up the space on the big end and crank, replace the return crank and eccentric to hold the coupling rods on and she was ready to be towed away or by centralising the valves, to take herself away as just described with 42763.

A straightforward job you might say. The only hazard present, although quite a real one, was the low parapet wall alongside, over which lay a considerable drop to the fields below. The precise distance could not be judged or seen as the early morning mist off the river and marshy ground below cast a blanket over the scene.

The eccentric and return crank were soon removed and fortunately the 8F had stopped in a position that enabled the little end pins to pass out between the spokes of the leading coupled wheel from behind the crosshead. After much grunting and heaving the crosshead was barred forwards enough to clear the con rod, despite the bent piston rod. All that remained was to bar the bent con rod off the big end crank and onto the ballast. In an ideal world this crank would have been positioned on the bottom centre but of course, in a case like this the ideal is rarely, if ever, present. Such was the situation now, with the crank almost at the top of its stroke.

After looking at it and pondering for a few moments, Sam McBride said,

Stand out the way. I'll soon sort it," and taking up a large pinch bar, he positioned the heel behind the big end and gave an almighty heave. With a clang and a crash the con rod shot off its crank, hit the edge of the parapet and disappeared into the mist below.

Hodgy's face was a picture and his demeanour was not improved by the resultant cheer which went up from the gang.

"We'll not have to maul that up onto the framing, thank goodness," one wit remarked.

Hodgy looked round, saw me and settled his beady eyes on his victim.

"Tha'll 'ave ta coom and find yon tomorrow if it's not foggy," he sneered.

"Suit me fine, that will," I thought and sure enough the following day broke clear and fine with the sun shining high in the sky.

Johnny Slater and me, for we were still apprentices then, caught a train to Elford and then found our way down to the flood plain searching both sides of the river for the Class 8F connecting rod but to no avail. It had disappeared completely, never to be seen again. Who knows, somewhere in the future, possibly hundreds or even thousands of years from now some futuristic inhabitant of this planet may unearth it, much in the same way that we are discovering Roman and Neolithic remains today. What will they make of it I wonder? That, for sure, is something we will never know.

As a postscript to this incident, another 8F eventually arrived, 'wrong line,' from Saltley and hauled both our 8F and its train of coal away to its destination, no doubt one of the power stations in the Birmingham area and we for our part returned to the railing job in Wychnor Sidings.

Another unusual and possibly unique incident occurred at Clay Mills one night when a Caprotti Class 5 came to grief near the level crossings there. Geoff German and his mate attended the scene and were surprised to find that the left hand cambox had come adrift and had been thrown onto the framing behind the cylinder where it was balancing precariously above the slidebars. Almost an impossibility you would think, considering that the engine and its train were accelerating from the Burton Station stop at the time and must have reached a speed approaching sixty miles per hour when the incident occurred. All Geoff and his mate could do was to secure the cambox in the position where it had settled by means of some wagon ropes and have the engine towed back to the shed where saw it the following morning. One of our redoubtable 4F's worked the train forwards, her driver and fireman no doubt wondering what they had done in life to deserve such misfortune.

My experience with the 4F in Derby Works came home to roost one wet Monday morning when I was acting as shedman in place of Les Bull who I believe was on holiday. A wire to the shed informed me that number 44091/16B had come to grief on the down goods road just to the north of the station. Joe Marsland (Marsy) was my mate and together we went down to the station to see what was required to be done.

44091 had broken the back cylinder cover on the left hand side and cracked the front one also. The tangled mess between the frames greeting our eyes had to be seen to be believed. I did at first consider calling out the whole breakdown gang, such was the task before us but following a brief chat with the bobby at the Burton Station North Box, who assured me that it was not causing too much of a hold up where it was, I decided to tackle it myself.

The slidebars were bent as was the connecting rod. This had bent inwards, striking the back gear eccentric which had also bent, twisting the expansion link as it did so. The brake pull rod between the centre and leading wheels had also bent, jamming the blocks hard onto the leading coupled wheels. Both siderods had bent also with the right hand side driving crank pin shearing off in the process.

The driver said that she had been quite a rough rider with everything between the frames rattling and banging more than was the norm with these engines. He had been just trundling along in the usual queue along the block when it just happened. He was a Toton man with his fireman, a passed cleaner, on loan from Kirkby as was 44091 also.

The Horninglow Bridge Tripper pulled the load of coal off the back of our sorry looking locomotive with Burton providing a Saltley Class 5 no less, to take it forwards whilst we had one of our spare Jockos, number 47464, to move 44091, as required, as we stripped her down prior to being dragged to the shed. No chance of working her back on one side under her own steam.

The Jocko arrived with some more tools and a bit more help in the shape of Joe Moore. The two Joes started by removing the right hand side rods whilst I crawled underneath to attempt to knock out the left side big end draw cotter and bolts. 44091 had fortunately come to a halt with this big end on the top quarter and in consequence, afforded some room to swing the hammer to knock them out. Having undone the securing cotters and nuts with some difficulty, one single blow saw the draw cotter fly out and hit the boiler bottom before crashing down alongside me and onto the ballast below. Now! It was rare for big end bolts on Midland engines to require much effort to knock out and fortunately these two proved to be no exception. After about half a dozen awkward blows the first bolt came loose as, likewise did the other one. With these two bolts out I knew we would succeed, as they presented the main obstacle of our progress.

I then turned my attention to the little end and slidebars. If I could manage to remove the slideblock on the inside then the little end pin would knock out to free the con rod and the job would be as good as done.

Having squirmed my way over the brake stretcher and under the motion plate, I found that 44091 would have to be pulled forwards about two spokes to allow room for the slideblock to come clear, once I had separated it from the back plate. Before I crawled out from beneath, I decided to remove the bent brake pull rod as it was holding the brake hard onto the leading wheels, as previously mentioned.

Being under tension, the first securing pin I attempted to remove refused to come free, as did the one at the other end. Joe Moore heroically clambered under the back end and spent a very hot few minutes lying under the ashpan slackening off the brake adjuster with a pair of Stilsons borrowed from the platelayers. This done, the Jocko pulled our 4F gently forwards the required amount and I scrambled back underneath. After some persuasion with the Brummegian Spanner (hammer and chisel), the slide block came away. It took a moment or two more to prop up the connecting rod and remove the little end gudgeon pin then everything was free.

The connecting rod was manhandled from between the wheels followed by the bolts, draw cotter and slideblocks. We tied the slidebars securely with the usual wagon ropes and I then turned my attention to the eccentrics. At least, with the con rod out of the way, I could stand up again. Kneeling on ballast is not to be recommended, believe me! I could possibly have left them in position without too much harm being done but decided to remove them just to be on the safe side. Joe Marsland offered to crawl underneath and do this for me but I declined his offer although my knees thought his offer was a good idea.

Twenty minutes later, both the left hand eccentrics were safely on the engine framing so the only thing left underneath to be removed was the big end itself. Having screwed a stretcher across the fork, the inside brass slid down to be removed when the stretcher was knocked out. It was but a moment then to lift the strap down, complete with the other half brass and pass the lot out from underneath. I gratefully crawled out behind them and straightened my back for the first time in over two hours.

All that remained was to remove the left hand siderods, the nuts of which the two Joes had already removed and the job was done. After moving 44091 backwards half a turn of its wheels with the aid of 47464, these were soon knocked off and split into two halves. With the aid of the relief crew from our 4F, the pair from the Jocko and ourselves plus a couple of platelayers, the various rods and pieces were soon loaded onto the framing where, with a few lengths of spun yarn and another wagon rope, they were tied down for the journey back to the shed.

The Jocko's fireman went across to the box informing the bobby that we were ready to move and thus ended another saga as far as Joe and I were concerned. Jimmy Mullet completed the strip down, following which she was proposed for Shopping and accepted for a 'Light Casual' which was rather surprising as the 4F's were being scrapped in ever increasing numbers about that time, towards the end of 1961. 44091 soldiered on for nearly three more years before being withdrawn and cut up at Crewe Works in 1964.

The two Fern brothers, Jack and George, had a call-out one evening when on the late shift. The 8 o'clock departure from Burton for Tutbury, The Tutbury Jinnie pull and push service, had run through the gates at Horninglow Station resulting in the inevitable pile of firewood and slight damage to the engine, an ex MR 1P 0-4-0T number 58080. The damage consisted of fractures to the vacuum brake and to the pull and push pipes on the engine front buffer beam.

A piece of rag and a wooden plug was soon fashioned with which to stop up the ends of the broken pipes and the train was then able to return to Burton under its own power. The passengers continued their journey to Tutbury in the comfort of two taxis hastily hired for the purpose. I recall seeing the engine concerned in the shed for repairs the following day and got the story, so to speak, from Les who was attending to the repairs. I was still a passed cleaner at the time.

To return to the maintenance of our Diesel fleet, consisting of eight 350 hp English Electric shunters and the Rolls Royce of course, George and I were kept fairly busy. With all eight 350 hp shunters arriving brand new and virtually together, they naturally all came up for various hourly exams together. The shedman, Wally and I attended to all the early and minor exams scheduled A to D, on overtime at week ends. However, the various shunting and tripping jobs on which they were employed, naturally not being of the same duration, meant that, in time, some of the engines slowly drew ahead of their consorts in hours worked; or should I say engine hours run; so that some Class E exams were being done during the week days.

D3569, being one such case, was kept in the shed on the Monday morning for the attention of George and I. A Class E exam involved the testing of the injectors, replacement of the exhaust valves, checking the inlet valves, fuel pumps and lines. Both the oil filters were changed and all drive belts checked for tension. Some of these belts were made up of a series of leather links and the belts so made had to be really slack before it was possible to remove a link and re-join the belt together, as I found to my cost in the early days of these exams. Each link overlapped the other by four holes with each integral pin passing through three links; a nightmare to join up when apart and round their pulleys.

The crankcase doors were removed to enable the big end bolts to be checked for tightness along with the seating of the little end pin and also for the crankshaft flexing. These last measurements had to be recorded on a special card and checked against the previous measurement. If more than 0.0150" (1½ thou') of flexing was recorded then the engine was not to be run until checked by an engineer from the Works. To my amazement, none of the six webs measured came within the ex Works measurement by 0.002" (2 thou') let alone 1½ thou. I thought about it for a while and decided to just tick the card and see what the next engine measured. After all, when using a micrometer, one person's touch was never the same as another's and I figured that the Works fitters would be more used to using one than me. A micrometer was very rarely used on maintenance of a steam engine. I mentioned this to Wally and as he also got the same result as me when he measured them, we both agreed that the best course of action was to ignore it, at least this once.

Initially, a replacement set of injectors was fitted each time an E exam was undertaken, the old set being returned to Derby Works for refurbishment. Soon however, a 'Hartridge Test Rig' was sent to the Depot and following a brief course of instruction, we were able to test and repair the injectors ourselves. This rig consisted of a fuel injection pump equipped with a manual pumping handle. The injector being tested was connected to the rig; both fuel and drain connections being attached. The pump was then primed by use of the manual pumping handle until the desired pressure was achieved, this being indicated by a reading on a gauge attached to the rig. At this point the injector should fire a fine mist spray, ejecting from the nozzle at a high velocity. If the nozzle was faulty the diesel would dribble from spray holes at some point during the pressurisation process, indicating that the nozzle required changing; all this spraying, of course, occurring behind a clear view plastic screen.

Dribbling was caused, in my experience, by one of three faults: either a damaged needle point, usually because a foreign body (particle of dirt) had found its way into the nozzle's fuel chamber; secondly, the integral piston on the needle was passing due to wear; or thirdly, just an ingress of dirt due to dirty fuel which the fuel filters hadn't sifted out, probably because the filters themselves were overdue for changing (not a fault on Burton's own Diesels).

A set of various pipes and fittings had been supplied with the rig to enable locomotives other than our 350 hp and Rolls Royce Diesels to be tested and as a result, we examined the occasional Type 1 and 2 Diesels of the Class 20, 24, 25 and 26, as they came to be known later.

But, to get back to our D3569, having dealt with the injectors and exhaust valves, these were refitted to the engine which was then barred over by means of a long rod supplied for the purpose with each locomotive. A series of holes were spaced around the fly wheel for this function and let it be said, George didn't find this task at all pleasant. It was unfortunately (for George) necessary to bar the engine over a number of times, both to check and adjust the tappets and bleed the fuel pumps and injectors.

Lubricating-oil changes were also a bit of a chore. Whereas the old oil was drained out into a 45 gallon drum positioned in the pit underneath, refilling the sump was a different matter altogether. A semi-rotary pump (not the most efficient piece of equipment ever invented) was screwed on to the top of the clean oil drum and its contents pumped into a two gallon bucket which was then poured by hand into the sump of the engine. This meant that it became a two man job with one of us passing the bucket up to the other all the time as the semi rotary pump hadn't the lift capacity to do the job all in one go.

Various ideas were tried to raise the oil drums sufficiently to allow the oil to be pumped directly into the sumps but with very little success. I have since come across many different pieces of equipment in outside industry, none too expensive, that would have made life so much easier but the Railway was always very frugal in supplying anything to make life for the maintenance men easier and of course, more efficient, particularly in the Running Shed. And of course, we still had to get the drum full of dirty oil out of the pit.

Whilst in the pit, the traction gearboxes had also to be lubricated, if such action can be called lubrication. The lubrication medium was such that even in the height of summer, it would not flow out of the drum and had to be prised out, it having a consistency like very thick treacle. In the depths of winter it had to be chopped out of the drum with a hammer and chisel in pieces roughly the size of a half house brick which were dropped through a door in the top of the gearbox. In cold weather, after standing overnight, the locomotives often had to see-saw backwards and forwards for some time before it would move continuously in one direction, such was the hold this lubrication had around the gears.

All the foregoing completed, the vacuum exhausters were checked over, drive belts adjusted and oil levels topped up, brake gear was adjusted and re-blocked if required, radiators topped up and antifreeze strength checked by use of a hydrometer. In the absence of an electrician, the indicator lights were checked and bulbs changed as necessary. Other jobs as required were attended to making the average cumulative time for an E Exam on a 350 hp shunter between two and three days; and all carried out in the smoke-laden atmosphere of the Running Shed.

After about twelve months of running, drivers' reports started coming in of certain locomotives not starting to move until the control handles were on notch two. Putting on my electrician's hat, I opened up the panel and had a look inside, after of course ensuring the battery isolation bars were not switched in. It soon became obvious that the cams on the main control shaft were working loose, requiring the control handle to be pulled round further than normal before the switches operated by the cams were closed. With a bit of trial and error, it was but a simple task to re-secure the cams in their correct place and sequence. However, when one considers how many of these panels had been made and supplied by the time our locos had been assembled, you would have thought such an obvious fault would have been rectified.

These units I believe, were made and supplied by the English Electric Company who also supplied the generators, drive motors and even the actual diesel engines on our particular eight locos whereas some of the power units supplied to these types of locos was of either Crossley or Blackstone manufacture. In general terms I always found the all English Electric 350 hp shunters to be quite good, reliable and efficient machines but considering their initial cost plus the ongoing maintenance they demanded to remain that way, I cannot really believe that they showed very much, if any saving, over the fifty or more year old steam engines they replaced; these going on and on with very little in the way of maintenance other than a squirt of oil around various places twice a day.

Some time during 1961 an electrician was finally recruited which alleviated the need for one of Derby's men to attend whenever a Class E exam was carried out. One Ken Peach, he and I gelled together straight away. Although he was a fitness fanatic unlike yours truly, we got on very well. Our happy Bug Ut gang were soon being entertained by demonstrations of his prowess and let it be said, there was no shortage of heavy objects around the shed for him to practice on, the demands for his ability not being too great with our small fleet of nine locomotives. He had an aversion for working on Sundays and thus was never at the depot when my little protégé number D2859 was On Shed.

On a Monday morning we would stroll down to Atkinson's Maltings for about 10.30 when she was scheduled to service the sidings there. While Ken did the electrical exam, I joined the driver Bernard and his guard at the 'Open Arms' therein to enjoy an excellent pint of Everards, sometimes having to drink Ken's pint as he was virtually tee total what with his fitness training and all. Oh! The hardships that sometimes faced the dedicated diesel fitter as he went about his daily toil!

As mentioned earlier, with the gradual increase in dieselisation, the odd Class A, B and C Exams started coming our way on Type 1 (Class 20), 2 (Class 24,25,26) and 4D (Class 44,45 and later 47). These we did according to the individual schedules to the best of our abilities, all without any formal training. This was a very sore point with us fitters as, whereas the drivers all attended training courses on the various individual types of Diesel locomotives, we had received no official instruction at all. Wally and I, I'm sure, would never have been sent to Rolls Royce had it not been to satisfy the warranty agreements of the said company.

Some fitters felt so strongly about this lack of training that they either refused to sign the exam card or added some caustic comment to it. This situation still hadn't been resolved when I left the Railway service some four years later. If it hadn't been for the unofficial two weeks that some of us enjoyed at Etches Park, I think it is fair to say we wouldn't have had much idea at all about how deal with Diesel loco repairs and servicing. Thus we muddled on.

The Diesel invasion wasn't the only event to herald in the 1960's for November 1961 saw the arrival of the Jubilees; no less than 18 of them, numbers 45557, 579, 585, 598, 610, 611, 612, 615, 618, 620, 626, 636, 641, 648, 649, 650, 667 and 668, all ousted from their usual haunts and duties by the all-conquering diesels. Previously allocated to Derby, Nottingham and Kentish Town where presumably the maintenance staff couldn't cope with their future care due to the demands made upon them by their 'paraffin can' replacements.

I had had very little to do with this class until their arrival as they were a rare beast at 17B until then. I seem to recall being accorded the 'privilege' of oiling-round underneath one during my early footplate days whilst on preparing duties; an extremely messy, dirty and unpleasant task involving clambering up amongst the oil and swarf to lubricate crosshead, small end and motion, situated as it was above the rear end of the bogie truck.

Needless to say, it wasn't long before George and I were handed an ME6 mileage exam which of course, found yours truly clambering up amongst all this filth once more. The outside motion was soon lying on the pit side as with any engine. Now to tackle the third set, hidden underneath.

A big end bolt cap nut had been obtained from Derby and I was pleasantly surprised to find how relatively easily the bolts came out after a dozen or so blows with the log-handled 12lb hammer. The con rod was barred forwards in the usual way to clear the big end strap which was soon swinging clear, about its journal. This big end assembly was at least half as big again as the more familiar Class 4F variety we were used to but it came apart in much the same way, by means of a stretcher across the fork end to release the inside half brass, once the draw cotter and glut had been removed of course; the glut incidentally, being an oblong piece of steel, roughly $\frac{1}{2}$" thick with a flat, tapered groove machined along the centre of one side, into which the flat side of the draw cotter slid, thus when knocked home, tightening the two halves of the bearings together; the length and breadth of the glut being determined by that of the back of the inner half bearing brass, inside which it was a snug fit.

If after adjustment to the bearing brasses, the draw cotter passed too far through the assembly, then a thin steel liner plate was inserted between the glut and the rear of the brass to take up the excess, the plate thickness being commensurate with the amount of adjustment required. To insert a liner plate of course, the whole assembly had to be dismantled but the experienced fitter could estimate the thickness required and insert the liner on initial assembly, thus avoiding himself a lot of extra work. Liner plates were carried in the stores of $\frac{1}{32}$" - $\frac{1}{16}$" and $\frac{1}{8}$" thickness for this purpose.

To determine the amount of adjustment required on an inside bearing, the two halves were stood on the bench together in the assembled position. The journal size was taken with outside callipers. This dimension was transferred to set of inside callipers and the swing measured between the assembled brasses by holding one leg of the callipers in the centre of the lower bearing and marking the free play on the upper half. If this free play was more than $\frac{1}{2}$" on say ex MR, LMS 2, 3, 4F's and 2P's then an equal amount was filed off the feet of each brass until the $\frac{1}{2}$" was achieved. Dependant upon the total amount filed off each brass on each side, a liner had to be fitted to take up the free space thus created. If say, a $\frac{1}{16}$" liner was required, I would fit two $\frac{1}{32}$" ones, one behind each half brass to maintain the optimum equal clearances at each end of the piston stroke within the cylinders.

The $\frac{1}{2}$" swing was increased to 1" on the Jubilees as their big end journals were considerably larger than those of the Midland Engines. I personally always had the Jubilee brasses re-metalled rather than apply the methods described above which also helped to keep Charlie, the coppersmith and Sid the machinist, busy although the real reason was that these being a Class 6 passenger engine, I liked to turn out a first class job.

Having removed the small end gudgeon pin, the con rod was soon lowered down by means of the rope pulley block and swung out to join the rest of the motion lying alongside. Now the fun really began; that of removing the crossheads. From previous experience with Mr. Stanier's Class 8F's and one of Mr. Fairburn's 2-6-4Tanks, I knew that the removal of these items was no sinecure. Just the removal of the draw cotters was bad enough let alone parting the crosshead from the piston rod. Indeed, such was the hold of the draw cotter on the 264 Tank that George and I eventually had to remove the bottom slidebar and turn the whole assembly over to enable us to knock the draw cotter out by direct blows to its inner end. The normal method called for the use of a suitable and substantial length of steel being passed through the spokes of the leading coupled wheel to be held by one of us against the underside of the draw cotter whilst the other knocked 'seven bells' out of the lower end with the inevitable 12lb sledgehammer. These proceedings could take anything from ten minutes to as many hours, with everyone in the shed having a go in the latter case. Then, once it was out, the crosshead still had to be parted. No wonder a mileage fitter had no trouble nodding off to sleep at night! And to think – we had three of these crossheads to deal with on a Jubilee!

By standing on a pit board and at the risk of a few grazed knuckles, I found that it was possible to apply some direct blows to the lower end of the inside draw cotter and I was more than pleased to knock the thing out with a series of mighty blows with my 7lb lump hammer. This method worked on both the Jubilees that I had an exam upon but some of my fellow fitters were not so fortunate.

So, with the draw cotters removed we set about parting the crossheads in the usual way. Eventually the two outer cylinder ones submitted to our attentions. All that now remained was the inside cylinder one.

Now, with these first two crossheads, along with all the other engines' crossheads I had split over the years, both inside and outside cylinder, MR, LMS, etc, I had utilised a nice tapered wedge, some 18" or so long, with smooth flat sides and highly polished from constant use. A quick look at the situation now facing us made it quite clear that this very useful piece of equipment would be of no use at all in this case. Instead, the blacksmith's shop at Derby Works had supplied us with a parting wedge some five feet long, beautifully forged but as rough as could be along its tapered sides, so an hour or so had to be spent upon preparing it, by firstly grinding then filing, before it could be put to use.

Over the top of the left hand outside slidebars, a hole was provided in the frame, through which this wedge was passed, then to enter the small end hole in the crosshead where the gudgeon pin fitted, to slot between the half moon and packing plates therein to tighten the parting gear against the button in the piston rod end, in the usual way. Then all that was required was the usual blows with a sledgehammer, applied standing outside in comfort on the shed floor, against the other end, some five feet away.

"Simple," you might say. "Much the same scenario as with the outside pair," you might add.

Yes, in theory, quite right but the amount of effort when applied to a short eighteen inch long wedge is more effective than when applied to one some five feet long where most of the energy is lost owing to the length along which it has to travel before taking effect.

"Rubbish! Nonsense!" you may cry and in theory you are probably correct but in practice you most definitely are not. The fact that the wedge is higher up doesn't help either!

Soon, George and I are exhausted, pounding away at this target some four feet up in the air. The noise of our efforts brings forth a number of our fellow artisans to watch the 'fun. Many are the suggestions forthcoming and, let it be said, are the blows applied by all and sundry in our aid; but to no avail. The set up at the crosshead is checked and some slight alterations made but still the crosshead remains resolutely attached, by nothing but friction, to the piston rod end.

I am led to suspect that the taper of the wedge is far too fast and feel that a narrower, more gradual lead would be better. As a second wedge had been supplied by Derby Works along with the one we were using, I prevailed upon Bob the blacksmith to attempt to draw it out and give it a more gradual lead. This he agrees to do whilst we persevere with the original one.

The gas bottles are brought out and the area of the crosshead where it connects with the piston rod is thoroughly heated up with the parting gear and the wedge assembly all under tension but still to no avail. Bob has done his best with the other wedge and I spend the rest of the afternoon cleaning it up, grinding and filing it smooth as with its twin.

As we are packing up our tools prior to going home at the end of the day, George gives the end of the tensioned wedge a few more blows, "For old times sake," as he puts it; only to be rewarded by a clatter as the parting tackle falls into the pit below. We both dash underneath in great anticipation and reaching for the big crowbar, ease the crosshead down its slidebars and away from the piston rod.

Using heat to assist in disassembling parts such as this is always a gamble and only used as a last resort (in desperation, some would say), the idea being to use the heat to expand the boss of the crosshead and hopefully release its grip on the enclosed piston rod. However, if it doesn't work, the heat transference to the said piston rod end, thereby causing it to expand also, has the opposite effect and increases its hold even more. In our case, George must have caught it just at the optimum moment; but who cares! The job was done! Why worry! Until the next time! As mentioned earlier, these solid crossheads were always a challenge.

I suppose, at this stage, the reader may be slightly puzzled as to what precisely a solid crosshead is and how it differs from any other type of crosshead. OK, I will endeavour to explain:

The crosshead is basically a block of cast steel which joins the small end of the connecting rod to the end of the piston rod, thereby becoming one of the most vital items in the transference of linear to rotary motion. To enable this crosshead to be attached to the piston rod a boss is cast into which the piston rod enters. The rod end is tapered and the inside of the crosshead boss likewise to match. A slot is cut through the crosshead boss and a similar one through the rod end. When the two parts are assembled with these slots lined up, a tapered steel wedge is driven through the slots to draw the two together and make them fast as one, hence its name: draw cotter.

In the early days when the whole assembly was complete, free space could still be found ahead of the draw cotter in the crosshead boss and inside at the rear of the rod. Whilst this was fine with the lower steam pressures in use at the time, as working pressures increased, a tendency for the piston rod to be driven further into the crosshead became apparent whilst the engine was in traffic, resulting in the draw cotter becoming loose and on occasions being thrown out altogether, thus bringing in its wake the risk of the piston rod becoming detached from the crosshead, the results of which, whilst on the move, being quite spectacular to say the least.

To alleviate this possibility the piston and crosshead tapers were so machined that when assembled, the piston rod all but came face to face with the inner end of the crosshead and the slot for the draw cotter was so machined that the cotter was in contact on all faces of the rod and crosshead, making in effect, a completely 'solid' assembly. The down side of this coming of course, when separating these component parts as described above, just one more of the crosses the locomotive fitter had to bear.

In the Works, on the fitting benches, where the need to build up and break down these separate items was required as the various parts were made, the fitters had sets of 'slip plates' which they inserted through the crosshead slots. These slip plates were made with a radius on one side to match the front and back of the slot, one having a slight relief where the rod came into contact on one side of one plate with the other having a relief where the crosshead boss contacted. These slip plates were inserted in such a way that when a tapered wedge was driven between them, the crosshead and rod were forced apart. I made myself a number of these plates in my time but enjoyed very limited success with them; but then, the newly manufactured jobs the Shop men were involved in hadn't been racing up and down the line for 36,000 miles or so! How did the lads in the Stripping Sheds at the Works go on? What methods did they favour? Perhaps I shall never know!

A smaller version of these stripping plates however, did work very well when parting valve crossheads, the one set that I made for myself serving me well, right up until I left the Railway service.

To get back to the mileage examination on our Jubilee, the rest of the procedures were as with any Stanier engine, or anyone else's for that matter, Messrs. Johnson, Deeley and Fowler included. Sufficient to say in conclusion, that the other wedge doctored by our blacksmith Bob, proved to be a much better and more effective tool and became favoured by most of the fitters in the shed.

The inside brasses of the Jubilees had two holes drilled laterally through the webs and into each of these holes was inserted a cartridge containing a substance which when overheated, gave off a strong aroma which I believe resembled aniseed. This brought the overheating bearing to the attention of the driver who was consequently able to take appropriate action to avert any further harm. As far as I am aware, this particular fate never befell any of our brood whilst they were in Burton's care though no doubt with 191 class members plus other modern inside cylinder locomotives, running about the railway over a twenty to thirty year time span, it must have occurred on occasion. I understand that the Patriots, Royal Scots, Pacifics and 2500 Class 2-6-4Tanks were all fitted with this refinement. Indeed, it was the failure of an inside big end which caused the LNER 4-6-2 'Mallard' to be kept out of traffic for a week or so following its 126 miles per hour sprint down Stoke Bank to achieve the world speed record for steam.

Our Jubilees were utilised on working our fitted and semi-fitted ale trains down to London and the West of England, a duty upon which our Crabs had performed so ably for a number of years and which consequently cascaded down to more menial and less demanding tasks in their turn. However, come the Spring Bank Holiday, the Crabs soon found their way out to the seaside again, working the excursion traffic out of Derby and Nottingham as had been the fashion throughout the fifties. Of course, our Jubilees went as well, when we had any about, for truth to tell, they rarely returned with the beer empties from London as they were utilised to take the places of recalcitrant Diesels that had either fallen by the wayside or shown some other form of reluctance to make their return journey north. As these new fangled machines began to find their way down to Bristol as well, it became a common sight to find our Class 6P's appearing at the head of the Newcastle and Bradford bound expresses once more, a duty with which they were more than familiar.

Every 12 to 16 days they would return to the fold for a boiler washout and repairs, and then it was out to battle again for another two weeks. But then, that was why they had been sent to Burton in the first place, as we had a full artisan staff and weren't encumbered with the all new conquering Diesels to any great extent so we were able to devote the time and attention to them that the staff at their previous traditional depots were not able to do. So, our Crabs still on occasions found themselves en-route to Somers Town or Westerleigh as before.

Some of the motive power units that turned up on these return workings, deputising for our 'borrowed' Jubilees, were interesting as well. Cricklewood invariably supplied London area Class 4F's, some of which were fitted with the LMS type ATC equipment which I believe was used mainly on the ex LT&SR lines. This equipment I seem to recall, was painted red and was not dissimilar to the BR version which was soon to become common.

The odd ex LNER B1 would also be a substitute on occasions. These were definitely unloved by the London men. London Crabs were a rare beast in the 60's if indeed any were still allocated there but that did not stop the Cricklewood foremen rostering anyone else's to work back to us. Judging by the condition of some of the motive power units managing to stagger in, I wondered what in turn their original duties had been covered by.

Saltley Crabs were a common replacement on the return run from the Bristol area or possibly a Bristol or Bath 4F, Barrow Road having no Crabs of their own. At least the 22A (82E) engines were in the main, well maintained.

Returns from Leeds, revealed much the same story, with the 4F performing the honours again, often Manningham locomotives.

1962 saw the arrival of the Black 5's once more into the fold. Much the same story applied to them, though as we moved on into 1963 things did start to improve with regard to the steam engines, at Burton at least. The Diesel availability was improving, no doubt due in part to the maintenance staff becoming more familiar with their charges.

During the late summer of 1962, Les Bull, now as you will recall, in charge at Overseal, applied for and obtained a salaried position at Derby, thus following in the footsteps of Joe Benson, so to speak. I was invited to submit an application for the vacancy which I duly did and was awarded the position forthwith.

Chapter 17

I'm in Charge

A week was spent with Les at Overseal learning the routine and on the following Monday I took over responsibility for the running of the depot.

There were six engines allocated to the shed consisting of one Class 3F, four Class 4F's and a Class 8F. All were Burton engines and returned there for boiler washouts at set periods, the usual way to effect these exchanges being by way of the Burton-Overseal Tripper (Burton Target 89) working.

The 3F spent most of its time working 97 Target which consisted of shunting Woodville Junction and Rawdon sidings, with the occasional trip down to Drakelow Power Station with a load of coal. The 4F's were variously employed, working 95, 96 and 98 Targets plus the 6.50 am. and 1.35 pm. Birmingham turns, these last two usually feeding into Hams Hall Power Station but occasionally working into Washwood Heath or Bromford Bridge sidings. The 8F was similarly utilised on these workings as well, doing two trips a day, one at 7.20 am and the other at 8.00 pm. ex Woodville Junction. These Birmingham turns were all booked to run over 'The Alps,' via Nuneaton Abbey Street and Arley Tunnel as described in the runaway referred to in chapter 4.

Oversea shed and yard. Photo: Authors Collection.

95 and 96 Targets worked out of Donisthorpe, Rawdon and Measham Collieries, with coal for Drakelow as required, each turn being of two shifts duration. 98 Target on the other hand, had been reduced to one shift, working off the shed at 9.50 am. and serving the Woodville Branch and Gresley Colliery. Several pipe works were situated in this area where the manufacture of earthenware drain and sewage pipes was carried out along with normal domestic items,

one of the most well known being the buff coloured, glazed mixing bowls of which most households had at least one example in their kitchens.

Within a couple of months of my tenure, the last of the 3F's at Burton, 43709, departed for its last run, to the scrap yard, the replacement being yet another of the ubiquitous 4F's. These, with their screw reverser, were not as popular on the Woodville Junction shunt as the old, pole reverse 3F's but such, as they say, is progress.

The shed itself was situated at the south end of the triangle formed by the Moira West, East and South Junctions, all movements, on and off the shed being controlled by the latter junction's signalbox, as indeed, was Overseal sidings alongside. Built as a joint venture by the Midland and LNW Railways at the turn of the century, the two-road, straight shed was constructed by the former, with the coal stage being the responsibility of the latter company. At some stage during the depots early history a turntable was added, this being situated behind and beyond the coal stage. At some 40 to 45 feet in diameter, it would just comfortably turn a typical MR or LNW 0-6-0 tender engine. However, this facility had been removed by the early 1950's along with its access road, leaving just the pit in which it once turned, to catch out the unwary on dark nights, as did happen on more than one occasion. Any engines requiring to be turned now used the aforementioned triangle.

The shed lay roughly on a north to south axis with the entrance at the southern end. Immediately to the right on entering was built the office, followed by the enginmen's cabin and oil-stores.

Within the office were the railway phones which were the old fashioned box type, fastened to the wall, whereby the operator lifted the receiver and pressed the appropriate code to call each location desired. This rang at every phone in the district and when your code rang you answered. After a while you became accustomed to all the various rings and in effect only heard your own code. In the case of Overseal Shed this was, I seem to recall, one short followed by one long beat (or was it the other way round?) One had to be very careful what you said over this rather open network as there was invariably some accidental listener or more likely nosey busybody, on any of the locations not being called, listening in to your conversation. Consequently, any juicy bits of gossip or rumour spoken on this 'bush telegraph' went round the area like wildfire.

During my first few days there I was naturally the main subject of discussion, being the 'new gaffer' in the area and most amusing some of it was as well, though on the negative side let it be said, some comments were quite alarming. These phones were on the far wall of the office so that anybody needing to use them had to traipse right through to do so. These consisted of drivers wishing to 'bell off' the shed, guards, shunters, platelayers and anyone else finding the need, very few of whom deigned to ask permission before doing so, simply bursting through the door without knocking and walking through without any sort of greeting.

This rather forthright attitude, I soon learned, was the typical nature of the district, this becoming more apparent as I got to move around my new area of activity. The locals, as the saying goes, really did call a spade 'a spade.' If some-

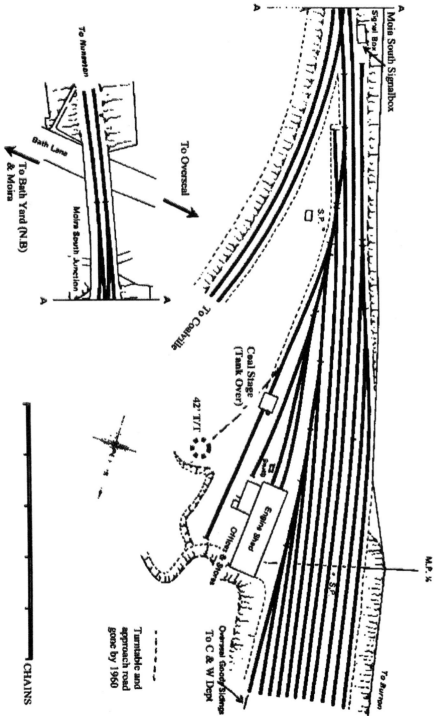

OVERSEAL 1958 track plan

Moira South Signalbox

Signal Box

To Nuneaton

Bath Lane

To Bath Yard (N.B)
& Moira

Moira South Junction

To Overseal

To Coalville

S.P.

Coal Stage
(Tank Over)

42' T/T

M.P. ¾

Engine Shed

Offices & Store

Overseal Goods Sidings
To C & W Dept

To Burton

Turntable and
approach road
gone by 1960

CHAINS

290

thing had to be said, it was said without fear or favour and 'To hang' with the circumstances. But, they were 'The salt of the earth' and would not let you down once you were accepted into their midst.

Other furnishings within the office consisted of a series of cupboards around two walls, all rather spartan but substantial in construction. In one of these, my comprehensive tool kit resided, under lock and key, with another, also locked, containing spare stocks of overalls, jackets and the like for issue to the shed staff, along with soap and the inevitable sponge cloths. Alongside the adjoining wall to the mess-room, my desk faced out across the breadth of the room, with a further cupboard to its left, containing various forms and other stationery.

The right hand space, adjacent to the door, was occupied by the stove; a piece of equipment that I can never recall being 'out of steam' throughout my two years at the depot. Many were the culinary delights produced on and around this glowing edifice, both by myself and the shed men; one Cyril Lee; in particular, but more of them later...

The whole room was painted in the usual cream and brown with the door picked out in red. The floor was paved with blue bricks, as was the shed itself. However, to bring a little warmth within the office, two pegged rugs; of the type grandmothers used to sit for hours making, with granddad's old suits and jackets cut into strips; graced the floor. Just how old they were no one seemed to know, for the oldest hand at the shed, one Bill Shelton, said they had been there as long as he could remember. Occasionally, when the weather was favourable, they would receive a steam clean, courtesy of a loco slacking pipe, after which, when dried, they looked like new.

Next door in the mess-room, a long table took up the centre of the floor, with two benches, one down each side, completing the dining furnishings therein. Along one side of the room a row of lockers for the shed staff was attached to the wall, whilst opposite, a huge fireplace kept the inevitable cast iron kettle on the boil. As well as keeping the mess-room warm and the kettle steaming, this fire provided background heating for my office, situated as it was behind the adjoining wall, not to mention providing a couple of shovels full of fire for lighting up each of the engines on Sunday nights. One of the fireman remarked that firing the mess-room grate was like firing a 4F only with better results. How many hundreds of tons of coal it consumed during its lifetime, all courtesy of the nearest tender out in the shed, I dread to think! Multiply this by all the similar fires in all the various sheds and goods yards and offices throughout the country, add all the 'frost fires' burning throughout the winters in these same loco depots, goods sheds, coal stages, water columns, etc. and there has been a few thousand tons of fuel burnt over the years throughout the land.

Above the fireplace, the Train Arrangement Board hung on a nail. On this was listed the eight turns worked. Against this the night chargeman chalked in the relevant engine numbers at his discretion unless I had left a note in the Night Book with some particular instruction regarding a particular engine or Burton Shed or Control had contacted him with other instructions after I had left for home. Typically, I might request that he keep an engine on 97 Target (Woodville shunt) so that it may be handy to change over with the Burton 89 Target at midday being required at Burton for boiler washout. This arrangement worked very well with a stud of five engines, all of the same type (4F's) but the 8F of course, was different. Apart from it not being the most suitable of shunting locos, it was most unpopular with both the drivers and the shunters in this role; thus this arrangement was rarely done. Another consideration was traffic requirements. A 4F was no substitute on its booked working, with the necessity for parts of the booked load being left behind in the siding.

On its booked turn the 8F was not due back on shed much before 14.45 hrs so the more usual arrangement was for the 15.30 prep and disposal set to take it down to Burton for change over, coaling up the replacement at the Burton stage while they were there to save time. As the Burton coalmen used to object to this arrangement, it meaning more work for them filling tubs; and who could blame them; I always rang ahead and spoke to the running foreman to get official sanction for this action. This was rarely refused, the usual arrangement being that a Burton set of men was organised to coal the replacement engine before our men had arrived; an excellent example of 'kidology' or 'The Judgement of Solomon' by the Burton foreman.

As the modern Stanier etc. tapered boiler engines required a boiler washout etc. every 12 to 16 days, as mentioned earlier, we usually received a replacement straight off washout, thus solving the problem, barring breakdowns, for the following two weeks. Similarly, it was most convenient to follow the same course with the 4F's when changing over, where possible. With these engines having a 28 to 32 day span between washouts we then had them for a full four week period. Even the 4F's were not free from the scrapping programme by now and consequently this ideal state of affairs was not always possible to achieve.

Another consideration causing complications to these arrangements was a local agreement peculiar to Overseal whereby only engines attached to tenders without coalrails were to be supplied; the reason being to enable the tenders to be coaled directly from the wagons alongside, thus saving the need to handle the coal twice as was the case when using a coal stage; the latter method only being used to coal the 8F, the tender height of which necessitated the use of a coal wagon under the stage, from which sufficient coal was unloaded onto the stage platform daily, prior to being shovelled into the Stanier tender.

Originally, only ex MR 4F's with the old Johnson type, round topped tender, were sent but as the later Fowler tenders became available; ex scrapped Compounds and the like; these were attached to all 4F's, ex MR or otherwise, thus making 4F's with original Johnson tenders as rare as hen's teeth, therefore compensations had to be made. During the last twelve months of the depot, even Fowler tenders without coalrails became more scarce, as these were all paired up with earlier members of the same class and in consequence generally became withdrawn earlier, the more common appearance of the coalrail variety becoming the norm.

This in its turn generated many letters being left for me by Mr. Gower, the night chargeman, which I passed on to Mr. Lewis, the Burton Shedmaster for his comments and attention as any replies I passed directly to him via the shed night book had little effect.

Mr Gower's hours of work were 22.00 to 06.00, six nights a week Sunday to Saturday morning, with my hours being 07.30 to 16.30. However, on Monday mornings Mr Gower's hours were officially extended to 08.35 so he could complete his weekly clerking duties and also allow an exchange of information between him and myself. In truth this rarely happened as all communication was carried out by notes left either in the night book or more personally by poking a note through his locker door.

I soon learned that when his grievances as described above got out of hand, leaving him a note in the night book suggesting he prepare and present his case for discussion between us at this hour on Monday mornings so thoughtfully provided by the company. This seemed to take the heat out of the problem and our official meetings never took place. Occasionally, George Swann, the senior Passed Fireman and elected LDC (Loco Departmental Council) representative, would request a brief meeting on some subject or grievance and naturally, Mr. Gower was often the originator.

In truth, I only met Mr. Gower twice. The first time, on my third Monday in charge, when I left him a note to wait so I could meet him and which lasted all of five minutes. The second occasion was when I had been called out by Burton to attend a misdemeanour involving the crew of the returning night Birmingham, at Woodville Junction. I decided to look into the shed at the same time, only to find the said gentleman fast asleep in my chair with his feet comfortably stretched out over my desk.

Not being sure as to the extent of my authority but realising I could not ignore the situation if I was to ever assert any control over the rest of the staff, I sent him home immediately, warning him that any further incidents would be brought to the attention of Mr. Lewis down at Burton. I signed him off at the appropriate time of 04.45 hrs so, truth to say, he got off lightly. However, I had displayed my authority, a fact which, as the jungle telegraph soon relayed, had not been lost on the other men at the shed.

A quiet word with George Swann, confirmed the correctness of my actions. He was my guide and mentor on a lot of problems with the rostering and general arrangements concerning what could and could not be done with the footplate staff, rules governing which seemed to be etched in stone.

A typical instance concerned two of the more junior passed firemen who, due to general sickness and holidays, were rostered for driving duties over a period of three consecutive weeks. The consequences meant that this re-allocation of duties along with their normal booked work would have caused one man to work five weeks of early turns and the other five weeks of lates. So, with the best intentions, thinking only of their welfare, I swapped their duties in the middle week of the three to give each of them a break from the continuous round of socially inconvenient duties over such a long period.

Oh, the uproar my actions caused! Firstly both men turned up for the early turn, one because he was rostered for it and the other because it was his official turn and he was claiming it. Other footplateman, not involved, joined in the ensuing argument resulting in the inevitable pandemonium. Fortunately, one of those present was George Swann himself. George was on driving duties virtually all the time, in place of Bill Shelton who was on long term sick leave. With the diplomacy of a saint, George managed to persuade the passed man, who should originally been on the late turn before my intercession, to go home and return at the later time for the late shift, all this occurring before I had even got out of bed.

When I arrived at my normal time Cyril the shedman was able to fill me in on the general gist of what had occurred. As George was on the first turn 97 Target, he was fortunately able to have a quick word with me when he finished at 09.50. As these arrangements for the following week had been posted since the previous Friday dinnertime, I queried why the concerned parties hadn't questioned the arrangements before. It was the old story. The man changed on to earlies wouldn't complain as it suited him (so I had got something right), the man changed to the late shift knew he could claim his rightful turn so he didn't complain, just turned up for earlies and the rest, who weren't involved at all, chose to sit back and let the gaffer get in a mess.

Another lesson learnt. Don't be Mr. Nice Guy, just stick to the book or should that be, the agreements. I felt duty bound to apologise to the late man when he came on but he only laughed and said, "Forget it." At least they never got to know at Burton which was a miracle in itself.

During my time at Overseal the 'Beeching Axe' was being sharpened and we were all fighting to retain our jobs; trying to justify our depot's existence along with everyone else. To this end I determined that no train in which we were involved would be cancelled because we could not supply either an engine or the crew to man it. With this aim in view most of the drivers and firemen accepted a considerable amount of inconvenience to keep the job going.

One of the main problems both I and Les in his turn, had to deal with was shortage of staff. On the shed staff side there was one short which meant, with a total strength of four, we were 25 per cent down in that department alone. Of these three, one was the night chargeman, leaving just two men to cover the full 24 hours shed duties, consisting of coaling the engines, keeping the ashpits clear, the yard and shed tidy and the care of any engines in steam. This would consist of five engines overnight when, of course, there was the redoubtable Mr. Gower to work with and one during all or part of the day which I inevitably looked after to help out.

These two labourers were Cyril Lee and Eric Woollett and they worked 12 hours per shift, turn and turn about, days and nights, six days a week with eight hours on Sundays when on days, the day man going home at 2.00pm and returning at 10.00pm at night. Between these hours the shed looked after itself, with the bobby in Moira South Box keeping an eye on the place from his elevated eyrie.

I was not happy about these eight hours when the depot was unattended but short of recruiting a third, or should that be fourth, labourer, there was nothing I could do about it. I made my feelings known to Mr. Lewis, the Burton Shedmaster which in effect took the onus off me being responsible for anything untoward that might happen during this time.

As the train numbering fraternity were now becoming more active with organised trips by coach all over the country, it could only be a matter of time before they discovered Overseal. However, Overseal was not quite so deserted on a Sunday afternoon as would first appear but more of that later…

Cyril and Eric were the complete opposites of each other. Both were excellent and faithful workers whose trust and reliability was without doubt but that was where the similarity ended.

Cyril lived at Lullington, where he had a smallholding. Here he kept poultry, raised pigs and bred turkeys for the Christmas table; and fine birds they were too. Had he not been ably assisted by his wife I doubt if he would ever have had the time for it all. His mode of transport to and from work was by motor scooter which always looked immaculate and never seemed to break down.

Eric lived in a small cottage on the edge of Swadlincote. His journeys to and fro were made astride various tatty motorcycles of questionable vintage and pedigree. Reliability was not a word which sat easily upon any of them but let it be said, no matter what, Eric always turned up at or near his appointed times. He had three great loves in his life: television, his small niece and the shed cat; not necessarily in that order. He proudly boasted to me that he had two televisions, one tuned to BBC, the other to ITV. When BBC 2 came out he had soon purchased a third set to allow that channel to be viewed as well as, when Eric was at home, all three sets would be switched on together. Living alone, he rarely went out socially, spending all his time watching television and tinkering with his motorbikes. The highlight of his week was when his young niece came to see him. He idolised her and talked of little else apart from, of course, his televisions.

There was a sort of fourth member of the shed gang in the form of Ted Brooks. Poor old Ted was an ex driver who had had to come off the footplate for health reasons. A very nice chap, he was physically unable to do much at all and just pottered about keeping himself busy day by day. One job he had made his own was the daily journey to the station at Moira to collect the mail. However, even him doing that chore worried me, particularly after he had been found lying by the line side one morning having fallen down, so I invariably walked up there myself if either the ganger or the Stationmaster hadn't brought them down for my by ten o'clock.

The Stationmaster at Moira was Mr. Frank Brazier. As well as being in charge of the station, he was also responsible for all the sidings and traffic movements in the district, including all coal trains out of the collieries ranging from Netherseal and Gresley in the West, Measham and Donisthorpe to the South and Woodville Junction and the Swad' Loop Line which included Cadley Hill Colliery at its far end. He liked to think that he was in charge of the Loco Depot as well but I, as had my predecessors, lost no time in disillusioning him on that score. He did however have a certain control in an emergency in my absence as will be revealed later…

As far as footplate staff shortages went, a pattern of cover for the lack of sufficient firemen had been established long before I took over the reins. This involved the middle 97 Target, first shift fireman staying on for an extra half shift and being relieved by the third shift fireman coming on half a shift early, thus enabling the middle shift man to be used for another shift entirely. This worked fine when all the firemen were in agreement but this was not always the case as some of the firemen had no desire to work any overtime other than that generated in the course of their normal working day, i.e.: by the late running on the Birmingham, etc.

The saving grace in these circumstances was that it was still possible to juggle things around amongst men off the other trippers as they all either came on shed or passed during the midday period to effect a crew change with the exception of the 98 Target, so an exchange of fireman was still possible. If, for some reason, the tripper was late, the crews would effect a changeover somewhere out on line. I was confident they would keep the job going somehow and truth to say, they never let me down. I only had recourse to borrow a fireman from Burton on two occasions during my time at the shed.

To keep the more co-operative fireman interested, I would occasionally offer them four hours on the shed, labouring in support of Cyril or Eric if they so desired. Naturally, they usually took up the offer though how long they stayed after I had departed for the station and my train home, I would rather not know. Certainly, as the DMU passed Moira West Signalbox at about 1640, Cyril could sometimes be observed astride his scooter, peering round the back corner of the Overseal Sidings Shunters' Cabin, hoping to catch a glimpse of me aboard the train before setting off for home. Now we know how he managed to rear all those pigs and turkeys! I don't know why he bothered really, as one or two of my staff had gone to great pains to make me aware of his movements, along with those of other people's as well.

That was another of my early lessons; that there was always somebody who would make it their business to 'tell the gaffer' about certain activities that the perpetrators would rather I did not know. This 'gossip' had to be considered very carefully before some, if any, action was taken and, let us not forget that the particular 'stool pigeon' and there was more than one, was always watching for signs and results of any reactions I might have to their information.

As far as Cyril was concerned, I reasoned that, in truth, no man could be expected to work twelve hour shifts on such a physical job, week in, week out, without some such perk or other being in operation so I chose to basically ignore it, just bringing some appropriate comment into the conversation at hopefully the right time. Just to torment him, I would sometimes sit on the opposite side of the coach or even better, ride in the guard's compartment, the benefit of this latter action being that I could see him whereas he had no chance of seeing me.

Eric, on the other hand, was never in a hurry to leave and even used to turn up when he had no need to. On Christmas Day and Boxing Day for instance, when he would go just to feed the cat. While he was there he would have a look round and shove a couple of shovels full on the fire in the mess-room, on the frost fires in the shed and under the coal stage; and all without a penny in reward for his efforts. As he was already working all the hours he could legally do, I could not approve any more payments for his efforts and consequently approached Mr. Lewis on his behalf. Although he agreed that the benefits of his presence had merit, he would not sanction the payments either so Eric, bless him, just carried on with his unofficial duties as before, free/gratis.

Within one month of my presence at Overseal, the National Union of Railwaymen, of which I was a member, called a national strike. This placed me in an embarrassing position, having just stepped onto the bottom rung of the management ladder but I felt that I had to join the protest as a loyal union member anyway. Most of the footplatemen were members of ASLEF and Burton requested a list of who was in which Union. This information was easier to obtain than I expected and I duly furnished the necessary list, unofficially mentioning its existence to George Swann at the same time.

Of the ASLEF members who asked, I told to sign on at their normal rostered times and inform Burton of their arrival by phone. Nothing was going to move on our bit of the railway in any case as all the traffic grades were NUR members to a man. Unquestioned support was also forthcoming from the miners, whose output provided about 90% of our local traffic so Overseal could be said to be well and truly out of business for the duration of the strike.

The far reaching effects of this action came home to roost very quickly in the Burton area and no doubt in many other places as well with the breweries' traffic reducing to a trickle, to quote just one example. To continue their output and maintain customer services they were obliged to turn to road transport, the management of which insisted on contracts of two years or more before closing their agreements.

As far as Overseal was concerned the coal traffic was maintained as before, there being no other, more efficient way of moving mass amounts of aggregate of any kind, even to the present day. However, the earthenware traffic soon dried up, with this business also moving to the roads.

Moira Station. Photo: H. Casserley

My daily journey to Overseal was made by catching the 0708 train out of Burton, Mondays to Saturdays, alighting at Moira Station and walking back, around the East to South curve half way, before following the path across waste ground around the edge of a field confined within the triangle and around one side of the turntable pit, to enter the shed from the eastern edge. When I became more organised getting to know people and becoming accepted, I used to have a lift round to the shed with the permanent way ganger, Harold Grew, who used to call at the station in his car every morning for his correspondence, etc.

Harold was a big, tall, upright, ex guardsman and very conscientious about his job. We became very good friends over the ensuing two years and many were the ex army stories we exchanged, amongst others.

On Saturdays I developed the habit of using my car for the journey to and from Overseal, as the return train from Moira was not until 1305 hrs, involving an hour's wait after my Saturday finishing time of 12 noon. Sometimes I would park by the shunters' cabin in Overseal Sidings and cross the line to walk down the sidings, approaching the shed from the rear. This cabin was one of the few items remaining of the old Overseal Station that used to stand on the opposite side of the Moira West, South Junction Spur to the Loco Shed. I understand that the station was closed in 1931, along with all the others on this line down to Nuneaton but unlike the others, which remained intact and open for goods and parcel traffic, was demolished, the passenger business being handled by Moira.

On other occasions I would park by the bridge over the Moira to Overseal road, alongside Harold's car, this bridge incidentally, being the northernmost arch of what was originally a five arch viaduct, the other four having been filled in some ten years before because of the effects of subsidence from the mine workings underneath. A series of steps were cut into the embankment at the southern end of the bridge which were climbed prior to crossing the bridge and entering the shed yard at the outlet point. This route could also be taken, continuing by road, to Moira Station as an alternative to walking along the line.

As previously mentioned, the Stationmaster at Moira, during my time at the shed, was Mr. Frank Brazier. His station workforce was headed by Bill Floris, who was the chief clerk. This worthy was also the pay clerk for the district and he used to walk down¹ from the station to the shed, following the route described earlier, every Friday lunchtime, with the wages for the staff, completely alone and unescorted. I questioned the safety of this practice with Mr. Brazier and suggested that the 97 Target (Woodville Junction Shunt) engine could be rostered to run, light engine, up to the station on Fridays to bring him down, taking him back afterwards with the unclaimed money. He pooh pooh'd the idea qualifying it by saying that he himself carried the earnings of the various signalmen and other staff, around the district without any problems. I subsequently found that he, in fact, carried the money in his car and indeed, quite a few of his 'customers' actually collected their own wages from the station.

That aside, when the weather was inclement, particularly during the 1962/63 winter when the snow around the East Curve was at rail height, I arranged for an engine to run up to the station to collect him and take him back; a duty that the footplate staff were only too happy to perform as Bill, apart from being the wages clerk, was also a very popular person in his own right.

Assisting Bill in his clerical duties at the station was Mrs. Jean Bacon. Jean was recently married and initially lived at Gresley prior to moving to Burton. I used to travel back with her on the train and when she and her husband moved to Burton she became a good friend of my wife and family.

Howard was the lamp man and an unenviable task he had, particularly during the winter months. He would occasionally pop into the shed on his rounds to have a warm and thaw out in front of our huge messroom fire with the inevitable mug of tea being forthcoming to heat the inner man. A small, quiet, inoffensive man, I doubt if he had an enemy in the whole world.

The station staff list was completed by two porters, brothers, whose names I have since forgotten. These two gentlemen were kept busy, not only meeting the passenger services but also handling the parcels traffic of which there was plenty. The railway was still the general carrier at this time. A considerable amount of goods was received from mail order companies which were just coming into their own at the time. Some of these items were quite inadequately packaged for the journey around the railway network. All the parcel traffic was sorted on receipt by the railway and allocated a destination number. I seem to recall that Moira's number was 49. This was written on the wrapper by the dispatcher at the receiving depot in blue crayon, the local address for final delivery being, naturally, the responsibility of the destination station. Here was where the fun started, as some final addresses were either torn, incomplete or occasionally non existent. How some of the items ever reached their final destinations is mystifying but between the two brothers and the van driver (who was based at Swadlincote), 99% of the parcels were delivered to the correct addresses, though what the customers thought of the state of some of their parcels I dare not repeat.

One extremely poorly wrapped carpet, for example, was that filthy from its contact with the floors of various brake vans and station platforms that it had to be partly unrolled to discover what its true colour was. Needless to say, the housewife concerned refused to accept it and was advised by the van driver, unofficially of course, which mail order company was best to order from and which to avoid. The carpet had to be returned to its originator, collecting no doubt, even more dirt in the process. And all this fun observed while I waited in the office for my train home. A siding off the down side of the line ran into a small goods shed where the intrepid pair dealt with any full wagon load traffic that materialised. The local coal merchant also had a wagon of domestic fuel standing outside. But enough of the station these details just being penned out of general interest.

Some of the tasks inherited on assuming responsibility for the shed really had no direct connection with the depot itself. One of these was meter reading. As the railway did not have its own water supply it had to purchase its water from the local water company, the same situation of course, also applying to the gas and electricity. Thus, I had the job of reading all the various meters weekly or monthly, depending on their source.

The main water meter was at the foot of the steps cut into the embankment by the bridge over the Moira-Overseal Road. This meter registered the supply to the shed and the water tank over the coal stage. This reading increased by thousands of gallons every week. The meter was exposed by lifting a grating on the floor which was kept fairly grass free by the constant foot traffic across it. Alongside this but further into the bank, under a small flap, was the domestic water supply meter which required a torch to read it. This only had to be read once a month and during the summer, had to be literally dug out to gain access.

For some time, I wondered why there was a separate supply for the domestic water and this mystery was solved when the company chemist paid one of his periodic visits. He told me that it was piped off the supply of the coal board, which had a purification plant based at the nearby Bath Yard complex. Here were their local engineering workshops and social club. Les told me they were very helpful there, should I need any engineering assistance, taking me down to the social club to introduce me to Mr. Grainger, the resident engineer. Whilst I never had any occasion to make use of the engineering facilities, I did cultivate the habit of having the occasional meal on Thursdays there with Mr. Grainger. This liaison with the NCB was actively encouraged by the railway and as we shall see later, had its benefits all round.

Another meter which required my attention was situated under a manhole down the side of Spring Cottage Bridge. This bridge spanned the Burton to Leicester main line at the point where the Nuneaton line diverged at Moira West Junction. Access involved climbing over the fence at the top of the bridge and scrambling part way down the bank to where a large concrete cover had to be lifted to reveal the meter underneath. This was a capped supply that had once served a water crane and cabin, the readings of which hadn't changed in years. I rarely bothered to check this meter for this reason and also because it took the strength of Samson to lift the slab, not to mention the fact that it was the occasional residence of an adder. I had a couple of confrontations with this venomous creature and let it be said, he was never pleased to be disturbed. Both adders and grass snakes abounded in this area though fortunately, the latter were the more common of the two.

The gas and electric meters were no trouble at all being sited side by side on the shed wall.

As mentioned, the company chemist visited from time to time to take water samples from the main tank supply for the engine boiler water. The water supply to Overseal was of a particularly hard nature and as such required softening before it could be used. This required yours truly adding a determined number of pellets into the tank on a daily basis. As this number could vary between fifty and nearly one hundred per day, each pellet being the size of a small tin of peas, a strategy had to be established to achieve this task as there were too many to carry up the ladder in one go.

Thus, I fashioned a strong hook in the blacksmith's fire one Sunday morning whilst at Burton MPD to service the Yorkshire shunter as explained in the previous chapter, to which I tied a length of wagon rope. This allowed me to haul up a sack containing some 20 pellets at a time for depositing into the container cage provided inside the tank near the outlet to the tender filler. Generally, I climbed the ladder up the side of the tank while Tommy Brooks filled the bags and hooked them on down below or in his absence Eric or Cyril would oblige.

Another occasional visitor was the Railway Fire Officer. This gentleman would arrive at Spring Cottage in his little, bright red van; his approach being signalled by the Moira West Signalman. He would knock the tops off our four fire extinguishers, take a small sample of the water therein, scrounge a cup of tea, and have a moan about the tarnished state of the brassware, then depart. About a week later, four sachets of some obnoxious smelling powder would arrive with instructions to change the water, add the powder and re-seal the extinguishers.

Why, I argued, could he not perform this replenishing operation himself during his visits? On this subject, the stationmaster also agreed, when I mentioned it to him, as he was also a recipient of this evil smelling powder. We argued that, as well as the extinguishers not containing the correct consistency of content during the delay between inspection and supply, the action made us responsible for the effectiveness or otherwise of the extinguishers. Thus, Mr. Brazier composed a letter explaining this, stating that such actions on our part did not incur blame on us should any untoward event occur and requiring a signature to the fact, absolving us, by the fire officer when he called. As he called at the station first, I was unable to witness his reaction though I am sure Mr. Brazier explained the situation to him in a way which he would find difficult not to understand. Sufficient to say that the subsequent visits were made by a more junior member of the brigade who brought his own powder and did the whole process in one go as one would expect.

Another bone of contention for the staff was the toilets. These were of the chemical variety and the only ones who enjoyed using them were the flies. Les had new Elson units installed two years before I took up the reins and they were now due for further replacement. However, the powers that be at Derby thought otherwise so I got George Swann to pen a letter for me to give to Mr. Lewis when he next came. He went round the corner to have a look for himself and the speed at which he returned confirmed that he was in agreement with me. He said he would pass the letter on to the DMPS (District Motive Power Superintendent) for his attention. This gentleman, one Mr. Bramley, had never visited Overseal in George's living memory, a record that I felt sure he was not about to break; and I was right.

I did manage to obtain a couple of gallons of sousing chemical and some toilet rolls eventually but the situation was far from ideal. Hardly a successful outcome to the problem but we decided to leave things as they were, not wishing to 'rock the boat' and draw too much attention to the depot, the Beeching situation being what it was.

Another little chore that required my attention was to check, however slight, for signs of subsidence of the shed walls. The north-west corner of the shed was subject to some slight movement, in fact by approximately one eighth of a brick's depth, a crack running down the complete corner, riser by riser. The civil engineer had painted the affected area white and then added some horizontal, numbered lines onto this painted area. Each month I had to measure the difference, if any, where the lines crossed the subsidence gap and send a report accordingly. During my first six months I perceived some slight movement reporting the findings as required. These brought quick responses from the civil engineer's department every time with someone coming to check my measurements, within the week. One of these confided in me that, if movements of more than one inch occurred within six months, a case for recompense was possible from the Coal Board. Sadly, after those first six months the crack never moved even the smallest fraction of an inch, right up to the sorry day the depot closed.

The daily routine that I adopted involved a quick walk around the loco yard on arrival. During this check I inspected the amount of coal remaining in the three wagons at the depot so I could record the amount of fuel used per engine over the previous 24 hours. Wagon labels were removed from any empty wagons, one label being sent to the station, the other to Burton in the daily letter bag via 89 Target, along with any other correspondence. These coal amounts were recorded in the appropriate ledger, the amount per engine being an estimated or calculated guess. Mr. Gower was quite good at this and entered his 'guess' for each engine in the night book for my information every morning, after all, he should have a good idea as he helped to shovel most of it onto the various tenders.

When 89 Target arrived and was shunting in the goods yard alongside, any empty wagons would be exchanged for full ones from the yard. A 'goods wagon return' then had to be completed and sent down to Burton every day so the aim was to keep the numbers down to a minimum thus cutting down demurrage charges. Whilst the wagons were still on the sidings alongside they were deemed to be still 'in traffic' and thus no charges were incurred. When a fresh load of, say, six or eight wagons of coal arrived, the shunters would try to persuade me to allow them to be pushed through the coal stage onto the spare road beyond in order to release siding space in the yard alongside. I soon learned only to agree if the wagons were not booked into the shed environs officially. The yard foreman however, would argue that they were then officially within the depot and we must take responsibility for them. I would point out that I was doing him a favour by freeing up the sidings and if he didn't like it, he could have them back. Fortunately, he only walked down from Woodville Junction occasionally, so these little arguments occurred infrequently. To be honest, the whole affair seemed rather childish to me but the Burton Chief Clerk was soon on the phone if I booked too many wagons 'on shed' so the game had to be played out to the full.

Next to be checked was the oil used per locomotive per day. These were set amounts, fixed by someone years before, being so many pints per loco per day, according to its class. As the full amount was rarely used, with the partly emptied oil bottles being just topped up, Mr. Gower again used his genius to guess these amounts used per engine. This was yet again entered into another ledger, the juggling of the recordings of the real amounts being used only becoming necessary when a particular drum became empty and the figures in the book indicated that there should be some left. A keen eye had to be kept on this situation as the discrepancies were as a result of us seeming to be supplying oil for every cycle, door hinge, etc and in one case even a car, in the district. After much correspondence to and fro, I eventually managed to persuade the civil engineers to repair the oils stores door and fit a new lock. With the usual railway efficiency, only one key was provided and it fell upon me to obtain another at my own expense so that Mr. Gower could have one also. A noticeable improvement in oil consumption was the result until he lost his key or mislaid it one night, with the result that he was instructed by Burton to break in. End of story then! With the situation soon back to the state in which it was before.

Some of these foregoing items may appear rather petty to the reader but it must be realised that all these consumables had to be paid for and contributed to the overall costs of running the depot.

Adequate sand supplies also had to be maintained as a considerable amount was used every week in the sand boxes of the Overseal stud of locomotives. This, as has been explained earlier, was brought from the dryer at Burton, being ordered a week in advance. The dried sand was stored in the old air-raid shelter; a brick built structure just outside the shed door. Where it was stored pre-war I have no idea. When it arrived, in a van, it invariably provided one of my willing band of work-hungry firemen four hours overtime unloading it.

All these chores, along with any sick notes, holiday requests and the like, together with various other items of paperwork completed, I was then ready to ring it through to Burton at the regular 10 o'clock call. This done, breakfast would be taken.

If Cyril was on duty he would have a roaring, red hot fire going. I would supply the bacon and sausage with him bringing eggs and occasionally, if Mrs. Lee had been baking, some hash browns as well. Mushrooms would also appear from time to time fresh from the field behind the shed. I was always a bit wary of these later items being poisonous, being a 'Townie' and having no idea which were edible and which were not so I always watched for Cyril to eat his first before trying mine, much as I enjoyed them. This, needless to say, became quite a source of amusement among the rest of the staff.

When Eric was on however, I would either supply and cook my own fry-up or for a change, have a tin of soup or perhaps beans on toast. All washed down of course, with copious amounts of tea, whoever was on shift.

Having digested this fare, if I had no other tasks outstanding, I might go up to the stage and help Cyril or Eric to shovel two or three tons of coal out of the wagon, ready for the 8F when she returned from Birmingham.

Most of our coal incidentally, was supplied from Clapwell Colliery in Nottinghamshire and quite reasonable stuff it was too, burning without making too much clinker. On the other hand, the excuse for coal received from Shirebrook Colliery, our other main source of supply was rather the opposite, clinkering up quite badly, yet I was told that these two mines were fairly near to each other.

Sometimes, among a new raft of coal, one of the old ex North Eastern Railway hopper wagons would appear. These I always re-labelled on to Derby where they could be tipped into the hopper of the mechanical coal plant. Derby, in return, would send us a normal wagon of coal and this was invariably ex Shirebrook. I wonder why?

At the bottom of the sidings nearest to the shed and behind the Moira West Signalbox, was located a shed which belonged to and was operated by the Gloucester Carriage and Wagon Works. Here, a considerable amount of minor repairs were carried out to various wagons defected in the district. It was presided over by one Mr, Topliss (I forget his Christian name). This gentleman was also a local councillor and some of his parishioners had developed the habit of visiting him whilst he was at work. Some of them chose to approach his workplace, which was well ensconced within the railway property, via the Moira Road Bridge and loco yard which I found quite disconcerting. That they were trespassing was without question but the safety aspect, with them wandering about the yard etc. was the main concern. Again, diplomacy was needed for, whilst not wishing to alienate Mr. Topliss, who could be very useful on occasions as we shall see later, there was the problem of where the responsibility lay should one of these parishioners meet with an accident on the way. After deliberating over the matter for some time I resolved a course of action when the next of these persons appeared.

This duly transpired in the form of a young mother complete with pushchair containing baby together with two other small children to hand. Spotting, through the office window, their approach down the yard, I met them as they neared the shed door.

"Can I help you?" I enquired. After all, she may have been coming to see one of the shed employees on some important matter; not an unknown scenario.

She explained that, in fact, she wished to see Mr. Topliss on a very urgent matter, beginning to relate her problem to me. I quickly stopped her, explaining that, as she was trespassing, she could be handed over to the railway police, (did the railway police even know where Overseal was? I thought) not of course, really having that intention, merely wishing to indicate to her the situation, intending then to escort her to her destination. Unfortunately, upon my opening remarks, to my uttermost shame, she began to cry.

Having calmed her down, I escorted her, as originally intended, along the side of the sidings to Mr. Topliss's little empire, intending on arrival, to let him know about my concerns and ask him to advise his parishioners to refrain from such visits, at least via the loco yard. However, with the best laid plans of mice and men, not to mention depot managers, he was not there, a note fastened to his vice advising us of his absence at a council meeting. With no alternative, I was obliged to escort the young lady and her retinue, back whence they came, pushing the buggy into the bargain. On reaching the road, I suggested that she find an alternative route for her next visit. What the good lady thought when she thanked me for my attention, I do not know but the expression on her face seemed to suggest the thought, "Pompous person," or words to that effect.

I did however, take a stroll to see Mr. Topliss the following day, mentioning the previous day's visit to the shed and expressing my concerns on the matter.

He, for his part, indicated his unease with the situation also but explained that, as he lived some distance from the area of the parish that he served, he felt he had to tolerate the inconvenience of these visits to his workplace. It must be remembered that, back in the 60's, fewer people had cars and in this area bus services were somewhat sparse. It transpired that the young woman in question had already walked with her family some two miles or more to this destination, with a further three or four miles more being necessary for her to reach Mr. Topliss's home.

To say that these excursions via the loco yard ceased would not be true and although I did manage to turn back most of these potential hazard-causing trespassers, some slipped through the net, so to speak. I must confess that, on at least two occasions, when confronted by elderly gentlemen with walking sticks, I personally escorted one to their intended destination, while getting Eric to take the other.

Most of the work at the Wagon Repair Shed came as a result of defects discovered by the local railway C and W Inspector. This gentleman, Harry Bird I think was his name, became a very good friend during my time at Overseal. He was quite elderly and very experienced. Nothing missed Harry's attention. He always had a full book of defects when he arrived at the shed some 40 minutes or so before we walked together, around the east curve to the station, to catch the train back to Burton.

During this time he would sit at my desk and attend to his paperwork, whilst enjoying a cup of tea with me, thoughtfully brewed by Cyril or Eric; one of many drunk during the day.

A common wagon fault, witnessed by me on more than one occasion, was when one wagon jumped over the buffers of the one ahead of it, usually during a rough shunt. Thus when the raft of wagons to which they belonged were hauled back out of the sidings with the buffer heads entangled, one or the other, if not both, usually became detached from the wagon, falling to the ground and adding their number to the many others already littering the sidings together with broken drawbars, buffering pads, etc.

One of the more unusual aspects of my appointed position at Overseal was the esteem in which I and presumably my predecessors were held in the local community. When, for instance, I took the letters up to the station myself, deciding to take the route via the road through the village, the locals would greet me with a friendly, "Good morning gaffer," "Nice day, gaffer," or some similar remark; all very disconcerting for a young man of some 26 years. This was apparently the welcome also reserved for the stationmaster, Coal Board managers and the like. For my part, I just used to reply with a cheery "Good morning," etc.

The subject of trespassing brings another incident to mind. On looking out of my office window one afternoon, I noticed a small figure moving about the yard which kept stooping down and straightening up again. On investigation I found it was an elderly lady, complete with sack into which she was putting, pieces of spilt coal from around the yard. When challenged, she explained to me in her defence that she was getting too old to climb about the local coal tips picking coal (a regular local pastime) and consequently had found this easier alternative source of supply. My heart went out to her as she was truly of a fragile appearance and I would dearly have loved to fill her sack for her but in reality, I was forced to empty it out and escort her from the premises. Although I felt bad about this action, in truth, had I not, the word would have gone around like wildfire and half the village would have been there, helping themselves in no time.

Just so that the reader will not think that being in charge makes one into a totally bad person, another situation which was to have a very far reaching effect, came about through a rather light hearted remark made over our very public railway phone system one afternoon.

Terry Wood, one of my faithful band of workaholic firemen, was sitting in my office having a break and a cup of tea whilst unloading a van of dried sand, which he was doing on overtime, having already worked a shift firing as described earlier. He was in the throes of a divorce and consequently feeling very down and depressed. From what he told me I gathered that a fair portion of the break-up was down to his other half being left alone for long periods of time, often a scenario commensurate with a footplateman's life. If anyone needed cheering up it was him.

The phone rang and it was Brenda from Burton Loco, ringing up about the coal supply situation; a regular request on this particular afternoon every week. I knew Brenda was also without a partner as I recalled she had mentioned to me she was 'in between boyfriends' only a few weeks earlier during one of our conversations. Of course, I already knew Brenda reasonably well from my regular conversations with her both over the phone and at the sheds and realised that her bubbly personality was just what Terry needed.

I therefore decided, as my wife put it later, to play Cupid by arranging for them to meet each other. On asking Brenda, she agreed to a meeting and as she was free that evening, I turned to Terry, telling him what I had arranged and asked him if he was also willing to make the meeting. He also replied in the affirmative so after explaining the details of the meeting location etc, I told him to forget the sand and get off home to beautify himself for the rendezvous I had arranged. Brenda was briefed as to Terry's appearance and car as, although he had previously started at Burton as a cleaner like most of our firemen, she could not recall him personally.

My word! I bet the phones were red hot that day after I had put my receiver down. Other than to casually enquire if he had made the appointment and receiving a big grin and an affirmative nod in reply, I said no more to either of them about it but from the noticeable improvement in their manner I presumed that things had gone smoothly. My wife and I were therefore delighted, to receive an invitation to their wedding some two years later when, sadly due to the machinations of the Beeching Plan, they were no longer in the railway's employ.

And the railway authorities didn't have that subject in the management course either!

After Christmas 1962 we received a new fireman or in fact a Passed Cleaner, who had transferred to us from Coalville with the express purpose of attaining the relevant number of firing turns to become registered. He had been told by some of our firemen that he would be out firing every day if he came to us. I was surprised to hear that this was not the case at Coalville. His arrival brought our footplate crews up to full strength, only to have it reduced again by the transfer of Peter McEvoy, to Crewe I think, only a month later. Still! It was nice while it lasted.

The new man's name was King. Unfortunately I can't recall his first name. He hadn't been with us long when he became involved in an incident one Saturday when on the afternoon disposing turn. This duty started at 15.30 on the weekdays but commenced earlier, around 1300 at weekends. Passed fireman Les Clamp was his driver and as with depots all over the country, they were disposing of an engine each, having five in total to attend to.

Having disposed of one of the 4F's, master King ran it up the yard to the dead end prior to reversing over the points to drop down by the coal stage to fill the tank. Now! This dead end was very short, only just allowing the Class 8F to clear the said points although allowing comfortable room for a Class 4F. Instead of terminating at a stop block it ended in a large mound of earth some six or eight feet high and our young 'driver,' misjudging the distance, finished up with the 4F's tender end well and truly buried therein. His natural instinct was to reverse his charge and drive it out but try as he might, neither he nor later Les, could persuade it to move. The only other engine with any steam left in the boiler that could possibly help to pull her consort out was another 4F but with only 60 lbs on the clock, their combined efforts also failed. After some deliberations, Les decided to re-light the 8F to raise steam in her. Having been looking forward to getting away to enjoy his tea at the normal time, all Les could hope for now was an early supper.

As Eric related the saga to me, with the 8F blowing off, she just managed to haul the 4F out of the bank. Then of course, they had to throw the fire out of her again and fill the tank on the Class 4 with the washout hose as by then she was completely out of steam.

I would have been completely ignorant of this incident had not Les come into the office on the Monday morning and told me about it. As he said to me, he thought it better to tell me himself as otherwise there was always someone else willing to 'spill the beans' so to speak. He offered to make out a report as was the official requirement but I told him not to bother. It wouldn't look good on his record, him being a passed man and Mr. Topliss and I straightened the damaged rail guards so no visible harm was done. I didn't hear any more about the event until Eric related the details to me the following week when he was back on days. I just told Les to be more careful in future and gave master King a pep talk as I was duty bound, at least though even that had to wait until the following week as he had been on the night Birmingham turn.

The next time round on this Saturday disposing turn, some thirteen weeks later, Les was once again cast in the roll of driver, again with master King as his fireman. As the wagon under the stage was well down for coal, Cyril asked him if he would push another one underneath later, ready for Sunday night, when he had completed emptying it.

Whether Les misheard what was said to him I am not sure but on pushing the full wagon under the stage and pushing the other one out, he failed to notice that the side door of the wagon was still down, resting on the coal stage floor. The wagon concerned was a standard 16 ton, steel, mineral wagon and as it was shunted back, the open side door acted like a knife and sheared off the brick column alongside the pedestrian entrance at the top of the steps. This column, constructed of blue engineering bricks, formed part of the supporting structure of the tank above.

As if this wasn't bad enough, the engine he used was the 8F, tender first and he discovered that the Stanier tender was also too wide to pass under the stage and the right hand rear handrail fouled the entrance, bending the rail and causing the tender tank to leak at the point where the lower end of the rail was welded to the tank.

I was working at Burton on the Sunday morning and Cyril rang the shed to tell me the bad news. As he explained that the 8F's tank was leaking badly and emptying to the point of the damage very quickly, I arranged there and then to have it changed over from Burton, telling Cyril to light the fire in it and endeavour to raise steam ready for the Burton men to bring it back.

As the only thing Cyril could say on the state of the coal stage was that, "It hadn't fell down yet," I decided to have a ride up in the afternoon to survey the damage so after dinner my wife and I, along with our six year old daughter and baby son, took a ride to Overseal. I didn't expect to see anyone at the shed as the place was officially unmanned, as explained earlier, on Sunday after-noons. A quick wave to the bobby in Moira South Box prompted him to slide his window open, presumably to shout some caustic remark but on seeing my wife and family he suddenly became lost for words.

The replacement 8F still appeared to have quite a good head of steam, judging by what was drifting up from the safety valves so I climbed up to check if the Burton men had thrown her fire out as requested, to find all was well with an empty grate and a full boiler, so no problem there at least.

The coal stage however, was a different story. The column of bricks in question was some four to five feet square and about twelve feet long, lying on its side, virtually complete, at the foot of the stairway alongside the 16 ton mineral wagon. A goliath could have picked it up and slotted it back into place but, not being blessed with such strength and stature, I realised that more conventional methods would be needed. However, as the tank did not look in danger of collapse, I felt it could wait until Monday morning when I would request an urgent assessment by the civil engineers. Many had been the little disasters at the shed I had managed to cover up over the previous months but this one was definitely beyond the ingenuity of even our most imaginative of men and certainly of mine.

As my wife, Judy had never previously visited my little kingdom I decided to give her the grand tour, starting in the office. As I opened the door the shed cat ran out and dived into the messroom next door. My daughter gave chase so we both followed her. What a sight befell our eyes! There was Eric, completely naked, standing in a cut down oil drum, in front of the large glowing fire, having a bath. I'm not sure who was most surprised, him or us. Fortunately the oil drum reached nearly waist height, his apparent method of entry being via the messroom table alongside, a seemingly hazardous journey considering the rather sharp looking sides of the drum. Quickly ushering my family back into the office, I left them there before returning to speak to him.

Apparently this was his normal practice on a Sunday afternoon when starting nights, with him coming to feed the cat and avail himself of the hot water ready to hand in the messroom kettle and the engines out in the shed which, although dead, still had quite warm water in their boilers. Sometimes he would return home to pursue his pastime of 'tele-viewing,' or alternatively, if perhaps the weather was bad or the television programmes were of no interest to him, staying to make a start on re-lighting the engines.

A character, Eric certainly was, amongst a shed full and a good worker to boot!

Members of the civil engineers department arrived in strength during the following week with two engineers and three workers to examine the coal stage damage; not, I hasten to add, to install a bath for Eric. They had expected a wagon load of scaffolding to have arrived prior to their visit but unfortunately it had not. While the engineers surveyed the scene and the three workmen made themselves comfortable in the cabin, tea brewed and sandwiches being consumed, I got busy on the phone trying to locate the missing scaffolding. The Woodville Junction Yard Foreman eventually tracked it down at Leicester Junction where it had arrived too late to be included in the day's tripper (89 Target) to Overseal. However, as it was reportedly almost certain to arrive the following day, the decision was made by the civil engineers and company to return in two days time.

As this period was over the weekend, it was on the following Monday that the one end of the coal stage became shrouded in a maze of tubing, a considerable amount purporting to support the weight of the water tank and contents, even though it had happily remained in place without any help during all the previous week. The actual rebuilding took about ten days, during which time our Class 5 and 8F went down to Burton to coal. In view of this extra workload, various sets of Burton men enjoyed ten days of overtime ferrying exchange locomotives back and forth.

Les's reward for all this extra work and activity, following the unavoidable enquiry, was sadly three days suspension with master King receiving one day as well. However, the union challenged this latter sentence and it was later rescinded and all mention of it removed from his record.

Over one of my lunches with Mr. Granger from Bath Yard, he mentioned to me that he wished to exchange the steam engine at Gresley Colliery with a fairly new diesel locomotive, then at Donisthorpe. I knew the steam engine, "Cradock" of old, having carried out a routine BR examination to enable it to operate over our sidings; these examinations being carried out every twelve months; but the diesel was new to me. Apparently its examination had been carried out by someone at the makers before its delivery some six months earlier.

In due course the expected letter containing the instructions to carry out these examinations arrived from the DMPS at Derby, along with the relevant forms for me to complete afterwards. Remembering an earlier occasion many years before when, as an apprentice, I had been sent to assist Joe Benson when he made his first check of the coal board engines under his supervision, I likewise requested some one to come with me to hold the other end of the tape, so to speak. To my chagrin a young engine cleaner was sent to assist me. Not that this was a fault in itself but I would have thought that a young apprentice might have benefited more in some small way from the experience. Still! He was a nice lad and I am sure he enjoyed his day out.

On the day I travelled to work in my car as its use made it more convenient to visit both sites in the same day. We went to Donisthorpe first to examine and take the measurements of the new diesel. BR had a special form on which to enter the details with which I was quite familiar as I had used them before at Burton when checking the brewery engines there. These forms had the outline of a typical six coupled diesel or steam locomotive against which the examiner entered all the required measurements where indicated. Height of cab; chimney; dome; safety valves; bonnet and fuel tanks; width of same; length over buffers, framing, wheel base; distance of overhang ahead and behind the coupled wheels; buffer height; buffer beam height; draw hooks, couplings, etc; these all being from rail level. Any item with less than two inches clearance from the rail had also to be noted, like rail guards, sand pipes and occasionally brake gear. Finally and most importantly the condition of the locomotives tyres was paramount. All these details were carefully taken and recorded for the new diesel, plus the type, make, builder's number and date constructed. I seem to recall that this particular locomotive was a Ruston six coupled, jackshaft drive, diesel mechanical, built in 1962 and very nice too as diesels go. Everything seemed to be in good order and I could visualise no problems that could be encountered on its journey to Gresley.

Not so "Cradock" however. I had no need to run the tape over her as I already had her measurements recorded on a copy of the form back at the shed. All that was required was to check the tyre profiles and have a quick visual check round; but Oh! Those tyres! As a result of her constantly working round the same tight left hand curve, working hard to push load after load of coal empties up a steep gradient to the colliery, returning down, braking hard with loaded wagons, the flanges on her right hand side had worn very thin, well past the minimum accepted standard of BR, whilst the left hand side flanges were hardly worn at all.

What a dilemma to be in! I knew that Mr. Granger was desperate to exchange these two locomotives and over our piece of railway was the easiest and most convenient way of doing it. I also knew that if I sent the measurements in as they were, BR would not allow "Cradock" to travel. So, what to do?

I decided to take the mail up to the station myself the next day (Friday) and use the national phone there to ring Mr. Granger and hopefully arrange to call on him on the way back. This I did, explaining to him the state of the tyre wear on "Cradock." I suspected that one of the reasons for the exchange was to try and even out the wear a bit more and thus get a bit more work out of her before the inevitable overhaul was required, there being no sharp curves at Donisthorpe as far as I was aware. Not, of course, that he would own up to this,

his reason being to monitor the performance of the diesel on Gresley's steep, sharply curved track.

After a long chat and a couple of whiskeys, followed by a nice lunch (and why not), I agreed to give it a go and try to get "Cradock" down to her new venue. I therefore sent in the report showing her flanges to be right on the minimum acceptable limit and hoped that Derby would agree to the move.

NCB 0-4-0ST 'Cradock'. Photo: L. Cairns.

Back came the confirmation with a rider to exercise all caution owing to the tyre condition, this being emphasised by underlining with red ink. It further stated that Mr. Brazier and I were to arrange the moves of the two locomotives at our convenience. All I needed from him was a guard and a brake van, the latter being a statutory requirement as the wheelbase of an 0-4-0 locomotive was of insufficient length to work the track circuit. I also had another purpose for the brake van; as I intended to load it with pieces of wood with which to pack the points at Woodville Junction, Moira West and South and Donisthorpe; together with a jack and re-railing ramps.

Thus the stage was set and was arranged for the following Sunday morning. I selected 'Lol' Saunders and Walter Lambell as driver and fireman and with Ernie Prewitt as the guard, we four set out for Gresley in the taxi thoughtfully provided by the coal board. Mr. Granger remarked, he would see us at Donisthorpe if we could make it. I replied that, if we didn't, I would be looking for another job and if so I hoped he would look favourably on me.

Ernie Tebbett, "Cradock's" driver, brought her down the bank from the colliery one last time and handed her over to our care. Lol backed her onto the brake van then reversed her back down the main line (in reality the Woodville Branch). A signalman had been booked on to operate the points for us to move out onto the line and as it was just a simple turn-out, we decided to risk it and inch out without bothering with packing at this time.

As Lol said, "It manages to get across the points in the exchange sidings every day without any trouble."

"Maybe it does and maybe it doesn't," I thought.

Soon we were trundling along towards Swain's Park where we had to wait for our travelling signalman to catch us up in his car and operate the level crossing gates. This done, we proceeded on our way to Woodville Junction with the signalman's remarks of, "See you at Donisthorpe," ringing in our ears. Mr. Brazier met us at the junction and when the road was set, watched Lol, Walter and myself as we inserted the hardwood packing between the blades and frogs of the points there.

When I was satisfied, Lol inched her forwards across the junction with yours truly watching those flanges all the way. Safely across and onto the level track of what was our true main-line; the Burton to Leicester line; we stopped and recovered the packing, having to repeat the process at Moira West Junction some half a mile further on. Here we had to swing round to the right which would put most of the sideways thrust onto the good side of the axle so I was even more confident here. However, I still intended to put the packing down. A long wait had to be endured first while a Desford to Matlock Sunday excursion passed down the line before Mr. Brazier would allow us to cross over onto the Netherseal line which, as you may realise, took us past the shed and over Moira South Junction. Next stop Donisthorpe.

With the same ritual of the packing observed at both the West and South Junctions we were soon rolling gently down the bank to Donisthorpe. Our travelling bobby greeted us and set the road for us to cross over into the colliery exchange sidings straight away. Lol was all for setting off immediately but I curbed his enthusiasm.

"Let us not tempt fate so near to home," I said. "We'll put some wood down just this one last time."

Was I glad to enter those coal board sidings. The new diesel was waiting for us just inside the gates so Lol and Walter climbed aboard to conduct the coal board driver back to Gresley as naturally, neither of them had a clue how to drive it themselves. Coupling up to the brake van the driver hooted up for the road as I joined Ernie in the van for the ride back up the bank where I would be dropped off opposite the shed, leaving the intrepid trio to complete the journey on their own.

As we set off up the bank, Ernie and I stood on the veranda enjoying the early morning sunshine, just in time to see "Cradock" drop off the road as her new driver started to take her to the shed. We both looked at each other and grinned.

"Touché!" was Ernie's comment, which quite surprised me, him being a South Derbyshire man and all.

I arranged for the brake van to be returned to the shed via 98 Target the next day so that I could recover my supply of wood etc which had depleted slightly overnight.

On arriving home the following Thursday evening I was greeted by a large pile of coal dumped in the street outside my house.

"Sign here missus," was the first my wife was aware of it when answering a knock on our side door and being confronted by a rather large and very dirty coal board lorry driver. And us with all gas fires as well! Still! My parents and neighbours were glad of it. I gather that Lol and Walter had a delivery also although I don't know about Ernie.

It made me realise how much our efforts were appreciated though Mr. Lewis told me that I was a fool to have done it. I suppose I was a bit foolhardy, looking back but my excuse was that co-operation with the coal board was of great importance to our very existence at the time; as my betters were always telling me. I wonder how he found out about it. But, as I have said before, there are no secrets at Overseal. Perhaps he was a bit narked that he never got any coal.

Another of our drivers, Charlie Moulton, had discovered the delights of holidays abroad. Not the everyday thing then that it is today. This pastime was made all the more attractive by the reciprocal travel arrangements that British Railways employees enjoyed with their continental cousins.

Naturally, the railway had a series of special forms which required completion. The privileged fares available were similar to those in this country. Indeed, it was possible to travel to some destinations completely free of charge, the only cost being in the form of port taxes, etc. The only down side to these arrangements was the six to eight weeks time period needed to allow all the travel documents to be completed and returned to the applicant. I, for my part, was surprised that more people did not take advantage of this facility. Had my family been a bit older, I certainly would. Johnny Close was the only other person at Overseal to try it, though a couple of our younger firemen did discuss the possibilities with me.

My concern was that these rather involved holiday and travel applications proceeded through the system without any delay on my part. Having started their bureaucratic journeys in the daily letter pouch via the Overseal – Burton tripper, I always phoned the appropriate clerk at Burton the following morning to ensure they had completed the first stage through the system onto his desk at least. After that of course, they were out of our hands until they returned, hopefully all complete, ready for the recipient's holiday.

Talking of holidays, another little occurrence comes to mind that happened one morning. I had been up the yard for some reason or other and was returning to my office when I thought I spotted Jack Harding, our junior driver, coming out of the office door. I thought nothing of it at the time. Nothing unusual about that in itself as he would have just booked on to work the middle, Woodville Junction, shunting turn (97 Target) and he could have been using the phone to enquire after a lift down to his engine to save the walk, for instance.

However, just as I had made myself comfortable in my chair he came back in and asked for a holiday form. As I got up to go to the appropriate cupboard for the necessary form he said, "No, no, me mon. Not out of there. One of them out of yon desk drawer."

Alarm bells now rung in my head for Jack was well known for his practical jokes. Sitting down again I went to carefully open the left hand drawer of my desk; the one that received the most use; the right hand one being used very rarely.

"No, no, not in there. In the other one," he added, pointing to the rarely used drawer.

"Oh. What are them forms called?" he puzzled further. "They're in there anyroad."

With great trepidation, I gently opened the relevant drawer expecting anything to happen, the look of anticipation on his face confirming my worst fears. As I opened the drawer further a grass snake was revealed, now comfortably curled up in its nice, new, dark haven. Fortunately recognising it for what it was, I reached inside, carefully took hold of the unexpected resident, lifted it out and handed it to him saying,

"Just hold this a minute Jack, while I look further inside."

His face was a picture. He had thought that I would have jumped out of my skin on being confronted with a snake, me being a "Townie" and all that. Had I not been on the alert his assumption would probably have been correct.

However, the incident was an indication that I had now been finally accepted into the fold.

Chapter 18

It's Not all Routine

Lest you should think that life in charge was all administration, this was far from the case.

Our main purpose in being was to run trains or at least to provide an engine and crew for the purpose, on every rostered occasion. This, as has been stated earlier we always managed to do.

The job in general became very much a matter of routine, when everything went according to plan, which it occasionally did.

The hours between twelve o'clock and two o'clock could be quite busy, for that was the time when the trippers came on shed, for crew changing and fire cleaning. Any repairs which were required, received my attention, such as brake adjustments, steam leaks, blocked sands, gland packings' and the like. If any repairs were booked overnight, the '4F' concerned was kept back for my attention in the morning, with it subsequently going out on the 98 Target working at 9.45am. With the '8F' advice was sought from Burton by Mr Gower, though usually the driver making the report would be able to assess the engine's suitability or not to continue at work. If not, this was normally changed overnight by Burton men bringing a replacement engine up; returning with the cripple, all while I was tucked up in my bed.

Things of course went wrong out on the line, from time to time as well.

Derailments were not an unusual occurrence, particularly in colliery yards' where the NCB's standard of track maintenance was somewhat inferior to ours.

The usual scenario was for the combined efforts of the footplate crew, shunters and NCB staff along with some ramps, re-railing the engine without to much bother. When the engine eventually returned to the shed, no one would have any idea how the railguards had got bent and the sand pipes damaged. The outcome being another task for me, putting everything right. This usually involved removing the offending part or parts, and if failing to straighten at the shed, taking them down to see Mr Topliss at his small wagon repair base; and beg the use of his gas bottles to apply heat to soften the metal up. He usually applied the heat himself, with yours truly officiating on the anvil with the sledgehammer. Can you wonder at me wishing to keep in his good books, for he could just as easily have shown me the door? After all there was no monetary reward for his labours from British Railways, and while he was helping me, he was not repairing wagons.

Some of these derailments were more serious than others. The most severe case during my tenure involving '4F' no. 44434, a regular Overseal engine. She had been pushed through the trap points down at Donisthorpe after failing to hold her load of empties whilst working 95 Target. The line here ran in a deep cutting and 44434 came to rest partly in the cess and leaning against the cutting side.

My phone was soon ringing, and in no time at all I was heading for the scene by light engine. On seeing the scene as described confronting me, my first thoughts were that the faith, which my footplate men placed in me, was going to be sorely stretched that day.

I immediately informed the signalman in Donisthorpe Box to request the breakdown train from Burton, which at that time still had its steam crane, though I couldn't quite see what use it would be with its maximum lifting capacity of 15 tons, in this case.

He informed me that control had already done that very thing, so apart from using the light engine to remove the undamaged part of the train, there was very little else that I could do until it arrived. Fortunately the derailment hadn't blocked the other running line, so the 'bobby' had introduced single line working past the sight. Mr Brazier when he arrived also found that he had little to do as a result of the signalman's action; so he offered me a lift back to the shed, which I duly accepted.

My other contribution to the saga being to contact Woodville Junction signalbox to suggest that they observe which way round the crane was marshalled in the breakdown train, so that if necessary, the train could be turned via the Moira triangle to enable it to be at the front. This was duly done, with the assembly running around the triangle as suggested. This action of course saving a considerable amount of time down at the accident site.

I would have loved to have been present down at the scene to assist with 44434's recovery, but of course it was now out of my hands. It was described to me on the following Sunday morning when I was down at Burton, giving my weekly dose of TLC to D2859. While the crane removed the derailed and damaged wagons, five in all; 44434 was righted with aid of jacks' and packing, and Sylvester; prior to being slewed across and back onto the rails, which had sustained only minor damage. The whole operation taking some seven or so hours to complete. No doubt the local hostelry which overlooked the site did rather well also, knowing the thirst of the Burton breakdown gang. Another derailment, which we did manage on our own, concerned a Stanier 'Crab' working the Nuneaton tripper. This engine, No. 42967 had been entering the field sidings on the opposite side of the running lines, to the shed, to collect a bogie bolster wagon which had been left there following some engineering work, the previous weekend. The approach to these sidings, two in number was by way of a double slip; a carry over from many years ago when this was the site of Overseal station, as mentioned earlier. It was over this double slip that the 'Crab's pony truck became derailed.

The Moira West signalman, under whose control the movement was being made, called me over the phone to attend, some five minutes walk away.

Giving Eric a shout, we both quickly walked down to survey the scene.

42967 was standing partly on the running road with both wheels of the pony truck sitting on the ballast between the blades of the double slip. Fortunately the shunter had observed the incident and stopped the movement before more damage was done. He had then dashed off back to Woodville

Junction sidings to fetch some rerailing ramps, though I was not aware of this at the time.

As 42967 also had a few wagons and a brake attached to her tender, the brake of which was fouling the Leicester to Burton main line, some prompt action was called for, otherwise our entire piece of railway would soon grind to a halt. Sending Eric back to the shed for a barrow load of timber packing, I started filling in the spaces between the points, rails and blades with some chair keys, a bag of which were lying conveniently to hand; having first of course informed the driver of my actions. (I didn't want him to try and reverse back onto the running line while my hands were in the way, in an attempt to rerail himself; an action not unknown in such circumstances, the end result of which usually making the situation worse).

Stainier Class '5' 2-6-0 No. 42948. Photo: P. Groom.

My intention was to make a solid hard wood base and slope behind each wheel, to afford a path for them to ride over, back (hopefully) onto the track.

As Eric arrived back on the scene with a nice barrow full of wooden blocks, thoughtfully collected over the years by my predecessors for just such an occasion, the shunter arrived back in his car with the rerailing ramps.

These cast iron castings are designed to rerail wagons of some ten tons or so on a straight piece of track, not a seventy-ton locomotive astride a set of points. Without further ado, despite my protestations, he proceeded to position them behind the two pony truck wheels as best he could. These ramps were designed to sit firmly onto the running rails with a cast arm leading down the one side to be positioned before the derailed wheel. This ideal position could obviously not be achieved while astride a set of points, let alone a slip, as the converging rails and blades got in the way.

I warned him that the weight of the engine would smash the ramps in such a situation, as they were unsupported underneath, but he ignored me and asked the driver to reverse anyway.

Eric and I took shelter behind the shunters cabin along with the Nuneaton guard, while the driver put 42967 in reverse and opened the regulator.

With a crack and a bang the front of the engine reared up in the air some six inches or so, before dropping back onto the rails. Bits of cast iron flew in all directions like shrapnel, one piece breaking a pane of glass in the cabin behind which we had taken cover.

To my surprise 42967 sat firmly back on the rails. But at what cost?

Two rerailing ramps, several special point chair castings and half a dozen sleepers, not forgetting the pane of glass. With a bit of patience and some careful packing, the damage to the points would probably have been minimal. But at least the shunter had the urgency of the situation at heart, so perhaps I should not be to hard on him.

The driver told me that it was the second time that day that he had been derailed by the pony truck with this engine, so I decided to make a close examination of the truck where it stood before letting it move again; blocked main line or not.

This inspection revealed a broken front spring hanger on the left-hand side. Such a defect rendered the engine a total failure where it stood. There was only one thing for it. That was to attempt to get the engine on to the shed without causing any further damage.

By now there were trains standing all round the place. Behind the West box, a Drakelow bound coal train could be seen waiting behind a Coalville '8F'. At the top of the bank from Donisthorpe one of our '4F's was stood with 95Target, also Drakelow bound, with another load of coal and not a hope of restarting it without assistance. Fortunately Bill Greening in the South box had held it there instead of allowing it on to the intermediate home signal protecting the points over which 42967 now stood. This meant that the 'Crab' could travel wrong line as far as his box, to then reverse and cross over straight on to the shed.

After consultation with the driver and the guard, the relevant wrong line orders were issued and 42967 and its trailing load eased backwards to clear the siding proper; before reversing to head forwards towards the South box. When clear of the west junction, its small train was uncoupled and left under control of its brakevan.

Her driver then eased our 'Crab' onwards towards the crossover by the South box. There was just enough room in front of the 95 Target '4F', to enable her to clear the points. Now the gamble to get her onto the shed, without further mishap. As she was to travel over the crossover in reverse, both the driver and I thought that we were in with a chance of success, and so it proved to be. But my heart was in my mouth as 42967 crept across, with me watching the left-hand side pony wheel and Eric and the fireman watching the other one.

318

There was one heart stopping moment as 'my wheel' hit one of the point frogs and literally bounced, but all ended well. With her standing safely down the bottom of the shed, I got on the phone to arrange first for a replacement engine for her train, and secondly a new spring hanger for the pony truck. As this latter item would have to come from either Crewe or Horwich works, I told Eric to let the fire burn out, as I visualised a few days delay waiting for the part.

While all this was going on, the Woodville Junction (97 Target) engine ran down onto the 'Crabs' train. She then reversed the whole lot down onto the front of 95Target before, with a concerted effort, both engines hauled the now combined trains off the bank. All in a days work for Overseal men!!

I removed the remains of the spring hanger with the help of Eric without to much trouble, in time to send it down to Burton on the return 89Target tripper. A set of Burton men duly arrived with another 'crab', a Hughes / Fowler parallel boiler one this time, and a Saltley engine to boot. The Nuneaton men bid us a fond farewell and ran back down to the junction to collect their train from where it now lay.

The Burton men were under the impression that they were to take 42967 back with them, and it was only Eric's vigilance that stopped them from moving her. They had made no effort to contact me at all.

As it was not a Wednesday, (I have forgotten precisely just what day it was) there was no midday train down the branch, so they had no alternative but to return on the 89 Target tripper. The daily Burton-Nuneaton-Burton tripper had already gone by; having been standing at Donisthorpe behind 95 Target earlier on, when this saga had began. After the dinnertime rush, one of my workaholic firemen asked me if I had anything for him to do to enable him to book twelve hours. So I set him the task of throwing 42967's fire out and disposing of her properly, then tidying up the loco yard, to complete his time. I had already hung a red lamp on her bufferbeam and added my 'Not To Be Moved' board, chalking a message to that effect on the messroom train arrangement board as well, for good measure. A note in the night book to keep Mr Gower informed, completed the formalities; and life went back to normal once more.

Another incident which occurred soon after the one related above, concerned one of our own engines; No. 44591 this time. She was working up the Woodville branch on 98 Target, when, following an unusual clattering noise, picked out by her driver's attuned ear above the normal rattling present when an engine is in motion, there developed an unusual knocking sound. Upon investigation, it was discovered that the left hand inside slide block had disappeared and thus the crosshead and little end was unsupported on the one side. Alvin Southerd, her driver abandoned his train and ran light engine back down the branch to stand at Woodville Junction to await my attention, as he did not want any disasters to befall while on the 'main line'.

When I arrived at the scene, some fifteen minutes or so walk away, I decided that as the little end gudgeon pin did not show any signs of working out; that we could risk a gentle run round to the shed.

Here, we positioned 44591 down the far end of the shed in a similar position to that which the Nuneaton 'Crab' had so recently vacated. With left hand big end set on the bottom quarter, I set about removing the little end gudgeon pin and the outside slide block; so that I could send them both down to Burton in the usual way. On 89 Target; which was actually shunting outside the shed as I worked.

Having supported the piston rod and connecting rod, it was but a few minutes work to achieve this, so I was able to get the relevant parts away in a very short space of time. The inside slide block keeper plate was still encapsulated by the little end gudgeon pin, but extremely badly damaged; so this was sent down as well.

A quick phone call down to Burton to have a word with Sid Booth the machinist, to give him the measurements to machine the replacement block too, and the job was in hand. He would of course have the gudgeon pin to make a new bush for, also. Sid was a very thorough worker, who kept a note of all the work that he did, and as such had probably already got the measurements that he required, recorded. But as 44591 had not been at Burton for long, I did not know whether she had had any mileage motion work done on her or not. But apparently she had.

'Ivant' Class 2MT 2-6-0 No. 46403 stands over Burton No. 2 ash pit. Photo: P. Webb.

She was a rare engine to us at Overseal as she had a tender equipped with coal rails, which as mentioned earlier, were 'de rigour' to us except in an emergency.

However, with scrapping programme continuing apace, coal rail fitted tender class '4's were becoming increasingly the norm.

Alvin and his mate took the '4F' off the returning 6-50am Birmingham with which to continue his work 'up the branch', finishing his day some half of an hour late, owing he said to a dirty fire; and who could argue with that.

I kept 44591 in light steam, as I knew that I could rely on Sid to pull out all the stops in his endeavours to get her back in service. My faith in him was not found wanting, for sure enough, on the arrival of 89Target the next day, all the pieces of motion were on board; ready for me to refit

Despite red lamps, 'Not To Be Moved' board, and the usual messages left in the mess room and night book; 44591 had in fact been pushed nearly half a turn further along the pit than where I had left her the night before. Apart from having bent my home made piston rod support, which had served me faithfully ever since I had started fitting; the unattached connecting rod little end had bumped the end of the crosshead. It was only by luck that the piston head had not been pushed through the cylinder end cover. A few inches more, and this would almost certainly have been the outcome.

Mr nobody was responsible of course, and for once the jungle telegraph did not reveal the perpetrator either. This in itself told me something, the very silence pointing the finger as it were.

Before I could start to refit the parts therefore, I had first to move the engine backwards half a turn. So I introduced Eric to the finer arts of the pinch bar, while I watched for a suitable position in which to effect the re-assembly.

Thus what should have been an half-hours task, took up the rest of the afternoon.

Burton had lent us an unusual engine to cover 98 Target while 44591 was out of action in the shape of an Ivatt Class '2' 2-6-0, which I seem to recall was a Kettering engine. Alvin was quite impressed with the comfort of this machine, which we hung onto for two days; though Mr Gower did not share his enthusiasm with its tender, as his little note in my drawer the next day bore testimony

I was tempted to reply in the vein that he should look on it as a punishment for his negligence, but decided to confine my comments to the usual, 'Owing to the current withdrawal programme, we had all to rally round and make do with what we got'.

However, Eric knew of my true feelings, so it would surely get back to him during the following week of nights.

Various tales about our night chargeman were related to me by Cyril and Eric, over the two years that I was in command. I was not naïve enough not to realise that the reverse was also the case, and therefore was able to use this trait of human nature to my advantage on occasions; though these pages are not a platform to air them.

The winter of 1962/63 started in the usual way with nothing exceptional beyond the normal frosts and low temperatures. Frost fires were lit in all the usual places, and life went on as normally as possible. But the temperatures plummeted towards the end of February, and the water supply to the shed froze up. Engines were able to get water at Drakelow and Nuneaton (Abbey Street) and from the NCB supply at Donisthorpe Colliery, this latter source only in emergency by kind permission of the local coal-board. Engines working 97 and 98 Targets' were unable to find an active water supply and thus their crews were changing their engines over with those on the 95 and 96 workings, to enable their tanks to be replenished at Drakelow. This water of course was also from a private supply, this time under the auspices of the CEGB (Central Electricity Generating Board) who lost no time at all in billing the Railway Company for its use.

Letters were soon in the post to me regarding this issue, so I resolved to trace the actual route of the supply pipe from its metered source at the bottom of the embankment on the Moira to Overseal Road.

I soon discovered that where it passed over the bridge towards the loco', the supply pipe was near to the surface as to be almost exposed.

This I realised would be a good place to start to try and thaw our supply out, as it was not at the tank end that the problem lay. The tank had emptied and dried up.

A compromise of opinions amongst the shed staff established an approximate course for the supply pipe from the end of the bridge to the foot of the tank. This I reasoned would be fairly deep in the ground as it had to pass under the Moira East to South spur lines as well as one road within the depot's confines. I therefore decided that frost fires would be lit and maintained right across the bridge above its course for the next few days to test the theory and hopefully achieve a favourable result.

The fires were lit some six feet apart and a coal wagon was hauled onto the bridge and its contents unloaded in numerous piles to keep them fed. When they were all burning brightly, I went across to Moira South Box to inform the signalman who had naturally been watching all the activity with great interest, just exactly what we were trying to do. All went very well until my departure at around 4pm. A note in the night book instructing the night staff to make the attention of these fires a priority, had a most unexpected reply the following morning.

Apparently, the local retain fire brigade had received a message during the early hours from a member of the public that the railway bridge was on fire, which of course technically it was. So without further ado, despite being told to the contrary by the signalman; they put it out. I bet Mr Gower derived a great deal of pleasure penning his note concerning the incident, in the night book that morning.

On arrival at the shed the next day and reading of the fire brigade's action, I helped to re-light them. Later on my way to the station with the letters, I went by way of the fire station, with the express intention of informing them as to what we were trying to do. But of course being a retain station manned by part timers', there was no one there to tell and the place was all locked up. When I arrived at the railway station, in the absence of Mr Brazier the station-master; Bill Floris the chief clerk suggested that I rang up Swadincote Fire Station to tell them, so that they could pass it on.

"Nothing to do with us," was the unhelpful reply, "Moira's in Leicestershire, try Coalville."

Eventually I managed to contact Coalville, who replied that although they didn't know where I meant, they would pass it on to the Moira brigade anyway.

I thanked them for their attention and also wrote a note, which I posted through the local fire station letterbox on my way back to the shed.

And do you know, they extinguished the fires again the following night.

After that I gave up. Whether we would have had any success or not, I really do not know, but I did feel fairly confident if we had been allowed to continue. At least the fire authority did not bill the railway for the call-outs. Maybe they thought better of it!

A report of these proceedings was written in reply to the next letter from the accounts department on the subject, and such was the way of things then; that nothing further was heard of on the matter.

The water supply was not restored until early in the May when, no doubt as a result of the winter weather, the rising main to the top of the tank had to be renewed as it had cracked.

Early in the March of that fateful winter, just when everyone was beginning to think that the worst was over, it began to snow. In no time at all it was up to rail level and still deepening. The walk around the East Curve when I didn't get a lift was akin to an arctic expedition, with the wind blowing at blizzard force along the top of the embankment. With the depth of snow approaching knee height, I abandoned this route altogether, opting for the longer course round by the road. One interesting point is worth a mention at this juncture. On first leaving the station by my normal route, my walk took me through the side of the goods yard and at one point, some fifty yards or so of ground would always be devoid of snow and actually steaming. This was caused by internal combustion, as the embankment at this point was actually on fire underground.

As Rawdon mine was beneath the ground here, the railway civil engineers blamed the coal board, who in their turn maintained that as it was a railway embankment; it must be the railway that was at fault. As far as I am aware, this has never been resolved. Even during the summer it was noticeably warmer over this spot, and always appeared dry even when it was raining.

On the morning of the first heavy snowfall, I was surprised to see a large completely white cylindrical object entering the shed yard with smoke and steam issuing from out of the top.

It revealed itself to be one of our '4F's which had been running up and down between Moira West Junction and Shackerstone all night in an attempt to keep the line open, manned by driver Loll Saunders and passed fireman Walter Lambell. They had been called out by the stationmaster for this purpose. They told me how they had had to charge some of the drifts to get through, and the impacted snow which adorned the engine bore testimony to their story, sticking to the engine as it did despite the heat from the boiler and smoke-box.

The 7.30 Birmingham (the 8Fturn) had been cancelled as it had not returned from its night run, courtesy of the inclement weather, so I enquired of control as to whether or not they wished the 7.30 crew to re-man the snowplough engine. They thought that this was quite a good idea, but suggested that it only ran between Measham and Shackerstone initially, as they hoped that the increased local traffic from Measham to Moira West would keep the snow under control there.

My 7.30 crew's face was a picture when I gave them the good news, as off they went to play Santa at the most southerly end of our area.

At least they could get water at Shackerstone as the supply had been restored there by then. Perhaps their local fire brigade was not so diligent.

This extreme weather was causing untold chaos throughout the country. Here at Overseal, we abandoned all attempts to run to the timetable; adopting an as required operation for the duration of the period.

The DMU's on the local passenger service made an effort to maintain their running times, but some fell by the wayside, due to the adverse conditions; being replaced by steam trains on many occasions.

My train up in the morning was often a substitute steam service with a whole variety of motive power at the head of a hastily assembled trio of coaches, invariably running late. No doubt because it hadn't been rostered until the DMU had failed to start, or had frozen up.

Ivatt Class '4's seemed to be the usual substitute motive power, with the odd '4F' or 'Black'5' turning up on occasions. Once I seem to recall a B1 at the front of our train. Goodness only knows where that had come from.

Some of the DMU's which did turn up, failed to complete the journey, though fortunately not while I was aboard.

On Wednesday morning's and indeed on Saturday's as well, an extra train was run to Leicester and back in connection with the market days in that city. This train was very well patronised, particularly from Moira onward; and usually consisted of two, three car units coupled together.

One particular Wednesday morning during this period of extreme cold and bad weather, Cyril happened to remark that it was rather late running by up the bank from Moira West to the station. We had a very good view of the bank from the shed.

Eventually the sound of a '4F' working hard was heard, so we rushed out in time to see 44434 pounding up the bank at the head of this six coach train, with passed fireman Les Clamp in charge.

It transpired that the DMU had made it as far as Gresley, only to expire in the station with fuel starvation. The driver had isolated all the engines and disconnected the drive to the gearboxes as will be explained later in the chapter. 44434 working 97 Target (Woodville Shunt) had been summoned to take the train forwards with Les insisting on taking the controls, much no doubt to the relief of the DMU driver; dressed as he would be in his nice smart green uniform suit.

Although he only signed for the road as far as Coalville, he had knowledge of the line through to Leicester, so allowed the DMU driver to conduct him for the rest of the way.

Terry Wood, his fireman described the scene at Coalville when a relieving driver appeared. Les apparently told him in no uncertain manner where he could go, embellished with certain Anglo-Saxon words when the Coalville man protested. After all Overseal passed firemen, George Swann apart, did not get many official driving turns of any sort, let alone with a passenger train; so Les was not going to pass up such a chance without a fight.

Returning light engine from Leicester, Les signed his road card as soon as he got back onto the shed. We had best draw a veil over how he got back as far as Coalville, before coming on to the piece of railway that he officially knew.

A rough diamond was Les, who would do his utmost to help the job along and never let you down.

When first introduced, the fuel pipes on the DMU's ran from the fuel tanks to the engines along the outside of the frames in straight lines. All very neat and accessible. Unfortunately, these pipes were not lagged and as a result the fuel in them froze up while running along, caused no doubt by the increased draught created, combined with the extreme cold temperature.

One DMU I was called to which had expired at Moira Station proved the case in point. On disconnecting one of these pipes to check on my diagnosis of fuel starvation, I was able, after a few very gentle taps to pull out a long straw of frozen diesel fuel; much to both the driver and the Station Master's amazement. With the aid of a blowlamp borrowed from Mr Brazier, I was able to thaw the offending pipes out and prime and restart the engines.

The unit was then driven back to Woodville Junction with Mr Brazier acting as guard to enable a shunter/guard to continue the journey back to Burton. No one was available who knew the road to Leicester, (the DMU driver excepted of course). (They should have asked Les!!).

The original guard had continued on the 'Midland Red' bus summoned by Mr Brazier to take the passengers on to Leicester, calling at all the booked station stops on the way, providing of course that the bus driver knew the way to where they all were.

Another DMU failure in Moira Station in the height of summer 1963 on a beautiful hot sunny day was of quite a different nature.

On the way up from its stop at Gresley a passenger had noticed a profound knocking and banging coming from beneath his feet, where all had been quiet and normal before. He drew the guard's attention to it, who immediately informed the driver of the situation. As they were passing Moira West Box at the time, the driver decided to continue if possible to Moira Station, which he duly did. Here, he got down and had a good look round underneath He didn't have to look far to spot the cause of the trouble. One of the gearboxes was jumping up and down, even with the engines just ticking over. He declared the train a failure (rightly so) and yours truly was sent for. Another bus was requested to take the passengers forward, and by the time that I arrived they were well on their way, courtesy of the 'Midland Red' again.

The gear boxes on these railcars are a separate item bolted to the under-frame, and connected to the engine on one side and the final drive gearbox over the bogie on the other by cardan shafts. They were manufactured by self-change gears and were relatively trouble free in service, at least while they remain attached to the railcar; which this particular one clearly wasn't.

Appraising the situation, it was fairly obvious that the only thing keeping it attached to the unit at all were the cardan shafts. If I disconnected them it would fall down and land in the four-foot between the rails, if it didn't fall on me first. As it had made it as far as Moira from Gresley in this state, I decided it was a worthwhile risk to try and get it down to the shed. So having isolated the engine by switching over the isolation switch provided (I was not sure just exactly what it did, but it stopped the engine turning, which was what I wanted). I then set about disconnecting the drive to the bogie. This being necessary as when the unit is moved, the wheels of the bogie would turn, as would everything else in the gear train.

A dog clutch was situated above the bogie, with the drive from the gearbox being connected to it via the cardan shafts as explained. To disconnect this dog clutch, a long toasting fork like tool is carried in the guard's compartment. At the end of each of the two prongs of the fork are hooks which when slid over the top of the bogie, engage in a 'T' bar on the side of this dog clutch.

When engaged, all that has to be done is to pull the fork towards you and turn through ninety degrees.

The drive is now disconnected and the bogie un-powered. This 'toasting fork' procedure just described, would have been carried out by the driver of the DMU at Gresley mentioned earlier in the chapter.

The DMU was now ready to depart for the shed by way of the East to South curve. The driver said that he did not know the road round there, whereupon Mr Brazier said "he does," and pointed at me.

The points went over, the dolly dropped off and we were on our way. Round onto the curve we went, passing under the junction starter with the left-hand arm pulled off. At the other end of the curve the home signal was off too, so we ran across the junction to stand on the bank, clear for the road to be set to reverse onto the shed.

Here the fun began. That DMU just would not reverse up the gradient and onto the shed. The driver informed me that there was already one engine isolated on the other car before the current disaster had occurred. Thus we only had two engines working, one on each unit. It should have been enough but it just wasn't. The driver decided to change ends to see if that made any difference, but it didn't.

Bob Greening in the South Box had been watching all this lack of activity, and realising from all the noise accompanied by the lack of movement that some assistance was required; had rung the shed where the 98 Target engine stood waiting for time.

My first inkling of this was to see it chuffing towards us, with Cyril hanging over the side of the cab with a big grin on his face, acting as driver. How many more rules are we going to break today, I wondered.

I dropped down onto the ground to couple up and giving Cyril the right away, we are soon over the ash-pit and safely on the shed. Hand-brake wound on and engines shut off, I quickly uncouple our '4F', and Cyril reverses her back into the shed. Now we have got our 98 Target engine trapped behind the DMU until such time as I can make it safe to move again.

The first thing to do is to secure the gearbox in its near normal position. A quick search through my stock of nuts and bolts reveals nothing long enough to reach down from its normal anchorage point to where it is hanging down, now.

I bet that Mr Topliss has something in his collection I muse, so grabbing a bike from out of the rack, I pedal off down the siding to his domain. Fortunately he is there and has soon come up with a couple of bolts of the right diameter and length. I scrounge a couple of nuts and some washers as well and am off back down the siding to do battle with the offending gearbox.

As a parting shot he remarks to me that as DMU's are coaching stock, he should have the job, not me.

"Be my guest" I reply, but he declined as I knew he would. Only a joke, more's the pity.

As I am slowly spannering the nuts up the long bolts to raise the gearbox back up into a secure position, with Cyril taking some of its weight with a long bar; Jack Harding, the 98 Target's driver arrived to book on for his turn.

I told him to sign on an hour early, and book the conducting time from Moira back on to the shed. This he did, saying that it was the easiest hour he had earned in a long time. Once I had got the gearbox back in place, I found that I could secure the other side with a much shorter bolt which I already had, but left the other long bolt in place to draw attention to the defect when it arrived back at Etches Park. It only remained to disconnect the two cardan shafts and stow them in the brake van to complete the job. I asked the driver what was wrong with the other isolated engine, as if it was to go to Derby under its own power; by far the easiest option; it was going to need it, judging by the trouble we had had just getting on to the shed. He said that he did not know as it was already isolated when he took the unit over, the driver he relieved being the one who would put the defect report in, when he signed off.

I had a look round, but could not see anything wrong with it anywhere, other than low oil level in the engine. So where could I get some oil?. Cyril suggested that I rang up the shunters' at Woodville Junction as most of them had cars. I gave him the honour of ringing up and Eureka!! One of them had got two full cans in his boot ready to do an oil change in two of their cars when they finished work that day. Within ten minutes he was walking up the siding with, one can in each hand.

I soon poured their contents into the engine and it then only required the driver to start them all up to see if it was all right. All three engines started, so with the aid of the toasting fork again, I re-engaged the dog clutch on the low engine and we were ready to go.

Cyril threw the two cardan shafts into the brake van along with the isolating fork, and I asked the driver to try a gentle run up the yard to test that the low oil level was all that was at fault with the engine. It seemed to be alright, so he reversed down onto the other road to release the 98 Target engine.

I phoned control to inform them that the DMU was now ready to return to Derby for repairs when I had organised a guard, and that the company owed me for two gallons of oil.

The guy on the other end of the phone laughed and thought I was pulling his leg, but I assured him that I was not. Cyril had paid the shunter for it, as I had not got enough money with me on that day.

When Mr Lewis came up on the following week, this oil money issue had still not been resolved. I had naturally re-embursed Cyril the very next day. The Chief Clerk at Burton with his usual stingy attitude, had flatly refused to sanction the payment, saying that that was what I was there for. To keep the job going.

As far as it went, I had to agree with him; but not to the extent of supplying and paying for my own materials. Mr Lewis for his part was full of praises for our actions in getting the unit back to Derby in such a short time, so that it could be repaired and returned to traffic without to much delay. However, he to seemed a bit reluctant to sanction the payment either; so I gave him a letter which I had prepared for the attention of the DMPS in person; for him to pass on which he was duty bound to do.

"Leave it with me and I will see what I can do," was his reply to this action, handing me the letter back as he said it.

"One week then," I answered and left it at that. As I was a little hot tempered in my younger days, I dare not pursue it any further at the time, lest I said something which I would later regret.

The problem was solved by booking me overtime, which I had not done, but as Cyril said, 'we won't be so soft next time'.

It is reasonable to say that if I had had to order the oil through the normal channels, the DMU would have been on the shed for the best part of a week. Alternatively it would have had to be towed back to Etches Park, which would have involved organising a special working with an engine, crew and guard. As Cyril said we will know better next time. But would we?. Or would we just do the same thing all over again?. Probably yes!.

During the sheds final year of operation, big things were going on at the southern end of our piece of railway. Namely, the electrification of the West Coast main line between Euston and Crewe. As this work progressed ever further northwards, amongst the train diversions in place; some of them ran over our lines. Mostly parcel trains for Manchester with the occasional fitted freight as well. The majority of these trains ran overnight and inevitably one of the engines on these trains came to grief at Overseal.

Travelling up to work on the usual DMU one morning, I glanced across towards the shed as was my habit as we crossed Moira West Junction, to see what appeared to be an '8F' still in the shed yard. So the 7.30 (Birmingham) hasn't run this morning, I assumed; a situation which did arise from time to time, usually because of the lack of a guard.

When I arrived down at the shed however, I found that the '8F' was in fact a Class '5', and a Willesden engine as well. Also that it was the only engine on the depot.

A quick glance at the night book revealed that she had run the left driving axle-box hot after leaving Nuneaton and had arrived at Overseal with the box actually on fire.

Mr Gower had sent 44528 out in place of her to continue on to Burton, where he presumed some more suitable power would be provided for the onward journey to Manchester. This was not apparently forthcoming so 44528 continued on with the train, no doubt losing even more time as she struggled with her heavy load. Just what her crew thought has gone unrecorded.

I rang up Burton to request an engine to be sent to work 98 Target, as we now had no engine to work this turn. They replied that at the moment, they had nothing suitable on the shed; but would do what they could when possible.

Round about 11 o'clock, a Burton set turned up with 43955, a Derby engine which they had been over to collect for us. They were relieved on the main line outside the shed by Don Toon and his mate, who found themselves starting their day some $1^1/_4$ hours late.

The Burton men took the Willesden Class '5', No. 45270 back with them, where she no doubt underwent attention on the drop-pit.

Another of these diverted trains to come to grief at Overseal occurred one bright sunny morning, when a Standard Class '9F' no less, failed with a stuck injector top feed clack.

As she pulled up outside the shed under clear signals, I knew that something was amiss. Clouds of steam were seen rising up from the far side of the cab as her fireman ran across to seek assistance.

I climbed up onto the running plate and tried a few tentative taps to the side and top of the clack box with my hammer, in a futile attempt to persuade the clack to re-seat. Not very hopefully, I might add. Ever conscious of the 250lb of boiler pressure contained within, it was only a bit of show; to let it be seen that something had been tried. I knew it and the driver knew it.

"Would you like me to fail it and offer you one of our wonderful '4F's," I asked him.

"Well its not very clever is it?" the London man replied.

"OK then, bring it on the shed and drop the fire, while I find you another engine" was my answer to that comment. If you are in charge, then you have to be seen to be in charge and tolerate no nonsense. Engines were conspicuous in there absence at that time of the morning, but I could soon have got the Woodville Junction shunt engine up.

"What are we going to get, that there wheelbarrow?," came the cynical reply.

"Just do it," I answered, and turned away to go back to the shed. As I was climbing down the steps he apologised and said that if he managed to go on to Nuneaton, would I wire for another engine there.

This I agreed to do, warning him that it was his responsibility now as I had made my opinion clear.

So ended another incident, or so we thought.

"I bet he doesn't stop here again in a hurry," Cyril commented afterwards.

Later that same day, I received a phone call from control asking me for a report on my part in the saga. Apparently, the '9F' had failed completely just short of Stockingford with fire having to be thrown out as she had run out of water and could not make it to the water crane there.

I said that I would send them a letter, as I felt that the driver was in enough trouble without it being broadcast around the district by our very public telephone system.

However, that did not stop the 'bobby' at Moira South ringing me about five minutes later to enquire as to his fate. Thus making my caution proved.

Apart from the obvious reason of being my superior and having Overseal under his ultimate control and responsibility, Mr Lewis also had another reason for visiting us on a Thursday's. He was coming to collect his eggs.

Apparently, long before my tenure at Overseal, a fire had occurred across from the shed by the field sidings', causing the boundary fence to catch alight.

Some quick action by the shed staff in taking an engine across to extinguish this fire with aid of the slacking pipe and buckets of water, had won the undying gratitude of the farmer concerned. Mr Lewis, who of course had had nothing what so ever to do with the dousing of the flames, being captain of the ship and receiving the rewards. The fact that a spark from a passing engine had probably started the fire in the first place, of course not entering in to the story. Thus every Thursday morning, someone from the farm would appear with a dozen nice brown ones; neatly packed in two egg boxes, tied together with string. Their approach being announced by the inevitable phone call from the South Box of "cluck cluck the egg man cometh," followed on occasions by other clucking sounds from all or some of the other phones in the circuit. The Palladium couldn't match this area for entertainment!!.

Mr Lewis on arrival would make himself comfortable in my chair as was his right, and drink my tea whilst eating his sandwiches and discussing the business of the day. The sandwich box would then change roles to that of egg carrier for the return journey.

One sunny summer afternoon of the last year at Overseal, I was sitting in my office writing the usual instructions in the night book for Mr Gower prior to leaving for the station and home, when Eric popped his head around the door to say, " Closey's coming up the bank. Let's' see if he makes it today."

Such was the boredom prevailing at the time, and desperate for some distraction to brighten the day, however mediocre. I nipped out of the office to watch the spectacle with him. And what a spectacle it turned out to be.

The bank in question of course being the climb from Donisthorpe up the ever-increasing gradient, courtesy of the mining subsidence; to Moira South Junction. Driver Johnny Close, who incidentally lived quite near to me at Burton, had the un-envious reputation of having to be pulled off the bank having failed to make the climb, more times than any other Overseal man. Hence Eric's remarks.

He had 44552 on 95 Target that day, one of our better Class '4F's, if such a beast existed. So we reasoned that he had a fairly good chance, what with the dry rail etc. But there is always one thing which on these occasions contrives to add a problem to the eventual success of many an event, and this day was no exception. The home signal protecting the South Junction remained steadfastly at danger. Looking to our right towards Moira West, a brake-van and the end of the previous train was still visible under the Spring Cottage road bridge. Obviously held at Woodville Junction signals'.

44552 could be heard pounding away up the bank like a 'good un' obviously working flat out with her heavy load. As she hove into view above the bank, that South Junction signal remained on, so with only yards to go Johnny had to shut off and apply his brake. Just as he did so, the signal cleared so Johnny threw the regulator wide open again in the hope of regaining the momentum which he had all but lost.

He managed to just clear the actual junction with the engine and we both thought that he had in fact managed to make it, when it all became to much for poor old 44552 who went into a violent slip and fractured the left hand driving crank pin.

The way those side-rods bent, twisted and straightened on the right hand side, the side incidentally that we were viewing from; defies description. I would never have believed that a piece of steel could have performed the gyrations that those rods did that day, had I not witnessed it myself.

Eric and I dashed across and dropped some brakes levers down on the following wagons before returning to the engine to survey the damage. Apart from the obvious damage to the side-rods, which would have to be removed before the engine could be moved again, both front steps were now bent outwards at such an angle as to possibly foul the adjacent running road.

As Eric and I set about removing the side-rods from 44552, the Woodville 'Jocko' arrived to couple on to the front to attempt to haul her and her train off the bank. The engine off the 6.50am Birmingham stood on the shed, as her afternoon turn had been cancelled, so I got her crew to bring her out also to couple ahead of the Woodville engine.

When we had removed the rods and loaded and secured them onto the framing, for which there was no shortage of muscle power, with all the crews to hand; the cavalcade was ready to move off.

With three '4F's, two of which were obviously 0-6-0's and 44552 now a 2-2-2, the wagons were soon on the move, even before Eric had lifted all those wagon brakes off.

Once the whole train was clear of the bank and on the level, 44552 was uncoupled, with the cancelled afternoon Birmingham '4F' taking over the train.

Back on the shed, a quick look round 44552 revealed no damage other than to the steps, as previously mentioned.

As I was examining her, Eric popped down the siding to see Mr Topliss to enquire if his gas bottles were full, and could we borrow them yet again please.

With the answer in the affirmative, the spare men (ex afternoon Birmingham) ran 44552 down to the wagon repair shop, where once again he performed his magic with the gas gun; while I wielded the sledge hammer. I did not want to cut the steps off if I could avoid it, much preferring to knock them back into place, or at least within gauge if possible. We managed to achieve this, so all that remained was for our crew to take her down to Burton for their onward attention. I think that Don Toon was the driver, with Mick Smith as his fireman.

With Burton informed, off they went with the 2-2-2 wheel arrangement '4F'. 'Make sure that you bring something back with you' was my parting comment to them. As mentioned earlier, in 1963, '4F's were being scrapped at any excuse, with very little wrong with them so I forecast that it would be the last time that we would see 44552.

However, her wheels were dropped out and sent to Derby Work's for repair; and thus refurbished 44552 returned to do battle once more on Donisthorpe bank and the like. She was eventually placed in store some fourteen or fifteen months later in September 1964, making her final journey to Cashmores', Great Bridge in January 1965.

Don and Mick returned with 44321 a Westhouses engine, which they said was quite the roughest '4F' that they had ever been on. So Mr Gower quite rightly allocated it to the Woodville Junction (97 Target) Shunt duty until such time as it could be exchanged for one of our own engines. I recall that the brake blocks were virtually none existent on this engine as well, necessitating me having to fit a complete new set, both engine and tender, to enable it to continue at work at all.

It was a rare event for me to have to change any brake blocks on a Burton engine, such was the standard of maintenance there.

As quoted before, the '4F's were being withdrawn and scrapped in ever increasing numbers as more and more diesel locomotives were coming on the scene. This in turn was cascading more modern steam locomotive types down the ladder to replace them on their more mundane duties. A direct result of this down loading at the commencement of the summer timetable for 1963, saw a Class '5' allocated to us to work the 95 Target turn.

Sure enough on the Saturday morning prior to the start of the summer timetable, the 89 Target ex Burton tripper arrived with Black Five No. 45059 at its head, still bearing its 17A (Derby) shed-plate. It was duly exchanged with one of our '4F's and left by the Burton men over our ash pit.

"I wonder what Gower will say when he finds out about this?," the Burton driver commented.

"It won't be very complimentary, you can be sure of that," I replied.

To quote the understatement of the year was only the half of it. A whole page and a half had been torn from the night book upon which to vent his thoughts, and pushed into my desk drawer; quoting agreements and expressing his displeasure in no uncertain terms.

I must confess to having a certain amount of sympathy with what he was saying, as I had had a go at coaling the stage myself on more than one occasion. It was enough for one man to do to keep the '8F' supplied, without having another Stanier tender to coal for the Class '5' as well. A note was left to the effect that I would forward his letter down to Burton for the attention of Mr Lewis, trying to explain the situation to him at the same time with regards to the ever increasing shortage of more traditional small tender fitted engines.

When Mr Lewis came up on the Thursday, ostentatiously to check on the depot, but as we know primarily for his eggs; I suggested to him that he might be able to exchange one of our Class '8F's for a 'Fowler' tender equipped one, to help to ease the problem. At the same time It would show that the management do listen to reasonable requests and grievances from their staff.

He said that he would look into it and see what could be done. As he had only a few more weeks left to serve before his retirement, I did risk mentioning that it would be a nice parting gesture on his part which would be much appreciated by the staff, if he could pull it off.

When he had gone I told Cyril the gist of the conversation, knowing full well that the jungle drums would beat loudly and Mr Gower would be in the know before I had returned the next morning. On informing George Swann the LDC man the following day, his only comment was that we would wait and see.

"Even if it happens," he added, "he'll (meaning Mr G) still moan about the coal rails."

Mr Lewis's replacement when he came was to my delight, my old mate from Derby Works days, one Michael Rowledge. We retired, as the saying goes to the Navigation Inn, our nearest hostelry; to discuss the business of the day and catch up on old times. A couple of pints later, as nothing had so far materialised with regards to a Fowler tender fitted Class '8F', I asked him to make some enquires about it himself, which he agreed to do.

"Shouldn't be to difficult," he said, "A couple of phone calls should do it. They've got engines they don't know what to do with these days."

So, well pleased I walked him back to the shed and down to his car, feeling quietly confident with the way the afternoon's events had gone.

Michael penned me a note which I received via the letter bag the following week, quoting that the official answer to his request was, 'there are none available owing to operating requirements'; the classic standard, can't be bothered with it statement. Not, I might add originating from Michael, but from the powers that be, (or try to be).

While all this deliberation was going on, one of our Class'8F's failed at Water Orton while working the night Birmingham, with leaking tubes. Saltley provided a Standard Class '9F' no less as a replacement, No. 92136; and we continued to use it on the job for the rest of the week. The favourite stabling point for the '8F' was on the coal-stage road in between turns, but this road was banned to '9F's in the official restrictions book. Imagine my concern therefore on the Saturday morning, to find the '9F' parked thereon. One of the Saturday morning Birmingham's was regularly being cancelled now owing to a shortage of guards', and this morning was no exception.

I poked my head round the mess room door to behold a rare spectacle for Overseal. A full set of men without a job.

"When you've finished your tea," the inevitable brew being to hand, "Could you very carefully bring your engine off the coal road and park it some-where else," I requested. To add strength to the matter, I pointed out the restriction in the book.

"Well I never knew that," was the reply. "I wonder why that is?."

"Probably because of the wheel-base around the curve," I suggested "Anyway, when you are ready, and take your time."

About half an hour later, control rang to order the '9F' to be taken down to Burton, so it was just a matter of driving off the coal road and straight out on to the line.

"Is it all right to take it round the East curve to turn, or do we have to go tender first?," was the somewhat sarcastic reply to my instructions.

"Look it up in your book," was my terse answer.

Standing outside the shed one lunchtime watching the shunting by 89 Target, while waiting to exchange the letter bags, another amusing occurrence happened. I am not quite sure how it came about, but between them the shunters' managed to put a bogie bolster wagon down two roads at once.

Bogie vehicles were not very common in our neck of the woods, and this one had appeared on behalf of the civil engineers department and carried a long but not particularly large girder upon it, the purpose of which, I have no idea.

However, there it now stood with one truck on one road and the other on the adjacent one. Fortunately the leading end came into contact with some wagons already down the siding before the rear end did, and with only a gentle impact (for a railway wagon) came to a halt with all wheels still on the rails. With the speed of light, a heavy rope was acquired from goodness know where, with which to haul it back. In their haste to put things right, the shunters' failed to notice that the bogie bolster had in fact locked buffers on one side with the wagon it had hit, which along with the five wagons behind it, were full of coal. Consequently, when an attempt was made to haul the bogie bolster back up the siding, it was not just that which was being towed, but the five loaded coal wagons as well. It is hard to believe just how far a rope will stretch before it breaks. It surprised me, I can tell you. The '4F' on the other end leapt forwards as it snapped with a loud tearing noise.

And guess who they sent for next. Mr Topliss of course. So I went down to give him a helping hand as he crawled beneath the first coal wagon and knocked out the cotter retaining the offending buffer in place. After removing the rubber compression rings, a few blows with the good old sledgehammer had the buffing head and spindle protruding through the casting. I then managed to lever it right out until it fell on to the ground with the aid of his large crowbar, and yet another crisis was over. The shunters' had tied the two ends of their rope together while all this was going on, and this time their efforts met with success.

With everything back to normal again, all and sundry disappeared back into their hidey-holes until the next time.

At this time, quite a lot of our loco coal was arriving on the shed in old wooden wagons stencilled, LOCO COAL. ONE JOURNEY ONLY. CONDEMNED WAGON. WIRE INSTRUCTIONS FOR DISPOSAL

This legend on the wagon sides, bode yet another form to fill in when the wagon was empty. I used to wait until we had three or four for disposal before sending a completed form down to Burton in the letter bag. By now the wagons concerned were back down the siding anyway, awaiting a last look over by Harry Bird prior to making their final journey to the breakers.

Some of them looked to my untutored eye to be in quite good condition, but then I suppose that it was the same for wagons as it was for the locos' that pulled them. There were just to many of them about.

Our Class '5' was frequently being borrowed over the weekends to presumably work excursions to various places. The usual arrangement was for it to change over with the engine on 89 Target on a Friday lunchtime. The change over engine was usually still a '4F', though not always a Burton one, with the occasional stranger turning up from time to time.

One of these oddities, kindly lent to us from Derby, was an Ivatt Class '4' 2-6-0. Within half an hour of it going off the shed to commence its afternoon duty, I received a phone message from Donisthorpe Box to inform me of the fact that its fireman had met with an accident. The Coal Board ambulance was taking him down to Burton Hospital, even as he spoke. As I had Terry Wood doing a bit of labouring about the yard following his early shift firing on 96 Target, I asked him if he would take over the fireman's duties until I could arrange a relief around tea time. I had another of my 'workaholic' firemen on 98 Target. I intended to get in touch with him to ask if he would swap over and complete the duty. This was duly arranged.

Now on these Ivatt '4's, the regulator handle is of the pull out type, a most unusual arrangement for an LMS engine. Furthermore it is duplicated on the fireman's side also, connected one to the other by a simple linkage across the firebox front. Hence, when the driver pulls out his handle, the one on the fireman's side comes out as well. Apparently as the injured fireman was bending forwards to operate the damper controls, the handle came out and cracked him quite hard on the head, knocking him out. Charlie Moulton the driver said afterwards that he went down as if he had been pole-axed. The coal board first aid man who was called to attend to him, quite rightly sending him to hospital.

I learned that this was by no means the first time that firemen's heads had come into contact with this duplicate handle, but not presumably with such dire consequences. Charlie brought his engine back up to the shed light engine, with the guard acting as second man, to collect Terry and thus continue his afternoons work. The fireman, whose name I cannot recall, was off work for two weeks.

The union took up his case for loss of earnings, obtaining reports from Charlie, the coal board first aid man and one of their shunters, who was present on the footplate at the time, with which to fight his claim. I for my part had to pen a character report for him also, outlining his experience on this class of engine, which was nil.

'Ivant' Class '4MT' 2-6-0 No. 43057. Photo: P. Groom.

The ASLEF representative confided in me after the enquiry that they had a whole file full of complaints concerning this class of engine, a number of which were about this same piece of equipment which was rarely if ever used. I believe that a small monetary settlement was paid in this instance, which would be most welcome to the recipient, as no sick pay scheme was in place at the time for railwaymen. Their only income when off work being the state payment.

Another of our overtime firemen was Ian Hall. I remembered him from my apprentice days when he was employed in the office as a list clerk. He must have transferred to the footplate grades, but I was unaware of this until I arrived at Overseal. He had one abiding fault however, which as has been seen earlier in this book; I once suffered from too. That of getting out of bed in the mornings. This particular week, he was rostered to work on the afternoon 96 Target, booking on at around 1/35pm. He was however also covering the first half of the middle turn Woodville Shunt duty (97 Target) that week, whose driver was Alvin Southerd.

On I think about the Wednesday lunchtime, say 12' o clock I received a phone call from Alvin saying that Ian had not turned up and asking how he was going to get round to the shed for engine duties?. He was shunting at Rawdon colliery sidings at the time, which was just opposite Moira West Box on the far side of the Burton to Leicester main line. Having no fireman spare on the depot at the tine, I left Cyril in command and went up myself. A raft of wagons was just being hauled out of the colliery with 44527 at its head. I went across and climbed aboard as she steamed by. Alvin was looking over the side watching for the shunters' signals and Les Skelton, the guard was comfortably stretched out on the fireman" seat.

A quick look at the gauge showed about 140lb on the clock, the glass showed a full boiler of water but the fire looked a bit run down. Les said that he had put a bit on it about half an hour ago and had just knocked the injector off.

They had been so busy he added, that Alvin hadn't had much time to see to her himself.

So taking up the shovel, I fed a few around the box. Probably three down each side with a couple under the door and one down the middle. I thought that I had done with firing loco's out on the line, '4F's in particular, and here I was with the shovel in my hand, yet again. Unbeknown to me however, all we had got to do was haul this raft of wagons up to Woodville Junction, about half a mile away and drop them onto a brake; ready for the afternoon Birmingham. Then we were right away to the shed. Les, being based at the Junction, got off and away we went. We arrived on the shed with a healthy fire, a full glass of water, 175lbs on the clock and the safety valves blowing their head off, due to my ministrations. All I could do was to drop the damper and open the doors.

Stan Kirby when he arrived off the morning 96 Target, decided to leave cleaning the fire until later as it wasn't in its normal run down state. The others present lost no time in telling him who the guilty party was. Obviously, he decided to keep his thoughts and opinions to himself when he found out.

Apparently the normal procedure was for the preceding fireman to clean the fire before the relieving man took over. This I decided was taking my temporary firing duties too far. If only Alvin had made me aware of what we were doing, I would have left the fire well alone.

Ian arrived about this time, full of apologies so I awarded him the honour of cleaning it, but Stan told him not to bother; no doubt more sarcastically than it is written here.

Just to rub salt into the wound he overslept again on the Friday, with the result that this time I found myself firing from around half past ten in the morning. There was a need to take a load down to Drakelow Power Station, an occasional requirement of the 97 Target duty, as mentioned in an earlier chapter.

Still with 44527, we set off with a full load of 24$\frac{1}{2}$ tonners.

Alvin had prepared a good fire before I got down to him, so with a full glass, hot fire and safety valves sizzling we were away, following the wake the mid-morning DMU to Burton.

Remembering to look back for the wave from Les, I gave Alvin the nod and we pulled out of Rawdon sidings and onto the main line. With all the train on the move, Alvin pulled the gear up about a turn and I opened the doors and fed another round into the box. Trying to remember all that I had learned about firing these fickle machines, I endeavoured to put up a good performance. I realised that any errors on my part would be much discussed back at the shed and all over the district.

Boxing her up just before we entered the tunnel at Gresley, I increased the opening on the blower to avoid the risk of a blowback. As we came out the other side I opened up and fed another round in ready for the climb out of Gresley Station towards Coton Park. The DMU was naturally well down the line by now, so with the back-un's off, we were sure of a clear run right into the Power Station.

Alvin dropped the lever down into full gear as we heaved our heavy train up the gradient out of the station and under the A444 road bridge. This brick-arched structure had suffered badly from mining subsidence over the years, and now stood on about six feet of packing between the ends of the arch and the original brick piers. 44527's exhaust was a joy to hear as it echoed off the side of the factory walls of Bonas's just beyond. The firehole doors banging in unison with every beat as she forged up the incline. Another two rounds onto the fire and we were over the top with a level and descending grade now before us all the way into Drakelow. The injector, which had been on throughout the journey had managed to maintain the water level down to about half a glass as we topped this last rise prior to descending towards our destination, so a quick top up was called for with the second one. A squirt round with the slacking pipe to lay the dust and I could relax on my seat for the rest of the way. I added one last round to the fire as we passed Drakelow box. We came to a stand in the full sidings there and 44527 lifted her valves, which filled me with delight I had mastered the dreaded 4F, at last I thought and said as much to Alvin.

"This is a good one," he answered, "There not all like this."

'Tell me about it', I thought. We had still to go back yet, no doubt with a full load of empties. But let it be said, I did feel quietly confident.

While Alvin went to the cabin to mash a can of tea, I got the rake down and pulled the excess coal ash and clinker from beneath the arch, lifting three or four pan fulls' out onto the ballast. Spreading the rest around the box, to my satisfaction, keeping it thin at the front and thicker under the door and down the sides. A round of fresh fuel added and I was ready for the return journey.

Alvin came back with the tea and after enjoying a lid full, we set off round the triangle to turn. This manoeuvre completed, we filled the tank prior to backing down to the empty side, collecting Les's brake-van on the way.

Dropping the brake on the back, we ran round to the other end, where the CEGB shunter coupled us up and Les gave us the load back. A mixture of 16ton, 21ton and 24½ ton mineral wagons, all empties of course, amounting to a full load for a Class '4' engine over this road.

The shunter was a bit intrigued as to who the strange fireman was, dressed in a shirt, pullover and serge trousers.

I am not sure what Les told him in reply, but they both went off laughing, whether at my expense or Ian's. Probably mine!.

"Any minute now," Alvin disturbed my thoughts so opening up the damper and closing the doors, I checked the water level for the umpteenth time and note the gauge, nicely on 170lb.

As we get the right away, 44527's valves lift again, no doubt as a result of opening the damper and lifting the blower.

Another two down each side with two more under the door and we ease down to the junction at the head of the triangle, still within the power station. Here the CEGB have their own signal-box controlling traffic in, out and around their site. They have two or three large six coupled diesel locomotives of their own for use within the complex. As I had not been inside the power station sidings before, I was most interested to see all that was going on.

An 'Overseal" 4F is working hard with a load of empty 24$^1/_2$ tonners as she passes Gresley Box and attacks the climb through the tunnel to Woodville junction. Photo: Authors Collection.

Another full train ran in from the Burton direction with a Toton '8F' at its head and crossed over in front of us, probably from the Nottinghamshire coalfields'. Behind him, another '8F' steamed by, this time heading up the branch in the same direction as we going; with another full train of empties.

"Probably a Coalville," Alvin said, "We will be following him I shouldn't wonder ."

And so it proved to be. The journey back to Rawdon is mainly uphill, apart from the welcome respite from Coton Park to Gresley Station; so I didn't put the shovel down for long on the return trip. We ran into Rawdon sidings with just under half a glass of water and 140lbs on the clock. I had not touched the fire since emerging from Gresley tunnel as I anticipated that we would be going on to the shed afterwards.

Passing Woodville Junction box, I had noticed our sleepy eyed fireman standing outside. He soon caught up with us and climbed aboard as we stood in Rawdon, full of apologies again.

Alvin got down off the footplate as he anticipated that I would have words to say to the gentleman.

In truth there was not a lot that I could say to him as he had turned up for his booked turn, the work which I had just done on his behalf being extra.

Threatening to exclude him from this extra work opportunity in the future; which formed a very lucrative addition to his income had him begging and pleading to still be included in the arrangement.

I suggested that he invested part of his next wage packet in the loudest alarm clock which he could find and left it at that. The annoying part of the whole episode on both days was that he still had to have the time booked to him, as I wasn't even meant to be there in the first place.

But it kept the job going, and truth to say, I had quite enjoyed the experience. And we arrived back on the shed in time for Ian to clean the fire for Stan Kirby.

Alvin, for his part seemed quite pleased with my efforts and asked me jokingly (I hope) if I was booking myself on the night Birmingham with him the next week, which I graciously declined. In bed that night, I could hear 44527 barking away in my mind as I dropped off to sleep. Firing a '4F'?. nothing to it !!.

So life went on at Overseal, running on a shoestring, rules being bent, sometimes almost to breaking point; every day.

Every week and some days within those weeks being a challenge, with all sorts of problems, some large and some small, being solved, time after time.

Ian never, as far as I was aware let me down again, so maybe he did invest in that loud alarm clock after all.

Chapter 19

An Indian Summer

During the first summer of my tenure at Overseal, whenever a special traffic notice appeared in the letter bag which affected our area of working, our shed was conspicuous in its absence when requirements for the provision of engines and or crew was needed.

Apart from the occasional ballast trains over various weekends, special excursion workings requiring assisting engines around the' Swad-Woodville Loop' were appearing virtually every Saturday and Sunday. These workings were all being allocated to either Burton or Coalville sheds.

During one of my discussions with George Swann, our LDC representative I mentioned this to him, asking if we at Overseal had ever covered duties in the past. He confirmed that indeed we had, though not for a number of years, as I had suspected. He felt sure that our men would be only to happy to cover such a duty should the occasion arise and added (surprise, surprise) that an agreement for the manning of these extra workings was already in place.

He went on to say that there should be a register somewhere in the depths of the cupboard with all the names of the drivers and firemen, turns worked, dates, etc, recorded; to enable as fair an allocation of duties as possible to be carried out. When he had left to take up his next duty, I had a good rummage round in the various cupboards until I had unearthed the aforementioned ledger.

Ballast trains I realised, being of a full days work or more; would not be too difficult to roster, but conducting and or providing assisting engines around the loop were a different matter, as the traffic was rarely heavy enough to constitute a reasonably full days work. With preparing and disposal time, I was looking at around six hours actual work in traffic if we were providing a pilot engine. As the journey time from Moira to Burton via the loop including stops at Woodville and Swadlincote was no more than 45 minutes each way, a single train working was out of the question, as I would not be able to support any claim for economic working which after all had to be proved to control's satisfaction, before they would consider allocating any work to us

Burton, I discovered worked these extra jobs with men out of the control link, who in all probability would have been sitting around waiting for a job in any case, particularly at weekends.

Coalville on the other hand, apparently booked a set of men on especially for the job; returning light engine from Burton if, as often happened; no reasonable return working was available. Two to two and a half-hours in traffic, maximum. This latter detail gleaned from the Moira West signalman.

A chat with the control obtained a promise that they would remind the train arrangers that we did indeed exist. This to my amazement culminated in a phone call from this very august body the very next week, asking me if I could provide an engine and two crews for a Donisthorpe ballast the following weekend. I immediately replied in the affirmative, and set out about making arrangements for the same.

To give the drivers a fair share of these extra duties, the passed firemen; who at a large depot would have had prior call for driving; were considered as just firemen for the purpose; this making thirteen drivers and thirteen firemen available for the extra work. This was how the local arrangement worked.

A study of the ledger revealed the next four men as listed for the duty. I then had to check if their Saturday and Monday rostered turns were affected by this extra work as the crews had to have a twelve-hour break between duties. If this was indeed the case, then the next man available had to be allotted the work. There was one thing for sure, if I got it wrong, I wouldn't have to wait very long before someone came bursting through the office door to point out the error to me. When George came on duty, I pointed out my findings to him, which he approved. He suggested that I personally notify the men concerned as well as just writing up the roster and alteration sheet, as Sunday work was, as has been seen; quite a rarity As he was to be one of the firemen, that only left three people to see. Of these, one of the drivers declined the duty; thus causing me to peruse the ledger further. Eventually all was settled and true to say, I was quite pleased with the outcome of my efforts to intercede on my staffs behalf.

Another ballast was forthcoming the following week, so with two thirds of my men now having had a Sunday turn, things were looking up. Interestingly, the roster clerk at Burton was at great pains to phone and inform me on both occasions of the impending duties. I got the impression that he did not think that we should have had the work at all, and no doubt had the appropriate men set in his mind to cover it, had I so requested. There was always much rivalry between depots in an area, vying for work and the opportunity to steal the odd duty, one from the other was a regular thing.

Quite a few ballast trains came our way during the ensuing months, sometimes relaying, but usually combating the effects of mining subsidence, with which the district was rife. If a relatively small ballast train was required, the wagons and brake would be worked up as part of the 89 Target working from Burton,. But with a larger load, the engine used for the 7-30 Birmingham which rarely ran on a Saturday, was used; with its booked crew running down to Burton to collect it. Otherwise it made a job for a set of Burton men who would only be sitting around in the canteen shuffling dominoes and drinking tea.

The two local football teams, Gresley Rovers and Burton Albion were both doing reasonably well in their respective leagues at the time and as a result, were generating the odd supporters special to convey fans to the away matches. I was quick to point out how ideally placed we were to provide the pilot engine for such events as we could justify the lay over time between the outwards and return journeys on such duties.

These 'footex' as they were called naturally ran on a Saturday and therefore it was assumed that we would not have any available motive power to carry out the work. I soon pointed out that 98 Target did not run on a Saturday, and therefore I did have an engine available for the job. But the powers that be thought otherwise and Burton got the work, using a 'Crab' and six coaches which managed the job unassisted; until one wet and windy day when one of the illustrious 'Reidinger Crabs' stuck on the bank out of Woodville Station, coming to a stand in the close confines of the single line tunnel under the village and the A50. After several setbacks and attempts, the Woodville 'jocko' was sent for to rescue the train, carrying on at the head, along with the 'Crab' as far as Coalville. It was fortunate that our 4F was still available as, with her fire rundown, she was only waiting for the 'footex' to come down the bank and clear the junction, before going onto the shed, where her fire would have been thrown out prior to her being stabled for the weekend.

As I have stated in a previous chapter, the 4Fs were being withdrawn ever more frequently, thereby posing an ever increasing problem in finding the right motive power with which to do the job. One particular occasion comes to mind with the 4F currently working the 96 Target being two days overdue a boiler washout. Having drawn Burton's attention to this fact, of which naturally they were aware; they replied that they just had not got a suitable engine on the place to swap it over with.

When I added that she was priming badly; not strictly true; but I knew that it would not be long before she was, such was our water supply, despite its constant dosing daily with tablets as mentioned earlier. They said that they would see what they do in that case.

Sure enough when 89 Target appeared, there at its head was a 'Jubilee', no less. Burton of course had quite a few of these on her books by now, these fine engines having been cascaded down the league tables by the all conquering diesels.

No. 45668 'Madden' was pristine in her very smart clean coat of lined green paintwork. Obviously very recently outshopped after a general overhaul.

"What are we taking back?" her driver asked as I exchanged the letter bags with him.

"You've never brought this up for us, have you?" I questioned in reply.

"'Fraid so" he answered, "Not exactly a coal train engine is she."

And so the exchange was made, with Bill Clemson and Terry Wood taking her off the shed at the start of their afternoon stint on 96 Target.

"Gower is going to love that thing turning up tonight," was Eric's comment. I knew what he meant as it would mean that he and Cyril would have no less than three Stanier tenders to coal, as well as one of the 4Fs with coal rails on her tender.

Stan Kirby was just finishing his turn on the early Birmingham and was hovering around hoping to be asked to do a bit of overtime about the shed. So I got him to help Eric to coal the stage, putting enough up there for the 8F off the second 'Brum', the Class '5' off 95 Target and now our 'Jubilee' off 96 Target as well.

About three o'clock that afternoon we all gathered out of the end of the shed to hear her come up the bank, and when she did; that superb three cylinder beat was a joy to listen to. Up she came like a good 'un', the beat slowly getting more prolonged as she reached the top.

"Terry's earning his money today," was Stan's remark as she hove into view, her exhaust shooting high into the sky. As she came by, I could see that the die block was right up at the top of the expansion link. Full gear, no less.

With half her train or more over the bank, Bill eased the regulator and 45668 blew off at her valves. Terry immediately leaned out of the cab and waved his hat to the assembled spectators.

What a fine happy crowd we were up here I reflected; which was more than could be said for some of the places I had been.

However this happy state of affairs was doomed to come to an untimely end in the not to distant future.

45668 continued to work the same job the following day, but following instructions overnight, Mr Gower put her on the 7-30 Birmingham the following day; with the' 8F' being kept on the 97 Target Woodville Junction Shunt, for change over at lunchtime; much to her driver Charlie Moulton's disgust. As mentioned before, the '8F's were not popular on this shunting turn.

When 45668 arrived at Bromford Bridge on her second run with the night turn, Saltley; at control's behest, pinched her for one of their turns; substituting 44172, a Rowsley '4F' in her place. This engine would not please Mr Gower either as she had a snowplough tender which as the reader may be aware, had a second bunker built inside the original Fowler tender; with sliding doors over the top.

The following day I was on the phone to Burton to complain about the unsuitability of the Rowsley snowplough engine for our needs, only to learn that Mr Gower had beaten me to the draw by moaning to them about it overnight. It was soon changed, and life went back to peace and quiet again. At least until the next time.

To return briefly to 'Madden'. This fine engine was placed in store some eight months after her debut at Overseal (spring of 1963).In the December of that year; making her last journey to Crewe Works the following month, January 1964, where she was cut up What a waste of a fine locomotive, withdrawn just over one year after her last overhaul. Such was the indecent haste to dispose of the steam engine in the face of the advancing diesel and electric power then coming on stream.

One sunny May afternoon in 1964, with Cyril up on the stage coaling the '8F' for its night run, I was sitting relaxed in my chair thinking of nothing in particular, the only sound being the '4F' off the 6-50 Birmingham gently hissing in the shed outside.

My reverie was broken by the buzzing of the phone on the wall to my left. It was the 'bobby' from Moira West Signalbox, and what he had to say was to change the life of myself and everybody else at Overseal forever.

"There's three posh limo's just drawn up with what looks like a load of gaffers in them, and there coming your way!," was his alarming message," Thought you'd like to know."

As I have mentioned before, you cannot creep up on this shed without being seen by someone, no matter which way you try.

I resolved to appear to be busy, as I had no idea whom they were, having received no prior notification of the visit.

So with ledger open and pen poised, the scene was set and I was ready. However they did not do me the courtesy of calling in my office first, but continued up the yard; where they stood in a group looking at the '8F' alongside the coal stage.

Its down to me then, I decided. So I left the office and walked down the yard towards them. There were seven of them in total, all dressed in dark suits and wearing black 'homburg' hats. Rather like a posse of undertakers, I thought, and as it transpired; not an unlikely simile either.

Six of them were strangers to me, the seventh being Mr Bertram Stanier; Sir William's brother, who I had met before.

"Can I help you gentlemen?," I enquired, in a more friendly tone than I really felt.

"Ah, Mr Fleming, there you are!, how nice to meet you again," Mr Stanier replied. "As we came along, I was telling my colleagues that this shed had been closed for twelve months, and here it is all in working order, with engines and everything. I hope you are going to help me out here!!."

'You haven't changed then', I thought, 'Still as out of touch as ever'.

I gave a sick smile and said to myself, 'It won't be long now then before we are closed. In any case if the place was closed, why did he expect to see me here; which he must have done; otherwise he would not have known my name'.

What I replied was that it was common courtesy to announce ones presence who ever you were, before wandering all around the place, as I was responsible for the safety of all visitors, irrespective of their status or standing.

'That's your career prospects out of the door, I thought', even as I said it.

Two of the entourage smirked at this comment, whereas the others positively glowered.

'I'll be lucky to be in charge of a brush next week', I thought, never mind an engine shed; on seeing their reaction.

However, I went on to try and sell the depot for the efficient unit it was, pointing out the nearness of the various collieries upon which we relied for our trade; emphasising the good relations we enjoyed with the local coal board. Also the very minimum amount of light engine running involved to reach our trains, and anything else that I could think of to present Overseal in a good and favourable light.

In fairness to them, who incidentally were never introduced to me; they heard me out and never questioned anything I said, though deep down I knew that I was wasting my breath. It was obviously already decided. Only when still needed to be settled.

I gave them the conducted tour and offered them all a cup of tea, which they refused. Probably got some thing stronger waiting in the cars.

Then, with barely a goodbye and without the handshake, customary on these occasions; they made their way back to the comfort(s) of the limousines and went on their way; presumably back to Derby.

Hardly had they passed through the gates at Spring Cottage, when the phone rang again .It was the 'bobby' at Moira West again.

"When do you shut then?," was his terse question.

I told you dear reader that they don't mince words around here, didn't I

"I have no idea," I replied truthfully," But I bet it won't be long now."

I rang down to Burton and asked to speak to Mr Lewis who was in his last weeks of office at the time, prior to his retirement. He said that he would come up the following day, (not his usual egg day) and we could discuss it then. Very wise, as neither he nor I wished to converse about such a serious and delicate matter over the very open railway phone system.

As George Swann was on the early Birmingham that week as the driver, I left him a note to see if he could arrange to exchange duties with either the 95 or 96 Target driver so that he would have a chance of attending the meeting with Mr Lewis and myself.

This he must have managed to do, as within minutes of Mr Lewis's arrival, he walked into the office; having apparently made a second exchange of footplates with the second shift 97 Target driver.

Mr Lewis had already heard of my less than friendly remarks to the septuplet of the previous day, and while agreeing with my attitude in principle; hinted that there were times when one should keep ones thoughts to oneself, and that this was one of them. And you can't argue with that!.

He had endeavoured to smooth things over on my behalf with the powers that be; putting my remarks down to the impetuousness of youth.

He, George and I enjoyed a very frank and informative discussion, the main topics being of course naturally the forthcoming closure; and the fate of the staff employed at the depot. Mr Lewis had a lot of good advice to offer and George for his part had already, with great foresight obtained considerable information on the subject from the union, in this case , the ASLEF. I for my part resolved to obtain the same from the NUR, of which I was a member. As a date for closure had not at that point been set, very little more could be done at the time, so after consuming the tea and biscuits which Cyril had provided, (where had those cookies come from) George left us to rejoin his fireman on the Woodville Junction Shunt.

As he left, the phone rang yet again and on answering it, Bill Greening's voice from Moira South Box announced, "The egg man cometh - - Cluck, Cluck, Cluck.." So Mr Lewis got his eggs after all, even though it was the wrong day. How did the vendor know?. Yet another example, if ever one was needed that you cannot approach Overseal without being seen.

I felt that on that day at least, he had earned them.

For the next few days, I was bombarded with questions concerning this very grave matter, but was unable to shed any more light upon it than was already known.

"Have you 'eared 'owt yet Gaffer," was the question ringing in my ears every day, and who could blame them. They were not the only ones at Overseal to be worried about their future. I was equally concerned myself.

In common with the rest of them, I to had a mortgage to pay; car payments to meet, children to clothe, feed and educate and a wife to provide for. My gas and electric bill had to be paid and the rates met. So we were all in the same boat. Or a least most of us were. Naturally some of the older drivers were more settled and presumably better placed financially as one would expect, but then that is the usual situation in any society.

The following week the official notice was issued, the date being set to coincide with the miners annual holidays, traditionally being the first two weeks of August. Thus our last working day became the last Saturday of July 1964.

When the date became known, very few were surprised as it was the obvious time to do it. Though, let it be said logic and the railway rarely go hand in hand in my experience.

Close on the heels of the notice came the all regions vacancy list for footplate grades. These were naturally perused with great interest by most of the staff, with some of the comedians; pretending to plum for the most outrageous and unlikely depots.

In truth, they all applied for either Burton, Derby, Toton or Coalville; with some of the older drivers and Cyril taking the redundancy offered.

As their chosen depots were not a foregone conclusion, I vowed to do all in my power that I could to ensure that they actually achieved the moves which they desired. I felt that I owed them my best endeavours in recognition of the unstinting loyalty that they in their turn had shown me during the previous two years.

The firemen in particular had endured considerable disruption and alteration to their rostered duties, not always at an advantage to them; financially or otherwise.

In most cases, the transfer to the depot of their choice was achieved without any problems at all; but in two instances this was not so. One was to Derby and the other one to Toton.

The Derby one proved to be a case of mistaken identity with another man of the same name, fortunately for our man but not him; junior in service to my driver.

The other instance concerned one of our senior firemen, who with his seniority would move straight into the position of driver, without having been a passed man at all. Knowing how we worked at Overseal with most drivers taking their turn on the shovel; he would have driven thousands of miles during his career, controlling loose coupled coal trains on gradients as fearsome as any in the country.

As more than one driver has told me during my time on the railway, "Any fool can start and drive a train, but it takes a man to stop them."

The passed firemen at Toton were none to pleased about this, as they were already being pushed back by the influx of redundant drivers at their depot, without having a mere fireman arriving in their midst and usurping them even further; which I suppose is understandable.

Approaching the union (he was an ASLEF man) didn't seem to help as they were already involved with the protest from the other side, so I resolved to write a letter to the DMPS (District Motive Power Superintendent) himself at Derby; to see if he could intercede on his behalf.

He replied to me personally, stating that he would draw the attention of his opposite number, the DMPS at Nottingham in whose district Toton had just been included, to the matter.

I do not know quite what transpired between them, but sufficient to say that our man obtained his transfer; taking effect from the first Monday in August, in common with every one else.

Two exceptions to these moves were our two senior active drivers, Charlie Moulton and George Caddy; who were to remain on the district, signing on and off at Woodville Junction where they would carry out the shunting duties; mornings and afternoons, turn and turn about.

A 350HP Diesel Shunter would be based at the junction for this duty, and during the preceding months would work out of Overseal Shed while the two drivers concerned received training on them under the care of a Burton driver, passed to drive them.

I received instructions to make one of the two men available for training on the following week, the arrangement being for the selected man to travel down to Burton on the first train; which left Moira Station round about 0630am. Having walked down to the sheds; meet up with the Burton driver and bring the Diesel shunter back to Overseal, where the initial instruction would be done by the Burton man.

This driver turned out to be Albert Clamp, a very gentle and pleasant man; gifted with untold patience. I knew Albert very well as indeed did both George and Charlie.

I arranged with the Overseal shunters to leave the siding which leads down to Mr Topliss's domain empty, so that it could be used for instructional purposes; and at the same time be handy for the shed; so that the usual cooking and mashing facilities would be to hand. Of course, one must not forget that these diesel shunters come equipped with their own electric cooking ring for the boiling of water and no doubt other culinary skills as well.

No cooking on the shovel on these babies!!.

On arrival on the shed, I had a brief word with Albert about the forth-coming training. One of the things which I did ask him not to do, was to avoid showing the trick with the brake stick.

"I don't know what you mean," he replied.

"That's all right then," I answered, although I knew that he did, and what is more he knew that I knew that he did.

The reader may remember that a standard brake stick, as used when pinning down wagon brakes; was just the right length to wedge down the dead mans pedal, with the top end jammed under the top of the recess provided for the drivers legs, the other end bearing down onto the depressed pedal; thereby holding it down and rendering its purpose as a safety back up useless. I figured that Charlie at least, if not George would work something out for themselves in the fullness of time, without having it pointed out to them.

Charlie Moulton was the first man to be trained, and he took to the diesel like a duck to water. After a couple of hours he was driving up and down the siding as if he had been doing it for years, so when the 89 Target working arrived from Burton, I arranged for him under the ever watchful eyes of Albert, to shunt the train while the Burton men parked their engine, a Class '5' on the shed out of the way. The same procedure was followed on the following day, and on the Wednesday I arranged for the shunter to be taken down to Woodville Junction, to enable Charlie to familiarise himself with all aspects of the work down there while he still had Albert with him.

Whilst down there at the Junction, the need to pull a train off the bank occurred twice; with the Diesel proving very effective in this role. The only snag being the longer time that it took to arrive on the scene; as its top speed is only 15 miles per hour.

I asked Albert if he had shown Charlie where the manual oil pump was, and how to use it.

He said truthfully that he hadn't as he did not know about it himself. So I took on the role of instructor, acting unpaid and did the honours for both of them, pointing out as I did so, that whereas on a warm sunny summers morning, the loco's engine would in all probability start; on a cold and frosty morning in mid winter, the chances were that after standing all night outside; it probably wouldn't, without a pump up first.

The traffic department requested an assessment of its performance from Mr Brazier, who passed it on to the Junction Foreman for his comments. The only downside which he could see was its unsuitability for working the occasional trip down to Drakelow Power Station; a current requirement of the 97 Target workings.

As I realised that such a proviso would be met by the new workings which would be introduced following the depot's closure, it could be concluded that the use of the diesel shunter was a complete success. The following week it was George's turn for instruction, with a similar routine being followed as on the previous week, except for the need to collect it from Burton, as it was already at Overseal.

On the Friday of that second week, George and Albert took the diesel back to Burton, with George travelling back on the 89 Target engine.

Both of them were very disappointed about this as they thought that they would be taking up their new jobs on the diesel shunter, straight away.

With more diesels coming on stream, the Burton—London ale trains were now being worked by new Type 2 Diesel locomotives of a type later known as Class 26 or 27, being numbered initially in the D53xx and 54xx series. These locomotives were all Cricklewood based, but worked by Burton, London and Wellingborough crews as previously when steam hauled.

However, having a higher availability they were rostered to other duties between the main workings to and from London.

One of these turns was the Burton to Nuneaton and return tripper, which passed Overseal on its return journey round about 11-30 in the morning. As I invariably had a spare driver most Saturday mornings sitting around doing very little, I asked them if any one wished to go on it down to Nuneaton on a road refresher, as although most of our drivers signed for it; very rarely was there a need to actually go right down into Nuneaton and on to the low level; the nearest normally being Abbey Street, when working the Birmingham turns.

I thought that the knowledge regained would stand them in good stead when those drivers who had elected to transfer to Burton or Coalville, made their move.

Johnny Close was keen to take up the offer and as he actually lived in Burton, quite near to me in fact; I arranged for him to start and finish there. As he could not sign on at Burton as his card was at Overseal, I told him to sign it on Monday morning, unless of course he wished to start from there and be picked up outside the shed. The drivers and firemens' cards, along with the shed staffs dockets were sent down to Burton in the letter bag on Monday mornings, with the new cards coming up in the Friday bag. Hence no harm done if he elected to start from Burton, which he did.

The following Monday morning I gathered that he had thoroughly enjoyed his day out, having driven the loco part of the way back.

The only other driver to take up the offer was Bill Clemson, who I gather also enjoyed the experience as well; joining the train at Overseal in his case.

Least you should think that I was channelling so much effort into the staffs welfare as to neglect my own, then let me inform you that this was far from the case.

I to was scanning the vacancies notices for suitable positions for which to apply, as indeed I had been for some considerable time; even before the closure situation came along. I had already applied for the position of Foreman Fitter at Barrow-in-Furness, but hadn't received an interview, Now along came a similar position at Rugby. As this was a Class One Grade vacancy, I didn't expect to even get an answer let alone an interview; but to my surprise I received notification to attend one at Euston for consideration for the position. A travel warrant was enclosed, so having arranged for a relief to cover my duties at Overseal for the day. I travelled down to St Pancras, and walked down to Euston to pass through the famous Doric Arch, now sadly no more; to attend the interview. There were some other applicants also present, and I was the last but one to be called in.

As soon as I entered the room and surveyed the members of the panel before me, I knew that my chances of securing the position in question were less than nil.

One of the panel was a person with whom I had crossed swords before; many years ago. A flash of recognition crossed his face as our eyes met, and I could tell from that instant that I had not a snowballs chance in hell of ever getting a job on the old LNWR anywhere, let alone Rugby. Still, I went through the motions, as did the panel.

As it progressed it became increasingly obvious that not withstanding the hurdles already mentioned; they had no intention of letting a Midland man, as they saw me; loose on their railway.

Had no one ever told them that the LNWR died on January 1st 1923, if not even earlier when the LYR amalgamated with them, a year before, in 1922.

But let it be said that I had come across this attitude at all levels before, both on the Midland and the LNWR sides. All I can say, to use a modern idiom is to grow up and "get a life."

The final interview was an ex apprentice from out of Derby works and as we had been chatting together while we waited, I decided to wait for him to come out. His interview was even shorter than mine, his impression of the panel being much the same as my own. As he had only completed his apprenticeship just over a month before, he did not expect to be appointed to the position; just attending the interview for the experience. It is after all never to soon to display ambition.

We enjoyed the rest of the day together around London, a place which he had never visited before; travelling back to Derby on an evening train, the last one we could catch and still make a connection with the 'Lincoln Mail' for my onward journey back to Burton. I often wondered how his further career progressed, but unfortunately our paths never crossed again.

With the threat of closure at Overseal now a reality, the atmosphere amongst the staff changed considerably, as would be expected. I for my part avidly scanning the vacancy lists as already mentioned, applying for any job which I thought I could handle, commiserate with its location. After all one had to live there as well with my family. One job which I did really fancy was on the Western Region at Leamington Spa. Although only a small depot, it was located in a nice town and furthermore, my wife had relatives in the area. But I never even got an interview.

After a few more disappointments, I realised that the situation arising was that of too many applicants chasing to few vacancies.

I applied for a casualty inspectors job, based at Derby and was surprised to find just how many men were being interviewed for the vacancy. Some of them quite senior to me in what had been established salaried positions until quite recently. This made me realise that as the 'Beeching cuts' bit ever deeper into the railway network, so the need for managerial staff would reduce as well; with current trend slowly swinging towards the academic types, rather than the hands on practical railwayman. Experience counting for nothing, when stood against the highly qualified college and university types; some of whom have never even travelled on a train in their lives, let alone worked on the railway.

Although this realisation didn't stop me from still searching, I didn't in truth anticipate much success in gaining a worthwhile position in the near future.

Meanwhile back at Overseal life carried on, all be it with a distinct atmosphere. Only George Caddy and Charlie Moulton knew what they were going to be doing. All the usual problems were still occurring as before. The firemen who were willing were still doubling up on shifts, and also doing the odd four-hour stint around the shed when not engaged in these extra firing duties.

While enjoying my lunch one Thursday down at the Bath Yard Moira Miners Welfare with Mr Granger, he casually asked me if I had ever been down a mine. I had to confess that I had not, but if he was asking; I was more than willing to go. He told me that there was a new cutter under test down at Rawdon colliery, and that I was welcome to accompany him the following day if I was free; as he was going down to witness it in operation.

With the parting comment, "Don't turn up in your best suit," we arranged to meet up at Bath Yard the next day at eleven o' clock.

Telling Eric that I was going down to Bath Yard on business, I made my way to our rendezvous, and was soon driving round to Rawdon in Mr Granger's car. On arrival, we entered the office where I was introduced to the colliery manager. Although I had taken my overalls with me, a brand new pair of coal board orange ones were produced for me to wear; along with a white safety helmet. With all three of us suitably attired, the manager lead us to the lamp room where we were issued with a lamp for our helmet, a belt to wear which carried the battery box to power it; a pair of knee pads and most important of all, a numbered tally; without which no one enters the mine. We also had to sign a declaration that we had nothing on our person might cause a fire, like matches or a lighter for instance.

At the entrance to the winding house, someone checked our tallies' prior to us entering the cage. This battered and dirty piece of equipment contrasted sharply with the spotless engine room which we had just left. On its floor, two sets of narrow gauge railway lines were fastened, placed to catch the feet of the unwary in the semi darkness; me included.

The man who had checked our tally's slammed the cage doors shut, and with a heart stopping lurch the floor seemed to drop away as the cage literally hurtled down the shaft at breakneck speed. The air thus displaced raised clouds of dust, which swirled around us as we fell, all in total darkness. Much as I would have liked to have switched my helmet light on, I declined to do so as neither of my companions had lit theirs.

What other surprises are in store I wondered, as we plunged down this hellhole.

At last we shuddered to a stop, the halt being almost as instantaneous as the start was. Someone outside threw open the cage doors to reveal a most unexpected sight; for there before us lay a huge tunnel, wide enough to drive two cars down side by side; and lit so brightly by rows of fluorescent lights, that I couldn't believe it. I don't know quite what I expected, but this most certainly was not it!.

My two companions guided me into a crude sort of passenger coach, constructed of heavy gauge steel with wooden seats. A battery powered locomotive hauled us off along the tunnel for at least I would estimate half a mile, before coming to a halt in an area of semi darkness. Here we alighted from the 'manrider' and after a few minutes walk came to large door. These doors are situated throughout the mine as an anti- fire precaution and are in pairs, the chamber in between being known as an air lock.

I hope I am right about this last fact.

After a few more yards, we all switched our lights on and turned off this main drive into a side tunnel.

Here we had to stoop as we walked as its height was only about five feet high. As we progressed even further down it the headroom reduced still more, until to walk at all required a crouching gait.

"Why am I here?," I asked myself," I must be mad to submit myself to such torture." The further we got down this tunnel or road as I think they call it, the air got thicker and heavily laden with coal dust.

Out of the gloom the managers voice declared that now was the time to put our kneepads on, and pads for our elbows as well. Then we dived off again, in to another side road; this one being even shallower than before, with a height of about three foot six inches only.

A feeling of claustrophobia was coming over me, not helped by the managers voice casually mentioning that we were now about nine hundred feet below ground.

"Quite the comedian, I don't think," I thought.

The coal dust in the air was getting quite thick by now. The view was only of the belt of coal; which all these roads seemed to have, rushing by on my right hand side; and Mr Granger's orange clad derriere in front of me, picked out in the beam of my lamp.

After what seemed an eternity, we came out into a wide chamber still of the same height but some thirty or so feet wide. Here, a group of miners were preparing to drive another cut into the seam of coal which formed the chambers far wall. I was pleased to note a series of hydraulic props supporting the roof behind me.

They were obviously awaiting our arrival before making another cut into the seam. The cutting machine had a series of cutters one above the other in a horizontal plane, mounted on a massive head which in turn appeared to be secured on the end of an hydraulic ram. When operating, the cutting heads rotate and as the ram pushes the cutters into the seam, some form of traversing system; presumably also hydraulic drives the whole machine across the face. The coal thus hewn is then fed down a shute onto a cross belt which is integral with the machine. This belt carries the coal onto the main conveyor, which then transports it to the pithead. Or so it all seemed to me.

With no cutting being done the forced air fans soon drew most of the dust away until it was possible to see with ease all that was going on.

Mr Granger was deep in conversation with the group of miners who I imagine had some fitters and electricians amongst them, while the manager tried to explain the foregoing action of the machine to me.

After about twenty minutes the machine was ready for the cutting demonstration and all hell was let loose.

The noise was indescribable, and the air was soon virtually solid with coal dust. I was very glad of the mask which one of the miners had given me, I can tell you. These conditions went on for about a quarter of an hour before the machine was stopped to enable some further adjustments to be made. These completed, the whole assembly was winched forward prior to making another cut across the face, this time of course in the opposite direction to finish up where it had started. But before this could be done, the unsupported area where the cut had just been made had to be propped up. I was well in favour of this action, as I could not get the fact that we were over 900 feet below ground out of my mind. I kept thinking that the ground had only got to settle a small amount; after all what is three foot six inches in 900; and we would be there forever.

But I hadn't reckoned on where those props were to come from. Some of the miners calmly did something to the base of the rearmost row, which caused them to retract. As they moved them out to reposition them in their new location, the ground fell in behind them. Despite the look of unconcern shown by my colleagues (they were all my mates now), I thought my end had come.

Get me out of here safely, and I'll never miss church again, was one of the thoughts racing through my head.

As the dust settled once more someone said ' shall we give it another go', and once again the cutting exercise was repeated.

Another session of examination and adjustment followed, the props were moved again and another cut was taken.

This time, knowing what to expect, I was not so concerned; but even so I was not sorry when it was time to leave.

Our return journey was much the same as the descent, except that we came up a different shaft. After handing over our tallies, my companions took me into the winding house where a beautiful steam driven winding engine was on view. This spotless machine had brought us up from the mine. The other hoist by which we had descended being powered by an electric motor.

After a shower, but still with a dirty shirt etc, I was entertained to a very nice lunch by Mr Granger and the manager. It was only when I was alighting from his car later, at the foot of the steps up to the bridge, that I noticed my shoes. The toes were completely ruined by all that crawling about.

It was an experience which I would not have missed for the world, but not one that I would wish to repeat in a hurry either.

Having been down there, and seen and experienced the conditions which those miners endured; day in and day out to supply the coal, I will stand up and say that it is worth £100 a lump, if not more.

Eric was quite amused by appearance on returning to the shed. On looking into the sliver of glass which served as a mirror, wedged somewhat precariously over the mantelpieces of the messroom; I could see what the cause of his amusement were. The coal dust from the collar of my shirt had transferred itself in a series of rings around my neck and the lower part of my ears. I was more than pleased that I had elected to travel to work in my car on that particular day; and thus did not have to suffer the journey home by train, in such a conditions.

The following week, I received a phone call from Jean at Moira Station which she relayed to me on behalf of my wife, to the effect that my dog 'Mick' had bitten the lady who lived next door to us.

This worthy lady, a dog lover herself; owned two pedigree poodles, the closer acquaintance of which 'our dyed in the wool' mongrel was desirous of making. Although she always spoke to our Mick whenever she saw him from her adjacent garden, she made no attempt to disguise the contempt with which she held him; a mere mongrel.

Just what the circumstances were which led up to his misconduct, I have no idea; but following the incident. My wife; fearing for the safety of our baby son and young daughter, declared that he had to go.

Now both my daughter and I adored our 'Mick', and he us in return. So much so in fact that if he could actually get out of the house when she went to school, he would follow her down to the bus stop and hide behind the hedge in the first garden until the bus came. Then he would dash aboard and hide under the stairs just as the bus pulled away from the stop. The end result being a phone call from school, for my wife to go down and fetch him back.

So what to do?.

After much deliberation, I decided to ask myself for permission to take him to work with me while I decided on a more permanent solution.

Permission forthcoming, (naturally) I duly loaded him in the car and off to Overseal we both went. 'Mick' always liked riding in cars, or as we have seen, any other kind of vehicle; so he loved it. His behaviour at the shed was impeccable. Cyril took to him straight away, and soon he was following him about the yard and shed, as if he had known him all his life.

When he wasn't lying at my feet in the office, he up the yard supervising Cyril emptying the ash pits or coaling the stage. This situation could not carry on for long however, so reluctantly I decided that his fate would have to be a one way journey to the vet.

I took him for the longest walk which he had ever had that night, during which he never put a foot wrong.

Then loading him into the car, we set off for his last appointment. But when I got there, I just could not take him in.

So we made yet another trip to Overseal on the following day. On arrival, Cyril asked me what I was going to do with him as it was Thursday, the day that Mr Lewis usually paid us a visit. In my anxiety for 'Mick's welfare, I had completely forgot about his possible visit. Although he did occasionally miss his visit because of other commitments, substituting a phone call instead; I could not leave such a situation to chance.

Charlie Moulton, who was on 96 Target that week came into the office with a tit bit for 'Mick'. He, along with most of the other staff was quite taken with him; and I coveted the hope that one of them might in deed take him on.

'Mick'. Photo: Authors Collection.

"Shall I take him a quick run around the field?," he asked.

"Be my guest," I replied, and off the pair went to have a run round the piece of land encapsulated within the triangle formed of the Moira West, East and South Junctions.

Charlie's engine by the way was standing in the adjacent sidings, waiting to collect some empties stabled there, for onward dispatch to Measham Colliery.

Mr Lewis arrived, and following the usual administrations, settled down in my chair to enjoy his sandwiches; washed down as usual with many cups of my tea, as Cyril waited on us with all the panache of a royal butler.

With Mr Lewis settled, Cyril beckoned me to the door, so making my excuses; I went out to see what he wanted.

"Come and look at this," he said, and lead me outside.

There, just passing the shed was 96 Target en route back from Measham to Woodville Junction. Over the side of the cab leaned Charlie, with our 'Mick' by his side looking forwards at the road ahead, like a true professional.

Charlie looked across and I gave him a wave onwards. As the '4F' went by, the rear end of 'Mick' came into view; tail wagging for all its worth.

When the engine came on to the shed for crew change and fire cleaning at dinnertime, Charlie mentioned to Cyril that 'Mick' was tied up in the brake van down at the junction.

Eventually 'Mick' was reunited with me at about three o' clock in the afternoon, having enjoyed a much better and more exciting day than his owner. Obviously this state of affairs could not continue, otherwise I would soon be in hot water. All the district was now aware of his presence, and it was only a matter of time before word spread down to Burton. Whether Mr Lewis was a dog lover or not, I doubted that he would condone 'Mick's presence at the shed.

But as far as I am aware, he never did find out, for which I was eternally grateful. Thanking Charlie the following day for keeping him out of way, he said that it was nothing adding that he had enjoyed having him along.

"He's a cracking dog," was his summary, "I can't believe that he would bite anybody!."

On the way home that night, I called round to see my Dad, who said that he would take him to the vets as I just could not bring myself to do it.

I am pleased to report that he could not take him either, and kept him as his own for the rest of his (Mick's) life, until he died at the ripe old age of seventeen years.

My Mother maintained that Dad thought more of 'Mick' than he did of her. Maybe he did, I am not at liberty to say. At least he did not argue or answer back!

Several meetings were held at Derby between the management, unions and LDC representatives, George Swann of course representing us at Overseal in the latter role.

On enquiring as to why I was not invited to be present at these meetings as well, he was informed that my position was only a temporary appointment and therefore my presence was not required. This was news to him as indeed it was to me also.

The only conclusion to be drawn being that the intention to close Overseal was already on the cards, Beeching's proposals or not, this to me, further explaining Mr Bertram Stanier's remarks previously.

Eventually the sad day came when I had to inform the respective crews to take their engines down to Burton on completion of their last shifts, prior to taking up their fresh duties at their new depots on the following Monday.

Cyril, who had opted for redundancy and myself remained for a further week, tying up loose ends and generally sorting out the artefacts of some ninety or so years of existence. I arranged for a van to be shunted into the shed on which to load the entire surplus stores etc, and this was collected by 89 Target on that last Friday. 44527 was the engine on that day, being thus the last steam engine to enter the shed, officially at any rate.

Charlie and George had travelled down to Burton to collect the Diesel Shunter on the previous Friday morning and thus, this engine became the sheds only occupant.

Within a few weeks, this practice also ceased with the engine being stabled down at Woodville Junction, Charlie and George signing on there already, of course.

In a very short space of time, the demolition men moved in; and my fine depot was no more.

I had enjoyed my time at Overseal, facing all the various challenges which were thrown up, but most of all for affording me the privilege of working with some of the finest and most loyal group of men it has been my good fortune to know.

Chapter 20

A Step Backwards

The Following day as usual I reported to administer more tender loving care to diesel D2859. However, Monday morning found me making my way down the long concrete path to the sheds again, in stead of standing on the station platform to await the 7.08 to Leicester D.M.U.

On arrival I hung up my coat up in the 'bug ut' and presented myself at the foremans office for work. Chargehand Ernie Gaskell was in charge and he asked me to go up onto the droppit and carry on there. So the last two years had gone full circle and I was back where I had started. George slotted in alongside me as I walked up there ,so it wasn't all bad.

We were soon involved with the refitting of axleboxes etc to a set of 'Austerity' trailing coupled wheels and thus life went on This locomotive completed, our next job was on a Class '5' with the usual trailing axlebox hot. Having removed the rear section of the coupling rods each side, she was positioned straight over the wheel drop table as there was very little other preparatory work to do apart from removing the brake pull rod and adjusting box.

The exhaust steam supply pipe was no longer fitted to this engine. It had been blanked off along with the auxiliary steampipe thereby leaving the exhaust injector to operate on live steam all the while. This practice was becoming increasingly common on all of the exhaust injector fitted Stanier locomotives like 8F's, Class '5's and Jubilees. Also the 'Rebuilt Scots' were so treated. This modification, if you could call it that; must have made the railway company quite a few pounds in scrap copper; though what the effect out on the line to the general boiler management of the individual locomotives was, I have no idea.

At least the problems of knocking off when closing and opening the regulator, commiserate with failure of the changeover valve to operate would be eliminated. A not infrequent occurrence as I was well aware of from my own firing days.

The BR Standard engines so fitted however retained theirs so far as I could tell, as did the odd ex LNER B1 which came our way. An interesting observation for which we will probably now never know the answer.

Of the examining fitters, Jack Fern and his brother George still held office as did Geoff German, now mated by Bob Cotton. Wally Gaskell now filled the third position, replacing Les Bull when he went to Overseal before I in my turn replaced him there. Les of course taking the vacancy created by Reg Cordon when sadly he had died following a short illness while I was away in the army.

Now Wally announced his intention to leave the railway service for pastures new, and I was asked to fill the position thus created. This I agreed to do. George however expressed a wish to stay on days so I inherited Wally's old mate, Gerald Love; who you may recall was Joe Benson's mate when I first took up my apprenticeship.

As has been mentioned already, I had had some experience of shed work already, when covering for the regular man either on a Saturday mornings or when on holiday or sick relief. Also along with Bob Cotton we had on occasions covered for the Fern brothers on a Saturday afternoons during the cricket season, as they both played for Rolleston, a local village team of some note in the local area.

The duties of the examining fitter or shedman, as he is more commonly known; consists of examining all engines arriving on the shed for boiler washout and 'X' repairs, findings of which are then entered onto the repair card, the precise title of which I have forgotten over the ensuing years; but which we will call the 'X' repair card.

On the front of this card are pre-printed a list of various tasks which have to be carried out by the repairing fitter. This list is all embracing and not particular to any class of engine.. On the reverse side of the card, any defects and repairs which the examiner may find are entered, along with any other jobs; usually ones which cannot be carried out when the engine is in steam; which have been deferred from drivers repair cards, submitted after each turn of duty since the last 'X' repair.

It was part of the drivers' job to complete a repair card or alternatively a 'No Repair' at the end of each turn of duty

A typical report would be, brakes to adjust or sands not working; piston glands blowing or cylinder drain cocks sticking. Injector nuts leaking or injectors wasting water, and so on. . When these cards were submitted, it was the shedman's duty to rectify the faults if possible, ably assisted by his mate who incidentally was graded as a Class 3 Fitter with a wage enhancement to go with it. Brakes and sands were his forte, along with other sundry tasks as will be seen.

Examination of all engines working passenger and full or partly fitted parcels and freight trains also had to be carried out and any defects found rectified. If not possible, a decision had to be made whether or not to fail the engine concerned as unsuitable for its rostered duty.

These examinations naturally included a brake test, wherein 21" of vacuum had to be created by the small ejector, pulling against a "5/16" leak disc. This disc was a round piece of brass so machined as to make a seal against one of the locomotive train pipes when clipped on to the open end of the hose. The 21" was imperative when working a passenger train, but when out on a siding and coupled up to a rake of freight wagons, 20" or even 19" was acceptable.

If on testing the vacuum, the desired 21" could not be achieved when adequate boiler pressure was available, there were various things which could be done to correct the imbalance.

On the ex MR engines fitted with Gresham and Craven's vacuum ejectors and also the 'Crabs' which carried a similar type of ejector box, it was usual to remove the male cone from the small ejector and give it a quick polish with a piece of smooth emery paper; with which no self respecting shedman was ever without. This, followed by a blast of steam through the box before replacing the cone and cap usually put things right. If not then the next thing to try was a couple of washers added under the relief valve spring to add a bit more tension to it. Failing this the flame lamp was lit and a thorough examination of all the pipe joints and fittings was carried out while the ejectors were in operation. Any leaks then present in the trainpipe would reveal itself by drawing in the lamp flame at the point of leakage. .If not successful after all these checks, then the actual fittings themselves become suspect; namely the ejector box or the drivers brake valve. This of course rendering the locomotive unsuitable for its allocated task and failing it because either the replacement equipment is not available or the time to fit it. If the locomotive is a foreigner, (i.e., One from another depot other than Burton), it would then usually find its way back home either light engine or on a lesser and unfitted working.

General view of Burton 'Midland' yard. Photo: K. Fairey

The Stanier and BR Standard engines very rarely seemed to suffer from vacuum problems, other than the occasional train pipe leak; the odd washer under the relief valve being all that would be required. Access to the innards of the ejector box being impossible in any case without first removing it from the engine; quite an involved job in itself.

With other engines like say an ex LNER' B1' for instance, they either worked or they didn't, as we had no spares to repair them with anyway. These LNER engines did seem to have a tendency to develop train pipe leaks, which we at least could attend to. One of the mates jobs was to check the cylinder mechanical lubricators on these passenger and fitted freight locomotives, topping them up as necessary and any other like fitted engines going out on other work, if requested by the driver.

I could never understand why this arrangement was in hand as I am sure that the driver was quite capable of checking and filling it himself. Did the powers that be not consider him intelligent enough to distinguish between the cylinder and axlebox lubricators and thus add the correct oil into each.

As already mentioned, any defects reported by incoming drivers on their respective engines required the attention of the 'shedman'. These cards were inserted into a box by the driver, and it was the shed fitters job to check this box periodically throughout his shift, and attend to the jobs so entered if possible. Some of the more involved jobs reported may be deferred to the next 'X' day, if not considered detrimental to the working of the particular locomotive. Foreign engines cards frequently being deferred by the terse legend 'FHD' (For Home Depot) in this instance.

Any faults found by a driver when taking an engine off the shed would also have to be dealt with by the shedman to the drivers satisfaction, before it could be allowed to leave the depot; the added pressure in these instances of course being to avoid a late start for the engines booked working.

Then of course reasons had to be provided to explain the delay.

Trains passing by the depot also required attention from time to time. News of this need usually being announced by the receipt of a telegram, sent at it's drivers request from a signalbox further down the line.

An example to illustrate this telegraph system occurred to Gerald and me quite early on during our new found career as 'shedman'.

The driver of a Saltley 'Crab' working a Birmingham to Derby stopper wired for a fitter from Wychnor Box, stating 'both injectors not working!!'.

I thought this to be a little odd as although the exhaust injectors were notorious for going wrong, the live steam one could usually be persuaded to function; albeit with some inefficiency.

So gathering a few tools together we walked out to await the arrival at Leicester Junction.

"When it comes," I said to Gerald, "Nip up onto the tender back to check if there is any water in the tank." This he did and found that the tender was actually about half full, which was in contradiction to the gauge which showed empty.

As I climbed up on to the footplate, the driver was instructing his mate, a very young passed cleaner to start throwing the fire out. A quick glance at the glass revealed no water showing at all, so his concern was at least justified.

Opening the water valve on the tender, just the merest trickle dribbled out of the overflow pipe of the live steam injector, so I quickly diagnosed blocked water valves inside the tender.

"Was the lid on the tank?," I asked Gerald, only to receive a negative reply.

Just then one of our preparing sets of men drew up alongside with another of our 'Crabs'. Indeed one which I had just completed examining for the 6/50 London.

The two locomotives were quickly changed over, and the Derby train went on its merry way, with a minimum of delay. The look on that young fireman's face was a picture of relief when he realised that he no longer had to bail out that huge fire which he had built up during his journey from New Street. Not so the Burton one however, an old hand and somewhat plump of stature.

I acquainted the driver of the situation and suggested that he run the 'Crab' down into the New Shed doorhole, where I could connect one of the boilerwash out hoses to the live steam injector overflow pipe and thereby force some water into the boiler that way.

Gerald and the fireman dropped off and dashed into the shed to prepare the pipe while the driver and I ran the engine round the yard to meet them.

I kept the firehole doors shut and we both had our respective cab windows open and the side sheets also, so that we could make an extremely quick exit off the footplate, if the fusible plug should melt. But would we be quick enough if it did. I for my part was perched on the fireman's seat ready to dive through the open window should the situation arise, though I doubt if the driver was agile enough to follow suit through his. It was with great trepidation that I climbed off my perch to drop down and change the points at the top of the yard and thanked my lucky stars that there were no other engines blocking our path down into the shed.

As we arrived, one of the boilerwashers was waiting to connect up the water bag and with one co-ordinated action, had it clipped on; with Gerald opening the supply valve.

I for my part opened the injector steam valve as with a rattle of the water lever, that reassuring sound of an injector filling the boiler came as music to our ears.

The driver looked across at me and grinned, as did the trio down below. We had saved the day and prevented the fusible plug from dropping with all the implications which came in its wake; let alone the damage caused to the firebox.

Arthur Warrington, the Running Foreman appeared and said that control wanted a report concerning the delay which amounted to little more than a quarter of an hour, and would she; (the Crab) be alright for the 11/10 London tonight as the Leeds engine was now going on the 6/50 London and the 11/10 engine going to Leeds (8/25pm).

"Lets get some water in the boiler first then I'll have a look when she's turned off," I replied adding," What are you going to do about this great fire?." I could feel our fireman's eyes burning in my back as I made this last remark.

"When you've done with this," Arthur turned to the driver, "Carry on with your booked work, otherwise we won't know where we are." Sighs of relief from you know who. And who could blame him.

Once stabled over a pit, I dropped down under the tender and removed the drain plug from under the tank; jumping back to avoid a wetting as it came free. However only a trickle of water ran out as I did so; Gerald having the same result at the front end when he uncoupled one of the intermediate water feed bags which were supposed to convey the water from the tender to the engines injectors. Some judicious rodding and poking up through the drain hole however soon produced the desired effect and with the tank draining down as per normal, we decided to have a well earned cup of tea while it did so.

Thus fortified I put on my wellingtons and with my inspection lamp in my hand, cautiously lowered myself down into the tenders water spaces. And what a sight befell my eyes.

My feet landed on a vast heap of coal at least two feet deep, commiserate with coaling under a hopper with the tank lid open, and more than once; by the amount of coal in there, it would seem. Saltley of course being blessed with one of these coaling towers.

More coal was spread some six to twelve inches deep over the entire floor of the tank from front to back, along with sundry pieces of wood, fireman's caps, a jacket and several lumps of cotton waste and rags. Of the filter plates which protect the water feed valves, only the frames remained, bolted in place; their inner mesh screens broken into small pieces and helping to block the feed valves; ably assisted by yet more waste rag and the jacket previously mentioned.

Gerald produced two buckets and a rope, on one end of which was fashioned a hook with which to haul the full buckets out for tipping into the coal space.

Well over thirty buckets of coal and other rubbish was removed from within that tank, and I still wasn't happy about it working a fitted train with my signature to its suitability, particularly as the screens were in such a state of disrepair. Thus I informed Arthur of the position and he in his turn substituted a Wellingborough 8F in reasonable condition as motive power for the late London job.

Attending the subsequent enquiry, mandatory in all cases when an engine fails whist working a passenger or fitted freight or parcels train; it appeared to be a case of nobody knowing anything as to the cause of the failure at all. A classic cover up if ever I saw one. The DMPS (District Motive Power Superintendent) appeared determined to put the blame on the Saltley examining fitter which I thought was somewhat unfair, as with the tank full of water; short of donning a diving suit (not part of the examination schedule), how on earth could he determine the conditions inside; and said as much.

I added that the preparation crew who had coaled the engine were more to blame than anybody for not ensuring that the lid was on before going under the coal hopper, only to be told to keep my opinions to myself.

"When I want your views on the matter, I will ask for them," one of the managerial retinue scowled at me; whereupon; I got out of my chair; walked out of the enquiry and caught the next train back home.

But then again, I was a little bit volatile in my younger days.

Strangely enough, some six weeks later when once again on the same afternoon turn; another telegram was received concerning this same train, also with injector troubles.

The motive power on this occasion was a 4F, also a Saltley engine. This rundown specimen duly arrived at Leicester Junction, in charge this time it transpired of two Passed Firemen. The water was bobbing in the bottom nut and both the crew were trying without success to persuade one or the other of the injectors to work. The tender gauge read half a tank full as before but nothing was coming out of the overflows of either one.

Gerald, as ever up on the back of the tank shouted that it was empty, so it was but a few moments work to draw forwards a few feet to enable the tank to be filled from the crane alongside.

The driver or fireman said that the gauge had shown full when they had left New Street, so they never suspected that it wasn't still working.

"Probably sitting on a pile of coal," I commented, relating the saga of the 'Crab' to them as the tank filled.

"Still it shouldn't have emptied in this distance," one of them replied.

So I had a quick look around and found one of the intermediate water bag nuts loose, where it was attached to the engine. It was but a moments job to tighten it up, as it; in common with every other one on the railway, consisted of a cup shaped brass nut with two lugs, one on each side to facilitate ease of hand screwing; followed by a couple of taps with the hammer on one of those lugs to finally secure it.

"What about the time lost?," I enquired.

"We'll soon square that," the one playing at driver replied. "The blasted scoop don't work so we have had to stop for water."

"But what about the telegram?," I persisted.

"What telegram?," an incredulous look met my eyes.

"Are you in the ASLEF or Equity?," I asked.

We all laughed, the bag came out of the now full tank and they were on their way again. Another satisfied customer.

Nothing more was heard about it for which I was pleased as I didn't fancy another run in with the DMPS and his gang.

The 'Crab' incidentally was No. 42823 and the 4F 44179.

An unusual request was received one dark cold and wet winters night when one of our firemen came in and asked us to attend the engine which they had just relieved by the relief cabin at the junction.

"My mate can't find the taps handle!!," was the odd reply when I asked him what the problem was.

Apparently the engine in question was none other than an ex LNER Class V2.

"Just my bloody luck to get something like this when I've got no lamp," the driver moaned. Meaning I presume, his cycle lamp; which it appeared he had dropped somewhere along the way; the consequence of which was that it no longer functioned. Probably, a broken bulb.

"And just wait until my mate looks inside that firebox," he added.

The V2's of course having a very wide grate compared with most of the engines which came our way. 9F's excepted of course.

After a bit of a look around the footplate with my inspection lamp, the driver declared himself happy with the controls and their whereabouts. As a further help to him, being a Burton man; I lent him my flare lamp to help him on his way. It was no joke to man an engine with which you were not familiar even in the daylight, let alone in the dark; but in steam days the crews were expected to do it; and work the train and keep time as well. Not like now days with the diesels, where if you are not familiar with them and haven't been on a course to pass out on a particular type; then you could and did refuse to work a train with it.

No; in steam days it was a case of just climb aboard and get on with it. Readers will recall my own experience with the Class O4 at Toton. But they were comparatively simple to work once you had mastered the Dreadnought Combined Ejector and Brake Valve or whatever it was called, and a fine engine it was to; whereas on a V2 there were valves, wheels and levers, handles and gauges everywhere.

Another dramatic encounter with one of Sir Nigel's masterpieces occurred down at Shobnall Sidings of all places one balmy summers evening. This time with a K3 No. 61861.

These engines appeared quite regularly at the head of one of the daily Colwick-Wychnor Steel trains which worked through Burton via Stretton Junction and over the Dallow Lane Branch, rejoining the mainline to Wychnor at Leicester Junction.

It was the custom to hold these trains at Shobnall until a path across the Junction onto the mainline was available, so that they could have a run at the bank between Wellington Street and the junction itself; a gradient of some 1 in 45, with their heavy train of steel bolsters.

This particular engine on getting the road, just emitted a roar up the chimney and no movement at all. Obviously a problem in the steam chest, like a broken valve ring; or worse.

Ex LNER K3 Class 2-6-0. Photo: P. Groom.

On receiving word of this contretemps, Arthur produced a Class '5' and a set of men in very short time, upon which we loaded a selection of tools before embarking on the short journey from the sheds down to Shobnall. The Colwick driver had discovered the cause of the failure by the time that we arrived. This proved to be a fracture of the pin which attached the small crosshead on the middle valve to the two to one arm which gave this said valve its motion via the two sets of outside valve gear.

He presented me with one half of the broken pin with the comment," You'll not be able to much with that laddie!!."

I had to agree with him on that point, so the decision was made to drag the K3 off its train and park it in a siding while the Class '5' carried on with its train. The Shobnall Jocko did the honours and the 'Blackie' backed down to take the K3's place.

"At least you'll have a proper engine to carry on with"; our Burton fireman's parting remark. His Colwick counterparts reply being unprintable.

Faced with the prospect of humping a large and heavy bag of tools back to the shed as I had no intention of leaving them behind on the K3 to arrive after I had gone home and probably get lost, I resolved to see if I could manage to isolate or centralise the Middle Valve and thereby get it back up to the shed with the remaining two cylinders.

Looking at the remains of the broken pin I thought that it looked to be about the same size as a brake block pin, so wandering over to the Shobnall Jocko I checked it out.

A quick word with her driver, my old mate Bob Shrive from my footplate days, and I was slacking off the brake to borrow one off her; leaving of course the other five blocks with which to finish her days work with. Gerald said that if the idea worked, he would bring a replacement pin back and refit it when we got back to the shed.

And so it proved to be. I managed to lever the valve back into its correct position and couple it up, all be it somewhat sloppily into the two to one arm with the brake block pin. I was quite pleased about this as there didn't seem to be any obvious way to secure the valve independently, or indeed to be sure that it was in the mid gear position.

Our driver tried a gentle trip up and down the siding, and as this was completed satisfactorily I went across to the signalbox to arrange the trip back to the shed.

On arrival, we left her on the New Shed ashpit and Arthur arranged to have her disposed and the fire thrown out before stabling her on a long pit in the shed.

Gerald, as promised nipped back down to Shobnall with a replacement pin for the Jocko's brake block. Everyone was happy, except perhaps the luckless fireman who had to throw the K3's fire out.

As the motion pin was of case hardened steel and the brake block pin only mild steel, I would allow 61861 to travel back to Colwick light engine. If the foreman thought otherwise tomorrow when he read my report, then that was up to him though I doubt that he would.

Eventually a wire requesting all the relevant motion parts was received from Colwick, these all being returned direct from Doncaster Works for refitting, some two weeks later.

After a day out tripping, which must have surprised a few people around the district she was rostered away on a suitable turn which would see her back onto the Eastern Region again. My own memories being of the heat when I was squirming about under that smokebox. The other bit of good fortune being the presence of a steam engine on the Shobnall shunting turn instead of the (by then) usual 350HP Diesel.

The mention of Diesels of course meant that these were appearing more and more on the shed, having taken over the duties of many of the steam engines normally terminating here at Burton. Indeed we were now having diesel workings originating at Burton, covering duties previously rostered to steam engines. These engines being mainly type 24 and 25 Sulzer Powered 1100 HP Type 2s, numbered in the 50XX to 52XX and 75XX series. Most of them had been built at Derby Works, some of them being brand new. The 53XX and 54XX variety built up the line at Birmingham by Metro Cammell were no strangers either, turning up in the main on the London Beer trains; being based at Cricklewood.

Class 44, 45, 46, and 47s also came on shed, known then as Sulzer Type '4's of course and numbered D1-10,D11-137, D138-193, and D1100-D1500-D1999, respectively. Rarer visitors were the English Electric. Type 3's and 4's and the various kinds of Type 1's. The Class 31's, then known as Crompton's numbered 55XX- and powered by Mirrelles 1250HP engines were also around, and in general proving to be more troublesome than most of their Diesel sisters. At least the notorious Crossley's kept away from Burton, which when one considers that they were all based at Derby; only twelve miles down the line , was quite surprising.

At least I knew a bit about these latter beasts, whereas the local introduction of most of the other types had occurred while I was up at Overseal.

This of course did not stop them going wrong while in the area, either going past or actually on the shed. The latter scenario gave me time to have a think, get the books out and reason it through; not I might add always with success.

Out on the line of course, as has been mentioned before; the case was very different, bull and kid-ology forming a useful part of the tool kit.

Engine faults tended to be concerned by and large with overheating with smaller locomotives of types 1 and 2, the type 4's being relatively trouble free in this respect while out on the road, although some trouble with cracked crankcases was revealed with this latter group at examination times. One thing which all the mainline types suffered from in the early years was that of brake power, or rather the lack of it when working unfitted freight trains, which were the norm' at that time.

As a consequence, various designs of brake tender were developed; and soon locomotives of all types could be seen with one or sometimes two of these vehicles coupled to them when working loose coal and general goods trains alongside their not so fitted steam counterparts. These brake tenders themselves created problems as they utilised old coach frames and bogies, and thus became an anomaly of C&W and Locomotive engineering.

Frequent calls to passenger trains were received during the winter months when the steam generators which were fitted to most of the main line engines developed faults and failed to heat the coaches, which at that time were all steam heated.

As has been mentioned earlier, boiler faults in my experience fell into three main categories,. Lack of water, Fuel injector faults or the settings of the electrodes to ignite the fuel and create the heat. Close attention to these three points usually met with success. .Another bonus with these units was that the fireman or second man as he was now known, was usually quite knowledgeable and enthusiastic about his charge; being I suppose quite young and keen to embrace this new technology. This enthusiasm could possibly be motivated by the alternative which could result in failure of the locomotive with the boiler fault and substituting it with a steam engine. A situation which struck fear into the heart of many young men, having sampled the joys of the all conquering diesel.

But I digress.

One of the more important parts of the examining fitters duties was the actual examination of the various locomotives which were to work the scheduled passenger and fitted freight trains from the depot every day, and any extras or special workings as required.

Most of these exams were carried out by the afternoon and night shift man, with the day fitter taking care of the locomotives in for Boiler Washout and 'X' repairs, his only regular freight working being the 1/35 Bristol. He may of course check over the 4/20 Bristol and 4/40 London if available.

The 6/50 London and the 8/25 Leeds were usually examined by the afternoon man along with the 11/10 London as well. An 8/35 Rowsley job was also on the board when I was engaged on this work prior to going to Overseal, but had ceased to be a regular working when I came back and took the position permanently.

Likewise most of the local passenger workings had been converted to DMU's which were based at other depots, the working rosters being modified accordingly. Burton drivers still enjoyed a percentage of this work, most if not all of it being of a relieving nature, taking over a unit already in traffic.

Only a few years before, I would have been kept busy on the night shift examining engines for the 5.45 Nuffields, the 6.03 Leicester, the 7.08 Leicester, the 8.20 Walsall, the push and pull locomotive for the Tutbury Jinnie Autotrain, a mid-morning Leicester on Wednesdays and Saturdays and a fitted freight for Mold Junction; this last working starting from the ex North Western shed at Horninglow, necessitating a nocturnal cycle ride in all weathers to carry out the exam.

Just prior to Horninglow shed closing in August 1960, I was working the night shift and having carried out the exam, decided to ride back through the town instead of the slightly more direct route via Derby Street and Wellington Street, it being a nice warm summers evening. So there I am at about 3am in the morning, riding down High Street with a short tommy bar , my small hammer and a couple of spanners in my saddle bag; the acetylene examination lamp swinging on the handle bars to light my way, when out in front of me stepped two gentlemen of the law.

They inquired as to where I was going and where I had been, and were very interested in the contents of my saddlebag.

It soon became obvious that (a) they had never heard of and were unaware of the existence of Horninglow Sheds and (b), they did not believe my story and were intent on taking me back to the Police Station for further questioning.

Well you cannot argue with them can you, or at least you can try but they will take no notice of you if you do. So off to the 'nick' we went, with one holding my arm and the other pushing my bike.

On arrival the duty sergeant was called and their version of the story told to him. He however had heard of Horninglow Sheds and apparently was aware of our nocturnal ramblings as well. So all that remained to be done was to contact the Midland Shed to confirm that I was indeed who I said I was

Just a phone call. Simple you might say. But not so on the railway.

The shed did not have a national phone, only the railway system; so either Burton Station or Derby Control had to be contacted first. The very fact that I knew this should have been of sufficient value to our erstwhile policemen to realise that I genuinely was who I claimed to be, but they would insist on persevering until eventually the required confirmation was obtained.

So we all had a cup of tea and I was free to go. They warned me about carrying articles which could be used for nefarious purposes through the town at night, whereupon I felt duty bound to point to them that they were the tools of my trade and without them I could not do my job.

Rather like them going out on patrol without their truncheon and whistle I thought, but deemed it prudent not to say so.

This Mold job incidentally was allocated to be worked by a Mold (6B) Stanier 'Crab', but many and various were the types of engines which turned up on it; including ex Crewe Works engines on running in turns; usually Class '5's with occasional Jubilee or Patriot. An 8F or an Austerity was not unknown either. A Birkenhead ex GWR 63XX 2-6-0 arrived on one occasion I am told, and the fitter that night spent some considerable time trying to reduce the 25″ vacuum peculiar to GWR engines at that time down to 21″; before being put right by the local chargeman. I hasten to add that the fitter was not me, though I do know who it was.

Even the steamers could catch you out, never mind the diesels!!.

Most of the engines on these fitted workings were our own Burton ones, and as a result of the high standards of maintenance which they received, presented very few problems for the examiner. Occasionally a foreign engine would be rostered in place of the usual Burton one for whatever reason, but this was the exception rather than the norm..

The same could not be said for the 8.25 Leeds however, for with this train; Burton was at the wrong end of the rostered working; it having originated from that northern city.

Leeds tended not to put their best engines on this duty, so one always had to pay particular attention to their condition. The fact that it had made the journey thus far south, being no guarantee that it would complete the journey back.

One night in particular stands out in my memory as an unmitigated disaster as far as locomotive availability goes. It was a late autumn evening and for some reason or another, a thick fog had descended and covered the Midlands. It was a real pea-souper.

The engine rostered for the Leeds was a Royal Scot whose number for some reason I have not recorded.

Even as it stood on the long road which ran out of the rear of the old shed, it was enveloped in steam all round the front end. There was so much steam escaping out of the cylinder drain cocks and all three piston glands were passing quite heavily that I climbed up onto the footplate expecting to find the regulator handle open. The glands were blowing that fiercely that the steam was not condensing for some two feet or so after reaching the atmosphere.

I couldn't send an engine out in this condition on a night such as we were experiencing with this dense fog. Now normally the odd turn of the reverser usually cuts the steam supply to one cylinder or the other, depending on the position of the valve. If I could indeed achieve this on the left hand (drivers side) piston gland, I could then strip it out and file it down to make a steam tight fit. Then at least the driver would be in with a chance of seeing where he was going.

I very gently started to wind the Scot into reverse away from the turntable to try to achieve this. I hadn't gone more than half a turn of the handle when I felt her move backwards onto her tender. So steam brake on and back into mid gear promptly. Spotting my old mate Dickie Smith coming round the table, I asked him to move it for me. He told me that he had prepared her and added that you only had to take the brake off and wind the reverser and she set off, without touching the regulator at all.

I decided there and then to fail her and said as much to Dickie.

"You might as well," he replied, "Because no self respecting driver is going to take it on a night like this anyway. I know I wouldn't."

So I gave the bad news to Arthur, failing it with the regulator valve passing dangerously. At least he never questioned any decision which I made.

The next engine which control came up with was an LNER B1. This had just come on to the ashpits off a job and the disposing crew had been given the task of preparing her as well for her next assignment, namely the Leeds.

As they brought her onto the turntable to turn her off for my examination, Les the fireman, an old hand jumped off and called me over to her.

"Come and have a look at this," he announced. "Not much point in turning her off until you've seen inside this box," referring of course the firebox.

As I followed him back and up into the cab, he reached forwards and opened the firedoors. I had noticed that the .injector was on as I climbed up and shining my lamp into the box and onto the tubeplate, I could see why.

Water was pouring down that tube plate in a torrent from one if not more of the main flu tubes.

These are the large smoke tubes which pass through the boiler and contain the superheater elements.

"A definite failure this one then," I declared "You might as well chuck the rest of the fire out and park her up."

"That's just what I thought," Les said, and back to the ashpit they went.

Back into the foremans' office to convey the bad news and look into the repair card box to find her ticket. Sure enough her last driver had booked the tubes leaking badly.

"He never said owt to me," was Arthur's reply when told him, and showed him the card.

"Dunno what we are going to have now," he added, "We've got nowt left."

However lurking in a corner of the New Shed was none other than Class 4F number 44408, a Normanton (55E)..engine.

"Have a look at her and see if she'll do the job," he commented after he had had a look down his list. What he didn't tell me was that she was officially bound for Bow Works for overhaul.

Golly, wasn't she rough!!. Everything was loose that could be loose and a few more things besides. At least she seemed to be reasonably steam tight. All her last driver had booked was 'engine riding rough'; no surprise there; and 'brakes to adjust'.

As both injectors worked well and she created 21" of vacuum with 150lbs on the clock, I decided to attempt to mackle her up for the journey back north.

While I thumped the big end draw cotters down and set about tightening up some of the eccentric rod and strap nuts, Gerald adjusted the brakes and filled the lubricator. As we were doing this, Dickie Smith and his mate came along to get her ready.

"This old gel's going now is she?," he remarked.

"Yes," I replied, "Don't look to close and find anything too serious will you," I added. "I've enough to do as it is."

"Better be quick then, They'll be on her soon," he answered, referring to the crew booked for the job." You won't be to popular with them. They'll think they've got that Scot until they see the board," meaning the train arrangement board.

When they did arrive, I was just climbing out from underneath with Gerald in tow, having helped him complete the tightening up of the slide bar bolts. As they climbed up into the cab to dump their bags and coats, we crept away and laid low in the 'bug ut', hoping that our attention would not be requested to return.

Within the allotted quarter of an hour, she moved out on to the turntable and off up the yard, to clatter past the shed en route to Shobnall Sidings where she would pick up her train and start her journey back to Yorkshire.

What would they say at Normanton when she turned up again, always assuming that she got there in the in the first place.

As this job was a lodging turn, I didn't see either of the crew until two nights later, when I was pleased to see that the job had a Class '5' booked to it. Not I might add in the first flush of youth, but sound in wind and limb; never the less.

I asked the fireman how he had got on with the 4F, the previous trip.

"She was a bit rough," he replied," but what can you expect with one of them."

I confessed about the Scot and he told me that I had probably made the right decision, as they had experienced the fog for most of the trip, only running out of it north of Masborough.

With all those DMU's now running about the district on local services, they occasionally required our attention on the way; usually down at the station as has been mentioned before.

Having had a little experience with these machines by now, both at Burton and at Overseal; they held no fears for me at all.

Some one in the traffic department, noting that some of these units were standing idle over the weekend had the enterprising idea of running a series of excursions to the sea side during the summer months, Skegness and Rhyl being the usual destinations. They proved to be so popular with the general public that soon as many as three, three car sets would be coupled together to meet the demand.

The inevitable happened and we were called to one of these Skegness bound trippers one sunny Saturday morning, The driver, a Monument Lane man had had two engine lights go out on his panel since leaving New Street, and now a third one was flickering also. All these troubles being concentrated on the rear three car set. The whole train was full to bursting with mums and dads and their offspring, all dressed in their summer outfits and armed with buckets, spades and bags of pop and sandwiches.

While Gerald checked the oil levels on the two stopped engines, I had a look at the third which though still running sounded rather rough and was obviously down on revs. The top, or rather the side of the engine; it being mounted on its side when fitted to these DMU's, was soaked in diesel fuel; which to say the least was rather unusual; and also a fire hazard. Closer inspection revealed a fuel line nut spurting out diesel right over the back of the unit, about midway across the width of the coach.

Being reluctant to try and reach it over the top of the engine amidst all the filth and fuel lying there, I decided to gain access by removing one of the inspection doors in the floor of the gangway; inside the coach. In any case, there was so little space between the engine and the floor of the coach, that it would have been difficult to effectively use the spanner.

I volunteered Gerald to go up into the coach and open up the trap door. However, when he got there; he found that the fold down ring handles securing the catches, were broken off.

So I had to wriggle my way in after all, having first shut off the engine by means of the local isolation button; of course.

A couple of quick taps with the hammer soon had the catches free, so with a heave; I pushed open the trap door. Down on top of me came a very nice light coloured bag, discharging its contents of drinks and sandwiches, all nicely wrapped; about my head.

The fascinated interest in the proceedings, on the face of the owner turned to one of indignation and downright annoyance, in less time than it takes to tell.

I quickly spannered up the offending leaking pipe nut, while Gerald endeavoured to spread calm on the troubled waters.

My extremely filthy hand then passed the bag and contents back up to Gerald and added," Get this trapdoor down and stand on it, while I knock the catches back." All in one swift movement and moment, while the unfortunate owner was getting his breath back.

This done, I wriggled back out and reset the engine isolator.

Running up the side of the train to ask the driver to try and restart the three engines, I must have looked an awful sight; as I now felt, looked and indeed smelt like the proverbial oily rag.

All those three engine lights lit up, so presumably; everything was all right. (Except of course for the bag of sandwiches).

Walking back down the platform, I tapped on the appropriate window to apologise to the unfortunate passenger; who on seeing me in my bedraggled state, could not find any words to say to me. Either I had touched his heart strings, or he made it a rule not to swear in front of his children. I am pleased to say; we will never now know.

The guard, a dour 'Brummie' said that he would sort it, adding that it was a daft place to leave his bag anyway.

"What does he think the racks are for?," he asked, adding; "At least he won't forget this day out in a hurry!."

So Mr passenger, if you should by any chance, read this litany; please accept my sincere apologies once again; some forty or so years later.

Round about this time, British Railways in their wisdom committed two acts of vandalism at Burton MPD.

First of all they declared the centre section of the old shed roof unsafe, and removed it. The contractors on the job used typical demolition methods by first sawing partway through the roof beams with power saws, then attaching the beams so treated to the drawhook of a convenient engine, usually an 8F which was then sent off out of the shed doorway, bringing the roof sections down behind it, much to the detriment of the turntable below and its handrails in particular.

This task completed and the debris removed, the roof was left open to for the elements to fall upon those below for the rest of the depots existence, until closure in September 1966.

They now moved into the other (New) shed where they removed the eastern most bay, followed by the side and end walls of this same section.

The reason for this last act of demolition being to provide access for a siding into a new diesel refuelling point to be built in the shed yard. The site of this being adjacent to the new shed ashpits.

Two mysterious circular foundations were laid alongside the south wall of the shed. These, it later became clear were to carry two fuel tanks.

The fuelling point itself consisted of two roads with the fuelling pumps between, housed within an asbestos clad shed; open at both ends.

During its construction, the whole site was screened off, as is now the way with such things; so very few of us had any idea just what exactly was occurring behind the boarded off area. However, by climbing on to the top of a tender stood on the new shed ashpit, a view could be had of what was going on inside. Not that we were to much the wiser for looking. An even better view of course could be had by climbing up the ladder of one of the yard lights, but it did not seem worth the effort.

The all conquering Diesel was appearing more and more, with the steam engines retreating to the scrapyards in ever increasing numbers. By the winter of 1964/5, the only pre-Stanier locomotive left on the allocation was Class 3F 'Jocko' number 47643, the remainder of the allocation being made up of Class '5's, '8F's and 'Jubilees'; with 350HP Diesel Shunters and of course D2859.

The steam engines were being changed virtually week by week as more depots either closed completely or went over to the more modern power. Just about any defect was enough to condemn an engine to the storage line, pending its turn to make that one last journey to the breakers.

It was obvious that the writing was on the wall as to the future of Burton as a depot, new fuelling plant or not.

Being only twelve miles from Derby, the distance was to small and clearly if one was to go, it was bound to be Burton.

Driver's report cards were listing items which would never have appeared even twelve months before. One startling report for instance stated, 'There are no springs on this engine', a Westhouses Class 8F. When I went to look there were just seven spring buckles hanging underneath the axleboxes. Where was the eighth?. Only a few months earlier, should a report of this nature have occurred, gangs of platelayers would have been scouring every mile of track over which the engine had travelled since leaving its last depot; lest a spring plate or some other part was fouling the running lines. Now, the foreman just shrugged his shoulders and sent it back to its home depot, light engine.

Goodness only knows what the ride was like with the engine riding on the axleboxes, the only two springs on the whole locomotive being on the pony truck. If the fireman had any sense he would stay on the tender. At least that had a full set.

The vacancy board had long been empty of suitable and worthwhile jobs for a failed redundant fitter in charge, so I started to scan the local papers for suitable alternative employment.

Much as I enjoyed my time on the Railway, I had become somewhat disillusioned of late with the way that things were going. I had witnessed the stress and trauma of redundancy at close quarters and could see the situation at Burton going the same way.

So it was with great reluctance that I handed in my notice to the shed-master, none other than Joe Benson with whom I had started my apprenticeship some eleven plus years ago. We had a little chat and far from trying to persuade me to stay said that he did not blame me for making the move to pastures new.

The last and final week in the Railways employ saw me on the afternoon shift. I was to finish on the Wednesday as I had two days holiday left owing to me, one being for working the night shift over the new year when I had the pleasure of opening all the whistles of the engines in steam; to welcome the new year in.

This final week was supposed to see the commissioning of the new diesel refuelling station, but as with many new installations; it was suffering from a few teething problems.

Gerald and I went across to observe a refuelling demonstration on one of our 350HP Diesel shunters, but the procedure was constantly being interrupted by blockages in the filters protecting the installation.

To clean these filters, it was necessary to remove the top plate of the filter box. This plate was fastened down with six or eight studs, the securing nuts for which were about eight or ten millimetre spanner size. But had our contractor demonstrator the correct size spanner to hand. I doubt it very much as he preferred to use a pair of mole grips no less; to undo them with.

My colleagues and I were not impressed at all by this characters cavalier attitude to his job, as we came away in disgust. When I finished my last shift on that Wednesday night, this new facility was still not working properly, and in consequence Joe would not accept it on behalf of the company. He was a fine engineer and a good railwayman, and only perfection would be acceptable to him.

The very last job which I did was to part two brand new Type 2 Diesels' in the old shed doorway. The intermediate flexible train pipe between the two locomotives was connected in a semi-permanent way by two, two hole flanges with the appropriate rubber washers in-between. One hole in each flange had a long ⁵/₈" diameter threaded stud; the other hole being left open. When these two pipes were brought together, the single stud in each flange entered the hole on the other flange; brass nuts then being run along the two studs and

The new diesel fuelling facility. Photo: Authors Collection.

tightened up to draw the two halves together and make a seal. The threads on these studs soon became damaged, making it very difficult to tighten and undo. I believe that a different method of securing these two pipes was developed later. I am surprised that they were tolerated for as long as they were. Indeed that such a method was ever contemplated in the first place, so obvious being the potential damage to the studs threads.

All the other intermediate connections were of the snap, clip or plug type; in various shapes and guises.

Thus ended my railway career on such a mundane task, undoing two $^5/_8$ nuts.

The following Monday I started a new career at the Drakelow Power Station, still with steam boilers; but this time of a very different kind and pressure. 2850 PSI no less.

I can honestly say that I had enjoyed my fourteen or so years in the employ of British Railways, and had circumstances been different; would probably have never left.

However I can thank Dr Beeching for one thing if nothing else. By in effect making me leave BR's employ, he put more money in my pocket than I would previously have dreamed of. The wages paid by the railway were far from good, and downright disgraceful compared with similar occupations in outside industry; as I was soon to discover.

I am afraid that as an employer, the railways had played on and taken advantage of its employee's loyalty and dedication for far to long.

Chapter 21

It's Not all Fun

Railways by their very nature, can be very dangerous places upon which to work and within that environment; no more so than the various shunting sidings, depots and locomotive sheds. Care has to be exercised at all times, but human nature being what it is; accidents did occasionally happen. While not always so, human life was sometimes threatened, sadly on rare occasions resulting in a fatal outcome.

A number of accidents were witnessed by or made aware of to me during my career, some quite amusing but others very sad.

An example of the former occurred very early on in my time at Burton. I am not precisely sure after all these years whether I had become an apprentice at the time or not, but I think that I had.

We were working in the new No.2 shed one morning when Jack Pullman, the shed man came onto the turntable with 58236, a venerable Class 2F 0-6-0.Her fire had been thrown out and she was low in steam pressure. Jack's mate turned the table to the first available empty road and secured the catch.

On receiving the tip from his mate, Jack opened the regulator to reverse her off the table onto the vacant road where she was to be stabled for a boiler washout. With a woosh up the chimney, old 58236 suddenly dashed off the table, along the empty road and straight into and through the wall behind; coming to a halt with her tender buried right up to the leading axle in a pile of bricks glass and dust. Her buffers were nudging the wall of the canteen, new amenity block on the other side; the impact shaking over some of the drivers lockers and scattering their contents far and wide.

Following the noise of the initial impact, the ensuing silence was quite eerie. Jack climbed down out of the cab, shaken but otherwise unhurt. What had happened was that the boiler had been overfilled, causing a carry over of water when the regulator had been opened, creating an hydraulic effect in the cylinders. When this occurs it is almost impossible to close the regulator and stop the locomotive, least wise not in the short time and space available in this instance.

Poor old Jack, a more conscientious driver than he did not exist on the railway; I very much doubt.

With the wayward 58236 hauled out and re-stabled elsewhere in the shed, the resultant hole left behind became known as Pullmans Avenue. Until the damage was repaired it provided us fitters with a very convenient short cut to the canteen and tankroom, and some were sorry to see the gap repaired. For herself, 58236 appeared none the worse for her adventure, only sustaining damage to her two tender rail guards.

These were soon removed and straightened with no delay to her return to traffic after her boiler washout. Thus is the power and strength of steam.

General view of No. 2 (new) shed, this small window behind 47643 marking the place where 58236 went trough the wall. Photo: Authors Collection.

Another event, if you could call it that, was witnessed by me one sunny morning, also in the new shed.

A similar scenario to the situation just described was played in part, this time the leading role being taken by a Class 3F, number 43652. Like 58236, she to was brought into the shed to be turned off for boiler washout. I forget the driver's name but he was obviously a quota man as he was working on his own while his mate was no doubt attending to a second engine out on the ashpit.

43652 had a reasonable amount of steam left in her boiler and a comfortable water level, so no problem there. Our driver wound the turntable round to nearly half way, before finding a vacant pit over which to stable his charge. The one he selected fortunately as things turned out; was the one adjacent to the avenue road; this being the one which passes through the dividing wall between the two roundhouses, linking them together.

On arrival over the pit, he correctly placed the reversing lever in mid gear, opens the cylinder drain cocks and winds on the tender brake.

He then returns to the turntable and proceeds to wind it back to the correct position when not in use, namely in line with the running in road. Imagine his surprise therefore when glancing back, he sees 43652 slowly rolling back down the pit where he has just left it, towards the turntable hole.

As she reaches the edge, the leading wheels reach out into space with the whole front of the engine in effect levitating in air; unsupported. This state of affairs continuing until the second pair, the driving axle also came to the end of the rails; where with an almighty crash the front end dived down to hit the floor of the turntable well with further forward motion being arrested by the side of the turn table itself.

The whole building shook with the impact, bringing showers of soot, accumulated over many years down upon those gathered below. Again an air of silence follows.

Hodgy is on the scene in no time at all, no doubt alerted to the disaster by the noise of the impact. He is quickly followed by the members of the break-down gang, mentally working out the amount of overtime that they would earn. At least they would not be paid a bonus, as that was only paid when the breakdown occurred beyond the shed environs.

The breakdown vans were brought down and a suitable wire hawser was selected. This was attached to the tender drawhook of 43652 with the other end hooked over the drawhook of a Crab positioned on the adjoining avenue road for the purpose. As one would expect, the turntable in the other shed was also set to line up with the avenue road upon which the Crab was standing to afford an extension of track upon which to run when setting back to haul the 3F out of the well.

The main obstacle to pulling 43652 back apart from the obvious, were the trailing sand pipes which had been bent backwards as the 3F did her nosedive. These were soon removed with the aid of the "hot spanner," (oxyacetylene gas bottles) and the stage was set for the exhumation of 43652 from her temporary resting place.

The Crab set back a couple of feet or so to take up the slack in the hawser, continuing for a further short distance until the 3Fs middle wheels were up against the sides of the turntable well wall.

Jacks and packing were then brought into play and the long and tedious task of jacking and packing 43652 up to something like level again with the running rails began; probably some eight to ten feet in all; as the turntable well at its inner or hub centre was easily that deep as it sloped towards the middle of the hole. The platelayers supplied some spare sleepers to supplement the packing and these were placed along the free space between the jacking area at the front of the turntable wall, when 43652 was jacked up high enough to allow them to be slid underneath longways in line and beneath the engines wheels. Two short pieces of rail were also positioned under the middle two wheels as well at the platelayers suggestion, though whether or not there presence made a significant difference is questionable, for as the middle pair of wheels slowly slid up the pit wall, their flanges located inside the two running rails on the pit end any way.

Of course all this preparation takes a lot longer to achieve than it does to write about. The Crabs driver had inched his steed back a few times during the jacking, on request, as with the 3F becoming more upright the middle wheels were easing back from the wall.

When the time came to pull them back onto the pit rails, all attention was centred in that direction and not the direction in which the Crab was going.

Came the moment and the driver opened his regulator, looking back for the signal to stop again, with hand poised on his brake. The Crab eased back and 43652s middle wheel set climbed back onto the pit rail ends as someone more alert than most shouted "Whoa!

On slammed the brakes and the cavalcade shuddered to a halt.

"What've you stopped for? Keep going," Hodgy cried.

43652 stood teetering on the edge of the turntable well, neither in nor out, if you follow my meaning.

Behind the Crabs tender only a about a foot or so of rail remained before it to would be emulating 43652s trick of diving into the turntable hole in the other (No1) shed.

Some bright fireman had turned the turntable away from behind the Crab to enable his own engine to run on to it, commensurate with the desire to leave the shed.

Thus the scenario, probably never equalled on any other shed in the country ever; nearly occurred with an engine in each table hole at the same time.

Suitably chastened, the rogue crew and their engine left the roundhouse and the turntable was repositioned behind the Crab as before. The initial move was completed with no more harm done and with 43652 securely back on terra-firma, with only the leading wheels hanging over the wall; she was scotched in front of all wheels, prior to the strain being eased on the hawser which now required to be relocated along the side of the 3F to complete the pull; as the angle was now too acute with the original set up.

The hawser was re-secured around the cab step and with a gentle pull, having checked the turntable was behind this time; the Crab hauled 43652 back to its original starting place, and life at the shed went back to normal again.

But why had it happened in the first place, you may well ask.

An examination revealed that when the disposing driver had wound on the tender handbrake, the gearing had jammed up solid on an accumulation of coal which had found its way over the ensuing years down the hole through which it passed in the tender floor plate to connect with the brake shaft.

On these old Midland engines, this foreplate rested on a large balk of timber into which were drilled various holes to allow the brake gear, water pickup gear if fitted, and drawbar pins to pass; the timber being covered by a steel plate, similarly drilled and forming the tender part of the footplate. On the later tenders the timber balk was replaced by a steel fabrication with considerable free space between the actual footplate and the tender drag box so the situation present would not have happened.

Our driver had in consequence been misled as to the setting of the handbrake that had not pulled the brakeblocks onto the wheels as he had been led to believe. Therefore he was absolved of all blame. Rightly so, I think you the reader would agree.

Another thing of course that was revealed was the hitherto unknown fact that the pit rails did in fact slope towards the turntable and its well. A fact which a spirit level soon confirmed.

A check round revealed that this one was not the only pit to have this unwelcome feature, no doubt brought on by settlement and the constant pounding of the locomotives on and off the turntable over the years.

It was a standing order to scotch the wheels of any engine upon which one was working in any case, along with the display of a (NOT TO BE MOVED) board; but following this incident; notices were issued reminding all staff of this fact.

This was not the first time of course that engines had made an excursion into the turntable hole. Indeed on the very day that I started at Burton, as I entered the shed for the first time; I was greeted by the sight of an ex London, Tilbury and Southend 4-4-2T engine nose down into the old (No. 1) shed turntable hole; having run through the doorway from off the ashpits. I don't know the details of this incident, but these Tilbury Tanks were fitted with steam reversers, an item of equipment which I gather did not endear them to the Midland drivers, who were unfamiliar with this piece of gear.

Not that I am saying that this item was the cause of the mishap, but there you are.

For the record, 43652 sustained very little damage other than the two back sand pipes and the inevitable front rail guards. Both leading axlebox copper oil pipes were crushed, not surprising considering the fall, and one of the middle axle pipes was displaced. On parting the engine and tender to attend to the brake gear, it was thought that the drawbar was also bent; so this was changed as well; though it looked straight to me.

The turntable ever afterwards had a pronounced kink to the handrail one side. Unexplained of course if you were not there when it happened.

Working up the Droppit one day, George and I had with us a young apprentice. A very willing lad by the name of Dave Bartram. Dave travelled to and from work upon an old and battered cycle, the tyres of which had covered considerably more miles than the manufacturer had originally intended. As a consequence, punctures were quite common, though his talent at repairing them was somewhat awry. He was thus occupied one afternoon around the far side of the droppit, shielded from authoritative prying eyes by the locomotive over the table, when the sound of an impact assailed our ears.

"What has he done now?" I questioned George "are you alright Dave" I further enquired.

On receiving an affirmative answer, we all three went outside to view the scene.

A black five reversing down the yard had collided with an 8F standing foul of the points off the old shed ashpits, tender to tender; the resultant impact causing both tenders to rear away from each other with only the flanges of the respective outer wheels preventing them from becoming completely derailed. The driver of the Class 5 being on the opposite side of the cab to the ashpits, not being aware of the other engines tender standing in the way. Not of course that that was an excuse, as vigilance is the order of the day at anytime; particularly in a loco yard; where everyone does their own thing without recourse to signals and signalmen.

Before this worthy could reverse his engine and move forwards, hopefully to lower the two tenders back down onto the rails, a reasonable assumption to such an action; Bert Sinclair no less, the senior running foreman is out of his office and on the scene, to call a halt to the proceedings.

Having viewed the situation from all angles, he suggests this very action to the driver, much to the amusement of the usual assembly of onlookers who always seem to appear on these occasions. Now Bert Sinclair was nobody's fool and viewed the gathering over his spectacles with much disdain. A discrete withdrawal seemed the best option, so we retired back to the droppit to view the proceedings from there.

The black five crept forwards away from the point of collision, both tenders slowly lowering themselves back onto the rails as it did so. Just when success seemed certain, something; possibly a buffer head snagged on the 8Fs tender and flipped the rear end to one side; derailing the trailing axle as it did so. The immediate and obvious outcome being that all traffic out of the old shed will now have to travel either by the coalstage or the avenue road into the new shed. Neither option, while being viable is ideal.

As the breakdown gang were already out on a job, it fell to the remaining fitters, me included to do the honours. The only lifting equipment available to us was one hydraulic jack. So thus equipped and with the aid of a few pieces of packing, we set out to re-rail the tender.

One of the mates removed the rear coupling and we set the jack up beneath the drawhook under the centre of the bufferbeam at a slight angle leaning towards the derailed wheel on the inside of the running road. We hoped to jack the tender up so that the wheels would slide up the side of the rails and drop back on when the flange of the outer wheel rose above rail level. It usually worked with an empty wagon of some five or six tons tare weight, but we were dealing with a thirty ton or so tender here. We wondered if indeed the jack was even capable of lifting the tender at all on its own. In an ideal world a jack under each side would have been a better option, giving more control when the wheels reached the point of re-railment, but what you haven't got, you cannot use.

So we pumped away with the one jack that we had. Eventually we were rewarded with success, as with a bump and a grind, the wheels dropped back into place. No other damage was sustained to either tender, so after checking the gauge of the wheels, with incidentally a trammel borrowed from the C&W department; ours being in the breakdown vans, the two engines continued with their booked workings.

Mr Sinclair thanked us for our efforts, and we all went home.

Minor bumps and collisions such as just described, while not being commonplace, were certainly not a rare occurrence. The only thing hurt was someone's pride, which is how it should be.

Moving round the yard of an unfamiliar depot is always more difficult than when on home ground, and is obviously made worse during the hours of darkness. Local hazards and peculiarities that may be obvious during daylight hours can catch out the unwary when night falls.

One particular night a Western Division class 5 came on to the shed to turn and fill the tank manned by a Bescot crew. Their usual path down into the new shed was blocked, so they ran down to the No. 1 shed to spin on the turntable in there.

Coming back out again they dropped down towards the coalstage to use the water column there, situated just before and to the side of the stage.

As the crane was on the drivers blind side his fireman stood on the outside of the cab looking backwards ready to call his mate to stop when the filler was alongside. Now there was a restricted clearance below the coalstage, adequate space when it was built with the old Midland Railway engines of the day in mind, but not for the more modern ones built out to the full loading gauge.

Ex MR Class 2F 0-6-0 No. 58130 stands over the No. 1 ashpit. The water crane behind marking the scene of the tragic accident described in this chapter. Photo: Authors Collection.

Thus when the front of the tender came alongside the stage wall, the poor Bescot fireman became trapped; further movement using him like a roller between the two before his mate could stop the engine.

As the fireman could not be released from his trapped position, the emergency services were summoned to assist. They in their turn were handicapped, as there was no road access to the depot; necessitating the fire brigade personnel having to manhandle all their equipment from about half a mile away.

The recently (then) formed hospital medical flying squad were also alerted and attended, one of their first actions being to inject a pain killer into the patient.

This they were only able to do by lowering a very small and thin nurse down headfirst into the gap between the side of the tender and coalstage wall. Eventually the fireman was released, by jacking the tender up onto one side, thereby tipping it away from the wall and increasing the gap.

As if that were not enough he then had to face a journey of half a mile on a stretcher to reach the ambulance. Sadly he succumbed to his injuries within a very short space of time following his arrival at the hospital.

His demise cast a spell of gloom throughout the depot for many days to come. A collection was made and sent to his family along with a letter of sympathy.

As a direct outcome of this incident following protestations from the emergency services, improved access was negotiated with the adjoining firms of Lloyds Foundry and Sharp Bro.'s & Knight Ltd; timber merchants. Whilst I am sure that both companies were willing to be of any assistance which they could in such an emergency, an agreement was made with the latter to allow ambulances etc to use its internal road system which reached a point very near to the bottom of the slope on the path from the Moor St entrance, immediately behind the depot; only a rather dilapidated fence separating the one from the other.

However when this arrangement was put to the test with another emergency, this time when one of the shed labourers had what appeared to be a heart attack, their gateman initially refused to let the ambulance in, and when he did; left the ambulance crew to find their own way to the point of access. Thus further negotiations were required. These arrangements were a great improvement on what had gone before, when the patient had to be pushed the full length of the path to Moor St on a bier. This contraption of great antiquity was constructed mainly of wicker with large wheels akin to the front wheels on a penny-farthing; and probably supplied by the Midland Railway. Even the journey down the path was not without its problems, the ever-present risk of a train standing across the boarded crossing half way along always being a possibility.

Another dangerous place was the boarded crossing that afforded access to the depot from the Oxford St direction. These boards traversed both the two tracks at the start of the Leicester line as well as the adjacent shunting spur, to continue over the up and down fast and slow lines of the Derby-Birmingham main line; plus the shed access road before reaching the depot environs.

A place calling for extreme caution even on a bright sunny day, and positively perilous at night or in foggy conditions. Sadly over the years this crossing claimed the lives of several victims, but not always so.

One young fireman in particular got away with it (if such is not too glib a phrase), sustaining a crushed leg which had to be amputated He subsequently returned to his duties firing with an artificial limb, for which I have nothing but admiration.

On a brighter note, one job which was afforded to our breakdown gang and in which I was personally involved had (and indeed still does to this very day) considerable historic overtones. Namely the removal of the incline plane winding engine at Swannington following the closure of the mine and its subsequent redundancy.

All the work involved was supervised by a team of archivists, and great care was taken to preserve the equipment for later restoration and display. To facilitate its removal, part of the winding house had to be demolished; it having obviously been built around the facilities in the first place; all those years ago.

As the "hot spanner" was not allowed to be used, some of the original fastenings presented considerable problems with their removal. I well recall spending some time with my hammer and chisel splitting some very ancient and extremely large square nuts; holding part of the bedplate down.

Interestingly, some thirty five years or more later when attending one of the (then) annual Coalville Railway open days, I came across a small exhibition presented by an embryonic preservation group; formed with the idea of rescuing and restoring the incline and its artefacts. During the ensuing conversation with one of the group members, he produced an example of an old square nut; split open in the manner just described. Could this be one of several nuts that I had removed in this manner; we wondered? It was certainly about the right size, some 1½" thread size, to have been used to hold the bedplate down.

The original winding engine is now safely installed in a corner of the National Railway Museum at York, where it can be viewed working on compressed air at regular intervals throughout the day. No doubt the preservation group have their eye on this priceless item. With the idea of eventually reinstalling it in its original place; but they have an awfully long way to go before this could even be considered. I wish them well with their project, sited as it is on what is arguably one of if not the first public railway in the world. (No letters of protestation please).

Endpiece

During the early years of the railway mania a line was constructed through Burton upon Trent by the Birmingham and Derby Junction Railway. It was completed in 1839 and brought into use in either the June or August of that year, different historical records claiming either month with August being the most favoured.

Be that as it may, some 125 years later in 1989, its one and a quarter centuries of existence and service to the town was considered for celebration, largely by the influence of the local Burton Railway Society; of which I am a member; and the Bass Museum.

The local council, initially quite keen, soon lost interest and the celebrations eventually degenerated to one parade of historical vehicles around the town which, though quite impressive, would not have happened at all without the input and influence of the Bass Museum.

A very prototypical model railway layout of Shobnall Sidings was also operated every Thursday and at week-ends by a team of volunteers within the Museum's complex.

Amongst the activities organised by the local Railway Society, such as street walks, etc., was a visit to the Lloyds Foundry Pattern Store. This was housed in what had been the old Midland Railway Motive Power building and later taken over by Lloyds, as the two establishments were side by side, divided only by a brook. So in effect, the Old and New Shed Roundhouses still existed, complete with Blacksmiths and Fitting Shops; gutted of course; and the Tankhouse.

As I had not set foot within these premises during the intervening twenty-five years since leaving the railway employ, I put my name down to attend and was one of the party, limited to twenty souls, selected to attend.

We met at the foundry gates by a very pleasant young official who introduced us to the person designated to take us round. On entering the building (sheds), one of our committee members pushed me forward with the remark, "Come on Dave. Tell us all about it."

Apart from an access door having been knocked through the wall adjacent to the foundry, the Old Shed was more or less as it had been. The pits had all been filled in, the turntables had obviously also gone; no doubt into the furnace to be re-formed into goodness knows what; and the floor had been concreted over as one would expect. Asbestos sheeting now covered the central bay, which had been removed by the Railways as unsafe just before I left but otherwise the structure was just as it had ever been, in my time at least.

Rows of orange painted racking filled the area, loaded with wooden patterns of all shapes and sizes, all bearing painted catalogue numbers for the benefit of those who needed to know. But within a few minutes, I personally was not seeing the racking. In my mind's eye I could see 3F's and 4F's surrounding the turntable, stabled on the various roads, with the old 8F and Class 5 or Jubilee occupying the long roads of the corner pits.

As we made our way round towards the site of the old lobby, to my delight the stores counter and window, still glazed, was still in place though bricked up on the farther side, a chalked legend alongside reading, 'All diesel keys to be left in the foreman's office.' Joe Benson had told me he had written that all those years ago when he was the last shed-master there.

On entering the New Shed, a breeze-block wall had been erected alongside the railway where BR had knocked out the easternmost bay, giving the shed an oblong appearance in contrast to its original square design. Here, was less racking, the floor being strewn with larger wooden shapes, the dimensions of which forbade storage in a more conventional manner.

Our guide was most interested to discover the reason for the one small window amongst all the other more usual, loco shed style, large, round-topped ones, positioned in the north wall, along with the obviously newer filling in brickwork. This was, of course, the site of 'Pullman Avenue.' Unofficially named so after my old mate Jack Pullman, who was in charge, or otherwise, of 58236 on that fateful morning when it had crashed through this same wall all those years ago.

A thoroughly enjoyable evening was had by all and, after consuming of several pints of the amber nectar at a nearby hostelry, I was told the following day that I had agreed to repeat my litany to the wider membership on a future club night. This I again agreed to, when stone cold sober and eventually assembled, by fair means and foul, some seventy odd slides to augment my discourse. As an outcome of the resulting lecture I became 'on the circuit' as it were and found myself repeating it to various like societies throughout the Midlands, The RNLI, my favourite charity, benefiting from the fees acquired.

Several times during my brief outing of fame, it was suggested that I get the text written down. Easy to say but quite a task to achieve. I gave the matter some considerable thought and, when a bout of ill health, more of a physical nature than a medical one, saw me incarcerated in hospital and later at home for a spell, I made a start on the writing. As starting is often the most difficult part of any venture, once begun, the incentive to carry on and finish the project becomes a matter of determination and will. And, to be honest, I have enjoyed it. So, some five years on, here is the result of my labours. An autobiography of one railwayman's experiences.

If some of the locations are a bit muddled and the conversations more typical of the individuals than truly factual, then I apologise. If I have offended anyone when referring to some of the characters who it was my good fortune to meet and know, then I am truly sorry.

After nearly forty years of toil and strife, though the odd detail may have become lost on the recesses of my mind, I am still a railwayman at heart. I could still strip down a 4F for a valve and piston exam or overhaul an injector or whatever without a second thought. Mentally, I could still fire one as well though physically that might be another matter.

I do hope that you, the reader, have enjoyed reading it as much as I have in writing it and, if you should have any criticisms, please be gentle with me.

Thank you!

The tour of Lloyds Pattern Store proved to be the first of several, all subsequent visits being under my sole supervision without any official Lloyds personnel in attendance, though one of their office staff, a member of the Railway Society, was usually in the party.

I would like therefore, to place on record the undying gratitude and appreciation of the Burton Railway Society for the kindness and forbearance of Lloyds in allowing us access to their premises. They even delayed the work of the contractors retained to demolish the buildings in 1997, by one week-end, to enable us to make a final, nostalgic visit to the site.

Interestingly, this foundry has received recent railway fame by casting a new driving wheel for the one cut away at Barry, for the preserved ex GWR King Class 4-6-0 No. 6023, 'King Edward II'. A set of wheels has also been cast for one of the BR Standard locomotives now preserved.

So if any preservation society out there requires any ferrous castings made, you know who to contact.

The most famous claim to fame however being the casting of the driving wheel for 60163 Tornado the completely new A1 Class locomotive.

Finally, no work of this kind can be achieved without the help and encourage-ment of others. All so freely given.

I would like in particular to thank my cousin Ken Speed for his computor skills, Mark Ratcliffe for the proof rreading of the manuscript, Andy Colson, Chris Canner, Peter Baumgarten, Dave Wright, Pat Webb, members of the Burton Railway Society, The Trent Valley Model Railway Society, Steve Warren, Derek Warren, my daughter Rosy, my son Ian and last but by no means least my wife Judith for her unstinting support throughout the project.